Praying with Saint John's Gospel

Daily Reflections on the Gospel of Saint John

Edited by Father Peter John Cameron, O.P.

MAGNIFICAT®

Publisher: **Pierre-Marie Dumont**
Editor-in-Chief: **Peter John Cameron, O.P.**
Senior Editor: **Romanus Cessario, O.P.**
Managing Editor: **Catherine Kolpak**
Assistant to the Editor: **Claire Gilligan**
Editorial Assistant: **Andrew Matt**
Administrative Assistant: **Nora Macagnone**
Senior Managing Editor: **Frédérique Chatain**
Editorial Coordinator & Permissions: **Diaga Seck-Rauch**
Iconography: **Isabelle Mascaras**
Cover Design: **Solange Bosdevesy**
Translator: **Janet Chevrier**
Proofreaders: **Claire Gilligan, et al.**
Production: **Sabine Marioni**

Contributors: **Father Timothy Bellamah, O.P.,
Father Herald Joseph Brock, C.F.R., Douglas Bushman,
Father Gary C. Caster, Father John Dominic Corbett, O.P.,
Father Lawrence Donohoo, Anthony Esolen, J. David Franks,
Father Michael L. Gaudoin-Parker, Father Anthony Giambrone, O.P.,
Father Stephen Dominic Hayes, O.P., John Janaro, Father William M. Joensen,
Heather King, Father Joseph T. Lienhard, S.J., Monsignor Gregory E. S. Malovetz,
Father Francis Martin, Regis Martin, Father Vincent Nagle, F.S.C.B.,
Father Jacob Restrick, O.P., Father George William Rutler,
Father Richard G. Smith, Father James M. Sullivan, O.P.,
Father Richard Veras**

Foreword

Father Peter John Cameron, o.p.

"ND IT WAS NIGHT." That's how Saint John the Evangelist ends the passage where Judas Iscariot slithers off to betray Jesus Christ (Jn 13:30). John's purpose is not to tell us the time of day, but to symbolize the oppressive darkness and evil that befall the world through the treachery of Judas.

First words

For the last few years, the parish where I have been offering Mass on Sundays is Saint Rose of Lima Church in Newtown, Connecticut. On the evening of the Sandy Hook School massacre, an impromptu memorial Mass was held...attended by nearly two thousand. Because "it was night."

It hurt to look upon the sea of faces wracked with darkness and desolation. In my head I kept repeating the first words of Jesus in the Gospel of John—a question: "What are you looking for?" (Jn 1:38). The crowds had come to God's house—not to a therapist, not to a counseling center. Clearly they were looking for something from heaven—something from God to make sense of the horror. What drove them was the intuition, the *expectation* that "the light shines in the darkness,/ and the darkness has not overcome it" (Jn 1:5).

The parish, the town had become instantaneously overwhelmed by catastrophic violence and inconceivable loss. Yet we sensed that someone had foreseen and tended to our need before it had a chance to crush us. "They have no wine," says the Mother of God to her divine Son at Cana (Jn 2:3). Mary sees what is missing long before that lack can rob the wedding feast of joy. And Christ responds with a flood of wine signifying the outpouring of God himself: "God so loved the world that he gave his only Son, so that everyone who believes in him might not perish but might have eternal life" (Jn 3:16).

Most likely many in the congregation that night had not been to church in a long time. They were like the Samaritan woman at the well who, through her history of consistently bad choices, had become alienated from others, alienated from God, even alienated from herself. But when Jesus gets her to think about her thirst, and promises "whoever drinks the water I shall give will never thirst; the water I shall give will become in him a spring of water welling up to eternal life" (Jn 4:14), she leaves her old life—her water jar—behind. She runs to town bursting with love, proclaiming this Good News to the world!

More than a few in those pews resembled the lame man who had lain by the Sheep Gate pool for thirty-eight years. They ached to hear Jesus ask, "Do you want to be well?" (Jn 5:6). But the events of that abominable day seemed to augur a bleak and dismal future. Yet, even at that Mass, we could hear Jesus whispering, "Rise, take up your mat, and walk" (Jn 5:8).

What the assembled multitude craved that Friday evening was a Presence. They had come to the Eucharist. Jesus promises in the Bread of Life discourse, "I will not reject anyone who comes to me" (Jn 6:37). In the wake of incomprehensible death, drawing close to Jesus Christ in certainty…eating his very Body and Blood was, they knew, the most reasonable thing to do. "Unless you eat the flesh of the Son of Man and drink his blood, you do not have life within you" (Jn 6:53).

Words of eternal life

Even when hundreds found themselves stuck outside owing to the limited seating in Saint Rose Church, they did not leave. Their staying put in the daunting December cold silently professed, "Master, to whom shall we go? You have the words of eternal life" (Jn 6:68). For all were counting on the life-giving words of Jesus Christ to give them a reason to go on living. As even non-believers in John's Gospel declare, "Never before has anyone spoken like this one" (Jn 7:46).

That night nothing could keep us from staying close to Jesus. Not the shame of our sins, which the atrocity made us face with new gravity. Sin gave way to the mercy of the Son of God: "Has no one condemned you?... Neither do I condemn you" (Jn 8:10-11). Not the blindness of our worldly ways, countered squarely by Christ: "While I am in the world, I am the light of the world" (Jn 9:5). No, we had drawn near to what our hearts told us we longed for the most: the Good Shepherd. Lost, alone, the voice of our Good Shepherd wooed us: "I came so that they might have life and have it more abundantly" (Jn 10:10).

Maybe we would not witness a miracle like the raising of Lazarus. But the Lord's assurance to the dead man's sister Martha seared our souls with hope: "I am the resurrection and the life; whoever believes in me, even if he dies, will live" (Jn 11:25). "We would like to see Jesus," our voiceless anguish begged (Jn 12:21). Came the response, as if from an empty tomb, "While you have the light, believe in the light, so that you may become children of the light" (Jn 12:36).

Children of the light...

We recognized that we had been called to share in the Passion of Christ to a degree no one ever could have imagined. And even as we grieved and wept, Jesus himself stooped to wash our feet (Jn 13:1-5), tears mingling with water in the basin. Each touch of his towel brought a new tenderness: "I will not leave you orphans" (Jn 14:18).... "I am the way and the truth and the life" (Jn 14:6).... "Remain in me, as I remain in you" (Jn 15:4).... "Take courage, I have conquered the world" (Jn 16:33).... "May all be one, as you, Father, are in me and I in you" (Jn 17:21).

Last words, lasting words

At that Mass we encountered the absolute answer to Pontius Pilate's infamous question: "What is truth?" (Jn 18:38). Truth is this Man, who looks at us in a way that no one has ever looked at us before. Even from the cross, with *our* agony in mind, radiating a peerless gaze of love, Jesus confers an incomparable gift: "Behold, your mother" (Jn 19:27). What was granted at the beginning— a Mother at Cana to anticipate and accommodate our need—is given now at the end and for ever to accompany us in our pain.

One month after the school shooting, Jenny Hubbard spoke to the people of Saint Rose of Lima Parish about her beautiful, red-haired, six-year-old daughter Catherine who had been brutally murdered:

> I find comfort that Catherine was called to a job much bigger than I can even fathom. I must remain centered on God's face. He will provide what I need to move forward. When we stop listening to our hearts, we stop listening to God's voice. We stop acknowledging that we are in this place for a very specific reason. I pray that we find comfort and solace knowing that God loves each one of us and will wrap each one of us in his arms when the days become too much.
>
> I pray that the world returns to their faith.

What made it possible for one so devastated by suffering and sorrow to speak with such conviction, such utter serenity? Only the fact of the Resurrection of Jesus Christ from the dead—an event more present and alive in her life than the absence of her beloved little girl. For us Jenny was another Mary Magdalene who "went and announced to the disciples, 'I have seen the Lord'" (Jn 20:18).

In the end, only one question seemed to matter…a question of the risen Jesus: "Do you love me?" (Jn 21:16). To answer "yes" is to know that we are loved.

INTRODUCTION
The Gospel of John

Father Francis Martin

Rabbi Aqiba once said: "All the ages are not worth the day on which the Song of Songs was given to Israel; for all the *Writings* are holy, but the Song of Songs is the Holy of Holies." Now that the Holy Spirit has finished writing the Scriptures, we can add to Rabbi Aqiba's remark the words of Origen, one of the earliest and greatest commentators on the Gospel of John, who died after being imprisoned and tortured for the faith: "We may therefore make bold to say that the Gospels are the first fruits of all the Scriptures, but of the Gospels that of John is the first fruits. No one can apprehend the meaning of it except he who has lain on Jesus' breast and received from Jesus Mary to be his mother also."

Word and Worship

Reading Saint John's Gospel is like looking into a lake whose deep waters are clear and breathtakingly beautiful: the more one gazes the more one sees. From the very outset we meet the central reality of the Gospel: the Word who is "turned toward God" and who is at the same time God himself, through whom everything that is came into being. This Word chooses a people whom John calls "his own" though they do not accept him. He finally takes on flesh and reveals his glory as being that of the Son of God. This occurs most especially in the act of love in which he dies on the cross and hands over the Spirit. John concludes the Prologue, an anticipated summary of his Gospel, by telling us: "God, no one has ever seen; the Only Begotten God who is dynamically present in the Father's bosom, he has made him plain to us" (Jn 1:18, author's translation).

As the Gospel begins, John the Baptist with the eagle eye of a mystic sees Jesus passing by and declares him to be the Lamb of God. Wouldn't it have been exciting to follow John's lead, spend time with Jesus, and finally attend a wedding party where "the mother of Jesus was there" and see him change the water of the old law into the wine of the new covenant! Now we begin to follow Jesus (not just with our eyes, but with our spirit) as zeal for his Father's house consumes him and he cleanses the Temple and predicts that when the ruined Temple of his own body lies in the ground he will rebuild it in three days. Jesus heals many, speaks with a wealthy and learned aristocrat in Jerusalem, then with a simple woman who is a "heretic" and a "sinner" in the estranged land of the Samaritans, and then finally with an army officer who pleads for his son and is rewarded.

All the worship life of his people is precious to Jesus and so he begins, by anticipation, to bring this worship to completion. At Passover, he declares that his teaching and his body and blood will be the new food in the desert. At the feast of Tabernacles, he tells us that he is the Light, the Pillar of fire in the desert, the healer of the blind. He is also the authentic source of the Living Water flowing from the rock of his side: "If anyone thirsts, let him come to me. Let him drink, he who believes in me. As Scripture says: 'From out of his midst there will flow rivers of living water.' Now he said this of the Spirit…" (Jn 7:37-39, author's translation). Also, at this feast Jesus calls himself the Shepherd of his new people: he will lay down his life for them and will lead them to the Promised Land of eternal life. Then, as the people rejoice at the feast of the Temple's rededication, Jesus teaches that he is the Temple and the Altar who will be himself the eternally valid sacrifice.

Self-Giving Love

Lastly, we learn how he loves us, even when we are dead in sin, when he weeps over the dead Lazarus and then calls him to life, thus predicting his own Resurrection. Then, as he prepares to give his life he is troubled: he is inviting us to join him. He tells us that his soul is troubled (he is in glory now but there is still the mysterious call, understood by the saints and mystics, to "make up all that still has to be undergone by Christ for the sake of his body, the Church" (Col 1:24, author's translation).

At chapter 13 of the Gospel, the large doors of Jesus' heart are opened wide. It is time now for us to ask the Holy Spirit to bring us into the "Book of Glory" (chapters 13-21). Access to this glory comes through obedience to Jesus, the Son of God: "If anyone loves me, he will keep my commandments, and my Father will love him and I will love him, *and I will show myself to him*" (Jn 14:21, author's translation). First we are presented with two traitors: Judas who betrays him and Peter who denies him. Since we are all traitors and deniers, we are to choose what kind of traitor we wish to be: hardened into despair or sorrowful into reinstatement.

In these chapters, listen for the voice of Jesus as it sounds in your own heart. He calls us his friends and dies for us willingly and saves us from eternal death. He invites us to love one another and lay down our lives for each other: "In this we have come to know love: he laid down his life for us. And we ought to lay down our lives for the brethren. If someone has this world's goods and sees his brother in need, and closes his heart to him: how does the love of God abide in him? Little children, let us not love by word and speech, but in deed and truth" (1 Jn 3: 16-18, author's translation). The glory of God, John tells us, is not in dramatic splendor but in the radiance of self-giving love; it is the law of the Trinity: "The world must know that I love the Father" (Jn 14:31).

The Radiance of Glory

The most glorious part of the Book of Glory (chapters 18-21) begins with the tawdry tale of betrayal, arrest, a self-interested and cowardly Roman official, flight and denial on the part of the disciples, torture by the occupation forces, denial of the kingship of God on the part of the leaders ("We have no king but Caesar" [Jn 19:15]). Where is the glory? Look into the pierced heart of Jesus, John tells us, and there you will see the ineffable love between the Father and the Son which spills over into the gift of Mary as Mother to the Church and the gift of the Spirit to befriend us. The Spirit gives us a care for the world that he shows us is in the wrong on all the basics: the real meaning of sin (refusal to believe), the ultimate manifestation of justice (the Resurrection), and who is ultimately condemned at the cross (Satan) (Jn 16:7-11).

The radiance of this glory is portrayed in four vignettes, remarkable for their quietness as they trace growth in faith. First, the perplexity of Mary Magdalene and then Peter and John until John begins to believe (Jn 20:1-10). Then, Mary's conversion when Jesus calls her by name and makes her "the Apostle to the Apostles" (Jn 20:11-18). Next, Jesus appears to the ten hiding disciples, proclaims peace, and creates them anew by breathing on them as on Adam at the beginning (Gn 2:7), giving them the power to release humanity from sin. Finally, Jesus appears to the eleven hiding disciples. He shows them that his body will bear for ever the marks of his passage among us and elicits an act of faith from Thomas. The reinstatement continues in chapter 21 where Jesus serves breakfast (note his affection for his brothers), reinstates Peter on the basis of his love, and speaks of the future for Peter and John.

What is the message of the Fourth Gospel? It is *agape*: God's affection for the human race, his forgiveness and care. It is as well a promise to be present to us: we cannot love what we cannot attain. And finally, it is an invitation to a transforming union with the Son of God who takes us into the very life of the Trinity and its outpouring into the world: "As the Father loves me, so I also love you…. As the Father has sent me, so I send you" (Jn 15:9; 20:21).

An Invitation to Saint John's Gospel
The Crucified Womb: Birthplace of Our Life

Andrew Matt

Standing in the kitchen, pouring oatmeal slowly into a bowl, I'm suddenly blind-sided by a small, accelerating tornado on two feet. Louis, my one-and-a-half-year-old son, whom we adopted at three weeks, is churning across the floor, shouting, "Dada!"

No reaction time—as soon as these two syllables reach my ears: Tears.

Gratitude in spades.

Unbidden. Inexplicable.

I spin around, scooping Louis up into my arms. He curls his little frame into my chest like a ball. "I love you, Louis."

I can hear his short breaths. If he wanted to, he could hear mine as well—rapid, uneven, labored. If he tried, he might even make out a muffled echo of his filial outburst of joy: "Thank you, Father."

Pure gift—this ricochet of joy from son to father to our heavenly Father catches me off guard. Now I'm fighting back sobs. Fighting back the overwhelming foretaste of what we've been made for: "In love [God] destined us for adoption to himself through Jesus Christ" (Eph 1:5) and "sent the Spirit of his Son into our hearts crying, 'Abba, Father!'" (Gal 4:6 RSV).

As I stand there embracing my little boy within the embrace of the Father, I'm transported back to Louis' baptism day.

There he is, asleep in Martha's arms, beside the baptismal font. He barely notices the water creating him anew. Martha is overcome with joy—beaming and weeping all at once. She looks like a young bride, or as if she's just given birth. And in a real sense she has—as a member of Christ's Body she's participated in the birth of a child of God. No wonder that from apostolic times the baptismal font has also been called the *uterus Ecclesiae* (womb of the Church).

I too participate in Louis' new birth, but it's through Martha's radiant joy that this sacramental event takes flesh for me—an event of supernatural adoption that mirrors how Martha introduced me to adoption in the first place. For it was through her serene enthusiasm that I warmed to the idea of pursuing the eventual adoption of Louis.

Back in the kitchen, with a ball of joy nestled next to my heart, I realize that the tears I'm unsuccessfully holding back aren't my own. I'd never be filled with this welling gratitude were it not for my wife.

The ricochet of joy widens, and comes full circle. I've been weeping Martha's tears the whole time—gifts of baptismal grace from our *Abba* above to his adopted children in the Son.

The Gospel of Adoption

The Fourth Gospel is written by the Apostle closest to Christ's heart, the Beloved Disciple Jesus adopts into his family from the cross:

> When Jesus saw his mother and the disciple there whom he loved, he said to his mother, "Woman, behold, your son." Then he said to the disciple, "Behold, your mother." And from that hour the disciple took her into his home. (Jn 19:26-27)

Saint John's whole Gospel flows from this "hour"—the hour of adoption. The Evangelist writes out of the experience of having been gathered up by Christ, placed in the arms of Mary his new Mother, and borne into the loving embrace of the Father.

This is the hour of our adoption too. When we look at John standing beside Mary, we are looking right in the mirror. What do we see? What the Church Fathers saw: the birth of the Church. A newborn babe—John, us—saying "yes" with Mary to Christ's "yes" to the Father.

What are we saying "yes" to?

Gifts.

First, a little Pentecost—the gift of the Holy Spirit: "...and he bowed his head and gave up his spirit" (Jn 19:30 RSV).

Second, Christ's lifeblood—the gifts of baptism and the Eucharist: "...and immediately blood and water flowed out" (Jn 19:34).

John gazes at the pierced heart of the dead Christ, open and empty—the very heart he laid his head upon at the Last Supper—

and he beholds the Father's heart of love. Alive. Beating strong. Filling him to the brim.

Years later, looking back, John invites us to gaze upon Christ's life-giving wounds of love: "See what love the Father has bestowed on us that we may be called the children of God. Yet so we are" (1 Jn 3:1).

So let us look again at this mysterious gift of our adoption in Christ—so huge that it sometimes seems invisible. Let us revisit a crucial passage in John's Gospel that sheds light on the "hour" of our adoption, taking note of the key word *koilias* ("womb/heart").

The Hour of Adoption

Saint John loves the language of birth and baptism. Right away we read: "Those who did accept [Jesus]…were born not by natural generation…but of God" (Jn 1:12-13). To Nicodemus, Christ says, "No one can enter the kingdom of God without being born of water and Spirit" (Jn 3:5).

But here is the most pregnant passage of all:

> Jesus stood and cried out: "Let anyone who is thirsty come to me… As scripture says, 'From his heart [*koilias*] shall flow streams of living water.'" (Jn 7:37-38 NJB)

Alluding to the source of the baptismal waters that will flow from his side (Jn 19:34), Christ literally calls his "heart" a "womb" (*koilias*), the same word Elizabeth uses at the Visitation: "Blessed is the fruit of your womb [*koilias*]" (Lk 1:42).

In choosing this word—it only appears once—John reveals Mary's viscerally indispensable role in generating our new life in Christ. For Christ's womb—like all of his fleshly existence—is a gift received entirely through Mary's "Yes" at the Annunciation.

At the second Annunciation, beneath the cross, Mary says "Yes" again—to John, her adoptive son in the Son, and by extension to each one of us. Mary thus utters her second "Yes" as *Mater Ecclesia*, receiving back from Christ a womb made ready to give birth to a multitude of new children.

Let us rejoice with John as adoptive children of Mary, sprung from Christ's womb to be living witnesses of the Father's mercy in a world thirsting for love.

Starting from the Beginning Every Day

Father Vincent Nagle, F.S.C.B.

*In the beginning was the Word,/ and the Word was with God,/
and the Word was God./ He was in the beginning with God.*
(Jn 1:1-2)

John begins by telling us, "In the beginning was the Word." This is an experience that we can have today, for not only was the Word in the beginning, but also our own beginning—and especially our beginning again—is in the Word. As a confessor you hear again and again the frustration of people who are there to confess what they have confessed so many times before. And you feel the fear of those who, having committed betrayals, are afraid that they have definitively and permanently undone the weave of life that had sustained them up to that point.

I sometimes say to them, "Do not be afraid. You are beginning again in Christ with this sacrament." I go on to say, "When you receive this absolution and offer your penance you will appear before God whole and spotless, his beautiful and unstained image, even as the first man and the first woman in the beginning. You will be like Adam at dawn on that first morning of his creation: naked and unafraid, his bare feet treading on the dew-specked grass, when everything was perfectly fresh and full of promise."

In front of our limits and failures, beginning again from ourselves fills us with discouragement or worse. "What beginning is there for me in my trying again? Don't I already know myself? Haven't I already been down that path?" So we sit and curse the darkness. But there is the creative word being spoken to us: "The teacher is here" (Jn 11:28). And suddenly our world is full of possibility, for we are looking at him, the Word who "was in the beginning with God."

This is what redeems us: that we, in every moment, can start from what is truly new and has the fullness of promise. We start by saying "you" to him, the Word who was in the beginning and is our beginning.

Dear Father, do not let the prison of my sins and limits keep me in darkness, but let me cling to your Word made flesh who was with you in the beginning and who is my beginning, he who lives and reigns with you and the Holy Spirit.

How to Face the Waves

Father Vincent Nagle, F.S.C.B.

All things came to be through him,/ and without him nothing came to be./ What came to be through him was life,/ and this life was the light of the human race;/ the light shines in the darkness,/ and the darkness has not overcome it.

(Jn 1:3-5)

Sometimes when I was a boy, out at the northern California beach, my brothers and I would scamper out to the rocks that stood out from the beach, and be thrilled as we watched the large waves crashing and shooting up in great foaming walls in front of us. It was dangerous, of course. If a wave had completely overcome the rock, the freezing water might have paralyzed us. And though we were all strong swimmers, the undertows and rip tides could well carry us out too far for numbed muscles. But we were betting that the rock we were standing on was a rock that would not be overwhelmed. It was exhilarating.

As we grow older and more conscious of our limits, we know with ever greater certainty that we need to be standing on something that the storms of life, the irresistible and sometimes violent forces of disintegration cannot overcome. But what can that be? What principle, project, power, or path can ultimately withstand the unstoppable ravages of the treacherous hearts of men and the implacable destruction of time? Nothing in this world, it may appear, can hope to withstand annihilation for long. After all, death is the black wall of nothingness that awaits every creature.

And yet, we dare hope. Amidst all of the noise and terror, a small and almost inaudible promise is being spoken. This promise comes from the depth of creation, from the very Word that God uttered so that the universe might exist. And that Word is saying, "Do not be afraid any longer, little flock" (Lk 12:32). This Word returned from the darkness of the tomb to say to us, "I am with you always, until the end of the age" (Mt 28:20). Life with him and in him is the rock upon which we stand, that is not overcome.

Loving Father, I can be so uncertain and doubtful about the goodness of this life you have given me. Let me gain confidence in the victory of your love through the glory of your Son who is our Savior for ever and ever.

Virtual John the Baptist

Father Vincent Nagle, F.S.C.B.

*A man named John was sent from God. He came for testimony,
to testify to the light, so that all might believe through him.
He was not the light, but came to testify to the light.* (Jn 1:6-8)

Antonella keeps up with Middle Eastern matters and visits internet forums where Middle Easterners express interesting judgments. A few years ago she stumbled across one forum in which the moderator, a very convinced Muslim and Jihadist sympathizer, conducted engaging, evenhanded, and wide-ranging conversations without angry diatribe. Antonella often visited the forum, and the two chatted about various topics.

Antonella noticed that contributors to the forum, almost all Muslims, would often make statements about Christianity or ask questions about it that were left unaddressed. A committed Catholic, she decided to offer this information where appropriate without comment. The moderator was impressed by her ability to approach these subjects without debate or defensiveness.

Their conversations became more personal, and the moderator asked more and more questions about Christianity. It came to a head when the moderator asked a question about how Christians saw God, and Antonella said, "God is love." The moderator demanded that she back that up with Scriptural quotes. These quotes led to an explosion on the part of the moderator who left the forum for many weeks. When communication resumed it was with a real sense of urgent discovery. Antonella brought into the conversation a friend who was a priest.

After some years it comes about quite casually that all three—the moderator, the priest, and Antonella—are to be in the same European city on the same days. For the first time they all meet face to face. When the moderator insistently entreats to be baptized into the Body of Christ, it fills the other two with a profound sense of wonder.

It has all left Antonella humbled. She is in no way this person's savior, this person's destiny, or even, physically, this person's companion. And yet, her presence to this person in a virtual space has led to a new life, a new birth, salvation. John the Baptist's vocation to "testify to the light" belongs to each one of us.

*Let my grateful and free dependence upon you through your Son
and Spirit, Father, make of me a sign, a light pointing to the Savior
of all mankind, Christ the Lord.*

Who Needs a Savior

Father Vincent Nagle, F.S.C.B.

The true light, which enlightens everyone, was coming into the world./ He was in the world,/ and the world came to be through him,/ but the world did not know him./ He came to what was his own,/ but his own people did not accept him.
(Jn 1:9-11)

There is a story about a monk with a reputation for holiness. Devout and compassionate, he fulfills his duty and extends himself to those in need. People say he has reached perfection. Doubtful that this is true, he asks God to show him the true state of his soul. This is granted, and the monk is so undone by the horror of what he sees that he says to God, "Let me pass my days in prayer and penitence asking for salvation, but please never permit me to see this vision again!"

This has helped me understand why it is so very often hard to recognize the one who has come to "his own." Why do "his own people...not accept him"? The answer is that in order for us to see who he is, we have to accept to discover who we are.

Who is he? The Gospel of Matthew says, "You are to name him Jesus, because he will save his people from their sins" (Mt 1:21). "Jesus" means "God saves." He is the savior, who comes to give the people "salvation/ through the forgiveness of their sins" (Lk 1:77). Who can accept the Savior, then? Who is "his own"? Only the one who says "yes" to what "the light" uncovers: the fact that we are sinners in need of salvation.

Who can accept to live with the terrifying sense that one's own choices have brought him to the brink of a well-earned dark pit of eternal fire? For most of us, I think it is only possible when we have already begun to feel the saving touch upon our arm of the one who draws us back from the abyss. Tearfully embracing him, clinging to him, and sobbing with all our might implies accepting our need for a savior. Let us ask for the grace to accept today our need for salvation, and enter into the light.

Merciful Father, the life of your Son on earth was brief and ended in great drama. May the compassion that brought him back to us from the pit of the grave fill us with the confidence to cry out, "Save us, Lord."

Who Is My Father?

Father Vincent Nagle, F.S.C.B.

But to those who did accept him he gave power to become
children of God, to those who believe in his name, who were
born not by natural generation nor by human choice
nor by a man's decision but of God.
(Jn 1:12-13)

The death of my father was a milestone in my life. I had written a letter to him when young in which I expressed my gratitude for being the son of a man who lived with such a strong sense of the need for justice, and who had given me a name that, thanks to him, was associated with faithfulness to one's responsibilities and commitment to struggling for the weak. Though in his final years he kept me at a distance due to an argument between us concerning Catholic Faith and politics, yet even this distance only made me reflect all the more upon all that I had received from him.

Seven months after my father's death, the founder of the Catholic movement that I belong to died. I had been given rebirth in the faith by this man's searing insights into beauty: the human being's suffering heart, his courageous openness to God in the world, and his childlike wonder in front of Christ and the mystery of our salvation. He had taught us to live fully the communion of the Church. I had dreaded this day, when we could no longer expect any new liberating word of encouragement or judgment from him. What shocked me was how much more this loss affected me than the loss of my own father had such a short time before. It was incomparable.

Our real father is the one who reveals to us our reason for making the sacrificial choice for life. How right we are to call priests "Father," as they place before us our origin and destiny. How undeniably the God revealed in Jesus is The Father, for whom our hearts are made, and in whom alone they are at rest. With all due gratitude to our earthly origins, yet in Christ we are indeed children "born not by natural generation nor by human choice nor by a man's decision but of God."

Father and Creator, your Son's Incarnation, Passion, and Resurrection have brought to us the fulfillment of the promise of our earthly creation. Let our salvation in your Son make us more grateful for our created origins.

The Light of Glory

Father Vincent Nagle, F.S.C.B.

And the Word became flesh/ and made his dwelling
among us,/ and we saw his glory,/ the glory as of the Father's
only Son,/ full of grace and truth.
(Jn 1:14)

There are moments when you can see the victory of love and truth in the humanity in front of you, moments that oblige you to recognize the mystery of God at work, when his glory becomes humanly visible. One such moment for me came when I went to visit a famous and greatly sought after old priest, the head of a very large community of lay and consecrated people, who had been sick for some years and was very weak.

I went up to the third floor and we had tea together. Even lifting his tea to his mouth cost him enormous strain. In his study I explained to him that, due to health problems, I was not able to work and was undergoing intensive and protracted treatments. He spoke of our Lady who, upon the departure of the angel, had had to sustain herself through memory and prayer. He repeated many times to me, "Don't be afraid! Ask her to help you in remembering Christ's victory in your life."

When it was time to go, I noticed him struggling to rise. I entreated him not to trouble himself. He managed to get up and walk me to the study door where I tried to take my leave again. Ignoring my repeated protests, he accompanied me to the landing, down the flights of stairs, through the door, across the courtyard, and out onto the street. I walked off down the very long sidewalk. When I finally reached the end, before turning the corner, I looked back and there he was still waving. I never saw him again.

Who was I to him? Someone whom he had barely known. Yet somehow the passion in him for my humanity knew no bounds. In the many months of darkness, pain, and sickness that followed for me, this memory was for me a light, the glory of the Father's only Son.

Father, you did not want us to live in darkness, far from your light
of truth and compassion. Show us today the saving face of your
Son who lives and reigns with you and the Holy Spirit, one God
for ever and ever.

The Hunger of the Religious Person

Father Vincent Nagle, F.S.C.B.

John testified to him and cried out, saying, "This was he
of whom I said, 'The one who is coming after me ranks
ahead of me because he existed before me.'"
(Jn 1:15)

A friend of mine said to me, "There are only two types of really fascinating people, the truly religious man and the anarchist." In the core of the human person there is a terrible hunger which if fully embraced will bring the individual to either violence on the one hand, as with the anarchist, or prayer on the other, as with the religious person.

Human acts of evil very often come from the wounds of strange and impossible longings that we find hard to understand. We do not know what exactly the object of our desire might be, what can ultimately fulfill us. Our temptation is to answer that desire by gaining, winning, or taking whatever we have laid our eyes upon. The anarchist is the one who rejects any order in the world except taking what has captured his or her craving at the moment, what seems to calm the infinite hunger at the time. We can sympathize with this position. We are all wounded by desire.

The fully religious person also is someone whose entire existence is in tension toward the fulfillment of this unnameable desire rising out of the core of our being. But this person knows that he cannot imagine or possess the object of desire. *It precedes us and exceeds us.* This person has understood that the only true path toward satisfying the hunger is waiting and making a constant entreaty that the mysterious object of our longing come and possess us.

John the Baptist is the very icon of the fascinating religious man. A man of the wilderness with all the wild and consuming hunger of the anarchist, but who has turned toward the mystery, not himself, to touch and heal the wound. He cries out announcing the coming of the one who "ranks ahead of me because he existed before me." This is the true human position, and it is thus with authority that the Baptist points us to our Savior.

Father, do not let me fear this painful hunger within my soul.
Rather let it consume me so that in all times and ways I will be
begging to see you in your only Son, Jesus my Savior, amidst the
dramas and joys of this life.

If You Listen, He Will Speak

Father Vincent Nagle, F.S.C.B.

From his fullness we have all received, grace in place of grace, because while the law was given through Moses, grace and truth came through Jesus Christ. No one has ever seen God. The only Son, God, who is at the Father's side, has revealed him.

(Jn 1:16-18)

A friend and I were sitting drinking beer outside a bistro in the city of Rabat, the capital of Morocco. Having that day completed a short training course, the next day we would depart for different towns to begin our two-year contracts as English teachers in Moroccan high schools. He looked over at me, with an intense expression that I could barely make out in the obscurity, and asked, "What do you want to do with yourself during these years in Morocco?" To my great surprise the answer—of which I had been previously unaware—rushed upon me with clarity and certainty. "I want to learn to pray," I responded.

I had for five years or more been an active Catholic, involved in many groups and initiatives, including leading youth retreats. Yet never had I really gone to my "inner room, close[d] the door, and pray[ed] to [my] Father in secret," as Jesus commands (Mt 6:6). I felt strongly that God was waiting to hear from me, waiting perhaps impatiently, since I had so often spoken of him and so seldom spoken to him one-on-one.

Awkwardly I began with a daily missal, a rosary, and some music tapes. It was not all that long—a question of months rather than years—before something surprising happened. I had been aware of his waiting to hear from me, but I had not expected that he was so anxious to let me hear from him. In so many ways, some clamorous, others exquisitely subtle, he communicated a gift difficult to define. I only knew that through this prayer to the Father in the name of the Son a treasure of purity, light, and truth was consigned, with eagerness it seemed, to my keeping. The Son does indeed reveal to us the Father, I discovered, and the Father gives to us his Son, even as Jesus told us.

Heavenly Father, you have revealed your yearning for communion with your children through your Son. Let us not hesitate or draw back, but come to you in the silence to show you our devotion and receive your life-saving Word.

Admit One

Father James M. Sullivan, O.P.

And this is the testimony of John. When the Jews from Jerusalem sent priests and Levites [to him] to ask him, "Who are you?" he admitted and did not deny it, but admitted, "I am not the Messiah." So they asked him, "What are you then? Are you Elijah?" And he said, "I am not." "Are you the Prophet?" He answered, "No." (Jn 1:19-21)

In the Jewish leaders' pursuit of the identity of John the Baptist, they press him: "Who are you?" This translation of the Gospel of Saint John does not have John replying, confessing, or telling them, but rather "admitting" in answer to their question. Translations sometimes point us to a deeper truth that is hidden within the meaning of the text.

The English word "admit" comes from the Latin word *admittere*, meaning "to let in," which is obvious enough to us who often see Admit One printed on most tickets. We seek admittance to the theater or the ballpark, so we buy a ticket to ensure just that.

The remarkable fact about John's "admittance" to the Jewish leaders is that he is allowing them to enter into something far greater than they may at first realize. John is admitting them into the greatest mystery there is—namely, the mystery of God himself. The last prophet of the old covenant brings them face to face with the fulfillment of all prophecies.

This would not be possible, however, if the Lord himself had not sent John the Baptist for this very purpose. In fact, the Latin *admittere* can be broken down even further into two words: *ad* and *mittere*, which mean, respectively, "to" and "to send." In other words, John is being sent to the Jewish leaders precisely so that they can gain entry into the mystery John preaches. The Father sends John, not only to proclaim the coming of Christ, but to open the way for that coming.

In admitting to them who he was not, John is causing them to search even further and deeper for the One for whom they are truly searching: not Elijah or a prophet, but the Messiah himself. The Lord has placed many people, events, and revelations in our lives for that same purpose, so that we too will search further and deeper for Christ.

Loving Father, admit me into the mystery of your Son so that I may share in his mission to the world, and be a means for others to come to know him.

The S-Curve

Father James M. Sullivan, O.P.

So [the priests and Levites] said to [John], "Who are you,
so we can give an answer to those who sent us? What do
you have to say for yourself?" He said:/ "I am 'the voice of
one crying out in the desert,/ "Make straight the way
of the Lord,"'/ as Isaiah the prophet said."
(Jn 1:22-23)

Years ago, just south of Cincinnati, Ohio, on the major interstate running through the hills of Kentucky, there used to be a stretch of highway that was notorious for accidents. In addition to being on a hill, there was a very dangerous S-curve in the road. Quite often, a tractor trailer would not slow down soon enough, and it would topple over, taking with it all the cars around it. Finally, after much planning and preparation, the civil authorities changed the pattern of the road so that the S-curve would no longer be as severe.

In our spiritual lives, we can be a lot like those trucks which traveled that section of highway. We carry burdens, weighed down by life, and still we move ahead. We pick up speed, though, as we move along, and if we travel along the straight paths of the Lord there will be no difficulties. But once we come to a turn in the road, we have to be prepared to slow down or even to stop altogether. If not, we run the same risk as those unprepared truck drivers.

The S-curves in our lives are our sins. They are "sin-curves" that take us off the path stretched out before us. "Make straight the way of the Lord" ultimately means to be freed from our sins—to be straightened out, so to speak. Sin slows us down as we move toward the Lord. We lose our momentum and even our resolve to be faithful. Sin causes damage to ourselves and very often to those around us. Sin can even be fatal and leave us wrecked at the side of the road.

When they reconstructed that highway, it was better than before, but it still wasn't completely straight. As the Lord reconstructs us, however, we will be—his paths will lead straight to the innermost depths of our soul.

Heavenly Father, remove in my life all that hinders your grace from having its full effect in me. Free me from my sins.

Bethany of All Places

Father James M. Sullivan, O.P.

Some Pharisees were also sent. They asked [John], "Why then do you baptize if you are not the Messiah or Elijah or the Prophet?" John answered them, "I baptize with water; but there is one among you whom you do not recognize, the one who is coming after me, whose sandal strap I am not worthy to untie." This happened in Bethany across the Jordan, where John was baptizing. (Jn 1:24-28)

The village of Bethany is a special place in the life of Jesus. Bethany is where he visits Martha and Mary: "Martha, Martha, you are anxious and worried about many things" (Lk 10:41); here he dines with Simon the Leper and his feet are anointed (Mt 26:6ff.); and it is here that he raises his friend, Lazarus, from the dead (Jn 11:1ff.). It is a place of great hospitality where Jesus is always welcome and perhaps feels most at home. In fact, Jesus spends the week before his Passion here in Bethany.

But, the Bethany of John the Baptist across the Jordan is not the same Bethany of Jesus. They were completely different locations, and it is strange that in John's Gospel he calls it Bethany since even to this day there is no evidence of a town being present in that locale.

The name Bethany itself can be translated as "house of poverty" or "house of misery." Perhaps this is why John refers to the area as "Bethany across the Jordan." It is John the Baptist's special role to prepare the way for the Messiah. How can he do that without pointing out our need for the Messiah, or in other words, the poverty and misery in our lives without him? By going to this Bethany we would be going "across the Jordan" and be washed in the waters of conversion. John's baptism assures no forgiveness, it just makes us ready to receive that forgiveness when it comes.

The earliest Church Father to wrestle with this scriptural geography of the two Bethanys seems to be Origen. He proposes that the location John has in mind is a place called "Bethabara." This is all the more fitting because of its meaning: "house of preparation." To prepare for Jesus' coming into our lives reminds us of Bethany all over again: it is here that we are freed from all anxiety, anointed by the grace of the Holy Spirit, and raised from the dead of our sin.

Most merciful Father, prepare me in my poverty to receive you in all your richness. Fill me with your grace and configure my life to Christ's.

Ecce Agnus Dei

Father James M. Sullivan, O.P.

The next day [John] saw Jesus coming toward him and said,
"Behold, the Lamb of God, who takes away the sin of the world.
He is the one of whom I said, 'A man is coming after me who
ranks ahead of me because he existed before me.' I did not
know him, but the reason why I came baptizing with
water was that he might be made known to Israel."
(Jn 1:29-31)

The voice finally cries out in the wilderness so that all may hear him clearly: "Behold, the Lamb of God!" *"Ecce Agnus Dei!"* Do we need to hear John the Baptist say anything else? Does he need to explain what he means by "lamb"? Does he need to give more details about God? It seems not for his listeners, as the meaning is perfectly understood: the Lamb of God is the sacrifice for his people.

These same words of John the Baptist are spoken at every Mass, repeated three times, actually, to help prepare us for Holy Communion as we beg the Lord to have mercy on us and to hear our prayer. The recently introduced translation of the Roman Missal changed slightly the words spoken as the priest holds up the host: "Behold the Lamb of God, behold him who takes away the sins of the world. Blessed are those called to the supper of the Lamb."

In other words, we pray three times for the Lamb of God to have mercy on us, and then he appears in the host held for us in the hands of the priest. Our prayer for mercy has been heard because the priest proclaims, as John the Baptist did: "Behold the Lamb of God." Perhaps this is the quickest prayer that has ever been answered. We ask for mercy; Christ appears before us.

It is significant to remember, though, that this moment in the Mass only takes place after the host has been broken. The "fraction rite" breaks the host, and it is when he is broken that Christ is held up in the Eucharist and proclaimed to be the Lamb of God once again. The Lamb of God is the sacrifice for his people. "Behold the Lamb of God!" Do we need to hear John the Baptist say anything else?

Loving Father, take away my sins and increase within me a desire
for the Lamb of God. Make Christ known through me.

The Seed of the Gospel

Father James M. Sullivan, O.P.

*John testified further, saying, "I saw the Spirit come down like
a dove from the sky and remain upon him. I did not know him,
but the one who sent me to baptize with water told me,
'On whomever you see the Spirit come down and remain,
he is the one who will baptize with the holy Spirit.'
Now I have seen and testified that he is the Son of God."*
(Jn 1:32-34)

There is a certain completion to John the Baptist's mission now,
it seems fulfilled in a way. He has done what he was sent to
do, but what exactly was that? We have all seen directions or
recipes that include the step: "Now add water." In a way, John the
Baptist just added water to the seed that needed to grow.

Seeds have been created in such a way that all of them need water
to begin their growth, but it is important that the water is added
at just the right time and not too early or too late. There are many
factors in the growth of a seed: temperature, soil, oxygen, and the
most important of them all is water. Water assures growth.

All seeds have a protective "seed coat" that keeps water out of the
seed itself. Once the conditions are right for growth, the seed coat
begins to let water into the seed. The seed then does two things: it
forms a root to go down into the earth for more water and minerals,
and a shoot to go up to the surface for sunlight and air. In a type
of analogy, the Baptist has added water to the Messiah, and Christ
takes root as he blesses with the Holy Spirit the water that is to be
used later for baptism, and he forms that shoot which reaches up
to the Father who proclaims him to be the Son of God.

In our own spiritual lives as well there is the need for the root
of self-knowledge and the shoot of divine grace. As we grow in an
awareness of ourselves, both our virtues and our vices, we become
all the more convinced of our own need for the Messiah. He alone
by the workings of his grace can save us. We need both a root and
a shoot to grow and we first needed the waters of our own baptism
to ensure that beginning.

*Eternal Father, thank you for the gift of my baptism. May the
waters that came down on me always assure me of your grace at
work in my life.*

The Unnamed Disciple

Father James M. Sullivan, O.P.

The next day John was there again with two of his disciples, and as he watched Jesus walk by, he said, "Behold, the Lamb of God." The two disciples heard what he said and followed Jesus.
(Jn 1:35-37)

We know from later verses in Saint John's Gospel that one of these two unnamed disciples is, in fact, Andrew, the first called of the Apostles and the brother of Simon Peter. What we do not know for certain, however, is the name of the other disciple. There are many theories. It could be Philip, since he appears also in later verses, or it could be the Beloved Disciple himself, John. Others speculate that it is simply a disciple of no consequence, and that is why he is not named, or possibly even a disciple who later fell away. In the end, we simply do not know.

This lack of a name, though, is not a dead end, but rather quite the opposite. One way to meditate on passages like these with unnamed figures is to imagine our own name being listed there. In fact, we are not rearranging past events but rather opening ourselves up for new events. Realizing ourselves in the place of the disciples helps to deepen our relationship with Christ, and gives us the means as well.

"The two disciples heard what he said and followed Jesus." What is most striking about this discipleship is how immediate it is. There weren't any long conversations or arguments. They didn't even need John the Baptist to repeat himself; they heard what he said: "Behold, the Lamb of God." They followed Jesus.

Many times we imagine things to be much more complicated than they really are. Actually, we ourselves are often the only reason why so many situations in our lives are so complicated. Our discipleship doesn't have to be. It doesn't have to be of little consequence either, nor end in falling away. We simply have to follow the example of that first unnamed disciple. Ready? "Behold, the Lamb of God."

Most merciful Father, make me a better disciple of your Son so that I will listen for him in all the moments of my life, especially those that are the most painful and difficult.

Timing Is Everything

Father James M. Sullivan, O.P.

*Jesus turned and saw [the two disciples of John] following him
and said to them, "What are you looking for?" They said to
him, "Rabbi" (which translated means Teacher), "where are you
staying?" He said to them, "Come, and you will see." So they
went and saw where he was staying, and they stayed
with him that day. It was about four in the afternoon.*

(Jn 1:38-39)

Every generation has its moments when time seems to stop and people remember exactly where and when they heard something that changed their lives: the collapse of the World Trade Center, the attempted assassination of Pope John Paul II, Neil Armstrong stepping onto the moon. Time has an infinite quality at those moments when it almost seems suspended.

"It was about four in the afternoon." The two disciples never forgot that time of first encounter with Jesus. What makes their recollection of the time all the more surprising is that their verbal exchange with Jesus is not about the greatest mysteries of the universe. They almost seem caught off guard when Jesus asks them directly: "What are you looking for?"

Jesus' question is sidestepped by the response, "Where are you staying?" as if they are following the Lamb of God to find his home. Jesus, always hearing the deeper questions in our voice, invites them closer: "Come, and you will see." And something in that discussion had an everlasting effect on those two disciples, for they never forgot the time that day.

In our own spiritual lives there are countless moments like "four in the afternoon." They don't only happen on special occasions years apart from each other. Jesus is always asking us, "What are you looking for?" and inviting us to "Come and see." In a special way each time we go to confession or receive Holy Communion, Jesus is speaking to us in the same way he spoke to those two disciples. What is it that the forgiveness of our sins affords us? What does the Eucharist do for us? We don't have to discuss the greatest mysteries of the universe; we just tell Jesus what it is we are looking for. "Come, and you will see." Time will almost seem suspended.

Heavenly Father, help me to follow Jesus throughout each day of my life, and help me to stay with him.

First Finding Our Own

Father James M. Sullivan, O.P.

Andrew, the brother of Simon Peter, was one of the two who heard John and followed Jesus. He first found his own brother Simon and told him, "We have found the Messiah" (which is translated Anointed).

(Jn 1:40-41)

Andrew finds the Messiah, and the first person he finds after that is his brother, Simon Peter. Why does Andrew go to Peter? Is it love for his sibling or just family loyalty that motivates him, or is it something deeper yet more obvious?

Imagine reading a great novel and thinking at the end of it, "I have to tell my father about this book." Or after seeing a great movie and thinking at the end of that, "I have to tell my mother about this movie." Here's the question: Why not do it the other way around? Why not tell your father about the movie and your mother about the book? The reason you don't is because whatever it was in the movie or the book had something specifically to do with an individual person. You are not simply telling another random person about a great movie or book. You want to tell a particular person a particular truth. This is why Andrew first finds Peter; he knew that Peter needed to know Christ.

Sometimes the ones who need the most "finding" in our lives are the ones closest to us, maybe even the members of our families. We might be hesitant to speak a word about Christ to them, yet, remembering the example of Andrew, who else could we first go to? Perhaps in the Lord's providential plan for our lives we ourselves have the gift of faith precisely so that we can be the one to bring these persons to Christ. Andrew brings Peter to Christ, and think of how many people have been brought to Christ through Peter. It all started with Andrew.

First finding "our own" to tell them about Christ is better than anything we could tell them about a book or movie. There is some particular truth that Christ wants us to share with them.

Loving Father, give me the courage to bring those in my family closer to Christ through my own example and life. Strengthen their faith, and help them to find Christ.

So

Father James M. Sullivan, O.P.

Then [Andrew] brought [his brother Simon] to Jesus. Jesus looked at him and said, "You are Simon the son of John; you will be called Cephas" (which is translated Peter).
(Jn 1:42)

This is the first time in the Gospel of Saint John that Jesus sees Peter with his own human eyes. There is recognition in Jesus' words to him: "You are Simon the son of John." It is not a question, as one might expect upon a first meeting, but rather it is a declaration. Some translations even have: "So you are Simon." This "so" seems to communicate a knowledge of Peter that Christ, as the Son of God, most certainly possessed. The "so" also points to the significance of this meeting. It adds emphasis and even poetry to their first coming together. "So you are Simon and now you are going to be Peter."

In all movies that get us to cry there is that collage of significant events in the midst of some suffering that brings everything back into focus. I imagine that in the midst of Peter's denial of Christ such a collage ran through his mind. There was the miraculous catch of fish after Peter had caught nothing all night. There was the terror on the Sea of Galilee as Peter began to sink while walking toward Christ amidst the storm. There was the glory of the Transfiguration on Mount Tabor. There was the rebuke of Peter's diabolical talk in dismissing the Passion. But this is the moment in Peter's life that defined him: "You are Simon the son of John; you will be called Cephas."

This singular moment forms Peter, but it accomplishes something even greater: this moment saves Peter. It brings him back to the Upper Room after the crucifixion. It prevents him from ever returning unchanged to the life he had lived before. This moment leads him through the contrition for his denial of Christ to the joy of his Resurrection. "Yes," Peter says, "I am Simon, but I will only be Rock (Cephas) by your grace."

Eternal Father, refresh my memory with all that Christ has done for me, the numerous times I have met him and felt his presence. Never allow me to forget the singular moments of grace in my life.

Being Found by Jesus

Father James M. Sullivan, O.P.

The next day [Jesus] decided to go to Galilee, and he found Philip. And Jesus said to him, "Follow me." Now Philip was from Bethsaida, the town of Andrew and Peter.

(Jn 1:43-44)

There is a great deal of "finding" in these verses of Saint John's Gospel. Andrew finds Simon. Philip finds Nathanael, after he confesses to finding the Messiah. But by far the most important "finding" is the one recorded above in Jn 1:43: "[Jesus] found Philip." What this implies is that Jesus was first searching for Philip. Philip was sought by Christ before he was found by him. "[Jesus] decided to go to Galilee."

One possible way to conceive of this "finding" is likening it to the various "treasure hunt" shows that are on television. Whether they are pickers, diggers, or storage locker buyers, all of these shows have one thing in common—the search for the truly valuable amidst the not so valuable. They simply go in pursuit of what needs to be found. They are willing to take the risk or gamble of looking through piles of worthless junk to find something of value.

With Christ finding us, it is his quest through all of the "worthless junk" in our lives that makes us convinced of his love for us. What is worthless is, of course, sin. Our sin is the rubble that surrounds us and through which Christ must dig in order to find us. But just as in those "treasure hunt" shows, the thrill is in the hunt itself. When we reflect on our lives and think of all that Christ has done and continues to do to find us over and over again, it convinces us of our value in his sight. We might be dusty or dirty or hidden away, but Christ has found us, and, in perspective, his search for us gives us the thrill not only of being found, but the thrill of knowing what he went through in order to find us.

Most merciful Father, thank you for sending your Son to find me amidst my sins. Fill me with a greater desire for Christ so that I may never live my life without him.

The Good from Nazareth

Father James M. Sullivan, O.P.

Philip found Nathanael and told him, "We have found the one about whom Moses wrote in the law, and also the prophets, Jesus, son of Joseph, from Nazareth." But Nathanael said to him, "Can anything good come from Nazareth?" Philip said to him, "Come and see." (Jn 1:45-46)

P robably by now all of us have become familiar with talent shows that highlight either the abilities or inabilities of its contestants. Some people get their big break, and others sadly just get broken. By far, though, my favorite entries are the ones who at first cause the audience either to laugh at them or simply to dismiss them as talentless. It could be their hair, their walk, or just their clothing. Even the judges seem to have made up their minds before the person has ever performed. Then the moment of surprise takes over them all as the frumpy middle-aged woman hits each note perfectly, or the geeky teenager sings a ballad worthy of an opera star. It's not only rooting for the underdog that I enjoy, but also the fact that all those who prejudged that contestant could not have been more wrong about the talent before them.

Is Nathanael's question the same thing? "Can anything good come from Nazareth?" Has he already prejudged Jesus and dismissed him? Philip responds with the only possible answer for such an interrogation: "Come and see." How can Philip explain every reason for his belief in Christ, for each line of Scripture that Christ has fulfilled? "We have found the one about whom Moses wrote in the law, and also the prophets...." Philip speaks with a certain confidence that only comes from one who spends time with Christ. "Come and see."

That's why talent shows have performances. It's not about what the contestants are wearing or how they're walking. It's about the talent that you just have to hear or witness in order to be convinced. The crowd may at first begin to laugh or mock, but once the talent is revealed, the crowd's objections are quickly silenced. Likewise Nathanael goes and sees. He is even silenced as he witnesses for himself the good that comes from Nazareth.

Loving Father, help me to come closer to Christ and to see him more clearly at work in my life. Free me from all doubt and fill me with greater confidence.

Two-Faced

Father James M. Sullivan, O.P.

Jesus saw Nathanael coming toward him and said of him, "Here is a true Israelite. There is no duplicity in him."
(Jn 1:47)

One of the most striking and perhaps even horrific figures of Michelangelo's *Last Judgment* is not to be found in his depiction of hell but rather in the glories of heaven. It is the figure of Nathanael, or, as he is commonly referred to, Saint Bartholomew. This saint catches one's eye because he sits before the triumphant Christ, holding what seems to be another man drooping from his hand. He just seems to hang there, lifeless. The drooping man is in fact the skin of this martyred Apostle who was flayed alive for his profession of faith.

It is ironic that Bartholomew is praised by Christ for not having any duplicity in him, and yet in his iconic depiction he often has two faces, the regular one and the one that belongs to his skin. He is "two-faced" then, and even though that phrase is never used as a compliment, it might help us to understand something about the spiritual life.

"There is no duplicity in him." There might not have been duplicity in Saint Bartholomew, but there was certainly a need for change. The two faces therefore can be the "before and after," so to speak. The man who Bartholomew was when he began to follow Christ was not the man he was when his life was over—there was the start and the finish. The two faces show the change that took place over time. It's important to keep both in perspective so that we will never forget where we started or how far we have come by the grace of God.

Another important feature of the skin of Saint Bartholomew that many scholars have pointed out is that it is actually a self-portrait of Michelangelo himself. Perhaps he too wanted to be freed from the "old man" of his sin so as to be born anew in Christ.

Eternal Father, continue to reveal to me my true self so that I will always serve you with an undivided heart. Free me from any self-deception or disordered attachments in my life.

The Blessed Fig Tree

Father James M. Sullivan, O.P.

Nathanael said to [Jesus], "How do you know me?"
Jesus answered and said to him, "Before Philip called you,
I saw you under the fig tree." Nathanael answered him,
"Rabbi, you are the Son of God; you are the King of Israel."
(Jn 1:48-49)

The question this verse raises is: "Why does the mention of a fig tree elicit the response of faith?" It doesn't seem that figs would have that effect on people. It is certainly true that Jesus knows Nathanael better than Nathanael knows himself, but the fig tree must have meant something particular for Nathanael. Jesus could have picked out any place to reveal to Nathanael where he saw him, but Jesus names the fig tree. Something happened under that fig tree that none of us will ever know, but maybe it was something that we can perfectly understand.

All of us have had moments in our spiritual lives when we have "felt" the presence of God, and at other times we have had difficult experiences when that perceived presence is nowhere on the horizon. What happens to us then? What if under that fig tree Nathanael had made a type of promise with God? Or even more intriguing, as he looked up at the leaves of the fig tree, he had made a bargain with God: "Unless you reveal yourself to me, I cannot give my life over to you. Show me the Messiah!" While bargaining with or challenging God are never acts of faith, perhaps God used them to bring Nathanael to faith.

"Before Philip called you, I saw you under the fig tree." Jesus' revelation to Nathanael about the fig tree gives Nathanael the greater ability to reveal who Jesus is: the Son of God. The sins and failings in our own lives can have much the same effect. Too often we think that our forgiven sins are of no use to us or to the Lord. Reality is quite to the contrary. These forgiven sins help us to trust in the Lord all the more.

Jesus later in the Gospels curses a fig tree, but this one he most certainly blessed.

Heavenly Father, I surrender all of the events of my life to you and ask that you use them for my holiness and sanctification. Help me to see your work even in the midst of my sins.

The Real Greater Things

Father James M. Sullivan, O.P.

Jesus answered and said to [Nathanael], "Do you believe because I told you that I saw you under the fig tree? You will see greater things than this."

(Jn 1:50)

Jesus promises Nathanael "greater things," but he does not say that they will necessarily be "happier things." The greater things may not be all that joyful at all.

One of the greatest truths of the spiritual life is found among the sayings of Saint Catherine of Siena: "Suffering and sorrow increase in proportion to love." At first this doesn't compute all that easily. We have it stuck in us somehow that we are made to be happy at all times. We are never to experience pain or even disappointment. When we love more, we are meant to suffer less. This is how God made us, but it is not how he is redeeming us.

The only way to see the "greater things" and, thus, the hand of God in our lives, is to see them in the midst of all the other things in our lives. One helpful way to think of this is a number puzzle like Sudoku or my recent favorite, Ken-Ken. Both of them require seeing both the little picture and the big picture at the same time. Each row and square (or section) has the need for the same numbers, for example, one through nine, but it's only by seeing the whole picture that you're able to solve the puzzle. That's a little like life: it's only by seeing the whole picture that you're able to see how it all fits together.

Not many people would accept crosses solely for the sake of suffering more, but when the great reward or blessing of the penance is revealed, they would. The "greater things" before each one of us may not be the "easier things," but in God's providence for our lives they are always the "better things."

"You will see greater things than this," such as God's grace supporting you in suffering and stronger love coming out of sorrow.

Most merciful Father, increase my trust in all your promises, especially that of my salvation. Help me to see the "greater things" in my life that always assure me of your presence.

Stay Tuned

Father James M. Sullivan, O.P.

*And [Jesus] said to [Nathanael], "Amen, amen, I say to you,
you will see the sky opened and the angels of God
ascending and descending on the Son of Man."*
(Jn 1:51)

"Stay tuned. There is more to come right after this." I'm not sure if this cue for commercial breaks is still used on TV, but I do remember it from my childhood television watching days. I suppose the network officials knew people would want to skip the commercials and begin "channel surfing" to find something more interesting. The "stay tuned" just encouraged you to wait through the next few minutes, and the "more to come" would be fulfilled.

Jesus in this passage seems to be telling Nathanael to "stay tuned" for the "more to come." If Nathanael thinks that Jesus' knowledge of him under the fig tree is miraculous, wait until he sees the events of the future. If Nathanael thinks that this is all the Messiah can do for him, he will be even more surprised.

In fact, there is no record of this vision ever being fulfilled in the Bible. Jesus promises Nathanael this vision, and therefore it must be interpreted as a private vision that was meant for Nathanael alone. Perhaps it was what he saw at the Ascension or even at his death. Whenever it was fulfilled it was meant to convince Nathanael all the more that Jesus is the Son of God, that he is the Messiah.

This promised vision also points to the "more to come" in each one of our lives. We don't have the words of Christ assuring us of some particular vision but most assuredly Christ does have visions in store for us. Each individual person saved by Christ will see God face to face in heaven. Heaven is not some amorphous blob of happiness; it is our own individual happiness. We will be united as saints with resurrected bodies and glorified souls. We will see each other as the Church lives her triumphant life for all eternity.

Stay tuned. There is much much more to come after this.

Loving Father, give me a vision of your glory. Increase in me the theological virtue of faith by which I can know you here on earth and see you one day face to face in heaven.

An Ordinary Guest, An Exceptional Promise

Father Vincent Nagle, F.S.C.B.

*On the third day there was a wedding in Cana in Galilee,
and the mother of Jesus was there. Jesus and his disciples
were also invited to the wedding.*
(Jn 2:1-2)

The wedding gives us a rare glimpse of the hidden life of Jesus before his public mission. He came as Mary's son, not as a prophet, rabbi, or savior. He came to meet his people as an ordinary guest. But there it began.

It happened thus for me. It was at a barbecue that I had the first real hint that *everything* might change. A good friend had invited me to a cookout at his house, but I was doubtful. He was no social butterfly and had never hosted any get-together, as far as I knew. When I had been to his home for dinner it was a Top Ramen instant meal and some salad. Now he was hosting a barbecue?

I just had to go to this barbecue. I was afraid that if I did not go, then perhaps there would be absolutely no one there. I did not want to take the chance of him facing that humiliation.

When I showed up there were at least thirty people there and someone was playing a guitar. What had happened? The people I met were interesting and humanly attractive. One, with piercing eyes, answered my question about who they were with these words: "We're people who think that being Catholic goes way beyond Sunday morning." Later we read some pages from a book written by a priest they knew. Who were they?

Both my friend and I later left to live in Italy in order to follow these friends more closely, and we found our separate vocations there. It was just a barbecue. Ordinary. Yet out of the midst of that celebrating company, something extraordinary was promised and present. Jesus came and comes into the ordinary world to fulfill the promise for something exceptional that the ordinary makes to us. He is a wedding guest among others. This knowledge lets us embrace the ordinary in our lives full of extraordinary expectation.

Father, you know I can despise what is ordinary because I do not perceive there the fulfillment of your promise of life. Let me remember your Son and embrace the ordinary, giddy with the anticipation of meeting your Son.

What Really Interests Me

Father Vincent Nagle, F.S.C.B.

*When the wine ran short, the mother of Jesus said to him,
"They have no wine." (Jn 2:3)*

I n the small New England city where I lived for some years,
I would sometimes see an elderly man wandering the streets.
He was clearly suffering under some kind of mental impairment,
with his jerky movements, wild stare, and open mouth. Mucus
often ran down his face, hanging off of his chin. As I drove by him
I promised myself I would stop and talk with him the next time.
I never did stop, yet he still haunts my conscience. Why? What is
he to me? Why do I feel this responsibility for him?

I failed to obey the promptings of the Holy Spirit, yet it is clear to
me why I felt called. There is a presence in my life that has changed
what would otherwise be a confused existence into an adventure
of love and truth. It has transformed sufferings, which would have
embittered me, and achievements, which would have convinced
me of the futility of existence, into part of a yearning for heaven.

That answer to the deepest need of my life is a presence that
desires to communicate itself. I can be lazy and disobedient when
I sense the need that others have of that presence, but I cannot
be indifferent. That presence renders their need interesting to me.

At the wedding, the host family is facing a public failure in
hospitality, a breach in their social relationships. The reputation
of an entire family, perhaps an entire village, is on the line. But it
is not Mary's family and it is not her village. Why does she care?
She cares because Jesus is there. There is a presence in her life that
awakens her to the need of others, making their drama something
that involves her. She does not hesitate. "They have no wine," she
says to him. She has obeyed the Spirit, and brought the need in
front of her to her Lord, her Son, our Savior.

*Father, let us obey the promptings of your Spirit, and let your
Son present in our lives communicate to the needs of the world.
We ask this through the same Jesus, our Lord.*

The Answer, Not the Solution

Father Vincent Nagle, F.S.C.B.

[And] Jesus said to [his mother], "Woman, how does your concern affect me? My hour has not yet come."
(Jn 2:4)

My friends and I watched as a huge crowd of men poured out from the Friday mosque services from all over the Middle Eastern city and formed a march numbering perhaps hundreds of thousands. We listened as they began to chant in insistent tones a phrase in Arabic that translates into "Islam is the solution." It struck me very much.

But Jesus, for his part, apparently does not see his own role as "the solution." At the wedding of Cana his hosts face a reputation-blotting humiliation, and his neighbors and fellow guests an embittering disappointment. In the Middle East, a failure in hospitality is neither soon forgotten nor forgiven. Jesus, however, does not of himself feel obliged to fix anything. His mother feels otherwise, of course, yet he demurs before her entreaty. How is it that this one, in whom a mastery over nature and the supernatural are about to be unveiled, does not feel called upon to use his power to "fix" the problems around him? Why is Jesus not the solution?

Jesus is the Savior, not the solution. He has not come to get rid of our problems because he does not see our lives, even the pain and trials, as a problem. He sees our life as an opportunity for freely saying "yes" to communion with the Father through him. He comes to meet us in the here and now so that always and everywhere we are not determined by the obstacles, but rather by the present prospect of communion that his presence offers.

He is not here in order to get rid of anything. If he were, eventually he would have to get rid of us as well, since sometimes it is we ourselves who are the problem for us and for others. But he has not come to get rid of us, but to save us.

God and Father, again and again I come to you looking for a solution and say to you, "Fix it!" Let me listen to the real questions of my heart and come to you saying, "Save me!" through your Son.

Muslims Made Me a Priest

Father Vincent Nagle, F.S.C.B.

[Jesus'] mother said to the servers,
"Do whatever he tells you."
(Jn 2:5)

I half-jokingly tell people that I am indebted to Islam for my priestly vocation. The story goes like this: while I was living in a neighborhood of families of the Muslim Brotherhood, a very serious Islamic organization, in Morocco, I would have discussions about God, faith, and religion with some men there. One evening, returning home after one such discussion—hurrying to reach my house before the packs of wild dogs arrived—I suddenly had a conviction that something they had been telling me was true: to declare belief in God necessarily entails obedience. A person who says, "I believe," to be consistent, needs to follow that with the question, "What is your will?"

As a Californian boy raised in a hippie community during the 1960s and 70s, I understood God as a fuzzy entity, far too undefined to command obedience. In those months, though, I had begun a serious dialogue of prayer with the Father of our Lord Jesus Christ. Now, standing under a bright moon, I had a clear perception of the fact that God is God and I am not. He gave me an intuition of his unutterable and terrible vastness and power. I saw that not seeking his will means losing the opportunity of entering into his life and love. Through my discussions with those Muslims, God the Father made me understand that not to acknowledge his authority means to play with him a game in which I would be the loser.

Had I not made that step, could I have later answered his call to the priesthood, something that frightened me so deeply? Even today, I am brought back to a true position by this short command of our Lady, which shows her as a woman to be reckoned with. In moments of confusion or fear, she leads me back to the hope and peace we have in Christ by her words, "Do whatever he tells you."

Almighty Father, let me rediscover the joyful freedom of obedience to your Word, who is Jesus the Savior and who lives and reigns with you for ever and ever.

A Door in the Wall

Father Vincent Nagle, f.s.c.b.

*Now there were six stone water jars there for Jewish ceremonial
washings, each holding twenty to thirty gallons. Jesus told
[the servers], "Fill the jars with water." So they filled them
to the brim. Then he told them, "Draw some out now
and take it to the headwaiter." So they took it.*

(Jn 2:6-8)

A woman was diagnosed with a deadly disease. She felt as if the
paths of life were blocked and the walls of death were closing
in. "With our Lord," I said to her, "these circumstances are
not a trap closing in on you. What looks like a barrier in your way
is really a doorway on your path. He is the key to opening these
doors. Walk with him, for he sees a way forward for you through
what is here, not despite what is here."

How does Jesus answer the request of his mother? She has pointed
out to him what *is not* there, the wine. He starts to answer this need
by looking at, as he always does, what *is* there. There are six stone
water jars.

Whether it is a question of feeding the famished thousands with
five loaves and two fish (see Jn 6:9) or of opening the eyes of the
blind man with spit and dirt (see Jn 9:6), our Lord always starts
with what is already there. Even in choosing his disciples, he starts
from the ones who have come to him (see Jn 1:39) or who are near
(see Lk 5:1-11). He might be tempted to curse their limits (see Lk
9:41). Yet for him the finite nature of the things in front of him is
never an objection.

Jesus does not see the limits of this world as a prison shutting us
out from the infinite. Instead these things and these people are like
gateways that open upon the possibilities for God's saving work.
He is always asking what his Father is doing with what is there.
Those inert and useless jars show Jesus the answer the Father is
giving at the moment. Let us allow Jesus to liberate us from our
prisons and live in excited anticipation of what the Father is doing
with what is here.

*Dear Father, I so often feel burdened and threatened by what is in
front of me. Let the presence of your Son, who is the Way, lead me
to embrace this path and come to everlasting joy with you through
him and the Holy Spirit.*

What Is Foreseen Is Not What Is Needed

Father Vincent Nagle, F.S.C.B.

And when the headwaiter tasted the water that had become wine, without knowing where it came from (although the servers who had drawn the water knew), the headwaiter called the bridegroom and said to him, "Everyone serves good wine first, and then when people have drunk freely, an inferior one; but you have kept the good wine until now."

(Jn 2:9-10)

I had a full schedule: working up to thirty hours a week, writing my thesis, taking tough courses, dating, volunteering at a rest home, being student body president, visiting my family, running a Catholic students club, and keeping up with my athletic practice. I was not looking for any new activities.

So when a friend informed me that he had met some interesting Catholics and was meeting with them once a week, I was not eager to accept his invitations to join them. He introduced me to them at a barbecue, but I still didn't move. Running into him at a weekday Mass, I told him that I was all studied out and headed for the movies. He reminded me of my promises to attend these meetings, and pointed out that the meeting was that very evening. Caught, I went with him.

Some months later it occurred to me that, though always pressed for time, I had not only never missed a meeting with these new friends, but even when they got together socially I would go, or at least pass by or call to say, "Hi." "Why?" I asked myself. It was because I could not live without the experience of Christ that I had met there.

This taught me that the answer to the great question in my heart could hardly be answered by the fulfillment of what I had in my mind, of the program that I myself had made. Anything that we could have anticipated would be too small for our infinite desire.

The headwaiter was in charge of making sure all went according to plan. But what delighted him was this unplanned thing. Indeed, only something unforeseen can respond to the unnameable pain in us, the indescribable hunger in our souls. Our very salvation is in the fact that he is not quite what we expect.

Father, I am too small to understand what my heart is waiting for. Help me to expect the unexpected acts that are your grace, acting through your Son our Lord Jesus Christ.

The Religious Revolution

Father Vincent Nagle, F.S.C.B.

Jesus did this as the beginning of his signs in Cana in Galilee and so revealed his glory, and his disciples began to believe in him. After this, he and his mother, [his] brothers, and his disciples went down to Capernaum and stayed there only a few days. (Jn 2:11-12)

There is a revolution in this passage. Just how great a revolution it is became clear to me one evening talking with a young couple who had just been received into the Catholic Church after growing up in devout Sikh families in Singapore. The woman had excelled at school and graduated from university with a bright professional future ahead of her. But she had fallen into a deep depression. Nothing seemed to help, and she remained inert in her home for many months. A young man (now her husband) from another Sikh family in Singapore heard about her predicament. He had secretly converted to Christianity and went to speak with her about Jesus. She agreed to look at the copy of the Bible he left for her disguised as a Tolstoy novel.

The Gospel repelled her. This "supposedly" holy man, Jesus, did something that no holy man in any Eastern tradition would do: he constantly spoke of himself. Instead of presenting his followers with a spiritual path, explaining to them the way to enlightenment, he pointed to his own person. We see this in the passage where the Evangelist records that "his disciples began to believe in him." She thought, "What about believing in the way he taught? Why believe in him?"

This "egocentrism" of Jesus wounded her sensibilities, and yet she could not deny that every time she read the Gospel, the words of this Jesus brought peace upon her. This figure, like no other, anchored her heart in hope, and light began to come into her life. This was a revolution.

The way to God is not a teaching or a spiritual practice. It is this person who is the way. In the end, she could not live without Jesus. She and her friend married and came to the United States where they continue to live this revolution of coming more and more to believe in him.

Gracious Father, let the words, the presence, the person, the work, and grace of your Son so capture my heart that all things might be lovely to me only insofar as I recognize him, my Savior, in them.

Sluggish, and Sitting

Father Vincent Nagle, F.S.C.B.

Since the Passover of the Jews was near, Jesus went up to Jerusalem. He found in the temple area those who sold oxen, sheep, and doves, as well as the money-changers seated there.
(Jn 2:13-14)

Jesus goes up to Jerusalem to celebrate the Passover, the wondrous liberation of the children of Israel from their taskmasters in Egypt. He enters the precincts of the Temple, the house of God. This was the place where he had spent three days as a boy, speaking with the elders and astonishing them with his answers. Perhaps no place on earth means more to him, and what does he find when he arrives, but the same old human hardness of heart.

There are the money-changers, seated, plying their trade. For Jews from all over the world come to Jerusalem for the feast, and they bring coins that must be changed, for a fee, into the Temple currency. Then they purchase oxen or sheep or doves to be sacrificed. Maybe the money-changers and the sellers of the animals are squeezing the customers. Hucksters right on the spot are notorious for doing so. But Saint John does not say, and I think it dangerous to assume it.

For then we might be tempted to fall back into the same self-satisfied comfort that the money-changers felt, and many of their customers too. "We aren't doing anything illegal," says one. "We've come a long way for this feast," says another. "It's not my fault that the Temple elders won't accept Roman coin," says a third.

They are within a shout of the Holy of Holies, and it doesn't stir them. It's the occasion for a little business, a little enjoyment, maybe a little worship in due time, but not the raising of the heart to God. It's as if Moses had sold tickets for people to see the burning bush—meaning no disrespect, of course. Always, always man resists the call of God. It is too strenuous to stand. Always, we fold God back down into our own affairs. We instruct him to take a seat.

Almighty Father, for whom the weight of the universe is as nothing, but who sent your Son to bear the dead weight of human sin: lift up our hearts, that we may rise to you and praise you without ceasing, through Christ our Lord.

Knotting the Cords

Anthony Esolen

[Jesus] made a whip out of cords and drove them all out of the temple area, with the sheep and oxen, and spilled the coins of the money-changers and overturned their tables.

(Jn 2:15)

Never in the Gospel accounts do we encounter Jesus *deliberating* about something. He's never perplexed, never in doubt. That is remarkable. So intimate is his union with the Father, that to hear the Father's will and to act upon it are one and the same. All the more, then, does this verse strike me, because although Jesus knows exactly what he is going to do, it must have taken him a little time to find those cords and to knot them up into a whip.

Picture the scene. It's a regular mart, people shouting, haggling, searching for coins, and there's Jesus patiently fashioning the whip that will soon reduce it all to confusion. Not his confusion, but theirs; and he must have been a man of imposing strength and stature and authority, because it appears that none of the hucksters dared to resist him.

He spills the coins forth, as he will spill the treasure of his blood, and he drives the money-changers from the Temple, *cleansing* it, making it a fit place of worship; and soon the Temple of his immaculate body will become the site of the ultimate cleansing sacrifice. Even the whip—the scourge, as we might well translate it—will find a place in the Passion, and Jesus will wear upon his body the marks of his love.

Now, that whip of cords wasn't anything like the instrument of torture the Romans used to cut Jesus to the spine. It must have stung, but it was meant to sting the conscience into waking. As Jesus bound those cords, tightening each knot with a thrust of his arms, what was he thinking of? The honor of his Father, surely. But also, I suppose, he cared for the safety of the dullest of the sheep that need the sting on the back to keep them from falling into the pit.

Father in heaven, you who chastise those whom you love and make them clean, spare not your loving hand from us, but lead us with gentleness and firmness to your eternal Temple, through Jesus Christ our Lord.

As Innocent as Doves

Anthony Esolen

*And to those who sold doves [Jesus] said, "Take these out of
here, and stop making my Father's house a marketplace."
His disciples recalled the words of scripture,
"Zeal for your house will consume me."*
(Jn 2:16-17)

You can tell something about a man, said the great theologian Romano Guardini, by the people who are drawn to him, and though the scribes and Pharisees often lurked about Jesus, keeping a wary distance, children seem to have rushed right up to him. Jesus loved them, and loved the harmless animals too. "Be as innocent as doves," he says to his disciples. And now in the Temple, amidst the uproar, he approaches those who sold doves, and says, "Take these out of here."

The doves were sold to people too poor to afford a sheep or an ox to sacrifice. Joseph and Mary had sacrificed two turtledoves when they presented Jesus in the Temple. But the dove also plays a most mysterious part in Scripture. Noah sent a raven forth from the ark, when the rains had ceased, yet the raven never returned. The dove he then sent forth did return, not having found a place of rest. Then after seven days, as if to seek a new creation, Noah sent the dove forth again, and it returned to him with an olive branch in its beak, a sign that all would be well. The third time Noah sends the dove forth, it does not return—not until the day Jesus was baptized in the Jordan, to fulfill all righteousness, and to show the Holy Spirit renewing the face of the earth.

It would be sweet to suppose that the dove sellers set the poor creatures free. We don't know. But it is to them that he explains his actions, saying, "Stop making my Father's house a marketplace." He wants them instead to turn the marketplace back into the Father's house, and that can't be done just by ceasing to trade there. They must catch the zeal of Jesus: the fire of the Holy Spirit.

*Holy Father, make us both innocent and zealous, aflame with the
love of the Spirit, so that we may be a means for the restoring of
your temples in the hearts of men, through Jesus our Savior.*

The Jews Seek a Sign

Anthony Esolen

At this the Jews answered and said to [Jesus], "What sign can you show us for doing this?" Jesus answered and said to them, "Destroy this temple and in three days I will raise it up."
(Jn 2:18-19)

After Jesus has driven the money-changers from the Temple, the authorities confront him and ask him for a sign, to warrant his right to do what he has done. They are looking for a divine passport.

It's clear that they don't understand, nor do they really wish to. After all, they are implicated in the cleansing, since they have allowed the Temple to be made into a bazaar, and doubtless they profit from it directly or indirectly. But they are angered rather than just embarrassed. Jesus' words, "my Father's house," must especially nettle them. It isn't simply that Jesus has claimed a proprietary right to protect the sanctity of the Temple. He claims a unique and intimate relationship with God. He does not shut the door against anyone who wishes to enter. He is himself the door; and the Jewish leaders sense this new world within, and hold their places stubbornly outside.

Who was he to behave as if he cared for the Temple more than they did? Who was he to call God *his Father*? They might as well be military police asking for papers. Then Jesus' reply comes as a further shock. Does he have the right to protect the Temple? Why, if they should tear "this Temple" to the ground, he will raise it up in three days.

We may remember that when the disciples tried to impress Jesus with the sights of Jerusalem, playing the part of religious tourists, Jesus told them that there would come a time when not one stone would be left on another stone. For his Father's house as an attraction, or as the guarantor of ordinary business and perfunctory worship, he cares not one bit. It is as if he and the Jews are speaking different languages. The language of love is incomprehensible to the world; it can only be understood by love.

Almighty Father, worthy of all worship, send down your Spirit to enlarge the temples of our hearts, so that genuine prayer and devotion may find a pure and spacious place within, through Jesus Christ our Lord.

The Temple of the Body

Anthony Esolen

The Jews said, "This temple has been under construction for forty-six years, and you will raise it up in three days?" But [Jesus] was speaking about the temple of his body. Therefore, when he was raised from the dead, his disciples remembered that he had said this, and they came to believe the scripture and the word Jesus had spoken. (Jn 2:20-22)

There is one thing worse than complete ignorance. It's that dash of something that looks like knowledge, while it conceals from us how ignorant we are.

The Jews squint at Jesus sidelong—one can hear their baffled laughter and their barely restrained scorn. "This temple has been under construction for forty-six years!"

Here Jesus might say, "I am speaking figuratively," and engage them in some pointed discussion of the reform of worship in the Temple. Then they might nod, "Ah, we see," and return to their dinners, placing Jesus among other reformers they have known, with some of them mildly in favor and some not. But Jesus never invites this kind of knowledgeable ignorance.

Nor should we be satisfied with it. For Jesus is and is not speaking figuratively. Yes, his disciples would recall these words, with the flash of surprise and recognition after the fact: Jesus was speaking about the temple of his body, and of his Resurrection. But let us not rest there. The Temple was the center of Jewish worship. Hundreds of thousands of Jews would soon arrive for the feast of Pentecost, from all parts of the Mediterranean world. But Jesus is the new Temple, the new high priest, and the new and eternal victim: where his body is, there will people worship the Father in spirit and in truth.

The Jews speak of human work: the forty-six years required to build so massive a structure. Jesus speaks of the work of God, a new creation. The Temple that the Jews prize will be destroyed. But the Body of Christ, slain upon the cross, will rise again, and death shall have no more dominion over him. The Church too is the Body of Christ, and looks in longing for the banquet of the Lamb, in that Temple not made by human hands: whose name is the new Jerusalem—which will endure for ever.

Almighty and ever living Father, bring us from every nation to our everlasting home, to the wedding feast of Christ and the Church, where we will enjoy the bread of eternal life, through the same Christ our Lord.

He Knows Our Hearts

Anthony Esolen

While [Jesus] was in Jerusalem for the feast of Passover, many
began to believe in his name when they saw the signs he was
doing. But Jesus would not trust himself to them because he
knew them all, and did not need anyone to testify about
human nature. He himself understood it well.
(Jn 2:23-25)

This verse, to my mind, is one of the saddest in all Scripture. Jesus has performed wonders, and people are drawn to him. But he cannot trust them. They are not his open enemies. They would be his friends. Yet Jesus "did not need anyone to testify about human nature," or, more precisely, about man, for he knew what was in man.

We have a precious glimpse here into the mind of the Beloved Disciple, meditating in his age upon Jesus the man and what he was thinking. Recall that John reclined upon Jesus' breast at the Last Supper, and when he heard Jesus say that one of them would betray him, the young man asked, "Is it I, Lord?" John too must then have been aware of his own weakness, yet he was the only one of the Apostles to be found beneath the cross. Perhaps his youth protected him. Here he suggests to us the great solitude and disappointment of Jesus. How Jesus longed to open his heart! Yet even his Apostles, who dwelt with him and ate with him and traveled with him over the rugged hills and deserts of Palestine, did not understand him, and would not stand by his side in his greatest need.

It is "human nature," we may say, but that's not quite true. It is fallen human nature. It is the old man, Adam. Jesus knows that frail old man, crippled and bent toward the dust. But the old man doesn't recognize him. Imagine an honest man in the company of liars, pickpockets, and cheats. Imagine a pure man in the company of "good" fellows telling filthy stories and eyeing the harlots. Imagine the Lord, pierced with pity for all the lost sheep, among the self-righteous, boasting of their virtue. Adam does not know him. But Jesus knows Adam, and comes to summon him to death and resurrection.

Loving Father, send down your Holy Spirit upon us to give us
courage and steadfastness, so that by your grace we may stand
before the Lord our merciful Judge, and hear the words we long
to hear: "Well done, good and faithful servant!"

Saint Nicodemus, Patron of the Shy

Anthony Esolen

*Now there was a Pharisee named Nicodemus, a ruler of
the Jews. He came to Jesus at night and said to him, "Rabbi,
we know that you are a teacher who has come from God,
for no one can do these signs that you are doing unless
God is with him." (Jn 3:1-2)*

Nicodemus sought out where Jesus was staying and came to
him at night. Not during the day: probably he didn't want
the leaders among the Sanhedrin to know what he was
doing. I imagine a college professor, weary of secular emptiness,
driving half-ashamed to an evening Mass, hoping nobody will
recognize him.

Nicodemus says, "We know that you are a teacher come from
God," because nobody else could have performed the miracles that
Jesus has wrought. I don't know that he's quite honest there. Yes, Jesus
worked wonders. But to whom is he referring? Even as Nicodemus
speaks, the wheels of envy are grinding, and the hour of darkness
approaches. Perhaps he's hiding a little behind that plural. He hasn't
completely separated himself from the elders, whose good will he
still hopes for. Nor does he submit completely to faith in Jesus.
He does not say, *I know that you come from God.*

In other words, he seeks assurances. "You must come from God,"
he says, but he is implicitly begging, "Please, I need more. I need
to know."

Jesus will be gentle with Nicodemus, but he won't indulge the
diffidence. We'll soon see what Jesus does, but for now I'd like to
dwell on the special weakness of the intellectual. The common
laborer may see Jesus cure a blind man, and what else is there to
ask? But the intellectual hesitates. In part that's because he is wary
of committing himself too soon. But in part it is only because he
fears to look foolish. *Other people* may believe that at Fatima the sun
danced across the sky—indeed, many thousands of other people,
across many miles, who saw it with their own eyes. They stand up
to give witness, while the intellectual shies away.

But Nicodemus does come to Jesus; and the true wonder, the
conversion of a human soul, is about to transpire.

*Heavenly Father, be merciful to us in our blindness and foolishness,
and look kindly upon the most timid motion of our hearts, that
we may gain in strength and wisdom, through Jesus our Savior
and Lord.*

Born Again

Anthony Esolen

*Jesus answered and said to [Nicodemus], "Amen, amen, I say
to you, no one can see the kingdom of God without being born
from above." Nicodemus said to him, "How can a person once
grown old be born again? Surely he cannot reenter his mother's
womb and be born again, can he?" (Jn 3:3-4)*

"No one can see the kingdom of God without being born
from above," says Jesus to Nicodemus, who is perplexed
as to what this could mean. How can a man enter his
mother's womb a second time?

Jesus raises the stakes. Nicodemus has just said that the miracles
Jesus has performed show that he comes from God. But now Jesus
implies that that knowledge isn't enough. To see the Kingdom of
God in truth, you must do more than draw conclusions from the
works you observe. You must be a new creation, "born from above."

Here the confusion in the English might, for once, illuminate
a truth. When Jesus says, "born from above," he's using the same
word that Nicodemus uses when he says, "born again." To be born
again is to be born from above: to be made utterly new by the grace
of God. We aren't then talking about a reincarnation. The womb of
the mother doesn't enter the picture.

Or does it? Notice that Jesus never relieves the pressure of a
conversation by saying, "I am only speaking figuratively." Why,
anybody can shrug and walk away from a figure of speech. That's
because Jesus is not speaking figuratively. It's instead the real physical
birth that is the shadow or the figure of a birth that is more real, with
the agony of labor more painful, and the entrance from one world
into another more radical. The whole creation, says Saint Paul, is
groaning in labor to see its fulfillment in the Kingdom of God. It's
here among us, but not here in fullness yet; as a child in the womb
is among us, but not yet.

And the mother is here too, bearing children for the kingdom:
our holy Mother, the Church. In that sense, the man encountering
Jesus for the first time does not reenter the womb. He has never
left it to begin with.

*Almighty Father, who sent down your Spirit to overshadow the
Virgin Mary, that our Savior might be born among us: send down
your Spirit upon the Church, and be pleased to number us among
her children, through Christ our Lord.*

Hovering above the Waters

Anthony Esolen

Jesus answered, "Amen, amen, I say to you, no one can enter the kingdom of God without being born of water and Spirit. What is born of flesh is flesh and what is born of spirit is spirit."

(Jn 3:5-6)

Far from making his assertion easier to accept, Jesus' description of what it means to be born again deepens the mystery. "No one can enter the kingdom of God without being born of water and Spirit," he says—and not "spirit" as some generic substance, but *the Spirit*.

His words, as so often in the Gospels, bring us back to the time before the Fall. Here, they bring us back before the beginning of time itself, when God first made the heavens and the earth, and the Spirit of God was hovering above the waters. Nicodemus is a learned fellow; he cannot miss Jesus' reference to water and the Spirit of God.

Then the Kingdom of God breaks into this world with an all-transforming, sudden violence—the kingdom which is at the same time like the tiny mustard seed or the leaven as light as dust. To see that kingdom is to be present at the re-creation of the world. It is to be at hand when God says, "Let there be light." It is to see Jesus, the light of the world. But it is to be present not only as an observer; rather, as a partaker, being made new.

To the ancient Hebrews, the waters of the ocean suggested chaos, the darkness of what has not yet come to be. So to be immersed in the dark waters, like Jonah when the sailors threw him overboard, is to slip back to the verge of nonexistence. That is why our baptism into the Church is a baptism into the death of Jesus, and therefore also his Resurrection. It is fascinating, then, to consider the difference between what makes Nicodemus uneasy—the suggestion of death and rebirth—and what Jesus knows he will soon undergo, for Nicodemus and for all of us. We should like to be born again without those threatening waters. The cross teaches us otherwise.

Almighty Father, who sent forth your Spirit upon the waters, let your Spirit breathe also upon us, so that we may be re-created in the image and likeness of your Son, through the same Jesus Christ our Lord.

The Secret Spirit

Anthony Esolen

"Do not be amazed that I told you, 'You must be born from above.' The wind blows where it wills, and you can hear the sound it makes, but you do not know where it comes from or where it goes; so it is with everyone who is born of the Spirit."

(Jn 3:7-8)

When the prophet Elijah went up the mountain to encounter the spirit of God, he did not find him in the fire, or the whirlwind, or the tempest, but in a gentle rustling sound, the still small voice; and he went and hid his face.

God first appeared to Moses in what at first seemed a merely puzzling thing, and not very big: a bush that was burning, but not consumed. When the spirit of God accompanied the children of Israel in the desert, it was "housed," so to speak, in the smallish ark of the covenant, in a tent.

When the Holy Spirit overshadowed Mary, and the Word was made flesh, the infinite God was huddled in the intimate smallness of the Virgin's womb.

There is nothing of lasting worth in this world that is not born of the Holy Spirit, and yet how hard it is to form an image of this most mysterious of the three persons of the Trinity! Even Jesus, speaking here to Nicodemus about those who are born of the Spirit, uses the "image" of something that has no image, the breath of the wind, which we see only when the reeds and the grasses are leaning, and which we feel against our cheek, often as gentle as a kiss.

So too are all those born of the Spirit. Where they come from, and where they go, the world cannot tell. Yet they usher in the Kingdom of God itself. Saints of incomparable glory are walking among us, born from above, and driving the only genuine history of mankind forward, and yet these people are often wholly unrecognized, just as an "important" fellow meditating political strategy might walk right past the burning bush, or the cave on Mount Horeb—or Calvary, or the empty tomb, or Christ himself housed in all the tabernacles of the world.

Father of love and gentleness, incline our ears to hear your Word, so that we may see the works of the Spirit and be faithful witnesses to them to all the world, through Jesus our Lord.

How Can These Things Be?

Anthony Esolen

Nicodemus answered and said to [Jesus], "How can this happen?" Jesus answered and said to him, "You are the teacher of Israel and you do not understand this? Amen, amen, I say to you, we speak of what we know and we testify to what we have seen, but you people do not accept our testimony."

(Jn 3:9-11)

Nicodemus is a well-respected teacher in Israel, yet he doesn't grasp the very meaning of Israel itself. He doesn't know that all the history of his people testifies to the silent work of the Spirit. Consider Israel, an undistinguished people in a dusty corner of the Mediterranean, overrun by one invader after another, and now managing a precarious compromise between their faith and their political submission to Rome. Yet it is Israel the little, not Rome the great, that will be the victor, in Christ. It is Israel, not the Roman emperors, who still speaks to the world and will speak so long as there are men to hear.

Poor Nicodemus suffers the farsightedness of the learned man: he cannot see what's in front of him. And lest he admit he has missed something, he would set the testimony of Jesus aside. So Jesus rebukes him: "We testify to what we have seen, but you people do not accept our testimony." Saint John strikes that note again and again: he is a witness, he has beheld the glory of God with his own eyes, he has even touched the Son of God with his hands!

So, in one sense, the work of the Spirit is not obvious. Who would survey a map of the world and point to Judea as the radiating center of human history? But that work is also right in front of us. Jesus says so, and Saint John repeats the testimony. He has seen and heard and touched. What then prevents Nicodemus from seeing?

Well, Nicodemus will see. That too is a work of the Spirit. But the Spirit that did not hurl Elijah from his feet will never compel us; love has nothing to do with compulsion. The Spirit blows upon us, and we need to turn and perform that most shattering of deeds. We need to open our eyes.

Father of all truth, grant us eyes to see the truth, and the courage to open our eyes; grant us ears to hear the truth, and the courage to open our ears; grant us voices to declare the truth from the rooftops, and the grace to embody the truth by our lives, through Christ our Lord.

Trusting Him in Great Things

Anthony Esolen

"If I tell you about earthly things and you do not believe, how will you believe if I tell you about heavenly things? No one has gone up to heaven except the one who has come down from heaven, the Son of Man." (Jn 3:12-13)

I magine a father with a crippled son. The boy needs to learn to walk again, and the father takes him by the hand, leading him step by step, but never supporting him entirely. The father understands that the boy must eventually walk without the support. The boy must trust the father, too, to know when to grasp his hand firmly, and when to begin to let it go.

Jesus here is like the father with the exact touch. It would be easy for him to say to Nicodemus, "Let's go over the miracles you say you have witnessed, and then let's review the history of Israel, and then we can define what I mean by 'born of the Spirit,' so that you may repeat our conversation to the scribes. Then maybe someone will jot it down in a gloss on a commentary on the Scriptures, and everyone will be content." Yes, content, and still hobbling. Instead, Jesus is calling Nicodemus to stretch his mind and heart and soul toward heaven. One after another now will come verses that explode upon us like the dawn of a new world. "You can do it!" Jesus seems to say. "Only follow me, Nicodemus!"

Jesus longs to tell Nicodemus of heavenly things. Everyone can try to speak of earthly things, but only one person can testify of heavenly things, and that is the Son of Man, who has come down from heaven. The implication is clear. "I am the one, Nicodemus! Will you trust me?"

Why not? If the words of Jesus teach us how to live holy lives in this world, filled with the Spirit, why should we not trust him also when he speaks of what he alone can speak? People who say, "I believe in the teachings of Jesus, but not in his person," contradict themselves. His teaching and his person are wholly devoted to revealing the Father.

Loving Father, take us by the hand and help us to walk in the light; do not allow us to rest content with what we know now, but show us more and more of your light: we ask this through the same light of the world, Jesus your Son.

The Serpent and the Tree

Anthony Esolen

*"And just as Moses lifted up the serpent in the desert,
so must the Son of Man be lifted up, so that everyone
who believes in him may have eternal life."*
(Jn 3:14-15)

When the Hebrews grew rebellious against Moses in the desert, God sent a plague of serpents to afflict them. Then Moses interceded for them, and God instructed him to erect a bronze serpent on a pole for the people to look upon, and all who looked upon it were healed.

It's a strange moment in Scripture. It recalls another serpent and another pole, a living tree, when the Enemy whispered to Eve, "You shall be like gods." Now Jesus prophesies as to the true meaning and fulfillment of that event in the desert. The Son of Man will be lifted up on the tree: the One who comes to crush the head of the serpent that spat his lies and his venom in the garden. He is the One with more than the antidote to sin. After all, the children of Israel who were healed still died before they reached the Promised Land. But Jesus comes to bring us life in abundance.

He's just said to Nicodemus that the Son of Man alone can speak of heavenly things, because he alone has come down from heaven. Now the motion is reversed: the Son of Man is lifted up, as the bronze figure was lifted up in the desert. We know that Jesus is prophesying his death upon the cross. Nicodemus doesn't know it, yet. But what he might understand is that Jesus means this "lifting up" of the Son of Man as one of those unknown heavenly things.

What sense could the poor fellow make of that? It's as if Jesus were saying to Nicodemus, "Let me tell you what heaven is like," and then began to speak of this lifting, to heal a sinful people. Imagine the dismay if Nicodemus knew that a cross would be the instrument! Is heaven then a tree of suffering? By no means. It is a life of love—total love.

Merciful Father, help us to keep always before our eyes the glorious cross of Jesus, that we may run to his arms thrown wide to embrace all the world, through the same Christ our Lord.

The Drama of Love

Anthony Esolen

For God so loved the world that he gave his only Son, so that everyone who believes in him might not perish but might have eternal life. For God did not send his Son into the world to condemn the world, but that the world might be saved through him. (Jn 3:16-17)

I comment upon this verse with fear and trembling. It is the whole of the Christian faith. God so loved the world, that he gave his only Son.

What do I know about love, I with my feeble heart, unless Jesus teaches me?

What is that "world," with all its tangled ways, its quest for power, its craven fear of suffering and death and love, its worship of greatness in every petty, strutting despot and every shiny, new idea, and its ignorance of humility and truth?

What is that "world," with knees for cringing before every stark staring idol manufactured by the heart of man, but no knees for God?

The world hated Jesus. He came into the world, but the world did not know him. He came to his own people, but they refused him.

The world will always hate him. I know this, because I am in the world. I know it the more painfully, because the world is in me.

Who nailed Jesus to the tree? I did. I sold him for thirty pieces of silver, or something more sordid still. I could not watch with him for an hour. I fled when they came for him. I kept silent while witnesses perjured themselves. I searched for an excuse to do away with him.

I loved him, and I did not love him. I know him, and I do not want to know him. I want to draw near him, and I hold back.

I walked through the valley of the shadow of death, which is the world, and would have stayed there for ever, but the Good Shepherd came for me.

The story of the world is the story of man: all of us together, and each of us alone. From before the foundation of the world, God so loved that world—so loved me, so loved you—that he gave his only Son.

Almighty Father, work in us the wonders of the love of Jesus: teach us to love as Jesus loves, so that we may know you as Jesus knows you, and dwell in the Spirit that is your love, the very flame of eternal love.

The Holy Name of Jesus

Anthony Esolen

Whoever believes in him will not be condemned, but whoever does not believe has already been condemned, because he has not believed in the name of the only Son of God. And this is the verdict, that the light came into the world, but people preferred darkness to light, because their works were evil.

(Jn 3:18-19)

Jesus says to Nicodemus that those who do not believe in the *name* of the Son of God are condemned. What does he mean?

The ancient Hebrews took names seriously: a name was an expression of a thing's essence. That is why, when God brings the animals to Adam to see what he would name them, it is a tremendous honor, and evidence of Adam's share in the authority and the wisdom of God.

It is also why the hesitant Moses asks God to reveal his name, before he goes to free the Israelites in Egypt. The name that God reveals is a name beyond names: I AM. That is to say: no name can limit me. I am the One Who Is. But then God says, "I am the God of Abraham, the God of Isaac, and the God of Jacob." That means more than, "These men happened to worship me." It means, "I am the God who revealed himself to your fathers. *I am with you.*" We don't know who God is unless we know of that love.

Jesus will attribute to himself that holy name: "Before Abraham was, I AM." But we know him by his given name: Jesus, meaning "God saves." And we know him by the title granted him in prophecy: Emmanuel, meaning "God is with us." All of these names are indeed one.

To believe in the *name* of the Son of God is to believe that Jesus and the Father are one: one in being, and one in their saving love for mankind. What matters here is not so much that people have heard the name "Jesus," as that they respond to the call and the person of Jesus, however he may show himself to them. To reject Jesus, then, is to say, "I can save myself," or, what amounts to the same thing, "I am my own." And that is darkness.

Merciful Father, teach us to honor the name of Jesus in our thoughts and our words and our deeds, so that we may walk in the light, and enjoy the freedom of the children of God, through the same Christ, our beloved Lord.

There Is Light, and There Is Light

Anthony Esolen

For everyone who does wicked things hates the light and does not come toward the light, so that his works might not be exposed. But whoever lives the truth comes to the light, so that his works may be clearly seen as done in God.
(Jn 3:20-21)

Just before the elderly journalist Malcolm Muggeridge entered the Church, he wrote an essay describing what he believed about the world. He compared it to a stage. On one side, the glare of bright lights, fame, glory, wealth, pleasures—and madness. On the other side, soft strains of distant music, darkness, suffering—and sanity. Most people, said Muggeridge, muddle through their lives somewhere between, tempted by the hard light of the idols, yet casting a longing look now and again toward where life really dwells.

People do not love the light, says Jesus to Nicodemus, because their deeds are evil. True enough. But those same people may love the spotlight, or the harsh glare of greatness and success and earthly delights, a glare as blinding as darkness. A petty thief may skulk in the night, but the biggest thieves bleach their sins in broad day. So the Pharisees who want to be seen by everybody at the same time don't want to be seen by anybody. The limelight glosses over a multitude of sins.

But the true light that has come into the world, Jesus our Savior, has overcome the world. Not with a more powerful glare; that would be to add darkness to darkness. He overcomes with the light of truth and love. It is the light of the Father's countenance.

If we walk humbly with our God, we will beg for that light. We will say, "I am now appearing before my loving Father," and we will pray for the grace to do worthy deeds in his sight. That's not showing off. We are saying, "All that I am is yours, and I beg you to show me what to do, and the better if I may do it quietly, giving you all the glory." One deed of such humility is like a candle in the darkness. More than we can know depends upon it.

Father of Lights, from whom come all good gifts, shed upon us the light of your grace, that we may see, and may walk in the way that leads to the country of perpetual light, where all the saints and angels behold your countenance in wonder, through Christ our Light.

Peace Comes Dropping Slow

J. David Franks

After this, Jesus and his disciples went into the region of Judea,
where he spent some time with them baptizing. John was
also baptizing in Aenon near Salim, because there was an
abundance of water there, and people came to be baptized,
for John had not yet been imprisoned.
(Jn 3:22-24)

As we hurtle through the days, time is water and wind, scouring the heart raw. There is no love without difficulties, be it love of children, spouse, or friends. And love has this trick that the more true it is, the more tempered and strong, the more it exposes the heart like a wound to the stinging atmosphere. When we love, we are not our own. Our fortunes are inseparable from those of the ones we love. If they suffer, we suffer. If they fail, we are cut.

And true love cannot be contained in the domestic round, where we have our family and friends. It seeks the common good, the good of each and of all. The philosopher Emmanuel Levinas speaks of being "hostage to the other." To love means to be responsible for the others, each in turn. We cannot build a little island of happiness, inured to the vicissitudes of the stranger. Love shakes open the prison of the self, pushes one out of doors, where the agony of every human sings in the bone.

When your heart lets itself in for the deep pain of the world—for the victims of rapacity, the depressed, for the victims of the culture of death, the abused children, for those trapped by sin: what is our cry, but for peace? "Come, Lord Jesus," becomes our heart's plea.

Jesus descends from Jerusalem to the abundant water at Aenon ("springs") near Salim ("peace"), having spoken to Nicodemus of the mystery of salvation: God loves us so utterly that he sends his Son into our twilight world. "The morning star" (Rv 22:16), in meteorite blaze, is cast into the chaotic waters of human existence, teeming with the monsters of death-dealing selfishness. This star, though, sweetens and pacifies our waters, yielding the crystalline flow of the baptismal font. Jesus is the fountain of peace because he has truly descended into our agonized existence, in sinless solidarity.

Merciful Father, cause the cry for your Son's return to rise up from the deepest places in my heart, so each hurting human heart may receive through him the fullness of peace.

A Book of Intricate Device

J. David Franks

Now a dispute arose between the disciples of John and a Jew about ceremonial washings. So they came to John and said to him, "Rabbi, the one who was with you across the Jordan, to whom you testified, here he is baptizing and everyone is coming to him." (Jn 3:25-26)

How easy it is to become enamored of our plans! A project has been entrusted to you at work. After spending months collecting data, seeking counsel, and imagining what can be done given available resources, you have the satisfaction of seeing your vision realized.

But our plans can never be the last word. New facts on the ground must be accounted for. Others, especially the young, must be given a chance to build. We must yield the stage.

We are stung. Am I worthless? Have I poured my substance into my work for nothing? This anguish is not of itself selfish. As the theologian Hans Urs von Balthasar points out, the poignancy of human existence has much to do with our drive to write something permanent in the watery medium of material and temporal existence. Anything we manage to build in the world will eventually pass away. It is tragic. Our spirit, our power to know and love, transcends space and time; the eternal is our atmosphere. So why do our works turn to dust in our hands?

John's disciples have been playing an essential role in the coming of the Messiah. But this particular role is at an end. They need to be reminded that their hopes and dreams, their plans, derive all their worth from the way they fit into an all-encompassing narrative. If we live in the wide-open realm of the Father's plan of loving goodness, we can give up our white-knuckle grip on our position, and flow. It's not easy. It's never easy to let go. It will feel like dying, like drowning.

The Father's plan is clear: for the groundless love he bears the world, he gives up his Son, to be staked like the serpent to a pole, so that everyone who believes in him might have eternal life. Everyone. "All Judea" once streamed to John; now "everyone" streams to Jesus—according to an intricate plan of divine devising.

Provident Father, grant success to the work of my hands, the success of participating in your eternal design for history. Grant me the serenity of entrusting all to you.

Every Good and Perfect Gift

J. David Franks

*John answered and said, "No one can receive anything except
what has been given him from heaven. You yourselves can
testify that I said [that] I am not the Messiah, but that
I was sent before him." (Jn 3:27-28)*

In the defense of life and marriage, we have exceptional allies in the evangelical community. However, you will still hear many of them speak of the sacraments of the Catholic Church as examples of "works righteousness."

The reality is exactly the opposite. The sacraments are dramatic parables of our utter dependence on God's goodness, dramatizations of his priority and our receptivity. We have no good, we perform no good, which does not come directly from the hand of God. All being, all doing well, begins in what Blessed John Paul II calls the Father's "dimension of gift." And nothing more clearly demonstrates the absolute priority of God's activity than the baptism of an infant, in which there is no "asking Jesus into one's heart" or any other such work of our own. Infant baptism shows the secret of every human life: God the Father gives every good thing. He draws to himself. He authors our "Yes" to him. *Within* this gracious initiative, we may cooperate, and indeed merit. But God is, in every good act, the First Cause.

John the Baptist reminds his disciples that "everyone" flocking to Jesus has been given into Jesus' care by God the Father. And he is reminding them that his own mission is given by the Father, a mission to go before the Messiah to prepare for this messianic ingathering.

Obedience is the key. John is pure docility. Jesus himself is obeying the Father, carrying out his plan of salvation. John did not dream up his baptism of repentance. He was inspired by God. And now he happily surrenders his baptizing work to be consummated as God sees fit. We are looking into the future of Church order, with Jesus erecting the sacramental structure founded on baptism.

Detachment from our projects is hard for us, but it becomes possible when we remember that God the Father, in his loving goodness, has written the script and runs the show.

Bountiful Father, make us ever more alive to the extent of your goodness to us. Give us the joy of praising you, in gratitude, as you should be praised.

The Wedding Feast of the Lamb

J. David Franks

"The one who has the bride is the bridegroom; the best man, who stands and listens for him, rejoices greatly at the bridegroom's voice. So this joy of mine has been made complete."
(Jn 3:29)

A wedding promises a future. It interrupts the apparent futility of the world, for this man and this woman are promising to love each other to the end despite the vicissitudes of life. And in the normal course of things, their love will give rise to children.

The mission of Jesus Christ is to transplant this flower of human love from earth to heaven, so that new life will have a second birth from on high in baptism. Incorporated into Jesus, made members of the Son, we mysteriously proceed from the Father! This is the mystery John the Baptist prepares for; it is the mystery Jesus reveals to Nicodemus. It is how the Prologue situates the Incarnation: "But to those who did accept him he gave power to become children of God" (Jn 1:12).

This supernatural rebirth in baptism depends on our being born of woman in the first place, so it is no accident that Jesus, the New Adam, first reveals his glory at the wedding feast in Cana—prompted by Mary, the New Eve.

John the Baptist senses the marital context for baptism. God the Father is drawing the people to Jesus, and so the plan of salvation is being consummated. The world as it is drawn to Jesus is the Church. Cana itself points beyond marriage and baptism to what enables a living, growing union between each person and Jesus: the Eucharist, the total self-giving love of Jesus on the cross.

John has always been merely a voice in service of the Word. Now he surrenders even that. His voice yields to the Word speaking. We too have our roles at the wedding feast. Water will become wine; wine will become blood. Your heart imbibing the self-gift of Jesus will become light, and joyful, and abundant, a fountain of water poured out for others to be drawn in. And the water cycle of the Spirit of love goes on.

Father of infinite love, bring to fruition all human love in the Spirit of your Son's total self-gift on the cross. Bring this about by the intercession of the Mother of your Son.

Precession of Desire

J. David Franks

"He must increase; I must decrease."
(Jn 3:30)

How secure is my place in the world? My place in the hearts of those I love? If things change, won't I lose my grip and fall? New management; new acquaintances; new variables. If we think of life as a zero-sum game, we will shore up our position by trying to keep others down. When we are afraid, we are closefisted.

In his total trust in the One who sends him, John the Baptist is utterly serene. The Christian need not be anxious, though the world should rock. When the Light blazes into the world, when the Word becomes flesh: it is not catastrophe; it is renovation. It is fullness, abundance, plenitude, prodigality. All that is asked of us is that we be open, and empty of self-assertion: "I, the LORD, am your God,/ who brought you up from the land of Egypt./ Open wide your mouth that I may fill it" (Ps 81:11).

Jesus comes, "full of grace and truth," as the true Atlas to shift the world on its interior axis back into the dimension of gift. For John the Evangelist, the "world" often denotes the *saeculum* (in itself good) as it has been closed in on itself (let's say "secularized"). When our desires do not come from the Father, a dark gravity arises that collapses upon itself. Paradise, in which we desire the fullness the Father wishes to give us, becomes the scorched earth of the dimension of concupiscence: the unintelligent realm of merely self-serving desire. Every time we sin, we are curving in on ourselves, our secularizing desires preventing us from standing upright.

The axis of the world runs through human hearts, and so the precession of dimensions—the change of pole stars—from self-serving desire to the currency of self-giving love, occurs person by person. It happens in baptism, which enables us to find in the Father's wise and loving will our hearts' desire—as John the Baptist always has.

Healing Father, release me from my anxious desires. Cause me to trust you as you bring me into the bright country of your gracious giving. Make me an instrument of your graciousness to my neighbors.

The Incarnation as Submergence

J. David Franks

The one who comes from above is above all. The one who is of the earth is earthly and speaks of earthly things. But the one who comes from heaven [is above all]. He testifies to what he has seen and heard, but no one accepts his testimony. Whoever does accept his testimony certifies that God is trustworthy.

(Jn 3:31-33)

These words are probably those of Jesus, placed here to tie together the dialogue with Nicodemus and the testimony of John. Baptism has dominated the Gospel so far.

Jesus comes from above: into this dangerous world leaps the Word of God. He falls into our hands. What happens when he is immersed in the Jordan in some sense simply manifests what his human life has been from the beginning: a submergence in the chaotic waters of human existence. The Word was made flesh: *Logos-sarx*. This does not simply mean that the Word assumes to himself a human body (he takes up a human soul as well after all).

Rather, we should hear the Pauline resonance: Jesus comes "in the likeness of sinful flesh" (Rom 8:3). What is sinful flesh? It is the human condition burdened with the futility of sinful desire. The Word becoming flesh means the Word descending into the suffering and darkness of our lives: like us in all things but sin. The emphatic creedal refrain is necessary because the solidarity of Jesus with our condition is so total: "For our sake [the Father] made [Christ] to be sin who did not know sin, so that we might become the righteousness of God in him" (2 Cor 5:21). Made to be sin, incarnate in sinful flesh: *but without sinning*.

That is, the article of the Apostles' Creed about Jesus' descent into hell should not be understood as referring only to Holy Saturday. In *Jesus of Nazareth*, Pope Benedict writes, as a private theologian, of Jesus' baptism in the Jordan: "His entering into the sin of others is a descent into the 'inferno.'" Later, he boldly states, "This descent [into hell] not only took place in and after his death, but accompanies him along his entire journey."

The Incarnation is submergence, for "our gaze is submarine," as T. S. Eliot notes. Jesus will not leave us alone to drown in our anguish.

Heavenly Father, make me worthy to act as a citizen of your Kingdom of love and radical solidarity. Give me a heart for the victims of the culture of death, and for all others who suffer.

Saint or Effigy

J. David Franks

For the one whom God sent speaks the words of God. He does not ration his gift of the Spirit. The Father loves the Son and has given everything over to him. Whoever believes in the Son has eternal life, but whoever disobeys the Son will not see life, but the wrath of God remains upon him. (Jn 3:34-36)

Before the foundation of the world, the Father dreamt up the idea of you, indeed of every single one of us, the one hundred and ten billion or however many humans who have ever lived on the earth—and all those yet to come. He said of each of us, "I choose you. I want you to exist and share divine life."

Divine life is the interplay of infinite knowing and loving. The Father simply is the handing over of the divine essence to the Son/Word, in their mutual Spirit of love. That is mystery enough, but baptism truly inserts you into that eternal procession. You, in your concrete personality, are now divinized.

Whenever my children throw a fit, no matter how annoying, a not meager quantum of amusement is to be gained in the spectacle of miniature and bootless rage. As we grow, our selfish enactments lose their humor, but a quality of self-parody remains, according to the mystic Adrienne von Speyr.

When we fail to love, when we sin, it is as if we are fashioning an effigy of ourselves. Sinful actions are parodies of intelligent actions. The seriousness of sin is that we really do have the power to cling to our effigy and assert, "*This* is my identity." Insisting on this identification is to pull away from reality. The ultimate withdrawal is hell. The wrath of God is his not *being able* to know and love us in our self-parody. His light becomes hateful to us in our darkness, and we burn ourselves in effigy.

But the Father created each one of us for one reason only: to be sanctified by the Spirit of his Son and so to enjoy eternal life, the life of divine knowing and loving.

The Father intends that, as saints carrying out the evangelical mission, we be ablaze with the Holy Spirit of wisdom and fruitful love—not smoldering stumps of firebrands, but stars wheeling and singing in heaven.

Eternal Father, give me eyes to see the ancient glory hidden in every person, and never let me forget that you have always loved me, so that I will not despair of my weakness.

Passing through Samaria

Heather King

Now when Jesus learned that the Pharisees had heard that
Jesus was making and baptizing more disciples than John
(although Jesus himself was not baptizing, just his disciples),
he left Judea and returned to Galilee.
He had to pass through Samaria.
(Jn 4:1-4)

Already Christ is having to pass through unfriendly territories in order to return home. Already he is being falsely accused. Already the Pharisees are jealous of his "success."

One of the most striking things about Christ is that from the moment of his public ministry he is under siege. He never does the "safe" thing. He doesn't court danger, but neither does he try to avoid it. He doesn't go around trying to mount a preemptive defense, but when attacked, he has a ready answer. He's at home everywhere and he has no home. "Foxes have dens and birds of the sky have nests, but the Son of Man has nowhere to rest his head" (Mt 8:20).

John's head will soon be presented to Herod on a tray, and already Christ has nowhere to lay his own. The Samaritans believed their religion was the one true religion, preserved intact from prior to the Babylonian exile. They were opposed to Judaism. We go the long way around uncomfortable situations, undesirable people, potential conflict. That he has nowhere to lay his head allows Christ to walk straight into them.

We are all called to pass through Samaria. We are called to love the person who triggers us, threatens us, challenges us. We are called to interact with the poor person and the rich person, with the condemned convict and the teenager struggling with his sexual orientation, with the woman who has had an abortion, with the married father who is having an affair, with the troublesome, the annoying, the persistent, the person who is poised to refuse our help. How clearly we can see the faults, the problems, the solution for others! Christ passes through Samaria in order to remind us how blind we are when it comes to ourselves.

Almighty Father, give me the courage to pass through Samaria.
Help me be willing to explore the uncomfortable parts of myself.

It Was about Noon

Heather King

So [Jesus] came to a town of Samaria called Sychar, near the plot of land that Jacob had given to his son Joseph. Jacob's well was there. Jesus, tired from his journey, sat down there at the well. It was about noon. (Jn 4:5-6)

The meeting between Christ and Mary Magdalene takes place at dawn. The meeting between Christ and the woman with the nard takes place near dinner time, at dusk. But the meeting that is about to take place between Christ and the Samaritan woman takes place at noon, in the full heat and full light of the day.

Noon is just when we do not want to meet Christ. We're tired from our own morning journey. We want to eat, to take a break from work, to gossip a bit, kvetch a bit, to congratulate ourselves, perhaps, on a job well done. We may have asked for God's help that morning, but by noon we're convinced, one more time, that we can manage on our own. By noon we secretly believe, one more time, that intelligence backed by will power will carry the day.

This is often true in the noon of our lives as well, and there's another reason we don't want to meet Christ at noon. We don't want to be subjected to the unforgiving glare. We don't want to be subjected to quite that much light.

Christ is tired. He sits down near the well that, centuries earlier, Jacob had given to his favorite son. There is a stillness here. A sense of expectation. Dust. Sun.

I often wonder what went through Christ's head at any given moment. Sitting by the well, is he rejoicing that his cousin John is baptizing so many? Is he thinking about the public life that is before him? He who is all light would have welcomed the light. He who had no darkness would not have been afraid of too much light. Does noon for Christ bring his deepest union with the Father?

His mind is too deep for us and it is also too clear, too transparent, for us. All we know is that when in the next instant a woman appears, he seems to have been thinking of her all his life.

Heavenly Father, make me as transparent as Christ. Help me to be willing to face the light of noonday. Allow me to stand by Jacob's well with Jesus.

"Give me a drink"

Heather King

A woman of Samaria came to draw water. Jesus said to her, "Give me a drink." His disciples had gone into the town to buy food. The Samaritan woman said to him, "How can you, a Jew, ask me, a Samaritan woman, for a drink?" (For Jews use nothing in common with Samaritans.) (Jn 4:7-9)

The heart of the Kingdom of God is the face-to-face human encounter. Politics may bring superficial (if much needed) change, but transformation takes place through relationship. To need something from a poor person, a marginalized person; to be fed, walked with, shored up, encouraged, instructed, loved by a person of a different color, demographic, sexual orientation, neighborhood, religion, or country is a humbling and shattering experience. Most of us spend our lives surrounding ourselves with enough money, prestige, and friends that we can stay in our own little self-created universe. To need something so badly—companionship, directions, guidance—that we are willing to step outside our universe: that's where Christ is.

I once found myself in Spencer, West Virginia, a town of seven thousand, in the northwest part of the state. I'd spent a lot of time alone that year; voluntarily, but still, I was lonely. One Friday afternoon I read in the local paper of a covered-dish potluck at the nearby community center. I made a batch of deviled eggs, mentally reprised my best stories, and set out for the twenty-five-mile drive.

When I arrived, I found forty or so people who managed to be both totally accommodating and totally, comically, uninterested in me or my "journey." These folks didn't need another friend. They had friends. They had families, by whom they were surrounded. They weren't remotely fired up to have an existentially tormented, temporarily homeless person in their midst. And yet for that night, they saved me. They gave me a chair. They let me sit in on the conversation. They shared their food.

We tend to think religion is all about rules, but our religion is all about vulnerability. It is about relationship with people with whom we "use nothing in common." That night, I said, "Give me a drink." And the people of Appalachia gave.

Blessed Father, allow me to be stripped down to the point where I am invited to ask a stranger for food, for drink. Help me to remember that, to the Samaritan woman, Christ was a stranger.

Living Water

Heather King

Jesus answered and said to [the Samaritan woman],
"If you knew the gift of God and who is saying to you,
'Give me a drink,' you would have asked him and
he would have given you living water."

(Jn 4:10)

"How can you ask me for a drink?" the woman asks. You are a Jew and I am a Samaritan. We have nothing in common. At the deepest level, she is asking who are you and who am I? Christ immediately meets the Samaritan woman at this deep level of their core identities. Immediately he transcends nationality, culture, religion, family, and gender and goes straight to God. He turns the question of who is doing the asking and who is doing the giving around. He says, in effect, if you knew who was saying to you, "Give me a drink," you would have asked him for a drink. You would have asked him for the water to slake your own thirst.

We want to make small talk. We want to be clever. We want to find out what the other person wants and decide whether and on what terms we'll give it to them. It's not far-fetched to imagine that the woman at the well was a bit of a flirt and a sexpot. It's not far-fetched to imagine that Christ very much appreciated beautiful women, and that he was the frequent recipient of their attention. He doesn't spurn female attention; he engages it and he cuts straight to the chase. He says, we're not going to play that game. He says, I'm way more interested in your spiritual well-being than that.

And yet Christ is for ever a poet and a troubadour. "He would have given you living water." He never nags or shames; he's never a wet blanket, nor a prude, nor anything less than a full-blooded, virile man.

Impossible to imagine the story of Christ and the man at the well. The living water is a parable about the confluence of the masculine and the feminine. Here at the well he slakes the holy longing of both women and men by showing us how to love one another as he loved us.

Loving Father, make me thirst for the living water, even though I don't want to thirst. Help me to be impatient with small talk, evasion, and manipulation.

The Cistern Is Deep

Heather King

[The (Samaritan) woman] said to [Jesus], "Sir, you do not even have a bucket and the cistern is deep; where then can you get this living water? Are you greater than our father Jacob, who gave us this cistern and drank from it himself with his children and his flocks?" (Jn 4:11-12)

How Christ must have loved women. How well he understood their thirst: for connection, to be cherished, to give themselves fully to a husband.

And how well he understood our feistiness! Dude, where's your bucket? That well is deep, baby! You're acting weird already and I suppose next you're gonna tell me you know more than our spiritual father, Jacob?

Jacob gave them the physical cistern, the water that to be sure temporarily slakes thirst, that sustained his children and family and animals, and that has sustained the generations since. But the cistern is deep. Christ will give them another kind of water.

Christ is simultaneously utterly practical and utterly mystical. He insists upon the humble responsibilities of our daily tasks, but he never lets the merely material stand in his way. He's thirsty, but he's more thirsty to instruct this woman. He's not concerned with a bucket—a bucket is needed, but a bucket will show up one way or the other, just as when the Temple tax needs to be paid, he will casually send Peter to the lake and instruct him to throw in his line and "take the first fish that comes up. Open its mouth and you will find a coin worth twice the temple tax. Give that to them for me and for you" (Mt 17:27).

Here, as so often, he chooses water—next to air, the simplest, most essential element of our being—to illustrate. Here, as so often, he is challenged: *Who do you think you are?* Who do you think you are, coming into an alien territory and plunking down by our well? Who do you think you are: a man, speaking to a single, unchaperoned woman? Who do you think you are: in one breath asking for a drink and in the next, though you have no visible means that would enable you to get *any* water, speaking of the "living water"?

But the cistern is deep. And Christ himself is the bucket.

Eternal Father, help me to remember that Christ is greater than my most cherished forebears. Help me to remember that Christ infuses even water with Life.

Eternal Life

Heather King

Jesus answered and said to [the Samaritan woman], "Everyone who drinks this water will be thirsty again; but whoever drinks the water I shall give will never thirst; the water I shall give will become in him a spring of water welling up to eternal life." The woman said to him, "Sir, give me this water, so that I may not be thirsty or have to keep coming here to draw water." (Jn 4:13-15)

Like all of us, the Samaritan woman wants to do an end run. She wants the wrong kind of miracle. She wants to be relieved of the humble duties of daily life.

In *The Reed of God*, Caryll Houselander writes of this misconception under which many of us labor. "There are many people in the world who cultivate a curious state which they call 'the spiritual life'… All the time spent in earning a living, cleaning the home, caring for the children, making and mending clothes, cooking, and all the other manifold duties and responsibilities, is regarded as wasted.

"Yet it is really through ordinary human life and the things of every hour of every day that union with God comes about."

Jesus never encourages us to avoid the duties of daily life. Instead, he imbues those duties with his supernatural love. He makes making the bed "living"—making the bed. He makes commuting "living"—commuting. He makes paying the bills "living"—paying the bills.

Neither does he arrange things so that, once we meet him, we need never thirst again. Tradition has it that one of Christ's seven last words on the cross was *Sitio*: I thirst. Christ himself thirsted, till the moment he died. We thirst and the thirst is slaked. We thirst and Christ gives himself to us, again. For years I thought: If only I could get through this dreadful wrong turn, if only I could heal myself from this mortifying character defect, if only I could free myself from this difficult relationship, *then* I might start to get somewhere! *Then* I could at last embark on the authentic spiritual life. Now I realize those challenges *are* the authentic spiritual life. Now I realize those difficulties are the Way and the Truth.

Eternal life springs from full participation in the present life. Every morning we are called, one more time, to pick up our bucket and trudge to the well.

Heavenly Father, help me to see that I don't have to do anything or to go anywhere extraordinary to find you. Help me to remember that you are extraordinary, not me.

You Have Had Five Husbands

Heather King

*Jesus said to [the Samaritan woman], "Go call your husband
and come back." The woman answered and said to him,
"I do not have a husband." Jesus answered her, "You are right
in saying, 'I do not have a husband.' For you have had five
husbands, and the one you have now is not your husband.
What you have said is true." (Jn 4:16-18)*

What you have said is true, in other words, but it's only the partial truth. It's the truth shaded. How easily Christ sees through our half-truths and subterfuges!

Sober alcoholics have been known to say of hitting bottom, "I was sick and tired of being sick and tired." The good news is that when we are sick and tired enough, we will thirst for the whole truth. Because our half-truths mask a deep and desperate hunger for connection, meaning, and love.

Christ is blunt but he's never mean. He doesn't say, "You've had five husbands and you're a harlot." He says, in so many words, "You've had five husbands and that's not working for ya, is it?" He says, "You've had five husbands and not one of them has slaked your thirst." He says, "No outside person, place, or thing is going to fix you, my beloved." He says, "Come to me, all who are weary and heavy-laden, and I will give you rest" (cf. Mt 11:28).

Because nothing makes us more weary and heavy burdened than the bondage of our own addictions. To try to get outside things to fix us is a full-time, 24/7 job.

The essence of the sin of the adulterous woman was betrayal, but the essence of the woman at the well's is compulsion. We all develop strategies to promote our search for love. Those strategies can harden into prison cells. They can become our organizing principles and our masters. Against all evidence, we come to believe that this man, or woman, will be The One; this relationship, or possession, or accomplishment will give us the validation that will make us whole. Other people can see our strategies, but we are generally blind to them ourselves.

Even when we are able to see them, we can't change on our own. We need something to replace the yawning void that ensues when we stop. We need the living water of Christ.

Almighty Father, help me to see the truth about myself and the strategies I employ to get what I think I want. Help me to align my will with yours.

The Hour Is Coming

Heather King

*The woman said to [Jesus], "Sir, I can see that you are a prophet.
Our ancestors worshiped on this mountain; but you people
say that the place to worship is in Jerusalem." Jesus said to her,
"Believe me, woman, the hour is coming when you will worship
the Father neither on this mountain nor in Jerusalem." (Jn 4:19-21)*

Christ is never interested in superficial "religious" arguments. He never asks: Who are the "in" people? He never asks, do you lean to the right or the left? He never asks, are you among those who worship on the mountain or among those who worship in Jerusalem?

He asks questions like: Do you wash the outside of the cup, no matter how corrupt you are on the inside? Do you make a big show of praying on street corners even though you treat your wife, children, and co-workers badly? Is it more important to you to follow a rule than to help a person in need?

More and more we see the truth of the German theologian Karl Rahner's observation: "The Christian of the future will be a mystic or he will not be a Christian at all."

To be a mystic does not mean being vague; it means being very clear on who Christ is and what he calls us to. It means to be very clear that there is a law, and also very clear that Christ comes to fulfill the law by infusing it with spirit. It means to be very clear that there are rules and also very clear that the purpose of the rules is to provide a framework within which to explode in love.

Here, Christ is telling the Samaritan woman all that and more. She clearly knows "the rules" about worship and public morals. She knows she's breaking them. She assumes, perhaps, that Christ is going to lecture her.

Instead, he expands to infinity all notions of both law and spirit. He says, in so many words, when you break the rules, the wrong isn't stepping out of line, it's that you harm yourself spiritually. He says, you feel guilty but the answer isn't to memorize the rules. The answer isn't to figure out whether the "good" people worship on the mountain or whether the good people worship in Jerusalem.

He says if you follow the rules out of love, you will enter the kingdom of heaven. He says, "Come to the living water."

Loving Father, help me to remember that Christ was above all a prophet, ever ancient, ever new. Help me to remember that the hour is for ever coming.

The Father Seeks Such People

Heather King

"You people worship what you do not understand; we worship what we understand, because salvation is from the Jews. But the hour is coming, and is now here, when true worshipers will worship the Father in Spirit and truth; and indeed the Father seeks such people to worship him. God is Spirit, and those who worship him must worship in Spirit and truth."

(Jn 4:22-24)

I often wonder whether God suffers. Without in any way trying to diminish or anthropomorphize God, in particular I wonder whether he suffers the anxiety of waiting—as we do, when we seek, knock, ask. Without questioning that God knows in the end, that good will triumph, that love will reign, that Christ will take his place upon the throne, I wonder whether, like us, God doesn't know exactly how that will happen. To give people free will, it seems to me, is to consent to not know, to wait knowing *that* but without knowing how.

To say God knows no anxiety, it seems to me, is also to say that the same God who created man could just as well have not created him, or could have created him to be a programmed robot. It's to believe in a God for whom we play no part whatsoever in ongoing creation.

Instead, we have a very particular God: a God who pitches his tent among us, takes on human form, and knows the excruciating anxiety of death. Who laughs and loves, goes to weddings and parties, sweats tears of blood in the garden at Gethsemane, and gives us his very Body so that we can break him—knowing that we *would* break him—and eat. Who says, "I'll be with you till the end of time" but does not add "pushing you around like puppets" nor "sleeping."

I wonder if God does not contain his anxiety. I wonder if God does not consent to be stretched as far as he can possibly go, and to hold, as Christ does on the cross, the stretched to the breaking point tension, without lashing out, without transmitting the suffering, but rather in love, as a mother holds that kind of tension in labor—and is then split apart in birth. I think God knows all about waiting.

"Indeed the Father seeks such people to worship him." How patient he must be.

Blessed Father, help me to worship in Spirit and in truth. Kindle my desire to be among the chosen. Seek me.

I Am He

Heather King

The [Samaritan] woman said to [Jesus], "I know that the Messiah is coming, the one called the Anointed; when he comes, he will tell us everything." Jesus said to her, "I am he, the one who is speaking with you."
(Jn 4:25-26)

Surely paradise must be very much like Southern California in early fall. Sometimes I wish those long afternoons would last for ever. One Friday near dusk last September, I decided to head out on foot to a seven o'clock Taizé prayer hour at Saint Francis of Assisi. First, though, I took a long walk, up and around the steep streets north of Sunset Boulevard, lost in thought, the air rich with the fragrance of lavender and wild fennel and sage.

Way up near the top of the hill, I ran into a shirtless man with a friendly look in his eye who was also walking. I gave him a quick once-over but he didn't seem crazy. He did have on two different colored socks—one green, one pink—and a "Legalize Weed" button pinned to his shorts, but he didn't seem crazy.

"Is this your regular walk?" he asked. "I saw you up at the crest."

"One of them," I smiled. "I'm out here all the time, wandering about."

"I live over by the Franklin Hills, but I thought I'd come over this way today. I've just had heart surgery so I have to be extra careful about getting my exercise. Beautiful, isn't it?"

We stopped and gazed out over the hills. The cypresses and palms were outlined in black, and the sky just beginning to turn pink.

"Beautiful," I agreed.

He produced a pack of Camels, lit one up, and luxuriously exhaled. "This time of year…you can see why it's called The Golden State."

I extended my hands, palms up, as if to embrace the whole world. "We love L.A." I summarized.

It was one of those serendipitous moments of communion that are some of the sweetest fruit of the contemplative life. And all the way down the hill to church, I thought, *That was Christ. I just ran into Christ.*

Loving Father, help me to remember that anointing comes in many different forms. Open my eyes to see your love, your beauty, your joy, and your people.

The Disciples Were Amazed

Heather King

*At that moment [Jesus'] disciples returned, and were amazed
that he was talking with a woman, but still no one said,
"What are you looking for?" or "Why are you talking with her?"*
(Jn 4:27)

I once had a spiritual director to whom I often brought problems I was having with my own spiritual directees. "They should be a teeny bit afraid of you," she said. "They're coming to the mountain. You want to make it clear that your time is important."

Christ seems to have set this same tone with his disciples. He is their friend, but he never pretends to be their peer. They know all too well that he doesn't suffer fools gladly. They are already sufficiently well versed in the fact that his ways are not their ways not to ask "stupid" questions. They know that if Christ is talking to a woman, culturally taboo though that is, there must be a reason for it. They know the question, "What are you looking for?" is likely to bring a confounding, unanswerable counterquestion.

The disciples are amazed. As well as they know him, they are constantly amazed. Amazement is central to our faith. Dogma is essential; the problem comes when we mistake dogma for the mysterious, ever changing, vital experience that constitutes our actual lives. When we jab our finger at the Catechism instead of consenting to feel what goes on every second in our hearts, bodies, souls, and minds. When we forget that religion is about relationship; when we forget that religion is open, roomy, a mansion. There are many rooms in my Father's mansion and let's not forget it's a mansion, it's not a barracks, it's not a psych ward, it's not a jail. It's a mansion. It's a mansion we get to heal in, to learn how to love in. It's a mansion.

And it's a mansion with constant surprises. The disciples know something interesting is bound to happen. They know Christ never does things idly or aimlessly or out of boredom. He is talking to a woman for a reason. They are amazed—and when we're on the right path, we're constantly amazed, too.

Eternal Father, help me to study the actions and words of Jesus closely. Help me to ask fewer questions and to keep my eyes and ears open.

Leaving Our Water Jar

Heather King

The [Samaritan] woman left her water jar and went into the town and said to the people, "Come see a man who told me everything I have done. Could he possibly be the Messiah?" They went out of the town and came to him.
(Jn 4:28-30)

One kind of conversion consists in the experience of discovering: I've been thinking all along that things were this way, and now I see they're that way! I thought the problem was my alcoholic husband; now I see the problem is the way I react to him. I thought I was living a life of sacrificial martyrdom; now I see I'm really afraid to break out of my egg and be fully born!

In the case of the woman at the well, the pre-conversion thought was perhaps along the lines of: *I'm just full of love and how sad for me, nothing ever works out!* The post-conversion thought is: *I'm not a victim; I'm actually kind of a predator. I'm trying to take the shortcut to love. I use men and I let them use me.*

When Christ is our companion, such thoughts don't lead to guilt or despair. They lead to wonder and joy. Because simultaneously with the discovery of who we really are comes the knowledge that we are loved, even in our blindness, even in our brokenness, even in our sin. Immediately we want more than anything to be worthy of that love. And our very next impulse is to drop our water jar, run back to town, and tell everyone in sight.

The Samaritan woman must have undergone a noticeable change for the people to have gone "out of the town and come to him." Often we slower ones discover that no one else is nearly as interested, if they're interested at all, as we are. Often we leave our water jar and no one goes out of the town and comes to see him at all. Often we lose interest and flag ourselves. But we still get to dip deep into the cistern and to refresh ourselves once more. Even if no one seems to be listening, we still get to tell about the man who tells us "everything we have done."

Heavenly Father, help me to be ready to leave my water jar. Help me to spread the word that Christ is the Messiah. Help me to bring Christ into my own town.

Finishing His Work

Heather King

Meanwhile, the disciples urged [Jesus], "Rabbi, eat." But he said to them, "I have food to eat of which you do not know." So the disciples said to one another, "Could someone have brought him something to eat?" Jesus said to them, "My food is to do the will of the one who sent me and to finish his work."

(Jn 4:31-34)

If the Samaritan woman leaves her jar, we can assume that she never dips it into the cistern and that Christ still hasn't gotten his drink. Which would mean that the whole time Christ is talking to the Samaritan woman he is sitting by the well tired and thirsty.

We know that Christ gives of himself fully, and the giving must leave him drained. We know from the story of the hemorrhaging woman (see Lk 8:43-48) that when she touches the hem of Christ's garment and is healed, he is aware "that power had gone out of him." We sense a certain power going out of him here. We sense that he has brought all his resources to bear and that he is gathering himself. He is thirsty, but he is replenishing himself at the Eternal Fount. He is physically hungry, but he is hungrier still to draw the woman at the well to the living water of the Father.

We have a Messiah who allows himself to be affected and changed by his encounter with the Samaritan woman. And that means he allows himself to be affected by his relationship with us. How alternately confused, frightened, bewildered, and challenged the disciples must have been. "Rabbi, eat," the disciples say, and he replies, "My food is to do the will of the one who sent me." My food is to finish his work.

What is the work that the Father began? His work is Christ, in us. Christ, who is for ever willing to encounter the stranger, the outcast, the unpromising person, place, situation. Christ, who consents to remain thirsty while giving someone else a glass of water. Christ, who does the will of the one who sent him while the world misunderstands, tries to give him things he doesn't need, and asks off the mark questions.

God gives us Christ to help us finish his work. Our job is to love.

Loving Father, help me to discern the will of the one who sent me. Help me to long to finish his work.

Sharing the Harvest

Heather King

"Do you not say, 'In four months the harvest will be here'? I tell you, look up and see the fields ripe for the harvest. The reaper is already receiving his payment and gathering crops for eternal life, so that the sower and reaper can rejoice together. For here the saying is verified that 'One sows and another reaps.' I sent you to reap what you have not worked for; others have done the work, and you are sharing the fruits of their work." (Jn 4:35-38)

"Others have done the work." Consider all the people who go into surrounding us with food, shelter, clothing, entertainment at any given minute of our lives. The people who have grown, packaged, and shipped our food. The people who have manufactured our shirts, our iPods. The people who have written the books and blog posts and newspaper articles that we read to keep abreast and to be fed. The people who go into surrounding us with comfort, ease, and convenience within which we can do our work and shine in the eyes of our peers and the world.

In the parable of the talents (see Mt 25:14-30), the bad servant buries his talents reasoning that the "master" reaps where he does not sow. Here Christ reminds us that God is always sowing. Here, Christ teaches that, far from reaping where he doesn't sow, he allows us to reap where we don't sow.

We depend on others for our physical goods, but we depend on others far more than we know for our spiritual goods. How would we learn humility except by seeing others bear hardships far worse than ours with nary a shred of self-pity? How would we learn gratitude except by observing that we are showered with gifts through absolutely no merit of our own?

In *The Shadow of the Sun*, the late Polish journalist Ryszard Kapuscinski writes of his time in Nigeria: "Many of my neighbors here have just the one thing. Someone has a shirt, someone a panga, someone a pickax. The one with a shirt can find a job as a night watchman (no one wants a half-naked guard); the one with a panga can be hired to cut down weeds; the one with a pickax can dig a ditch. Others have only their muscles to sell."

How like Christ to allow us to share the glory of the harvest for work we haven't done.

Blessed Father, make me ever aware of the fruits I reap from the labor of others. Help me to be willing to share the fruits of my own labor.

The Woman Who Testified

Heather King

Many of the Samaritans of that town began to believe in [Jesus] because of the word of the woman who testified, "He told me everything I have done." When the Samaritans came to him, they invited him to stay with them; and he stayed there two days. (Jn 4:39-40)

Christ constantly stretches himself beyond his "comfort zone." Would you want to hang out with strangers for two days, eating their food, adapting to their schedule, putting up with their kids? Often we want to spread the Gospel to the ends of the earth, but on our terms. We want to sow the seed, but to people whom we handpick.

I was once asked to speak for a charismatic Catholic women's prayer group. Their approach was somewhat different than mine. A certain portion of the program was devoted to speaking in tongues. They seemed fixated upon miracles. When I got up to the microphone, several of the women gathered around, placed their hands on me, and prayed.

I did the best I could. I told my story. I said that the miracles I'd experienced tended to take place over a long period of time and after a lot of inner work. I said that a miracle for me was to refrain, for once, from the sharp retort.

Afterward, I felt like I hadn't done a very good job, or said what they wanted to hear. But then I thought, how do I know what people hear? How do I know whose heart is broken? How do I know who is struggling with an erring husband, a drug-addicted daughter, a fruitless job search?

How we long for everyone to "speak our language." To get our jokes. To have our taste. To "get" our elevated "spirituality." Such thoughts only prove we are not elevated at all—only Pharisees who are completely missing the point.

We need to remember that none of us is the keeper of miracles. We are hardly the arbiters of miracles. How do any of us know the day when we are hot, put-upon, and thirsty, and Christ himself appears to us, with his own special word, at the well? How do we know the day when we can be Christ for someone else?

Almighty Father, help my hardened, discriminatory heart. Help me to remember that everyone is struggling, everyone is suffering, everyone longs for a compassionate word.

Because of His Word

Heather King

*Many more [Samaritans] began to believe in [Jesus] because
of his word, and they said to the woman, "We no longer believe
because of your word; for we have heard for ourselves,
and we know that this is truly the savior of the world."*
(Jn 4:41-42)

As a writer, how carefully I choose my words! As a human who is constantly trying to get people and situations to go my way, how many hours I have spent thinking: If only I say it the *right* way, they'll understand! And as a Catholic convert who wrote a memoir about my stumbling journey to Christ, how my heart soared when I thought, now all my lapsed Catholic friends will see the light! Now all my agnostic friends will see that Christ is the Great Reality! How clear I will make it, how accessible! How people will simply fall to their knees and laugh and weep and worship when they see that Christ is one of us!

Of course no one—or no one I'd hoped—saw anything. My friends politely congratulated me and never mentioned the book again. From my family—resounding silence.

There is one group I never expected to respond to my book: priests. How much we owe to priests, stumbling men like you and me, marked out for sainthood in their misunderstood, lonely office. How far they have gone toward showing me the gallantry, respect, and support that have shored up my life and my work. They are a stand-in for Christ, just as I am a stand-in for the Samaritan woman, as we continue to carry out our long conversation by the well.

Christ himself never gilds the lily. He says what needs to be said and leaves the results to God. He calls us to a church, and he knows that church will be just as broken, as exasperating, as slow to see its faults as we are. He calls us to spread the Gospel to the ends of the earth, but he never says we will live to see the harvest.

We do what we can, but in the end Christ's Word, not our word, will convert hearts. Let us stay close to him, always, and listen.

Blessed Father, help me to let you choose the words. Help us to remember that apart from you, we can do nothing.

Why He Came Back

Regis Martin

After the two days, [Jesus] left there for Galilee. For Jesus himself
testified that a prophet has no honor in his native place. When
he came into Galilee, the Galileans welcomed him, since they
had seen all he had done in Jerusalem at the feast;
for they themselves had gone to the feast.
(Jn 4:43-45)

When the Twin Towers fell to the ground, killing thousands of innocent people, among its victims were police and fire personnel who surely knew that by entering the maelstrom of collapsing steel and concrete they too would die. They went in anyway. Playing it safe was not an option. Nor was it with Jesus when, entering Galilee, a place where his own kinsmen had previously tried to kill him, he knew that the certainty of rejection and death could not be far off. Unlike those in Samaria who, amazingly enough, received him as "the savior of the world," the Jews, in striking contrast, conspired to have him crucified. Yes, they appeared welcoming at first, but it was mostly boilerplate, the flapdoodle of folk eager to see yet another rabbit pulled from the hat. That God should come to his own, the lost sheep of Israel, and find that they not only do not wish to know him, but are determined on having him killed, is testimony to the perversity of the human heart.

So why does he not tarry longer in Samaria? How tempting it must have been to linger among those on whom he had left so favorable an impression. Because it was not the Father's will. The world's salvation was to come through the Jews, in the very teeth of their rejection of the One sent to bring it about. Thus will Jesus return to Galilee, there to await his destiny, the mysterious Hour toward which everything moves in the Fourth Gospel. And while he had succeeded among the Samaritans, it hardly follows that he should remain there to rest upon his laurels. Success is not a criterion of discipleship. Only fidelity matters. How completely Jesus evinces this by his readiness to return, moved by such love of the Father that he will prove it by loving even his enemies to the end.

Heavenly Father, you sent your Son into the very jaws of death
to save all that was lost. May we too be ready to suffer for others.

The Real Sign Awaiting Us

Regis Martin

Then [Jesus] returned to Cana in Galilee, where he had made the water wine. Now there was a royal official whose son was ill in Capernaum. When he heard that Jesus had arrived in Galilee from Judea, he went to him and asked him to come down and heal his son, who was near death. Jesus said to him, "Unless you people see signs and wonders, you will not believe."

(Jn 4:46-48)

While still at Cambridge, the young Richard Crashaw, destined to become England's premier Catholic poet, entered a competition in which he was asked to write about the miracle at Cana. It took awhile to produce the following, which, incidentally, got him the prize: *"The shamefaced water saw its Lord, and blushed."* How nicely it captures the whole transformative effect of grace upon nature. When Jesus shows up, miracles happen. "For the grace of God has appeared for the salvation of all men," writes Paul to Titus (2:11 RSV). What is grace? God's pleasure poured out upon the world in the gift of his Son. Can there be any doubt that the world will dutifully sit up and take notice? Especially when it sees an outpouring of such signs and wonders as can only be wrought by God? Like turning water into wine, which is the sort of wizardry designed to dazzle any crowd. Even highly placed pagan officials will gravitate to Galilee on the strength of that. Everyone will soon be looking for Jesus, drawn by the marvels he performs. And why not if, in the case of the royal official, a dying son needs deliverance?

Yet so thin is this man's reed of faith that Jesus rebukes him for it. And all of Israel as well stands rebuked for its want of faith. Because with the coming of Christ, the true Logos leaping across the heavens into history, what people really need to see, to move resolutely toward, is not the gaudy display of power, but the encounter with a *Presence* on whom the Father's favor rests. Let that be the sign, the sheer proximity of God in the guise of a servant who wishes only to move companionably among us. Let that be the wire of wonder we trip over—the miracle of Jesus himself, whose mission is to build the bridge over which in faith we can all journey back to God.

Loving Father, teach us to draw close to Jesus, near to the source, who is himself the real and abiding sign of your mercy.

The Exceptionality of Jesus

Regis Martin

The royal official said to [Jesus], "Sir, come down before my child dies." Jesus said to him, "You may go; your son will live." The man believed what Jesus said to him and left.
(Jn 4:49-50)

"Once the Incarnation happens," an old professor of mine used to exclaim, "nothing remains the same!" The far-reaching impact of that eruption, he insisted, would result in the most salutary subversion of the entire existing order. A clean sweep, in other words, leaving in its wake nothing untouched, undisturbed. Nothing less than the infinite God himself—"whose center," Dante tells us, "is everywhere, whose circumference nowhere"—choosing to encompass a space so finite, so narrowly circumscribed, as to end up stretched upon a cross. What could be stranger? It quite unsettles everything. "If we no longer experience the shock of that," writes Henri de Lubac, "may not the reason be that our faith has lost its cutting edge…?"

Surely the royal official who has come to importune Jesus is close to knowing this. Why else is he here if not because of the exceptionality of Jesus? That here is someone who possesses this amazing capacity to reconstitute the cosmos. Why, he can even turn a couple hundred gallons of water into wine! How cool is that? And, besides, where else can he go? Certainly his appeal is heartfelt. A son is about to die and, desperate to save him, a father goes off to find the One he *knows* has the power to make a difference. So does Jesus fly at once to the side of the stricken child? No. Because for all that the official urges him to go, it is not necessary that Jesus actually be there. When you're God, the laws of physics no longer apply. Of course the royal official does not know this yet, which is why Jesus, in order to stretch the man's faith, puts him to the test, telling him to go home *for his son shall not die*. So the man sets out, fortified by a faith he does not fully possess but, please God, is moving toward. He is not far from the kingdom.

All-powerful Father, awaken in us such simplicity of faith that whatever we ask of Jesus in your name we may receive with childlike confidence and trust.

Beginning Anew with Christ

Regis Martin

While [the royal official] was on his way back, his slaves met him and told him that his boy would live. He asked them when he began to recover. They told him, "The fever left him yesterday, about one in the afternoon." The father realized that just at that time Jesus had said to him, "Your son will live," and he and his whole household came to believe. [Now] this was the second sign Jesus did when he came to Galilee from Judea. (Jn 4:51-54)

"To live is so startling," writes Emily Dickinson, "it leaves but little room for other occupations." What can this mean but that whenever wonderment strikes, the soul withers and dies if it does not allow itself to become so enraptured by the experience as to feel quite helpless to be anything else. To find oneself drawn to, riveted upon a reality whose magnetism arrests the attention is a good thing; indeed, it is something so wonderfully, captivatingly good as to keep the soul in its grip for ever. Like Coleridge's Ancient Mariner, one is held by the sheer glitter of his eye. And isn't this what needs to happen to the royal official on hearing the news of his son's recovery? That thanks to that miraculous moment when Jesus pronounces, "Your son will live," the man needs to feel the tremor of bliss, of rhapsodic delight every time he remembers the mercies of Jesus. "Memory," the poet Pavese reminds us, "is a passion repeated." Well here is a memory to shape the whole trajectory of his life. To know that on a certain day, at a moment of which he is given no advance warning, something fabulously, extraordinarily special took place. The missile found its mark, leaving him, all at once, *surprised by joy*.

Again, the poet Pavese: "How beautiful it is to begin. The only joy in the world is to begin…to live is to begin, always, and every instant." How easy to imagine the royal official going through life, taking up the usual round of affairs, all the while in secret thrall to the truth that everything has changed. To live deep down the certainty of having been ravished by God, the influx of whose grace leaves him (and now his family!) in a state of constant stunned surprise, of gratitude for gifts neither he nor they could ever have given. All because of Christ. Who brings all things new simply by bringing himself.

Loving Father, you have given us a world filled with the wonders of your Son. Give us hearts eager and grateful to welcome him.

The Sheep Gate

Heather King

After this, there was a feast of the Jews, and Jesus went up to Jerusalem. Now there is in Jerusalem at the Sheep [Gate] a pool called in Hebrew Bethesda, with five porticoes. In these lay a large number of ill, blind, lame, and crippled. (Jn 5:1-3)

The ill lie at a gate. The gate has five porticoes. The ways that we are ill, blind, lame, and crippled often prove to be an opening, a portico. But this is not just any gate. It is the Sheep Gate and near it lies a pool.

We're reminded of the parable of the sheep and the goats (see Mt 25:31-46), where Christ says we will be judged "sheep"—his friends—based not on the sharpness of our eyesight or the perfection of our limbs, but on whether we were compassionate to "the least of these." In order to be authentically compassionate, it seems, we need first to offer up our own wounds to be bathed, to be baptized.

The wounded healer is a Christ-like archetype. My friend I'll call Peter, victim of a random shooting at the age of seventeen, has been in a wheelchair for forty-one years. He can't get up off his mat and so, with his sense of humor, his patience, his generosity of spirit, his utter lack of self-pity, he ministers from there.

But there are mats and then there are mats. Sometimes we are called to be healers by accepting that we must stay on our mat, and sometimes we are called to be healers by getting up off our mat and walking. Peter himself has picked up many mats. He picked up the mat of sobriety. He picked up the mat of caring for his aging mother, all the way up to her death.

I once asked him what time he had to start getting ready for a 12:30 PM gathering where many of us sober alcoholics and addicts regularly meet.

"10:30?" I ventured "Ten even?"

"Six," he replied.

"Six!" I pictured him laboriously rising, fixing breakfast, showering, dressing, getting into his car, driving.

"Not a minute later," he added cheerfully. "I live by minutes and inches."

An inch to the pool. A minute of love, stretching to infinity.

Dear Father, comfort the crippled, the lame, the blind. Help us to bear our infirmities of mind and body with patient endurance.

Wanting to Be Well

Heather King

One man was there [at the pool] who had been ill for
thirty-eight years. When Jesus saw him lying there and knew
that he had been ill for a long time, he said to him, "Do you
want to be well?" The sick man answered him, "Sir, I have no
one to put me into the pool when the water is stirred up; while
I am on my way, someone else gets down there before me."
(Jn 5:4-7)

To suffer with our fellow wounded is a beautiful thing. Often the ill can understand one another as no one else can. But sometimes the line between compassion and pathology becomes thin. Sometimes we can get a little too comfortable by the pool. Sometimes we begin to enjoy our suffering, to identify ourselves with our suffering. Sometimes we begin to believe that we cannot get well. That belief becomes our organizing principle, and then a possession, and then a chain.

We can make efforts to get well but subconsciously the efforts can be halfhearted. Subconsciously, we can come to prefer eliciting pity or even contempt rather than shouldering the obligations of "normal" life. Subconsciously, we can become terrified of what getting well might mean. What might we be called to? What new responsibility might be ours? Who or what would we be if we were no longer *by* the pool, but *in* it along with everyone else?

A priest friend once noted that nowhere does Scripture say, "God helps those who help themselves." In fact, he pointed out, God helps those who can't help themselves. But you have to want to be helped. You can't be at cross-purposes with your deepest self. That in thirty-eight years not one person has come along who is willing to carry the paralytic to the pool strains credulity. "Prayer is the daily admission of one's weakness," observes Father Bernard Bro, o.p., and sometimes our deepest weakness is that we've come to prefer sickness to health.

God can work any way he sees fit. He sometimes heals us when we didn't ask to be healed and may not even particularly want to be healed. But to long to be healed, and for a long time not to be, is heartbreaking. In that case, says Christ, we can ask ourselves, "Do I truly *want* to be healed?" We can continue to pray for the willingness.

Blessed Father, don't let me get too comfortable by the pool. Help
me want to be healed. Help me to be willing to be willing.

Rise and Walk

Heather King

Jesus said to [the sick man], "Rise, take up your mat, and walk."
Immediately the man became well, took up his mat, and walked.
Now that day was a sabbath.
So the Jews said to the man who was cured, "It is the sabbath,
and it is not lawful for you to carry your mat."
(Jn 5:8-10)

Reading the Gospels through, it seems Christ is constantly shadowed by prying eyes, gossiping tongues, and the kind of interfering spoilsports who can't bear to see another succeed. Faultfinders, nitpickers, the people with so little life of their own that they hang out looking over other people's shoulders and taking notes.

We know these people. They wouldn't dream of missing Mass and they also wouldn't dream of actually returning a smile, or pressing a neighbor's hand at the Sign of Peace. They'll make a big show out of praying the rosary, then cut you off without a pang in the parking lot. The worst of these, and Christ knew it well, are the spiritual busybodies. These are the self-proclaimed "guardians of the faith," with their magnifying lenses and checklists, who make a cottage industry out of checking the religious "credentials" of their brothers and sisters.

Their response is never, "Praise be to God, you're walking, man!" Never, "Can I give you a hand there with your belongings?" No, these are wet blankets who can't rejoice that after thirty-eight years someone is up and running again. They purse their lips and cross their arms and, with a sour look, say, "It is the sabbath, and it is not lawful for you to carry your mat."

These are the people who, when you're struggling to stand, kick you to the ground. These are the people who will watch you writhe as they brandish their Catechism. These are the people who killed Christ.

We know these people because they are ourselves; and worst of all, they are often ourselves; criticizing and carping at and pouncing on ourselves.

Christ was never about hairsplitting or nitpicking or elevating a rule over a human being. "Rise and walk," he said. And then give a hand to the next guy who's trying to rise.

Loving Father, help me to live my own life fully. Help me to rejoice when my neighbor is fully able to live his or hers.

The Hidden God Unmasked by Love

Douglas Bushman

[The man who was healed] answered [the Jews], "The man who made me well told me, 'Take up your mat and walk.'" They asked him, "Who is the man who told you, 'Take it up and walk'?" The man who was healed did not know who it was, for Jesus had slipped away, since there was a crowd there.

(Jn 5:11-13)

What do Zorro, the Lone Ranger, Superman, and Batman have in common? They all have unique costumes that identify them as do-gooders while concealing their real identity. People expect these heroes to use their extraordinary talents to help those in need, especially in situations of injustice. Yet no one knows who they really are.

God reveals his love in Jesus, yet his humanity masks his divinity. In today's passage, Jesus heals the formerly ailing man, who knows he has been loved, but he does not know who it is that loved him. He is like those who seek God, knowing that they owe their existence to him, but not knowing who he is. He is like the poor attended to by Blessed Teresa of Calcutta; they know her compassion for them in their diseases and desperation, but they cannot know her deep, inner motive until they come to faith.

God's act of love always comes first. He does not wait to love us only after we come to know him. In this his love is impatient. In contrast, he does wait to be acknowledged, and in this his love is patient. In the next passage it becomes clear that Jesus wants this man to know who he is. Above all, he wants to be known as the one who loves. He wants all to know that his love is powerful, that it heals and transforms. This is the deep meaning of Jesus' miracles, and of the places of pilgrimage for those in search of God's healing love, like Lourdes. Jesus meets us in our needs, thereby giving us hope that there is a love strong enough to overcome evil and suffering. Our hearts do not deceive us when we long for liberation from evil and suffering. Nor does faith deceive us when we acknowledge him, making our own Saint Thomas' words: "My Lord and my God." Jesus is the Lord and God who loves us!

Praise and thanks to you, eternal Father, for revealing your love in Jesus. Help me to continue his mission of disclosing your love, so that the world may know you as the Father who is rich in mercy.

God Always Has More to Give

Douglas Bushman

After this Jesus found [the man who was healed] in the temple area and said to him, "Look, you are well; do not sin anymore, so that nothing worse may happen to you." The man went and told the Jews that Jesus was the one who had made him well. Therefore, the Jews began to persecute Jesus because he did this on a sabbath. (Jn 5:14-16)

When recovering from surgery, a follow-up appointment to assure that everything is progressing as it should is normal. Should the surgeon make an unscheduled house call, inquiring not about the patient's recovery but his financial preparation for retirement, that would surely trigger surprise. A doctor's concern is about bodily health, right? Regarding financial planning, he should mind his own business, right? Certainly, unless one's doctor is also an expert financial advisor!

In today's reading we see that Jesus has more that he wants to say, because he has more to give. God's love is concerned with the whole person, body and soul. The doctrine of the resurrection of the body confirms this. But, people are tempted to pay too much attention to the body, to the point of neglecting their souls. To counter this, Jesus' miracles of healing are always associated with faith and forgiveness of sins. Healing the man's body is a sign of another kind of healing—the inner healing of his soul. He was eager to receive God's love through Jesus to mend his body. Is he just as eager to receive God's love to mend his soul?

The greatest wound to our souls is the absence of love. That is what sin is, the absence or diminishment of love for God as a result of loving something else, some created good, like our own bodies, too much. In sin there is too much love—for a created good—and not enough love for the uncreated Good—God. Sin is a deficit of love for God. Jesus' words for the good of this man's soul, "do not sin anymore, so that nothing worse may happen to you," are meant to draw his attention—and ours, too!—to the higher order of love for God. He wishes to draw us from the gift to the Giver, because from the infinite fullness of his love God always has more to give.

Merciful Father, I am heartily sorry for having preferred the good of my body over the good of my soul. Help me to love you, who are deserving of all my love, with all my heart, mind, soul, and strength.

God's Love Never Rests

Douglas Bushman

But Jesus answered [the Jews], "My Father is at work until now, so I am at work." For this reason the Jews tried all the more to kill him, because he not only broke the sabbath but he also called God his own father, making himself equal to God.

(Jn 5:17-18)

Building a perpetual motion machine and finding a self-renewing energy source are elusive. What does it say about man, a time-bound creature, that he seeks something that time neither decelerates nor arrests? Since man is made for love, the real search is for an unending, undiminishing love. This love cannot be human or man-made. It must be divine. It can only be encountered, and to encounter it, it must be revealed.

In Jesus we encounter the everlasting love that we seek. To reveal that it is divine, his healing love acts on a sabbath. This provokes a question: only divine love can accomplish such a prodigious beneficence, but can divine love contradict itself by transgressing the precept to imitate God by resting on the sabbath? Jesus knows the sabbath's true meaning because he knows the Father: "No one knows the Father except the Son" (Mt 11:27). God rests after six days of creation because his love is fulfilled; nothing is left undone, creation is complete. When by sin his love is rejected, everything changes. There must be a new creation. God's love cannot rest again until it is fulfilled again, when men open themselves again to his love. God's love does rest until Jesus loves "to the end" (Jn 13:1) and men "come to know and to believe in the love God has for us" (1 Jn 4:16). "This is the work of God, that you believe in the one he sent" (Jn 6:29). Bringing men to faith in God's love is the work of that unending love that all seek.

The crippled man cannot plunge himself into the stirred waters that heal and laments not being loved: "I have no one to put me into the pool when the water is stirred up" (Jn 5:7). This stirs Jesus' love, which remains stirred and at work until it is fulfilled and can rest when we are with him in heaven.

Father of all consolation, I thank you for the grace of being plunged into your Son's love in the water of baptism. Grant me the grace worthily to celebrate his love that is at work still in the Eucharist.

He Chose Us

Father George William Rutler

Jesus answered and said to [the Jews], "Amen, amen, I say to you, a son cannot do anything on his own, but only what he sees his father doing; for what he does, his son will do also. For the Father loves his Son and shows him everything that he himself does, and he will show him greater works than these, so that you may be amazed." (Jn 5:19-20)

An architect has no difficulty finding his way around a house he has designed. He knows where every door leads. Christ speaks with casual familiarity about everything in heaven and earth since "the Father loves his Son and shows him everything that he himself does." At the age of twelve, Jesus spoke of the Temple as though he knew every inch of it because the design is his: "In times past God spoke in partial and various ways to our ancestors through the prophets; in these last days, he spoke to us through a son, whom he made heir of all things and through whom he created the universe" (Heb 1:1-2). His relationship with his Father is hard for mere humans to understand, precisely because it is not a human invention. If Christ were simply our theory, he would be easy to figure out, and he would not be a mystery at all. Without the help of the Holy Spirit, the human intellect always misunderstands Christ, "for no prophecy ever came through human will; but rather human beings moved by the holy Spirit spoke under the influence of God" (2 Pt 1:21).

The ultimate truth about Christ is that he has no beginning or end, and he shares that eternal existence with this Father through the bond of love which is the Holy Spirit. So when Jesus speaks lovingly of his Father, he is revealing to the human race something of the holy Trinity. It took many centuries for bishops and theologians to find language adequate to describe this Three-in-One God, because they did not design him. "It was not you who chose me, but I who chose you" (Jn 15:16). To the narrow-minded who believe only small things, the things that God does are only inconvenient problems. But to the large-minded who recognize in Christ "the radiance of his Father's splendor" (cf. Heb 1:3), everything he does is amazing.

Almighty Father, I praise you for shedding the radiance of your love through the holy face of your Son who is one with you and the Holy Spirit now and for ever.

Our Eyes at Last Shall See Him

Father George William Rutler

"For just as the Father raises the dead and gives life, so also does the Son give life to whomever he wishes. Nor does the Father judge anyone, but he has given all judgment to his Son, so that all may honor the Son just as they honor the Father. Whoever does not honor the Son does not honor the Father who sent him." (Jn 5:21-23)

One learns from hard experience that it is all too easy to type one wrong letter in a word and completely change the meaning. *U* and *I* are next to each other on the keyboard but that does not make Bill a Bull. It becomes more problematic if you add a letter. Add an *i* to "run" and you get "ruin." The Nicene Creed came to us after a long struggle over the little Greek letter iota, which is like our *i*. Add it to the Greek term "same substance" and you get "similar substance." To make clear what the Divine Mind revealed to human minds about himself, the recent translation of the Creed says that Jesus is "consubstantial" with the Father.

What the Father does, the Son does. Both Father and Son give life and they both judge. Jesus does not contradict this when he says the Father judges no one, but gives all judgment to his Son. Saint Augustine explains that while the Father judges with the Son, "no one will see him in the judgment, but all will see the Son, because he is the Son of man, even the ungodly who will look on him whom they pierced."

Jesus is declaring his divinity, as he will say bluntly to Philip: "Whoever has seen me has seen the Father" (Jn 14:9). In the rabbinical story, Job longed to see God, "Whom I myself shall see: my own eyes, not another's, shall behold him" (Jb 19:27). That tattered man in an Eastern desert was far removed from the Victorian lady, Cecil Frances Alexander, who shared that same hope, but also knew, as she wrote in her children's hymn, that the Father had shone his love through the human eyes of his Son: "And he feeleth for our sadness/ And he shareth in our gladness/ And our eyes at last shall see him, through his own redeeming love."

Almighty Father, grant the grace needed to recognize you in your Son, that on the day of judgment I shall not be ashamed to look at him who looks at me every day of my life.

Life More Than Existence

Father George William Rutler

"Amen, amen, I say to you, whoever hears my word and believes in the one who sent me has eternal life and will not come to condemnation, but has passed from death to life. Amen, amen, I say to you, the hour is coming and is now here when the dead will hear the voice of the Son of God, and those who hear will live." (Jn 5:24-25)

What is now called the "Big Bang" was originally called the "First Atomic Moment" by the Belgian priest, Father Georges LeMaître, who developed the theory and had no easy time persuading other physicists to accept it. Some thirteen to fourteen billion years ago there was a vast explosion that set in motion all that exists. We may say in a technical sense that God does not exist, because he is pure Being, and so while all creatures "exist," they come from him who purely "ists." This is not fanciful wordplay, for the Word who made all things has no beginning or end. Yet he came into the world speaking with a human voice. "And the Word became flesh" (Jn 1:14). When the daughter of Jairus, and the son of the widow of Nain, and Lazarus heard that voice they were restored to life.

The Word is not satisfied that we exist. He wants us to live beyond mere existence. For existence ends, but life united with the Source of Life can never end. There is a story that a young musician, often said to have been Fritz Kreisler, saved his money to buy a fine violin, only to find that it had been sold to a wealthy collector of musical instruments, who kept it in a locked cabinet. He would not sell it to the youth but let him play it to hear how it sounded. The collector was so moved by how the instrument could "sing" that he let the young man have the violin. Human existence becomes true life when the voice of God sings through the soul by faith. Saint Irenaeus says, "The glory of God is man fully alive." To live a half-life, existing without God, is to be condemned to a locked cabinet, where potential is unrealized. To be freed of that banality through faith is to pass from death to life.

God our Father, who have spoken to us through your Son, may I open my ears to hear that Word every day, and may I open my mouth to praise him who gives me life.

Life and Judgment

John Janaro

"For just as the Father has life in himself, so also he gave to his Son the possession of life in himself. And he gave him power to exercise judgment, because he is the Son of Man."
(Jn 5:26-27)

The leaders of the people oppose Jesus. They are even trying "to kill him" (Jn 5:18). Jesus doesn't fight back. He doesn't try to destroy his enemies. Instead he bears witness to the truth about himself and the Father. Jesus knows that his very identity consists in being "from the Father," and thus he offers himself—in every circumstance—as the gift of the Father's love.

As a human father, I often need to discipline my children. But I want them to learn that my authority is not based on any strength of my own, but rather on the fact that God has given me to them as a father, to teach them about his love and show them how to live.

Recently, I had to be firm with one of my girls. It would have been easy to vent my frustration and gain her cooperation through fear: "Just do it, or else…!" But instead, this time, I sat her down and said, "God gave me to you as a father to help you grow and become the person he wants you to be. It would be much easier for me to say, 'Do whatever you like,' but God wants me to help you learn what is good, and he wants you to trust my judgment here, even if you don't understand it. That's why you obey your parents. They are gifts to you of God's love." I think this helped her to obey me with a sense of trust, and of being loved.

Jesus doesn't try to win arguments, or use his great power to terrify people into submission. He bears witness to the truth about himself, the truth about the Father's love. Throughout life, the Father seeks to embrace us in love, through his Son Jesus. The meaning of life is accepting the embrace of God's love and loving him in return, and therefore it is by this love that we will be judged.

Loving Father, give me the grace to recognize in the presence of your Son Jesus that loving embrace that draws me to my fulfillment in you, and grant that I might respond with love, gratitude, and trust.

The Resurrection Is Already at Work in Us

John Janaro

"Do not be amazed at this, because the hour is coming in which all who are in the tombs will hear his voice and will come out, those who have done good deeds to the resurrection of life, but those who have done wicked deeds to the resurrection of condemnation." (Jn 5:28-29)

Through Jesus, God gives himself to us in love. He gives us a share in the mystery of his divine life. But he doesn't force us to accept this great gift. Love doesn't impose itself; it seeks a response in freedom from the beloved.

Still, God never changes. His love for us always remains true, for he himself is Love. And we cannot be "neutral" or indifferent in front of God's never-ending love for us. Our final destiny depends on whether we accept or reject this love in the actions of our lives.

If my wife brings me a cup of coffee out of love, and I just take it and ignore her, I have not received her love. Indeed, I am being rude, and this diminishes me as a person. On the other hand, if I recognize the gesture and say, "Thank you," I experience her love by responding in love. I grow as a person. I become a more loving person. And through the responsive love of my gratitude, my wife's love gives me joy.

But if I continue to be rude every day, I will get worse. I may become resentful. I will start to hate the intrusiveness of this loving gesture. My morning coffee will begin to torment me. My wife will still love me, but her love will only remind me of the selfish person I have become.

We can only receive love by giving love in return. Our freedom makes it possible to say "yes" to God's love, and be transformed by it so as to share in his joy. But it also means that we can refuse to say "yes." If we thus reject God's love in our lives, we can condemn ourselves to being eternally closed, resentful, and tormented because the One who creates us is Eternal Love.

Loving Father, open our hearts to receive your love through your Son Jesus Christ. Grant that we might grow in love for you throughout our lives, so that we might rejoice for ever in your glory.

The Father's Testimony

Father Francis Martin

"I cannot do anything on my own; I judge as I hear, and my judgment is just, because I do not seek my own will but the will of the one who sent me. If I testify on my own behalf, my testimony cannot be verified.
But there is another who testifies on my behalf, and I know that the testimony he gives on my behalf is true."
(Jn 5:30-32)

From the mouth of the Word made flesh we catch a glimpse of the fire of love that is the life of the Blessed Trinity. While the One who is speaking is revealing to us the decisions of his human will, he is also revealing a secret about the depth of his relation to the Father: he is not seeking his own will but "the will of the one who sent me." We catch a glimpse of that interaction in Jesus' prayer in Gethsemane: "Take this cup away from me, but not what I will but what you will" (Mk 14:36). Meditating on this Gethsemane scene, Saint Maximus the Confessor tells us: "We are saved by the human decision of a divine Person." Human salvation is worked within the confines of human existence: this is the will of God. When alluding to the Gethsemane prayer, the Letter to the Hebrews, interpreting the prayer of Jesus through the words of Psalm 40, sums up Jesus' prayer this way: "As is written of me in the scroll,/ Behold, I come to do your will, O God." The Letter then adds: "By this 'will,' we have been consecrated through the offering of the body of Jesus Christ once for all" (Heb 10:7, 10).

When Jesus, in the text we are meditating upon, claims the witness of the Father on his behalf, he is sure that the Father will testify to the reality of his Son and to the depth of their union and oneness of their will. To receive this testimony we must gaze on the cross and, by faith and love, penetrate the wound in Jesus' side and heart. Then, we may be granted entrance to that secret place where the Father's eternal gaze of love is for ever bearing witness: this is the Father's testimony which is for ever true.

Father, lead me to that place of testimony and enable me to cling fast to your will always and remain in your truth.

The Baptist's Testimony

Father Francis Martin

"You sent emissaries to John, and he testified to the truth. I do not accept testimony from a human being, but I say this so that you may be saved. He was a burning and shining lamp, and for a while you were content to rejoice in his light. But I have testimony greater than John's."

(Jn 5:33-36a)

Jesus, out of love for his adversaries, appeals to yet another testimony: that of his precursor, John the Baptist. By this means he hopes to lead them to the truth. John spoke of his own ministry as that of "baptizing with water," a conversion rite he used to bring people to renew their commitment to God and be prepared for the One who would "baptize in the Holy Spirit." This expression of John's would evoke in the minds of his hearers all those places in the Old Testament which referred to the definitive act of God on behalf of his people as a "pouring out of the Spirit." Recall, for instance, the words spoken by Saint Peter on that first Pentecost as he quoted the prophecy of Joel (see 3:1): "I will pour out my Spirit upon all flesh,/ and your sons and your daughters shall prophesy,/ and your young men shall see visions,/ and your old men shall dream dreams" (Acts 2:17 RSV). And there are so many similar prophecies and promises. All of these prophecies point to the need for special divine aid in responding to God's loving initiative. At Pentecost the Father, by pouring out the Spirit of his Son, brings this promise to a reality.

Every generation needs this same outpouring, as Pope Benedict reminded us in his remarks after reciting the *Regina Caeli* prayer with the crowds on Pentecost 2008. On that occasion he spoke of the grace of an experiential faith: "Let us rediscover, dear brothers and sisters, the beauty of being baptized in the Holy Spirit; let us recover awareness of our Baptism and our Confirmation, ever timely sources of grace." This recovery of awareness of the foundational graces of our Christian life is at the heart of Pope Benedict's call to the Church to be renewed through a personal encounter with the living Christ.

Jesus, let the deep recesses of my heart echo your desire to have me know you better, love you more faithfully, and make you known in this unsettled time of concern and fear.

Jesus' Works as Testimony

Father Francis Martin

*"The works that the Father gave me to accomplish, these works
that I perform testify on my behalf that the Father has sent me.
Moreover, the Father who sent me has testified on my behalf.
But you have never heard his voice nor seen his form, and you
do not have his word remaining in you, because you do not
believe in the one whom he has sent."*

(Jn 5:36b-38)

Jesus now invokes further witnesses to his identity, namely, the works that the Father gave him to accomplish and which indeed are the testimony of the Father himself. As we behold the miracles of Jesus, we see revealed the action of the Father who, in his essential activity of creation and giving life, makes known the reality of his Son. Thus, we see in one and the same regard the Son and the Father whom he makes known. Failure to know the Father is a direct result of not believing in the one whom he has sent. When we come to know the Father, three desires are satisfied: the desire of the Father to be known and to be in a personal relationship with us; the desire of the Son to bring us to share his relationship with the Father; and the desire of the Holy Spirit who stirs us to this knowledge and who cries out with us, "*Abba*, Father!" The whole purpose of the "works" is to bring us into this intimate relationship. Later, when Philip asks Jesus, "Master, show us the Father, and that will be enough for us," Jesus responds: "Whoever has seen me has seen the Father.... The words that I speak to you I do not speak on my own. The Father who dwells in me is doing his works" (Jn 14:8-10).

One dimension of the "works" which Jesus does and which reveal the Father is his action in our souls and spirits. It is a worthwhile practice at times to go over our life and reflect on the works that Jesus has done already in our life. Sit down as soon as you can and reflect and write down where you see the works of the Father in your life, and ask the Holy Spirit to testify to the reality and majesty of Jesus: this is the way to come into contact with the witness of his works.

*Blessed Father, please open my heart to embrace the witness you
bear to me through your action in my life.*

The Scriptures Bear Testimony

Father Francis Martin

"You search the scriptures, because you think you have eternal life through them; even they testify on my behalf. But you do not want to come to me to have life."

(Jn 5:39-40)

Next, Jesus challenges the notion that one can have eternal life through the Scriptures. They are not the source of eternal life, they are witnesses to its source who is Jesus. In order to have the life to which the Scriptures witness, we must come to Jesus. In John's Gospel the word "come" often indicates an act of belief in Jesus. Jesus promises the first two disciples who ask where he abides: "Come, and you will see" (Jn 1:39), and Philip promises the same to Nathanael (Jn 1:46). Later, in chapter 6, Jesus states on three occasions that coming to Jesus is a work of the Father (see Jn 6:37, 44, 65). In this passage Jesus is challenging his audience who fail to act on the witness of the Scriptures and believe in the One who can give them life. This is not to imply that the Sacred Scriptures cannot bring life. Pope Benedict said in his homily at the opening of the 2004 Synod: "Only the Word of God can profoundly change man's heart so it is important that individual believers and communities enter into ever increasing intimacy with his Word." Saint Thomas once said that for those who study the Scriptures with an open heart, there are "unspeakable delights." This occurs when believers go to Jesus with a desire to learn about him and to learn from him. The Blessed Virgin Mary is our model. We read of her that "she kept all these things, reflecting on them in her heart" (Lk 2:19). Then too, Saint Paul speaks of the Word at work in us: "And for this reason we too give thanks to God unceasingly, that, in receiving the word of God from hearing us, you received not a human word but, as it truly is, the word of God, which is now at work in you who believe" (1 Thes 2:13).

Father, you sent your divine Word who works in us with power—please make us active disciples.

We Must Act on the Testimony of Scripture

Father Francis Martin

"I do not accept human praise; moreover, I know that you do not have the love of God in you. I came in the name of my Father, but you do not accept me; yet if another comes in his own name, you will accept him. How can you believe, when you accept praise from one another and do not seek the praise that comes from the only God?"

(Jn 5:41-44)

At this point, our Lord Jesus calls his opponents (and us) to look at the source of their resistance to him: it lies in egoism. Accepting Jesus means accepting his offer of salvation. Accepting Jesus' offer of salvation means acknowledging that we need it. Acknowledging that we need salvation means that we are not self-sufficient. Here Jesus uncovers the source of our self-centered rigidity: we do not really trust Jesus and his offer of salvation, so we make up a "salvation" of our own and try, using our own resources, to achieve this self-styled salvation. This can be money, power, popularity, or even "good works" like large donations, serving on the boards of charitable organizations, etc. These are good things, but they are meant to *follow* our self-surrendering act of faith, our acceptance of the *gift* of salvation. All the praise and adulation in the world does not replace a simple act of faith and an acceptance of this gift. That is why Saint Thomas Aquinas' first question concerning human happiness is whether or not it consists in honor. He answers that this is impossible because honor lies in the one honoring, not in the one honored. If someone honors me, that is a credit to them. The honor may or may not be deserved but it cannot create my happiness since honor is in the one honoring.

Excellence is in the one honored—if the honor is deserved. That is why Jesus points to the inevitable uneasiness and frustration of seeking happiness in being honored: "How can you believe, when you accept praise from one another and do not seek the praise that comes from the only God?" Let us risk our self-protecting attempts at religion, and accept instead the praise that comes from God himself.

Blessed Father, protect me from my instinct to stay clear of you rather than accept your gift and the freedom that follows from it.

Receiving the Testimony
of the Old Testament

Father Francis Martin

"Do not think that I will accuse you before the Father: the one who will accuse you is Moses, in whom you have placed your hope. For if you had believed Moses, you would have believed me, because he wrote about me. But if you do not believe his writings, how will you believe my words?" (Jn 5:45-47)

I n order to understand these words we must think of other Jews who, in their faith and trust in God, pondered the words of Scripture and began to understand the contours of God's plan for Israel, and the world. Think of Simeon who was awaiting "the consolation of Israel, and the Holy Spirit was upon him." When he took Jesus into his arms he blessed God, saying: "Lord, now let your servant depart in peace, according to your word;/ for my eyes have seen your salvation/...a light for revelation to the Gentiles,/ and for glory to your people Israel" (Lk 2:25-32 RSV). Think especially of Mary who, in the light of the Holy Spirit, was prepared to understand what was being asked of her at the Annunciation because, here as well, "the Holy Spirit was upon her." Notice in our Johannine text that Jesus says: "if you had believed Moses, you would have believed me." Observe that in the two Resurrection appearances recorded by Saint Luke, the risen Jesus leads the disciples to an understanding of the Old Testament Scriptures. The two disciples on the way to Emmaus exclaimed: "Were not our hearts burning [within us] while he spoke to us on the way and opened the scriptures to us?" (Lk 24:32). In regard to the disciples huddled in the upper room in Jerusalem: "Then he opened their minds to understand the scriptures [the Old Testament, of course]. And he said to them, 'Thus it is written that the Messiah would suffer and rise from the dead on the third day and that repentance, for the forgiveness of sins, would be preached in his name to all the nations, beginning from Jerusalem'" (Lk 24:45-47). Saint Peter says of this gift of Old Testament prophecy: "You will do well to be attentive to it, as to a lamp shining in a dark place, until day dawns and the morning star rises in your hearts" (2 Pt 1:19).

Heavenly Father, please open my mind to the understanding of the Scriptures; I want my heart to burn with delight in the presence of your Word.

Prayer upon the Heights

Father Stephen Dominic Hayes, O.P.

After this, Jesus went across the Sea of Galilee [of Tiberias].
A large crowd followed him, because they saw the signs
he was performing on the sick. Jesus went up on the mountain,
and there he sat down with his disciples. The Jewish feast
of Passover was near. (Jn 6:1-4)

We now begin a new section—the two miracles that precede Jesus' "Bread of Life" discourse in chapter 6. In today's verse, it is Passover time, and Jesus' actions evoke the days of Moses and the great deeds of the Exodus. As Moses went up Mount Sinai with the elders of the people, so Jesus ascends the mountain with his disciples; the crowd, like the populace at Sinai, remains below.

I have visited the traditional site of the miracle while on pilgrimage in the Holy Land. There is a church overlooking the Sea of Galilee built on the height there to serve pilgrims. The air was filled with the smell of flowers, and the wind was blowing. I remember being mightily impressed by the solitude of the place, and the silence of it. A mountain is a natural place of prayer—the sky is bigger, and heaven seems closer. It's easy to leave the busyness of one's daily concerns back in the valley. The mountaintop is a natural stage waiting for God to enter and show himself. God showed himself on the heights of Israel to Abraham, Moses met him on Mount Sinai, Saint Patrick prepared for his ministry atop Mount Eagle, and Saint Benedict built his monastery on Monte Cassino.

In our passage, Jesus ascends the mountain as a new Moses. This implies that he goes up the mountain to commune with his Father, as Moses communed with God in the days of the Exodus. Moses came down the mountain with a law whose weight human flesh could not bear, as Saint Peter witnesses (see Acts 15:10). When Jesus descends the mountain he comes to nourish the souls and bodies of those who wait hungry below with his own presence: a new bread from heaven, and the sacrifice of a new and better Passover.

Father Most High, you brought Moses to Mount Sinai so that your people might learn holiness; through your Son's example may we begin all our work by first lifting our eyes and hearts to you, from whom comes our help.

Food That Nourishes

Father Stephen Dominic Hayes, O.P.

When Jesus raised his eyes and saw that a large crowd was coming to him, he said to Philip, "Where can we buy enough food for them to eat?" He said this to test him, because he himself knew what he was going to do. Philip answered him, "Two hundred days' wages worth of food would not be enough for each of them to have a little [bit]." (Jn 6:5-7)

When I was in seminary, I had a professor who tried to illustrate the objective reality and order of the created world by pointing out that humans can't eat rocks. Stones don't nourish the body, and if anyone were so foolish as to try to eat rocks, he would certainly break his teeth on them. God has made stone and bread for different purposes, possessing qualities radically different from each other. Jesus refuses to make stones into bread during his temptation in the desert (see Mt 4:1-11). However hungry he is, he will not use his divine power to provide himself nourishment in a way apart from his Father's establishment of the creation. Yet now he will use the divine power to multiply the loaves and fish to feed a crowd. He does so to prepare them to receive a supernatural nourishment.

In this miracle, there is a sense in which Jesus transmutes stone into bread. At Sinai, Moses descended the mountain bearing the Word of God carved on tablets of stone, appropriate to a law too heavy to be humanly borne, as Saint Peter testifies (see Acts 15:10). When Jesus comes down the mountain, he gives the crowds at the bottom not stones, but his own sacred Person—revealed as the Bread from heaven come down to feed the world (see Jn 6:51). In his perfectly obedient humanity—body, blood, soul, and will—he manifests the law given by Moses made concrete in human life and action—his own. But he will do more than simply demonstrate human perfection. This miracle of the loaves also presages his institution of the Eucharist, by which his holy humanity, the perfect incarnation of the Word of God in its fullness and the ancient law of God now come in Flesh, will be in Holy Communion a heavenly Bread to feed the souls of each one of us. This Bread will be nourishment unto eternal life.

Loving Father, we thank you that you ordained that sinners should not be crushed for ever by the holy weight of your Word, but through Jesus, the Bread from heaven, might find a medicine for our sins and a foretaste of immortality.

The Bread of Angels

Father Stephen Dominic Hayes, O.P.

*One of his disciples, Andrew, the brother of Simon Peter, said
to [Jesus], "There is a boy here who has five barley loaves
and two fish; but what good are these for so many?"*
(Jn 6:8-9)

Andrew's concern that the five barley loaves and two fish are insufficient for the needs of the five thousand echoes almost exactly Elisha's doubt in Elijah's ability to feed one hundred men with twenty barley loaves (see 2 Kgs 4:42-44). Yet the outcome will be the same: by the grace of God, by a deed of the divine power, not only will all be satisfied, but there will be some left over. God's graciousness always provides not only "enough," but more than enough. His blessings overflow: "You open wide your hand/ and satisfy the desire of every living thing" (Ps 145:16). Similarly, when God feeds the people through Moses in the Exodus, his gifts are marked with superabundance: God fills the desert with manna, mysterious bread divinely and copiously supplied (see Ex 16:4-30). When the people then ask for flesh to eat, he supplies quail in such abundance that they actually become sick with it (see Nm 11:18-20).

In the hands of the boy, the five loaves and two fish seem completely inadequate to feed the crowd. Placed in the hands of Jesus, this small gift will be more than sufficient for a task that seems impossible. There will be twelve baskets of fragments left over from a beginning that could be placed in its entirety in a single basket. There is a deeper meaning as well: in the events of the Exodus, Moses promised bread and meat to the people, but it came forth from heaven, from the hand of God. The bread and fish are placed in the hands of Christ, and are multiplied there. Thus Christ is identified as truly divine. The Power that fed the multitude in Exodus from heaven in ancient times now works manifestly and abundantly through the open hands of Jesus, to feed God's flock with richer fare than earthly bread and meat: his own Presence and indestructible life.

Father of heaven and earth, who fills the earth with food and provides the necessities of every living creature, we thank you for our daily sustenance, and even more for the supersubstantial gift of your Son Jesus' presence in the Holy Eucharist.

Shepherd of the Flock

Father Stephen Dominic Hayes, O.P.

*Jesus said, "Have the people recline." Now there was a great deal
of grass in that place. So the men reclined, about five thousand
in number. Then Jesus took the loaves, gave thanks, and
distributed them to those who were reclining, and also
as much of the fish as they wanted. (Jn 6:10-11)*

J esus feeds the crowd while evoking Israel's sacred past and
prophesying the further revelation of God's mysteries. What
Moses did with manna and quail, he now renews with bread and
fish, and preparing his disciples for the revelation of a new manna—
the Eucharist of Bread and Flesh he will institute the night before he
ascends the cross of his sacrifice. He feeds the crowds miraculously
and completely, "as much as they wanted."

Saint John notes that the men recline upon the grass. The early
Church Fathers see in this an allusion to the divine Shepherd of
Israel, who makes his flock lie down "in verdant pastures" (cf.
Ps 23:1-2). Jesus "spreads [a] table" before them (cf. Ps 23:5) that
evokes, not only God's mercies to his people in the Old Testament,
but clearly prepares the way for his institution of the Eucharist.
As on the night he is arrested, Jesus takes bread, gives thanks (in
Greek: *eucharistēsas*), and distributes the broken loaves and fish
to his disciples to feed the crowds who have joined Jesus as table
companions. In Matthew, Mark, and Luke, this language is part
of the institution narrative of the Eucharist; in John's Gospel, it is
a prelude to Jesus' discussion of the Eucharist that will constitute
the rest of chapter 6.

How richly we are fed by our Good Shepherd! I only vaguely
remember my first Holy Communion at the age of seven, but the
light, dry touch of the host upon my tongue, and the meaning of
it, is one of the fundamental and formative experiences of my life
and self-understanding. I can't live without receiving him who has
been so good to me, and who has fed me with his Presence since
my childhood. Every day that I serve him as a priest this miracle is
renewed for me, as he places in my hands his own life and Presence
to nourish the people he loves.

*Heavenly Father, through Jesus your Son, you make sinners your
table companions and saints your intimates; grant that we may
always grow in love of him who suffered the cross and through the
apostolic ministry continues to make its fruit manna for pilgrims.*

Superabundance of Grace

Father Stephen Dominic Hayes, O.P.

When [the people] had had their fill, [Jesus] said to his disciples, "Gather the fragments left over, so that nothing will be wasted." So they collected them, and filled twelve wicker baskets with fragments from the five barley loaves that had been more than they could eat. (Jn 6:12-13)

The arithmetic is amazing: five loaves plus two fish minus full belly servings for five thousand people equals twelve full baskets of fragments left over. Jesus has fulfilled the words of the psalm: "They all look to you/ to give them their food in due time/.... When you open your hand, they are filled with good things" (cf. Ps 104:27, 28b). What is even more arresting is that Jesus has accomplished what the psalm describes as appropriate only to God. Saint Hilary of Poitiers notices something else about this verse—that even after the crowd has eaten to satiety, each of the twelve Apostles holds a full basket. They have in fact left over more food than they started with, because there is no lack of power in Jesus' ability to provide. As long as they are with him, not one of Jesus' company will ever lack for sustenance.

Jesus' command to gather the fragments also makes a point to the Apostles about the ministry which they will have after the Resurrection. Entrusted with the ministry of feeding the flock of the Good Shepherd by preaching and sacrament, Saint Hilary points out that they are furthermore entrusted with the task of gathering; through Christ, their work will feed thousands upon thousands in the future, but the twelve full baskets signify that they will never be left short of nourishment to provide for God's people.

How splendid and rich is the table Jesus sets for the flock entrusted to him! Whether we come to him in church to hear the preached Word or to receive his presence in Holy Communion, whether we approach him in silent prayer or by opening up a text of Scripture to meet the risen Lord, he feeds us. He who is Bread from heaven as well as the Word made Flesh feeds those who accept him with measureless abundance, with eternal life itself.

Father of the Word Incarnate, every grace comes down from you through your Son Jesus and the Holy Spirit's power; grant that, summoned to holiness in Christ, I might enjoy his active presence in me as he shepherds me toward glory.

Crowned by the Father

Father Stephen Dominic Hayes, O.P.

When the people saw the sign [Jesus] had done, they said,
"This is truly the Prophet, the one who is to come into the
world." Since Jesus knew that they were going to come and
carry him off to make him king, he withdrew again
to the mountain alone. (Jn 6:14-15)

In 1804, attempting to emulate the greatness of Charlemagne, Napoleon Bonaparte had himself crowned emperor of the French in Paris. He required the presence of Pope Pius VII for this. The pope, who was virtually a prisoner of the Napoleonic government, was supposed to crown Napoleon in the traditional manner. Instead, however, Napoleon snatched the imperial crown from the pope's hands and put it on his own head, thus making it clear that it was by his own hand he was seizing the imperial dignity.

How different is Jesus' approach to the crown the crowd wishes to offer him! They want a savior on their own terms, and this Prophet, whose advent is foretold by Moses (see Dt 18:15-19), and in whom the miraculous power of God is so visibly manifest, becomes their hope of political liberation from pagan Rome.

Jesus will have none of this. Authentic kingship always comes from above, because it is a participation in the authority of the God who is King of the universe. It is God who gives kings their crowns; one cannot truly steal authority from the hand of the Almighty. Jesus understands this. The only one from whom he will accept crown, kingdom, and authority is his own Father in heaven, who first gave kingship to human beings as a gift when he set Adam over the world to share in his lordship of it. The only crown that Jesus will accept from human hands is the crown of thorns, which specifically and deliberately mocks the kingship Jesus is receiving from his Father as the new and perfectly obedient Adam. The kingdom his Father is giving him has the cross for a throne, whereby the tree of pain that human beings invented to keep each other enslaved becomes the royal seat upon which Christ the King separates good from evil, and begins the judgment of the living and the dead.

Father and King of the universe, your Son Jesus has made me a partaker of his life and spiritual authority; grant that through his grace I may master my pride and sinful inclinations, so that I may reign with him in the glory of heaven.

The Blessing in the Water

Father Stephen Dominic Hayes, O.P.

When it was evening, [Jesus'] disciples went down to the sea,
embarked in a boat, and went across the sea to Capernaum.
It had already grown dark, and Jesus had not yet come to them.
The sea was stirred up because a strong wind was blowing.
(Jn 6:16-18)

The text for today's meditation mentions only the absence of Jesus. Setting out for Capernaum by boat—a fairly short trip—a storm blows up and catches the disciples by surprise. These sudden storms on the Sea of Galilee turn it into a very dangerous place, particularly if the winds are from the northeast. The disciples, according to the map, would be blown into the depths of the sea, away from every shore and source of aid.

If you've ever been in a storm at sea, or even in a storm while boating on a large lake, you won't forget it. The sky is gray, the waves are gray, and the water is everywhere—down your neck, up your nose, in your eyes and mouth and clothes. In a very wild storm, you don't try to go anywhere; you just try keep the nose of the boat into the wind. If the waves get over the gunwales, you might find yourself capsized and drowning. Death feels very close as you fight wind and water and wave. And you pray, intensely.

When you and I find ourselves out of our element, we pray. We may not readily think of God when things are going well, but when our world is overwhelmed and we feel no solid ground beneath us, when the torrents of our difficulties pound down upon us like the ancient Deluge upon the sons of Cain, then we know we are feckless, helpless. Then we pray for a Savior. This is a blessing and a gift. The mercy of the storm is that it reminds us that we cannot captain our lives by ourselves. Like the disciples in the boat, we peer into the wild wet chaos around us in the hope of finding a rescuer—one who can be, as we cannot be, the Lord of the storm.

Father of mercy, Lord of heaven and earth, through the work of your Son Jesus, teach me to be vigilant in seeking you, who remain my protector and Savior amid the evils of the present age.

Lord of the Storm

Father Stephen Dominic Hayes, O.P.

When [the disciples] had rowed about three or four miles, they saw Jesus walking on the sea and coming near the boat, and they began to be afraid. But he said to them, "It is I. Do not be afraid." They wanted to take him into the boat, but the boat immediately arrived at the shore to which they were heading.

(Jn 6:19-21)

Jesus' walking upon the water reveals his divine identity. He has just fed the crowds in a manner that recalls God's deeds in the time of Exodus; now he evokes the primary event of Passover: the passage of the Red Sea waters. Psalm 77 remembers that day as God's visitation of his people: "The waters saw you, O God;/ the waters saw you and shuddered/…. Through the sea was your way,/ and your path through the mighty waters,/ though your footsteps were not seen./ You led your people like a flock/ under the care of Moses and Aaron" (cf. Ps 77:17, 20-21). Jesus is more than a new Moses; he demonstrates the specifically divine attributes of Israel's ancient Savior. In him, God visits his people in power. The Apostles find themselves rescued like the Israelites of old, unexpectedly under the divine hand brought swiftly to safety on a farther shore (see Ex 14). There's no hint that the imperiled Apostles understand all this. Their sudden danger and swift rescue leave no time for deep theological reflection.

Like the Apostles, you and I seldom do theology in the midst of personal disasters. When my mother was dying, my familiar world and that of my adult siblings dissolved as she made her passage out. Suddenly, we were orphaned. Suddenly, the new "elder generation." To understand that her death was the occasion of grace and blessings for all of us required distance from the pain of the event. But what was absolutely clear to us in the midst of our personal storm was that God was with us and her—and in the moment of the storm, that is sufficient. In Jesus, the full power of divinity resides, and that is sufficient for any disaster. He will rescue us in a way of his choosing, and that is a grace sufficient for all things.

Shepherd of Israel, through your Son Jesus, continue to guard me and bring me to the verdant pastures you have promised; draw me through the turbulence and sorrows of this present life to the peace of your kingdom.

True Seeking of Jesus

Father Michael L. Gaudoin-Parker

The next day, the crowd that remained across the sea saw that there had been only one boat there, and that Jesus had not gone along with his disciples in the boat, but only his disciples had left. Other boats came from Tiberias near the place where they had eaten the bread when the Lord gave thanks. When the crowd saw that neither Jesus nor his disciples were there, they themselves got into boats and came to Capernaum looking for Jesus. (Jn 6:22-24)

In these verses the Evangelist implicitly presents the state of confusion experienced by the crowd. They are perplexed about why Jesus isn't still there among them on the day after he had satisfied their hunger. Their curiosity is aroused by the fact that he appears to have left after his disciples. Thus, in their eagerness to find Jesus, they avail themselves of some passing boats to go in search of him.

This scene suggests a thematic thread woven through the whole fabric of John's Gospel: the mysterious identity of Jesus. For instance, John the Baptist points him out to his own disciples as the "Lamb of God" worth following (see Jn 1:36). He likewise draws back from the people's acclaim in preference to Jesus: "I am not the Messiah.... He must increase; I must decrease" (Jn 3:28, 30). The Evangelist explains that Jesus, being God's Son, bestows heavenly life "from above" (Jn 3:31), the Spirit's gift without measure. Jesus' mystery is also indicated in his disciples' understandable bewilderment to find him talking with a Samaritan woman and refusing the food they brought by responding: "I have food to eat of which you do not know" (Jn 4:32). Being entirely sustained by the Father, his life is simply thanksgiving. His sharing of the divine mystery becomes gradually unfolded in the course of this Gospel through his repeated "I AM" statements.

Fascination about Jesus isn't enough. Nor is a seeking of him to benefit from what is hoped to be gained from him or from what he promises. This may be the initial stirring of faith. It isn't yet authentic discipleship, which requires adhering to him as uniquely revealing God as "Father," whom he knows as the wellspring of abundant, eternal Life.

The human heart's search for happiness, as Saint Augustine says, can only be satisfied by God, by and for whom it is created.

Merciful Father, grant that our seeking of your Son may be not for hope of passing gain or advantage, but for the joy of knowing you through him.

Motivated by Working in Love

Father Michael L. Gaudoin-Parker

And when [the crowd] found [Jesus] across the sea they said to him, "Rabbi, when did you get here?" Jesus answered them and said, "Amen, amen, I say to you, you are looking for me not because you saw signs but because you ate the loaves and were filled. Do not work for food that perishes but for the food that endures for eternal life, which the Son of Man will give you. For on him the Father, God, has set his seal." (Jn 6:25-27)

Jesus bypasses the crowd's natural curiosity. He goes directly to their inner motive for seeking him. Knowing they want to find a solution for their temporal needs, he challenges them to consider the significance of what they see him doing and receive from him. He compares his work to life-sustaining food. Earlier he already tells his disciples: "My food is to do the will of the one who sent me and to finish his work" (Jn 4:34). He wants to interest and involve people in this same work, which gives an eternal meaning to all temporal human endeavors. This work must motivate and undergird everything in living. It carries its own reward, since it is oriented toward fulfilling God's will. It indeed supplies a new energy and dynamism.

A mother once recalled how when her little child was dangerously ill, she sat on the edge of his bed for a whole night. Her one thought was for her son's recovery according to God's will. She didn't feel any physical weariness or discomfort, because she was sustained by her loving attentiveness.

The lives of the martyrs present inspiring examples about the implications of what it is to be truly a Christian, not only in name but *in deed*. They witness to Christ's desire to please the Father through the complete gift of self. For example, as he faced the ordeal of terrible suffering, Saint Ignatius of Antioch was entirely focused on becoming "the pure bread of Christ" rather than on making eloquent professions of faith. In this he imitated what he handled in the holy food of the Eucharist, in which the supreme labor of love, the "work of our redemption" is carried out.

In our times of consumerism, Servant of God Chiara Lubich taught that prayer opens us to become part of God's "economy of communion," through which we discover how to care for our neighbors' needs by sharing their lives.

Almighty Father, may we live more deeply what Jesus your beloved Son showed us about praying that your will be done on earth as it is in heaven.

Faith in God's Wonderful Works

Father Michael L. Gaudoin-Parker

So [the crowd] said to [Jesus], "What can we do to accomplish the works of God?" Jesus answered and said to them, "This is the work of God, that you believe in the one he sent."
(Jn 6:28-29)

The answer that Jesus gives to the crowd's question expresses the entire purpose of proclaiming the Gospel. His answer in turn issues a challenge. It calls for a response that entails more than can be made by words. To say that we believe in him as the God-sent Savior is one thing. But it is quite another matter to *live* what with our lips we profess in the Creed about God's saving deeds brought to fulfillment in Jesus. This living faith costs not less than everything. Its qualitative value can never be properly assessed or described in human terms.

This lived faith, experienced on an existential level, is nevertheless not merely a subjective feeling of being saved. Believing in God's act of saving us through sending Jesus into the world means becoming personally involved and completely committed to realizing, that is, making real the purpose of the wonderful design of God's work of love.

No work is as wonderful as God's creation of humankind, for which the Psalmist often gives praise in awe considering human fragility. Incomparably more wonderful in beauty and dignity is the work of the new creation brought about through baptismal faith in Christ. Being God's "handiwork" or work of art, we are, as Saint Paul says, "created in Christ Jesus for the good works that God has prepared in advance, that we should live in them" (Eph 2:10). In his words to the crowd, Jesus is thus calling them to entrust themselves to this new reality of God working in them, rather than to rely on their own efforts and works.

This mystery of being plunged into God's wonderful work is recalled at Mass when a little water is added to the chalice of wine. This gesture symbolizes our becoming diluted wholly into the rich reality of Christ, who fulfils the Father's work in transforming our humanity by sharing it.

Heavenly Father, in praising you for Jesus showing us your wonderful works, may we be faithful instruments of your love.

Reading the Signs of the Times

Father Michael L. Gaudoin-Parker

So [the crowd] said to [Jesus], "What sign can you do, that we may see and believe in you? What can you do? Our ancestors ate manna in the desert, as it is written:/ 'He gave them bread from heaven to eat.'" (Jn 6:30-31)

These two questions imply that the crowd understands that Jesus is asking them to believe in him as the one sent by God. They are no longer looking to Jesus to satisfy their material needs, but to assuage their spiritual yearning for the long-desired Messiah. They want some miracle that would confirm his claim and offer evidence of his divine power. They thus act in accord with their tradition of believing on the basis of receiving convincing miraculous signs. Insofar as Jesus claims to be someone greater than their Moses, he is being asked to present a more outstanding demonstration of his credibility than their Lawgiver.

Jesus is no magician. He doesn't wish to bedazzle the multitude easily excited by spectacular stunts. He isn't out to seek popularity nor does he succumb to the intrigue of those wishing to make him their political liberator.

John's Gospel, unlike the Synoptics, doesn't have Jesus confronting and dismissing the Tempter's wily attempts to seduce him in the desert. Yet, the question of giving a sign already emerged when he was asked to justify his act of cleansing the Temple. Outwitting the challenge of profiteers of piety, he states: "Destroy this temple and in three days I will raise it up" (Jn 2:19). The Evangelist explains that this is a prophetic utterance of his victorious Resurrection over death. Jesus refers to this elsewhere as "the sign of Jonah" (Mt 12:39). Only through his paschal sacrifice in conquering death would the crowd's questions be answered, for then the "hidden manna" becomes revealed.

Saints like Francis or Mother Teresa knew how to read the signs of the times by asking the right questions that lead to hope. They focused on the implications signified in the "Bread from heaven," where the deep value of material things and the worth of human life are communicated.

God our Father, lead us to appreciate Jesus' gift of life in the form of Bread, so that we may attend to our neighbors' hunger for the truth of love by our self-giving.

Our Daily Bread

Father Michael L. Gaudoin-Parker

So Jesus said to [the crowd], "Amen, amen, I say to you, it was not Moses who gave the bread from heaven; my Father gives you the true bread from heaven. For the bread of God is that which comes down from heaven and gives life to the world."
(Jn 6:32-33)

The poet Gerard Manley Hopkins calls God the "giver of breath and bread." His awareness was rooted in recognizing deeply that God alone is the true provider: "Lord of living and dead." The expression "bread from heaven" occurs in the Old Testament accounts of Israel's deliverance from slavery in Egypt. Recalling this event that changed this people's history, Jesus corrects the notion that Moses sustained them during their hard times of desert wandering. He alludes to Psalm 78 that praises God for providing his people daily with manna. The significance of this food is mysterious in multiple ways as regards its source, appearance, duration, and its prophetic purpose. The Hebrew word "manna" means "What is it?" The fact that the manna would spoil if kept beyond the day it is gathered implies complete trust and dependence on God, who is aware of our needs in deeper ways than could ever be imagined. This is why Jesus teaches us to pray for "our daily bread."

This prayer finds its fulfillment in the Eucharist. Following the interpretation of some Fathers of the Church, Saint Thomas Aquinas in a beautiful hymn states that this sacramental food for wayfarers is "the Bread of angels." Why? Because just as angels feast on the life-giving Word, so too all people, both rich and poor, need to be fed by Jesus, the Word become visible and accessible for their earthly journey. Moreover, only through God's self-giving love poured out in this sacrament do we receive the nourishment and strength to be messengers, like angels, of his Good News of hope giving faith to others.

In these days of a much-needed New Evangelization, there isn't any better way to proclaim the Gospel of the Eucharist than by our becoming ourselves bread broken for a new world.

Loving Father, since you alone know our deepest needs, nourish our minds and hearts by your Son's presence so that our whole lives may witness what we celebrate in the Eucharist.

Believing to Understand

Father Michael L. Gaudoin-Parker

So [the crowd] said to [Jesus], "Sir, give us this bread always."
Jesus said to them, "I am the bread of life; whoever comes to me
will never hunger, and whoever believes in me will never thirst.
But I told you that although you have seen [me], you do not
believe." (Jn 6:34-36)

The people misunderstand Jesus' words about God being the wellspring of all life. To clarify this he points out that he himself is the Bread of Life. He thereby undersigns God's covenant with his chosen people to be their sole support and staff of life. In other words, he assures them of *standing under* all creation, since he, the Word from the Father, is the unique source of its meaning as its vitalizing substance.

This truth is already proclaimed at the beginning of John's Gospel: "All things came to be through him,/ and without him nothing came to be./ What came to be through him was life." This life is perceived through him, for as the Word of the invisible God he is revealed as "the light of the human race" (Jn 1:3-4). Later, in confronting those who refuse and hesitate to believe him, Jesus states: "I am the light of the world" (Jn 8:12).

As elsewhere in this Gospel, Jesus here affirms the basis of his credibility by using the phrase "I AM," which echoes the divine name "Yahweh." Only obstinate blindness, not mere misunderstanding, can resist the meaning of the truth of his divine being from God.

Yet, there are those who waver, even like one of his disciples: the words of others aren't enough for Thomas. He has to see and touch the wounded Lord, who points out that they are more blessed who believe without seeing, like Mary. By remaining steadfast in the darkness of the cross as she *stood under* the wounded Healer, Jesus' Mother is the model of faith.

By first believing, as Saint Augustine often pointed out, a person comes truly to *understand* the Bread that satisfies the human heart's deepest hunger in the Mystery of Faith. This mystery, though our senses deceive us, is what "many prophets and kings desired to see" (Lk 10:24). Indeed, it is that "into which angels longed to look" (1 Pt 1:12).

Merciful Father, through faith in the Eucharistic mystery, deepen our understanding about how to reflect with consistency your Son's true light and life to those needing to behold it.

Recapitulated in Christ

Father Michael L. Gaudoin-Parker

"Everything that the Father gives me will come to me,
and I will not reject anyone who comes to me, because
I came down from heaven not to do my own will
but the will of the one who sent me."
(Jn 6:37-38)

These words convey a sense of Jesus' outreach in love to all creation. They articulate his Father's gratuitous desire to unite all people under and in him. Jesus tells Philip at the Last Supper: "Whoever has seen me has seen the Father" (Jn 14:9). He welcomes all whom the Father gives him: "Come to me…. Take my yoke upon you and learn from me" (Mt 11:28-29). Before his Passion he says: "When I am lifted up from the earth, I will draw everyone to myself" (Jn 12:32). On the cross he cries out: "I thirst" (Jn 19:28).

Jesus' yearning is expressed tenderly in his image of a hen gathering its chicks under its wings. This is depicted in a mosaic in the chapel facing Jerusalem where Jesus wept because he was rejected in his efforts to convert that city. Recalling Jesus' words, Saint Anselm of Canterbury has a prayer in which he calls him our mother.

Saint Paul states that God's whole purpose is "to reconcile all things" to himself through Christ (Col 1:20). He elsewhere describes this mystery in the imagery of recapitulation: "to sum up all things in Christ, in heaven and on earth" (Eph 1:10).

In the second century, Saint Irenaeus was the first to take up and develop the multifaceted meaning of this imagery. He relates it to the Pauline teaching on the unity of the Body of Christ, under whose headship all members of the Christian community are at-oned in communion.

The imagery of recapitulation implies that all fragments of creation, like words and syllables on a parchment scroll, are wound around the Word made flesh. It also suggests that just as in a musical composition a theme is repeated and developed, so too Christ, the joy of human desiring, is the theme song played out in the lives of his faithful. The Jesuit poet Hopkins writes: "Christ plays in ten thousand places,/… To the Father through the features of men's faces."

Heavenly Father, as your Son sought nothing for himself but only to draw us toward fulfilling your design, may your Spirit unite us to attract others to you by our lives.

Christ's Pledge of Future Glory

Father Michael L. Gaudoin-Parker

"And this is the will of the one who sent me, that I should not lose anything of what he gave me, but that I should raise it [on] the last day. For this is the will of my Father, that everyone who sees the Son and believes in him may have eternal life, and I shall raise him [on] the last day." (Jn 6:39-40)

In these verses Jesus raises human hope beyond all dreams and desires. All that is required is faith in him. This is what he asks of Martha, who approaches him after her brother Lazarus' death. She meets his challenge, responding: "Yes, Lord. I have come to believe that you are the Messiah, the Son of God, the one who is coming into the world" (Jn 11:27). He responds to this woman's trusting faith in him, as he does at Cana to his mother's faith-filled confidence that he has power to transform the young couple's embarrassment into festivity.

Jesus calls Lazarus out of the tomb, however, not merely because moved by compassion nor by his own deep sorrow at his friend's death. Rather, this action reveals his uniquely intercessory role as the eternal High Priest "always able to save those who approach God through him" (Heb 7:25). Faith and confidence placed in him participate in his own utter reliance on God. This is clear in his grateful prayer for Lazarus' rising from the dead being a sign of his own: "Father, I thank you for hearing me" (Jn 11:41).

Promises are easily made, not always kept. Jesus' assurance of eternal life is more than a human promise. It fulfills the covenant prophesied: "With age-old love I have loved you;/ so I have kept my mercy toward you" (Jer 31:3). He is the divinely effective Word made flesh, who, as God says through Isaiah, "shall do my will,/ achieving the end for which I sent it" (Is 55:11).

He is the Good Shepherd who carries out his mission from the Father to lose no one. Seeking out those in the "valley of death," he goes ahead to prepare a banquet for them in their eternal home. At the Eucharistic table we already have a pledge and foretaste of future glory. We become an Easter people, whose song, as Blessed John Paul II said in Harlem, is "Alleluia."

Loving Father, through, with, and in Jesus' gift of the Eucharist we praise you for enabling us to savor the joy to come as our hearts become transformed in the Spirit of love.

Identikit of Jesus

Father Michael L. Gaudoin-Parker

The Jews murmured about [Jesus] because he said, "I am the bread that came down from heaven," and they said, "Is this not Jesus, the son of Joseph? Do we not know his father and mother? Then how can he say, 'I have come down from heaven'?"
(Jn 6:41-42)

Seeing the crowd's eagerness to be taken in by Jesus' promise to provide them with a lasting supply of food, some of the Jewish authorities ("the Jews") in their midst feel that he is a threat to their power base. They start spreading suspicion about his claim to bring about such an extraordinary deed. They point to his ordinary origins, since his human kith and kin are well known to all. Where did this mere son of a carpenter learn how to offer more than what people obtain by the sweat of their brow?

The real question here as throughout the Fourth Gospel concerns the mystery of Jesus' divine identity. This presents the great challenge. This perspective is already set out in the Prologue. Although many of "his own people did not accept him," to those coming to believe in him "he gave power to become children of God." This new humankind arises "not by natural generation nor by human choice nor by a man's decision but of God" (Jn 1:11-13). This new breed shares in Jesus' fullness of "grace and truth" because, as he explains to Nicodemus, it is "born from above" (Jn 3:3, 7). It is sustained by Jesus himself, God's new gift of bread from heaven.

Through this bread Christians become directly linked to the mystery of Jesus' paschal gift of himself. Their communion with him expresses the genetic code of their identity. Without disparaging natural family ties, Jesus states that this identity means being freed from enslaving self-love and bonded in God's design of brotherhood. As he says at the Last Supper, "I have called you friends, because I have told you everything I have heard from my Father" (Jn 15:15).

Discovering this new freedom, Venerable Dorothy Day was empowered to sacrifice all, even her relationship with a common-law husband, as she learned to feed others on Christ's law of love bestowed in his bread from above.

Merciful Father, ever grateful for your Son giving us himself as bread from heaven, we ask you to free us from self-love so that we rise above others' opinions in seeking to fulfill your holy will.

Drawn by Love

Father Michael L. Gaudoin-Parker

Jesus answered and said to [the Jews], "Stop murmuring among yourselves. No one can come to me unless the Father who sent me draw him, and I will raise him on the last day. It is written in the prophets:/ 'They shall all be taught by God.'"

(Jn 6:43-45a)

Jesus doesn't just silence the spread of malicious talk about his qualification to speak in public. Rather, he reaches out to his opponents by reminding them of words that would have been familiar to them. Citing words from the second Book of Isaiah, he expresses his confidence that whoever gives him a fair hearing does so only because of being open to the work of the Father in drawing people to him. On another occasion, when further murmuring breaks out against him, Jesus replies in the clearest manner to the leaders' fear about their people being misled by someone who hasn't been through their Scripture schools: "My teaching is not my own but is from the one who sent me" (Jn 7:16).

Teaching means more than bookishness. It requires not what Blessed John Henry Newman called "notional" knowledge, but rather the assimilation of wisdom acquired through experience. Without this, as an old saying has it, no matter how learned a person is he is like an ass carrying books. Being the Word—"The only Son…who is at the Father's side" (Jn 1:18)—Jesus is attuned, as no other ever has been or is, to communicate the fullness of life. In him the joy of desiring is fulfilled. He alone is able to raise human awareness and enlighten the heart to see God is love.

Years of searching the paths of sense knowledge, pleasure, and philosophy led Saint Augustine to acknowledge finally that God etches into the human heart a longing that only he can satisfy and bring to rest. In a sermon, this great African pastor comments on Jesus' words about the Father drawing us to him. As a sheep is attracted by a fresh green twig, he says, so are we by grace. We can't raise ourselves by a muscular voluntarism. Our virtue itself is inspired, sustained, and brought to perfection by surrendering to God's amazing grace of love.

Loving Father, transform our hearts to be ever grateful for your Son showing us that in your will is our peace through the grace of your Spirit.

Facing God in Christ

Father Michael L. Gaudoin-Parker

"Everyone who listens to my Father and learns from him comes to me. Not that anyone has seen the Father except the one who is from God; he has seen the Father. Amen, amen, I say to you, whoever believes has eternal life."

(Jn 6:45b-47)

What Jesus says expands the key notion of John's whole Gospel, stated in the Prologue: "No one has ever seen God. The only Son, God, who is at the Father's side, has revealed him" (Jn 1:18). He extends his revelation to everyone. No one is excluded. The Word of the Father is inclusive.

God's people learned to appreciate that their being nourished on manna was continued in a spiritual sense through the Torah or Law, which is life-giving "bread." But they couldn't see the face of their Benefactor. Jesus uncovers new facets in understanding what being fed by God means. Belief in him is spirit-nourishing. Nothing of the past is discarded. All that had gone before is a necessary preparation. Israel had received partial knowledge of God in various ways; now God speaks through his Son, "whom he made heir of all things and through whom he created the universe" (Heb 1:2). In Saint Paul's words: "now that faith has come, we are no longer under a disciplinarian" (Gal 3:25). The Prologue of John's Gospel states: "while the law was given through Moses, grace and truth came through Jesus Christ" (Jn 1:17). He shows God's face as that of our Father turned toward us.

Faith in Jesus is crucial since he continues and completes the gracious way to true Wisdom. He can offer Wisdom because he is divine Wisdom, which, as John repeats, descended from God. He communicates what he sees the Father doing. Saint Jerome thus pointed out that ignorance about the ways of God in the dispensation of the former covenant amounts to ignorance of Christ. By believing in him we are offered a new nourishment. At last, through him—the visible "image of the invisible God" (cf. Col 1:15)—we are enabled to feast our spiritual sight on God, in whose presence we can face one another. To use our technological jargon, he interfaces us with God and ourselves.

Loving Father, fill us with a longing to see you as our Father and thus to recognize one another as called to be your children.

Sacramental Realism
Father Michael L. Gaudoin-Parker

"I am the bread of life. Your ancestors ate the manna in the desert, but they died; this is the bread that comes down from heaven so that one may eat it and not die. I am the living bread that came down from heaven; whoever eats this bread will live forever; and the bread that I will give is my flesh for the life of the world." (Jn 6:48-51)

Though he has no account of the institution of the Eucharist, as in the other Gospels, the Beloved Disciple points to the Eucharistic gift in Jesus' promise to give his entire self ("my flesh"). He presents Jesus' "heart-to-heart" tone of voice, which, as Blessed John Henry Newman recommends, pertains to the depth of communication. Access is gained to the eternal well-being of communion with him through the intimate act of eating (literally, "chewing").

For a second and third time in these verses Jesus claims to be bread from heaven. He goes on to emphasize the reality of this food as life-giving for all people by saying it is his flesh. His language is not mere metaphor, but powerfully imbued with a realism that startles his hearers even more than his assertion about offering something more enduring than the manna. This realism presents a promise containing a prophetic utterance about both his death and the sacramental memorial of his world-saving sacrifice.

On two other occasions earlier in this Gospel, Jesus announced his sacrifice for the life of the world. The first was in the Temple, when he stated that his body would be raised up though killed; the other in his encounter with Nicodemus, whom he assured: "just as Moses lifted up the serpent in the desert, so must the Son of Man be lifted up, so that everyone who believes in him may have eternal life" (Jn 3:14-15). His promise to give his flesh in the form of bread recalls John's succinct description of the Annunciation: "the Word became flesh/ and made his dwelling among us" (Jn 1:14).

This flesh, as the Church Father Tertullian says, is the key of salvation. For, by entering and assuming our human condition of weakness, fragility, fickleness, and sin—as "flesh" signifies in the Bible—Jesus raises us to share his eternal glorification by the Father.

Merciful Father, we thank you for your Son's realistic way of satisfying our yearning for eternal life through communicating his whole self to us in his sacramental gift.

More Than Food for Thought

Father Michael L. Gaudoin-Parker

The Jews quarreled among themselves, saying, "How can this man give us [his] flesh to eat?" Jesus said to them, "Amen, amen, I say to you, unless you eat the flesh of the Son of Man and drink his blood, you do not have life within you. Whoever eats my flesh and drinks my blood has eternal life, and I will raise him on the last day." (Jn 6:52-54)

To the nagging question of the Jewish authorities, Jesus adamantly repeats what he has already been saying. By adding "unless" he emphasizes that there can be true life only by eating and drinking his flesh and blood. This is not cannibalism, abhorrent to any civilized people. Rather, Jesus is at pains to communicate the essential need to participate in him, in his eternal communion of life drawn from the Father, the wellspring of all authentic being.

Jesus' use of "unless" isn't to threaten people to be converted. Thus, he speaks to Nicodemus about the necessity for baptism; he insists on taking up one's cross to be his disciple. Being humankind's friend he issues here the gentlest invitation to consider the purpose of living. In his "high priestly prayer," Jesus asks his Father to glorify him for communicating eternal life to all flesh over whom he has received authority.

Jesus' self-gift causes pause to reflect on a total change of perspective about the quality of human existence. As Socrates said, an unexamined life has little value. Greed induced by consumerism ushers only death into the human heart. Jesus assures abundant life at his table where the present tense matters: "eats…drinks…has eternal life." Our being is enhanced in him now, so that life is worth living, as Venerable Fulton Sheen pointed out in TV talks prepared before the Blessed Sacrament.

By discerning what we receive in the holy food of the Eucharist, Saint Paul teaches, our focus is turned to our neighbors' needs and to Christ's real presence in them. We become open to live as a community of hope as we learn to behold material things afresh, transformed into bearing spiritual reality.

More than merely providing food for thought, Jesus presents the flesh and blood experience of eternal life, which is to know "the only true God" and him the divine emissary.

Eternal Father, raise our sights to behold your Son's presence relating all persons and everything we handle in the new creation of eternal life.

Abiding in Life

Father Michael L. Gaudoin-Parker

"For my flesh is true food, and my blood is true drink. Whoever eats my flesh and drinks my blood remains in me and I in him. Just as the living Father sent me and I have life because of the Father, so also the one who feeds on me will have life because of me." (Jn 6:55-57)

In the third verse here, Jesus points to something deeper than saying merely that the Father sent him. His phrase "living Father," which occurs nowhere else in the New Testament, indicates that God is his very life. This is highlighted by the words he adds. The whole sentence progresses from linking his own vital relationship with the Father to his followers' crucial bond with himself. This enlivening connection is made possible through their being nourished on him—that is, by partaking of the true food and true drink that he would provide through the sacrificial gift of his flesh and blood.

The words "because of" are closely related to the notion of remaining faithful and steadfast. This fidelity, however, consists not only in believing in Jesus, as in discussion with the crowd in earlier verses. Rather, it entails consuming him. Here Jesus introduces the significance of remaining. This involves total adherence of commitment and at-onement with him that has its basis on and is strengthened by feeding on him.

The notion of remaining or abiding is often expressed in John's Gospel. At the Last Supper, Jesus describes what comes about through close relationship with him. In the allegory of the vine and the branches he says: "Whoever remains in me and I in him will bear much fruit, because without me you can do nothing" (Jn 15:5). The Beloved Disciple begins to learn how to remain in Jesus' presence from that first moment when the divine Master responds to his question about where he dwells: "Come, and you will see" (Jn 1:39).

Blessed John Henry Newman recognized that Christ's "kindly light" leads homeward during our earthly pilgrimage. After his conversion to the Catholic Church he wrote to a friend about the comfort he discovered in having his room next to the chapel where Christ's abiding presence radiates Life.

Loving Father, teach us truly to believe and abide in you so that our lives may be fruitful in witnessing to the abundant life flowing from your beloved Son's sacramental gift.

Medicine of Immortality

Father Michael L. Gaudoin-Parker

"This is the bread that came down from heaven. Unlike your ancestors who ate and still died, whoever eats this bread will live forever." These things [Jesus] said while teaching in the synagogue in Capernaum.
(Jn 6:58-59)

The fear of death permeates human experience. Its reality tends to frustrate every desire or plan about the future. Anxiety over the transitory nature of existence can't be allayed by human reason or scientific achievement. The people of Israel were kept aware of this reality in the psalms, expressing their reliance on God alone in times of adversity. However, despite being fed on manna, as Jesus reminds the crowd, their ancestors died.

However, the bread that Jesus offers is different. It has a life-sustaining quality that transforms the mortal condition of all creatures. This is sin-blighted as a result of humankind's first parents defying God's design for their well-being. By seeking merely what is "pleasing to the eyes" (Gn 3:6), they forfeited a taste for the wholesome wisdom of experiencing the lasting beauty and goodness of truth.

This can only be appreciated by receiving life as God's generous gift. Unlike the first Adam, Jesus seeks only to please the Father. He assures his disciples that doing the will of his Father is like food for him. In his promise to give himself as the heavenly bread of life, he perfects God's work of saving love for creation. He brings about a new creation that is implied in his statement: "My Father is at work until now, so I am at work" (Jn 5:17).

By partaking in faith of Jesus' flesh and blood in the appearances of bread and wine, the fruit of the paradise tree of life, we are restored and united. Alluding to the water and blood from Jesus' pierced side, Saint Thomas Aquinas says that this is divine Wisdom feeding humankind "with the bread of understanding,/ and...the water of learning to drink" (Sir 15:3). Jesus, the wounded healer, casts out all fear, even that of dying. As the martyr Saint Ignatius of Antioch puts it, his Eucharistic love is "the medicine of immortality."

Father most merciful, we praise and thank you for casting out our fear as you heal our divisions by your love manifest in your beloved Son's sacrament of communion.

What's So Shocking?

Father Gary C. Caster

Then many of [Jesus'] disciples who were listening said, "This saying is hard; who can accept it?" Since Jesus knew that his disciples were murmuring about this, he said to them, "Does this shock you? What if you were to see the Son of Man ascending to where he was before?" (Jn 6:60-62)

The sayings of Jesus can still seem as hard and difficult to accept now as they were when originally spoken. Fortunately, Jesus' response to human incredulity is to push us even further. He doesn't coddle us or modify his words; he expands them. Our murmuring is always met with greater and more astounding claims, like "the Son of Man ascending to where he was before."

Simply put, Jesus wants us to be shocked! He comes to confront our preconceived ideas about God, ourselves, human relationships, and indeed the entire created order. The words he speaks are meant to establish a fresh, exciting horizon, one that frees us from complacency and breathes new life into our suffocating, constricted hearts. Jesus wants us to witness his ascent because where he was before is exactly the place we were always meant to be. This can indeed be shocking.

And yet, it's no more shocking than God becoming man, incarnate of the Virgin Mary. This truth lies at the heart of the Christian claim and guarantees that with God, all things are possible (see Lk 1:37).

Jesus can therefore assert that his flesh is real food and his blood real drink (v. 55) because his humanity establishes an entirely new direction for human life, an unimagined way of being in the world. We can be like children who roll their eyes at the seemingly unreasonable and outlandish things their parents say, or we can embrace what's said because we trust the one to whom we are listening.

Although it's painful for me to admit, I was a chronic "eye roller." My mother and father often prefaced what they said with, "Now don't roll your eyes…" However, over time I learned how my parents' words were always directed toward my well-being. What initially seemed challenging continually proved to be true. Like Jesus, my parents wanted my life to ascend to heights beyond what I could ever possibly envision for myself.

Heavenly Father, help me truly to hear the sayings of your Son and to accept them with all my heart, for he speaks them solely for my well-being and redemption.

Back to the Beginning

Father Gary C. Caster

"It is the spirit that gives life, while the flesh is of no avail. The words I have spoken to you are spirit and life. But there are some of you who do not believe." Jesus knew from the beginning the ones who would not believe and the one who would betray him. (Jn 6:63-64)

When God entrusted dominion of creation to Adam and Eve, there was a real chance they might lose sight of the "spirit and life" by which everything came to be. Satan exploited this by enticing Eve to doubt what she knew about God because of what she could see in front of her (see Gn 3:1-6). While the fruit was "pleasing to the eyes" and "desirable for gaining wisdom," it was, in the end, of no avail. She and Adam were left with something far worse than indigestion; they were left separated from God's life.

From the beginning Jesus has known "the ones who would not believe" and even "the one who would betray him," because he knows how easy it can be for us to determine and to reduce life only to that which can be seen, touched, heard, felt, and tasted. While our physical senses enable us to experience the goodness of creation, they are meant to lift our hearts and minds to the Creator. From the beginning Jesus has known that there would be those who would not believe this.

Nevertheless, Jesus comes to us on behalf of the Father offering a whole new way of seeing, hearing, and of being fed, a way that sustains life within God's kingdom. Jesus' words are truly "spirit and life" because they satisfy the hunger for God that came about the moment the eyes of Adam and Eve were opened (see Gn 3:7).

The celebration of Thanksgiving can help open our eyes to the importance of Jesus' words. The anticipation and the enjoyment of dinner frequently end with a reminder that "the flesh is of no avail." Seeing the meal set before us can make our eyes become "bigger than our stomachs," such that it is easy for us to eat more than what we should. The result is never pleasing. This has been the case from the beginning, because "the flesh is of no avail."

Almighty Father, increase my capacity to believe so that I can see, hear, and be fed on the spirit and life that come from the words of your Son.

Keeping the Right Company

Father Gary C. Caster

*And [Jesus] said, "For this reason I have told you that no one
can come to me unless it is granted him by my Father."
As a result of this, many [of] his disciples returned to
their former way of life and no longer accompanied him.*
(Jn 6:65-66)

The disciples who return to their former way of life have misunderstood what Jesus says to them. They no longer accompany Jesus because they have failed to recognize that access to him has already been granted by the Father. Jesus' words are in no way meant to imply partiality or exclusivity. Rather, they are spoken to reveal the graciousness of the Father who wants no one to perish and longs for the salvation of us all (see 2 Pt 3:9). The ones who leave have listened, but they haven't heard. They have looked, but they haven't seen what's already been given them.

Today, we may live in the "age of information," but our advance in communication through electronic technology merely reinforces how easy it is to hear only what we want to hear. Emails, tweets, text messages, and posts on Facebook are regularly misinterpreted. It's easy to project sentiments and emotions onto other people's words which are not actually conveyed. We may have increased our ability to communicate more easily and more expansively, but we continue having the same kinds of experience as Jesus. "That's not what I was saying" was as true in his day as it remains in our own.

The remedy for the misunderstanding that led many of his disciples to depart is simple: Keep following! The best way to understand and to experience the extensive and inclusive love of the Father is to accompany his Son, especially when we are confused or uncertain. We have to let Jesus continue to explain for us the height and breadth and depth of his words.

We do this as part of the company of his friends that constitutes the Church. Her Scriptures and teachings, her sacraments and traditions offer us the chance to hear what Christ is truly saying, and they safeguard us from using what we think we heard as an excuse to "return to our former way of life."

Loving Father, give me the strength to accompany your Son as a member of his Body, the Church. Open my ears that I may hear all that you long to teach me so that my life may be filled with your gracious presence.

In the Right Place

Father Gary C. Caster

Jesus then said to the Twelve, "Do you also want to leave?"
Simon Peter answered him, "Master, to whom shall we go?
You have the words of eternal life. We have come to believe
and are convinced that you are the Holy One of God."
(Jn 6:67-69)

L ate one night while praying before the Blessed Sacrament, the spiritual director of the seminary asked me, "Are you thinking of leaving?" I told him that I was actually sitting in the presence of the Lord grateful that I was just where I was supposed to be. I didn't explain myself as clearly as Peter, but the sentiment was the same. "Where else could I possibly go?"

The intimacy with which Jesus questions the Twelve makes clear that he understands how difficult discipleship can be. Jesus' words are indeed "spirit and life," but they do exact something from each one of us. We not only have to let go of what we thought we knew and believed, we also have to fight against sentiments and sensations, drives and desires that once seemed just a natural part of who we are. Once we step toward Jesus, we begin to see God, ourselves, others, and the created order in an entirely new way. This new way of seeing is often unsettling, instilling a sense of fear: "What or who will I become if I keep following him?"

Once we are convinced that Jesus is "the Holy One of God," this fear begins to fade. Speaking these words with Peter, and from our hearts, allows for what Pope Benedict XVI described as eternal life spilling over into our lives, and our lives spilling over into eternal life. This vibrant reciprocity, a gift of the Spirit united with our spirits, prevents us from ever walking away.

The conviction of my vocation was strengthened by my time in the seminary. Our conviction about the truth of Jesus is strengthened by being part of his community. That's why Jesus addresses his question to the Twelve; they represent the Church. It's also the reason Peter answers not just for himself alone. Jesus is therefore reassuring us that participating in the life of his community is exactly the place we need to be.

Eternal Father, let me never walk away from your Son and experience ever more the gift of eternal life which he came to bring.

Betrayal

Father Gary C. Caster

*Jesus answered [the Twelve], "Did I not choose you twelve?
Yet is not one of you a devil?" He was referring to Judas,
son of Simon the Iscariot; it was he who would betray him,
one of the Twelve. (Jn 6:70-71)*

The offer to share God's life and love has been extended to all of creation. Every member of the Church, like the Twelve, needs to be reminded that each of us has been chosen by God. Like Jesus, we can all think of, and name, those we might classify as devils. However, we should never forget that just like Judas, they too were offered God's friendship. The rejection of God never results from our having been left out or excluded. Rather, it comes about after having seen just what's being offered.

Judas betrays Jesus because he cannot accept the way in which Jesus teaches about God's kingdom and goes about establishing it. Lucifer betrays God because he cannot accept serving a plan that seems so unimaginably beneath him. What is important to remember is that in each instance, the Lord is clear about his intentions. Sadly, both Lucifer and Judas think they know a better way.

Although the way in which the angels experienced being chosen is radically different from ours, the possibility of betrayal is just as real. The first serious sin I committed was an act of betrayal. I will never forget the pain I intentionally inflicted upon my elder sister simply because I was mad at her. I risked our friendship in an attempt to make myself feel better. In the end, I was the one who suffered.

Just like Judas and the Twelve, the Church continues to learn the depths of God's intentions as she continues on her journey toward everlasting life. Yet Satan still lurks about, for ever God's betrayer. His singular aim is to instill within our hearts cancerous doubts about the truth of God's love for and belief in us. Any tug we feel or leaning we have toward accepting Satan's poisonous whispers incline us toward betrayal. At such times we can easily silence him by saying, "Go away! Jesus has chosen me!"

Loving Father, your Son has chosen me to share your life and be filled with your love. Let me never betray this precious gift through jealousy, suspicion, or doubt.

Liturgical Celebrations

Father Gary C. Caster

*After this, Jesus moved about within Galilee; but he did not wish
to travel in Judea, because the Jews were trying to kill him.
But the Jewish feast of Tabernacles was near.*
(Jn 7:1-2)

Jesus' decision to move about within Galilee is a tremendous act
of charity. He is not avoiding those who have plotted against him.
Rather, he is offering them a chance to change their minds. The
upcoming Jewish feast of Tabernacles is an opportunity for them
to rethink their plans. At least it should be.

The seasons and celebrations of the Church's liturgical life are
meant to provide the same opportunity to each of us. By participating fully in the life of the Church we are drawn into the mystery of
God's saving love in Christ from a host of different sides, aspects,
and profiles. Each solemnity and every season offers us a chance
to reflect upon our lives so that Christ can move within them more
freely. Jesus wants his presence to be intimate and never remote.

Most often the reason Jesus seems distant, moving about
everywhere else than where we are, is due to attitudes and actions
that put his presence to death. The sacramental and liturgical life
of the Church helps us grow ever more in our ability to recognize
the obstacles that impede the Lord from drawing closer to us.

Thus we should look forward to and welcome each season, all
solemnities and holy days, and every Sunday. We should gladly
and frequently celebrate the sacrament of confession. We should
willingly build our lives on the foundation of daily meditation,
opening ourselves to the Lord, speaking and listening to him from
the interior of our hearts.

Jesus wants to move about within every dimension of our lives.
He wants them to become unique "feasts," individual expressions
and celebrations of his loving presence in the world.

*Eternal Father, grant me the grace to participate fully and faithfully
in the sacramental and liturgical life of the Church, so that your
Son may move within the whole of my life more freely.*

Bad Publicity

Father Gary C. Caster

*So [Jesus'] brothers said to him, "Leave here and go to Judea,
so that your disciples also may see the works you are doing.
No one works in secret if he wants to be known publicly.
If you do these things, manifest yourself to the world."
For his brothers did not believe in him. (Jn 7:3-5)*

When we were boys, my older brother and I built all sorts of models. His were perfect; they looked just like the picture on the box. Mine were always a disaster; always! My problem: a complete lack of patience. My brother, on the other hand, painstakingly took his time. He could wait weeks for paint and parts to dry. He followed every detail of the instructions and was even an expert at affixing decals. Frank's models were always works of art.

Perhaps a lack of patience with Jesus' methods leads his brothers to urge him toward Judea. Although they have seen his works, they fail to recognize that Jesus is building something that requires great care. They do not understand that Jesus' works are part of a plan formed by the Father long ago. There is no need to rush. When the last part of the plan is in place, people will marvel at what God was building.

Perhaps the need for Jesus' works to be seen in the open stems from a lack of belief. The more people who share his brothers' position will make it easier to stop what Jesus is doing.

My brother tried as best he could to slow me down, to teach me the best way to build my models. He was as patient with me as he was with everything he built. I would try to follow his example and heed his advice because I really wanted my models to look as good as his. Unfortunately, I just couldn't wait.

By refusing to go to Judea, Jesus teaches his brothers patience. The deliberateness of his actions will, in the end, make it easier for them to see just what God has been up to. Jesus knows who he is and exactly what he's up to. In time, so will his brothers.

Almighty Father, let my life be modeled on the life of your Son. Fill me with greater patience so that you can continue to build me into the person you have always known me to be.

The Time Is Right

Father Gary C. Caster

So Jesus said to [his brothers], "My time is not yet here, but the time is always right for you. The world cannot hate you, but it hates me, because I testify to it that its works are evil. You go up to the feast. I am not going up to this feast, because my time has not yet been fulfilled." (Jn 7: 6-8)

Time can be an enemy or an ally. It can move too slowly or pass too quickly. When we're young time often drags on; as we grow there just never seems to be enough of it. Time seems to be ever beyond our control and we seem to be ever its subjects.

Jesus is well aware of the hold time has over his brothers. He sends them to the feast in order to free them from the constraint of waiting. By their decision to continue following him, the time is right for them to be in the world in an entirely new way. Jesus is encouraging them to take their place in time because he knows they have begun living outside of it.

The reluctance of Jesus' brothers to go up to the feast of Tabernacles is not only rooted in a fear of being hated, but also in their need for something further. For this reason Jesus tells them that his time has not yet been fulfilled. He is trying to teach them that God has already given them what they need to be freed from the "evil works" of the world. In their friendship with Jesus, God has given them the most definitive sign of his unyielding love and commitment.

Once we begin following Jesus, the time is right for us as well. Instead of asking God for signs, or waiting for "just the right moment" to be living embodiments of his saving love, we should accept what's been given us through baptism. We have been incorporated into the life of Christ, and thus God dwells within us. The time is always right for us to contradict the works of the world by concrete acts of love which show that, indeed, Jesus' time has been fulfilled.

Jesus needs those who have feasted on his Body and Blood to show all peoples of the world that, in him, indeed their time has come.

Gracious Father, the time for manifesting your love is always at hand. Give me the strength to make your love real in the concrete conditions and circumstances of my daily life.

Without Force or Fanfare

Father Gary C. Caster

After [Jesus] had said this, he stayed on in Galilee.
But when his brothers had gone up to the feast, he also went up,
not openly but [as it were] in secret. The Jews were looking
for him at the feast and saying, "Where is he?"
(Jn 7:9-11)

Thanks to YouTube, Facebook, reality TV, and other social media, the lives of those with less than admirable civic and social virtue are now elevated to the status of celebrity. Far too many people are obsessed with men and women whose only claim to fame is being famous. At least the Jews had a reason to be looking for Jesus. After all, many of them had witnessed the works he was doing on behalf of God.

This is, perhaps, the main reason Jesus comes to the feast after his brothers go up to it. He has no desire to draw attention to himself. The works that he performs are not meant to point back to him but are meant to point toward the Father. By waiting for the feast to be underway, Jesus knows that the attention of the people will be centered on the celebration. Their shift in focus will enable him to continue working among them without becoming a spectacle.

By staying in Galilee, Jesus teaches us an important lesson about God. He never barges into our lives with force or violence or seeking his own acclaim. Rather, God comes to us with little or no drama or flourish. In the midst of undertaking our daily tasks and attending to our responsibilities, God comes to us, as it were, "in secret." He moves about within the contours of our lives; not apart from them.

Therefore, the undertaking of God's Spirit in our lives is generally imperceptible. While this can sometimes lead us to question "where God is," the decisiveness Jesus shows in choosing when to go up to the feast should encourage us that God is always where we are. Through, with, and in his Son—that is precisely where God has chosen to be, so there is no reason to question or be concerned when we can't seem to find him.

Almighty Father, grant me the confident assurance of your presence in my life so that I might attend to all that you ask of me and serve you faithfully.

Speaking Out

Father Gary C. Caster

And there was considerable murmuring about [Jesus] in the crowds. Some said, "He is a good man," [while] others said, "No; on the contrary, he misleads the crowd." Still, no one spoke openly about him because they were afraid of the Jews.
(Jn 7:12-13)

At some point in our lives, we've all had the experience of not saying something because we were afraid. Physical safety, job or relationship security, financial stability, and the opinion of others can all inhibit our ability to say what's on our minds or speak the truth. Therefore it's easy to empathize with the crowds who discuss Jesus in secret; they are afraid for their lives, even those who think Jesus misleads people.

This fear that prevents the murmuring from becoming too public aids in deepening our understanding of the cross as the focal point of faith and the absurdity of Saint Paul preaching "Christ crucified" (see 1 Cor 1:23). For the Romans, crucifixion was the ultimate humiliation, and anyone who stood and watched the crucified was considered to be as guilty as the victim. The fear of being associated with Jesus crucified should have kept the mouths of Christians silent concerning Jesus and his death upon the cross. Yet, from the beginning, the early Church gave magnificent testimony to the message of the cross. Through the gift of the Spirit, "the crowd" of Jesus' followers was finally able to find its voice.

The willingness to associate with the man who died like a condemned slave or violent criminal has led many to lay down their lives. Men, women, and children in every age have not remained silent. They have stood valiantly against those who think of Christianity as harmful. From the beginning, the Church has been nourished and strengthened by the blood of those who were not afraid.

It can be as difficult today as it was in the first century to associate with Jesus. There are many groups that seek to silence Christianity permanently. Only beneath the cross of Christ will we find our voice and be free from whatever inhibits us from proclaiming to the world, "[Jesus] is a good man!"

Almighty Father, let me stand with Mary and the martyrs at the foot of the cross so that I will never be afraid of proclaiming the goodness of your Son before all the world.

Learning from Above

Father Gary C. Caster

When the feast was already half over, Jesus went up into the temple area and began to teach. The Jews were amazed and said, "How does he know scripture without having studied?" Jesus answered them and said, "My teaching is not my own but is from the one who sent me." (Jn 7:14-16)

Whenever someone tries to test my knowledge of Scripture, I usually say, "I don't memorize it; I live it!" While this is certainly not the most charitable reply (and one of the reasons why I go to confession regularly), it does, in my mind, relate to what Jesus tells the Jews in the Temple area.

We know that anyone with enough patience and willpower can memorize the Bible. We also know that anyone with interest and acumen can study Scripture. However, neither of these is a guarantee of faith. That knowledge of Scripture which is a fundamental feature of authentic relationship with Christ isn't necessarily found in a classroom.

While studying the Scriptures with others or in school can enhance our knowledge of Christ and relationship with him, it will never take its place. The knowledge of Scripture that best informs our relationship with Christ only comes through prayerful meditation. In quiet reflection the "One who sent Jesus" instructs our minds and touches our hearts concerning everything that has been written down, preserved, and handed on. Although commentaries, reflections, and learned insights have a role to play, it is always at the service of that which the heart discovers through an interior openness to the Spirit working with one's own.

Those listening to Jesus in the Temple area witnessed the sort of vibrant reciprocity that should exist between what is studied and what the Father speaks and illuminates in the recesses of the mind and heart. Prayerful meditation on Sacred Scripture actually inspires greater study, which in turn expands our ability to reflect prayerfully on God's Word.

Years ago I met an uneducated African-American woman who talked of Jesus as if she had witnessed his life firsthand. Sophie could answer correctly any question posed to her, however theologically astute, because she had been taught from above. She didn't memorize Scripture; she lived it.

Eternal Father, calm my mind and quiet my heart so that I can learn from you all that Sacred Scripture has to teach me about the height and breadth and depth of your love.

137

The Secret to Fulfillment

Father Gary C. Caster

"Whoever chooses to do his will shall know whether my teaching is from God or whether I speak on my own. Whoever speaks on his own seeks his own glory, but whoever seeks the glory of the one who sent him is truthful, and there is no wrong in him."
(Jn 7:17-18)

There's a long list of suggestions about what can lead to human happiness. Much of what's on the list, like money, class, power, and fame, is arbitrary and illusory. Someone can possess all of these—and more—yet remain unfulfilled and unhappy. Countless stories, both old and new, illustrate this point.

Many of us first encountered the truth of this when we were young and found that the thing we wanted most didn't really measure up. There are a lot of discarded Christmas toys that can attest to this. The recognition that the heart yearns for something greater than what was initially thought continues to move people toward a lifelong search for meaning and fulfillment.

In speaking to the Jews, Jesus addresses something greater than the source and truth of his teaching. He describes exactly that which will fulfill the longing in the human heart for justice, peace, beauty, joy, and happiness. He knows well that no created thing, human relationship, or social category could ever answer our questions about meaning, purpose, and happiness. Doing the will and seeking the glory of "the one who sent him" is the only way toward the contentment, fulfillment, and peace for which each of us longs.

Hopefully Jesus' words opened the minds of his listeners to consider his life from an entirely new perspective, and they were able to see just how it was the answer to their question. Hopefully they came to accept that doing the Father's will was the only thing that would fulfill them.

Discussions about the truth and source of Jesus' teaching will not end until he returns in glory. In order to be freed from such idle talk and speculative distractions, we have only to live as Jesus did. In him our search for meaning is ended and our path to contentment, fulfillment, and peace has been found.

Heavenly Father, let me live always in your truth by seeking in all things and at all times to do whatever is in accordance with your will.

Keeping the Law
Father Gary C. Caster

"Did not Moses give you the law? Yet none of you keeps the law.
Why are you trying to kill me?" The crowd answered,
"You are possessed! Who is trying to kill you?"
(Jn 7:19-20)

Two months into one of my early assignments I told the bishop that the new position would probably kill me. I was sent to a place where a priest was not wanted, the bishop disliked, and the people believed the ministry belonged to them. One person wrote to every bishop in the country demanding I be removed because he and his wife thought I was possessed.

One month later I nearly died. While recuperating from emergency surgery, I asked my bishop if I would be getting a new assignment. He replied, "No. I need you just where you are." While I wasn't particularly pleased with his response, I did do what I was told. The years I spent in that assignment ended up being some of the best years of my priestly life.

While following the law is often difficult, encouraging others to do so can be even more challenging. All of us resist being told what to do by anyone and for any reason. Because of this, we think of freedom quite simply as the ability at all times and in every situation to choose for ourselves. We bristle at the suggestion that someone else, even God, knows what's best for us. This tension, called concupiscence, is a result of original sin, and can very easily lead to the death of God in a person's life.

Jesus speaks to the crowd about the law in an attempt to move them away from what they think is best, to that which actually is. Their failure to keep the law has set them on a course of self-destruction. Those who walk this path are possessed by their own sense of what's good and true and beautiful. As the fulfillment of the law, Jesus offers us what he offers them: namely, an opportunity to rediscover the truth of human life within the context of God's providential care.

Almighty Father, you gave the law to prepare your people for the coming of your Son. Let his life govern and guide me in all things, and keep me firmly fixed within your providential care.

Indelible Marks

Father Gary C. Caster

Jesus answered and said to [the crowd], "I performed one work and all of you are amazed because of it. Moses gave you circumcision—not that it came from Moses but rather from the patriarchs—and you circumcise a man on the sabbath. If a man can receive circumcision on a sabbath so that the law of Moses may not be broken, are you angry with me because I made a whole person well on a sabbath? Stop judging by appearances, but judge justly." (Jn 7:21-24)

I was sixteen years old the day my father was baptized. While "the work" performed that day left an indelible mark upon my father's soul, it also left one upon the members of his family, especially my mother. The grace that moved my father to seek private instruction in the faith and accept baptism, confirmation, and Communion, imprinted itself on each of our lives in ways we continue to discover. On that day, God may have given the gift of divine life to my father, but God also enabled my father's life to be a means of grace for each of ours.

When the patriarchs and Moses gave the people circumcision, they were actually preparing the people for sacramental life. The custom of marking the body with a permanent sign of belonging to God was but a precursor to marking the soul—which gives life to the body—with an everlasting sign of being a member of God's family. Jesus is teaching the crowds about the continuity between what he is giving the people on behalf of God and what God had given the people through Moses and the patriarchs.

The sign of circumcision was meant to be an indelible reminder of the covenant that existed between God and his people. At the heart of this covenant was God's promise to redeem and restore his people, no matter the span of their sins or the egregiousness of their rejection. Because of the abiding mark on their bodies, they knew that God would one day make the whole people well.

Jesus heals a man on the sabbath in order that the crowd might recognize that the fulfillment of God's promise is at hand. The physical healing is but a sign that Jesus has come to inaugurate a new Sabbath, a new day of rest from the re-creation of the whole person, whose entire life will now be marked by the very life of God.

Eternal Father, through the grace of the sacraments you have permanently marked our lives with the promise of your loving care. Grant me wholeness of life so that I might live for ever your Sabbath rest.

Speaking Openly

Father Timothy Bellamah, O.P.

So some of the inhabitants of Jerusalem said, "Is he not the one they are trying to kill? And look, he is speaking openly and they say nothing to him. Could the authorities have realized that he is the Messiah? But we know where he is from. When the Messiah comes, no one will know where he is from."
(Jn 7:25-27)

In the midst of powerful men looking for a chance to kill him, Jesus speaks openly. These authorities, by contrast, are unable to say anything in return, and can only intimidate the people of Jerusalem. For their part, the people can only murmur. Gripped by fear, they are also unable to speak openly (Jn 7:12-13). Those trying to kill Jesus cannot speak their minds because their minds are full of hate; the townspeople cannot speak their minds because theirs are full of fear.

Anyone who has ever regretted speaking openly can understand their discretion. After all, boldness with words often brings trouble. Sometimes people learn the hard way that in dangerous situations it can be useful to let discretion have the better part of valor. But Jesus has no such reservations because he knows that his words have a power all their own. In the face of hostility he speaks fearlessly because he speaks his words not on his own, but with the Father who dwells in him (see Jn 14:10). More powerful than a two-edged sword (see Heb 4:12), his Word will not be thwarted by hatred or fear.

Those who try to proclaim Jesus Christ soon realize that the Gospel still meets with hostility. Some listeners respond with silence, prevented by their malice from responding honestly. Others are checked by fear. But when Christ confers on his disciples the task of proclaiming the Gospel, he also offers them confidence in the power of the One whom they proclaim. The first place where this power takes effect is in our hearts, liberating us from slavish fear and giving us the power to become children of God (Jn 1:12). When we realize that Christ has the words of eternal life, we find that we need not be anxious about the threats of those who choose to live in hatred or fear.

Heavenly Father, grant us the grace to proclaim the Gospel with the courage of your Son, our Lord, Jesus Christ.

Knowing the One Who Is from God

Father Timothy Bellamah, O.P.

So Jesus cried out in the temple area as he was teaching and said, "You know me and also know where I am from. Yet I did not come on my own, but the one who sent me, whom you do not know, is true. I know him, because I am from him, and he sent me." (Jn 7:28-29)

One of the first things most people want to know about those they meet is their place of origin, where they are from. And whether we like it or not, people often size us up by focusing on where we are from. Such information can be revealing, but also misleading, since there is much more to be known about every one of us than that. Anyone judging others merely on the basis of their hometown is likely to be misled.

Passing such judgments on Jesus, the people of Jerusalem are disastrously blinded to his true identity. Taking him for nothing more than a Galilean, they conclude that he may be safely ignored. In our own thoughts about Jesus, we can make the same mistake.

None of us has seen him in his native place or heard his local accent, but we have grown up hearing about him and have formed certain opinions of him. These can lead us astray, because he has come from an origin we have not seen, the Father. Understandably, people often protest when others try to judge them by their place of origin, but Jesus redirects the inquiry of the people of Jerusalem by crying out his true origin, and so reveals his true identity—he is the One from the Father. With this cry Jesus allows us to know him and his Father in faith. He also teaches us about our own origins, and so shows us something about ourselves. Like him, we come from God, but unlike him, we have come forth as creatures, not as sons by nature. Crying out his identity as the one sent by the Father, Jesus invites all those willing to listen to share in his eternal Sonship as adopted sons and daughters of the Father. It is this unutterable origin and destiny that is the first thing we and others should know about ourselves.

Almighty Father, grant us the wisdom to recognize your image in all people that we might serve you in drawing them into the beatitude you have prepared for us.

The Familiarity That Breeds Wondrous Love

Father Timothy Bellamah, O.P.

*So [the chief priests and the Pharisees] tried to arrest him,
but no one laid a hand upon him, because his hour had not yet
come. But many of the crowd began to believe in him, and said,
"When the Messiah comes, will he perform more signs
than this man has done?"
The Pharisees heard the crowd murmuring about him to
this effect, and the chief priests and the Pharisees sent guards
to arrest him. (Jn 7:30-32)*

Familiarity breeds contempt, as the saying goes. It's often difficult to respect those we know well. And even the famous people we know from afar show us their feet of clay once their human failings become public. The people we imagine to be great so often disappoint us once we really get to know them that we are unaccustomed to finding true greatness, true virtue, in anyone we know well. And so it is that we come to treat those familiar to us with contempt.

Such is the problem the people of Jerusalem have in recognizing Jesus. Knowing him only as the Galilean carpenter's son, they take him for someone of no great importance. Christians still stand at risk of falling into the same trap. With respect to Christ this tendency is calamitous, because it prevents us from seeing that familiarity with God has the opposite effect. The more we come to know him in faith, the more we recognize our own failings and his greatness. The more we see his splendor in faith, the more we recognize his power and goodness, the more we are filled with awe. In the words of Scripture, under the familiar signs of bread and wine, and in the people we meet, Christ comes to us in the most familiar of appearances. If we are too skeptical, too proud, to accept him in faith, we can expect to find ourselves treating him with the same contempt as his kinsmen. Quite likely, we will become bored with the Mass and the Church, supposing that we have it all figured out. And yet, should we profit from such occasions to become familiar with Christ, we will find ourselves captivated by the One who offers us something completely new—freedom from sin and eternal life. Such is the familiarity of wonder and love.

*Blessed Father, help us to come to know your Son, so that we may
see the daily wonders of your providential care for us.*

The Lord's Plan

Father Timothy Bellamah, O.P.

*So Jesus said, "I will be with you only a little while longer,
and then I will go to the one who sent me. You will look for me
but not find [me], and where I am you cannot come."*
(Jn 7:33-34)

I f even the best laid plans of mice and men go astray, what can we expect of the worst laid ones? Most people know how easily even the most carefully prepared projects can be brought to nothing by unforeseen circumstances and events, even when they have pursued them with the best of intentions. Sending guards to arrest Jesus in order to kill him, the chief priests and Pharisees follow the worst of plans with the worst of intentions. But he has other plans and tells them he will be with them only a little while longer. He will be arrested and killed in his time, not theirs, when he wills to allow it to happen and not otherwise. They have foreseen neither that the one they want to kill is life itself, nor that their plan for his death is part of his plan for our eternal life.

All of us need to plan well to live well, and our own day-to-day plans will probably never be as vicious as theirs, but they can still lead us into the same trap as the one that caught them—trusting in our own cleverness to find the happiness we seek. There is only one plan that can bring us that, God's, which we take part in by our trust in his Son. When we seek our well-being and that of those dear to us by confiding only in our own wits and good intentions, even our smartest plans are apt to end up looking silly. But if we confide our endeavors to the One who can will only what is good for us, they will draw us into his plan for us and those dear to us. To all who receive him and believe in his name, this Light of the World gives "power to become children of God" (Jn 1:12). Whatever we may think of our own plans, his cannot lead us astray.

Heavenly Father, help us to seek our happiness only in you, so that our every work may come to completion in you.

The Only Journey That Matters

Father Timothy Bellamah, O.P.

*So the Jews said to one another, "Where is he going that we will
not find him? Surely he is not going to the dispersion among the
Greeks to teach the Greeks, is he? What is the meaning of his
saying, 'You will look for me and not find [me], and where
I am you cannot come'?"*

(Jn 7:35-36)

People now often travel greater distances before lunch than most people in Jesus' time did in their lifetimes. And we move about in ways they could not have imagined. But modern technology has left some facts of life unchanged. Before we can arrive at any destination, we still have to know where we are going and how we are going to get there, and we need a reliable means of transportation. It is understandable, then, that people spend vast sums on such means. Whether moving about by planes, trains, or automobiles, people normally go to great effort and expense to travel well. And yet, our preoccupation with traveling well can lead us to take for granted that our most important journeys are to be undertaken in a nice car or a good seat on a plane, and that we have no place better to go than to work or to the beach.

To the people of Jerusalem, Jesus describes a journey neither they nor we can imagine—in his humanity he returns to the one whom he never left in his divinity. As a man he is off not to this or that city or town, but to take his place with his eternal Father, whom he never left as his divine Son. Where he is going we cannot go for the simple reason that we are not God. But if we cannot follow him, what does all this matter to us? By his return to his Father, Jesus shows us our destiny: life with the Father. We cannot go there on our own terms, in our own time, or by our own means, but we do have a way, and it is he. By his cross Christ offers himself as our way, both for living rightly in this world and for passing from it to our final destination.

*Loving Father, grant us the grace to go forward in peace to you,
the one goal of all our labors.*

The Thirst That Leads to Eternal Life

Father Timothy Bellamah, O.P.

On the last and greatest day of the feast, Jesus stood up and exclaimed, "Let anyone who thirsts come to me and drink. Whoever believes in me, as scripture says:/ 'Rivers of living water will flow from within him.'"/ He said this in reference to the Spirit that those who came to believe in him were to receive. There was, of course, no Spirit yet, because Jesus had not yet been glorified. (Jn 7:37-39)

Everyone knows something about thirst, but few people living in modern societies ever have to endure the agony of a life-threatening lack of water. Jesus' immediate audience knows well that having enough of it is a matter of life and death. When our Lord invites those who thirst to come to him and drink, he talks about a matter more serious than a routine drink from a water fountain. He teaches us about our spiritual survival. Without his gift of the Spirit, we are goners. Why? Because it is by the Spirit that our sins are forgiven and we are made sharers of the divine nature. This is why we can have no reconciliation with the Father without the Holy Spirit.

When Christ made this exclamation, the Spirit had not yet been given, because it was by his cross that he won for us the victory over sin and death. His Resurrection from the dead is the cause of ours. Saint Thomas Aquinas says that Christ is the Word, not just any word, but a Word breathing forth love, the love that is Holy Spirit. He goes on to say that the Spirit's work is to conform us to the one whose Spirit he is, making us sharers in God's nature. As his love knows no limits, Christ makes his offer to anyone who thirsts for it. At Jesus' exclamation, we would do well to ask ourselves, for what kind of life and peace do we thirst? Is it only the life and peace of material comfort and security? If it is "for this life only we have hoped in Christ, we are the most pitiable people of all," as Saint Paul tells the Corinthians (1 Cor 15:19). But if we thirst for Christ's precious gift, we can expect the Spirit to flow from within us.

Merciful Father, direct our steps to your Son, that we may always drink of his gift of the living waters he offers those who come to him.

Living as God's Children

Father Timothy Bellamah, o.p.

Some in the crowd who heard these words said, "This is truly the Prophet." Others said, "This is the Messiah." But others said, "The Messiah will not come from Galilee, will he? Does not scripture say that the Messiah will be of David's family and come from Bethlehem, the village where David lived?"

(Jn 7:40-42)

Most of us usually would rather agree than disagree with those around us. Unpleasant as they are, disagreements result from misunderstandings, arising when various people know different aspects of the truth of something, while none can see the whole truth clearly.

Jesus' teaching is such that it leaves the crowds in disagreement. His instruction, the most sublime ever to come forth from a human voice, leaves his audience not in a state of wonder, but in a mood for argument. Their disagreement arises from their failure to understand him fully. Realizing that he speaks God's words, some call him a prophet. Recognizing him as God's anointed one, others call him the Messiah. Aware of his Galilean background, still others cast doubt on his identity as the Messiah. All of them have bits of the truth, but fail to realize what they don't know: though raised in Galilee, he was born in Bethlehem; though born in time as man in Bethlehem, he proceeds eternally as God from the Father.

We have the benefit of the Church's understanding of the Gospel, but it would be tragic for us to presume that we have Christ all figured out, losing our sense of wonder and forgetting that at present we see in a glass darkly, as Paul tells the Corinthians (see 1 Cor 13:12). There remains much for us to learn about Christ and ourselves. Returning by the cross to the One who sent him, he finds his human destiny in his divine origin. Coming from God as creatures, and not as sons by nature, by grace we wondrously take part in that same destiny. As John the Evangelist tells us: "We are God's children now; what we shall be has not yet been revealed. We do know that when it is revealed we shall be like him, for we shall see him as he is" (1 Jn 3:2).

Heavenly Father, you know all things. Enlighten our minds so that we may please you in living by faith until the dawning of the day when we shall see you face to face.

The One Who Speaks Like No Other

Father Timothy Bellamah, O.P.

So a division occurred in the crowd because of [Jesus].
Some of them even wanted to arrest him, but no one laid
hands on him. So the guards went to the chief priests
and Pharisees, who asked them,
"Why did you not bring him?" The guards answered,
"Never before has anyone spoken like this one." (Jn 7:43-46)

Who wouldn't want to see a miracle? In Jesus' time, many people, such as Herod, took an interest in him only because they wanted to see him work some wonder (see Lk 9:9; 23:8). Even his more faithful followers asked for them. It's easy for us to imagine that some sign from God would make us unshakable in our faith, supposing that if only we could have some portent or some miraculous healing, then we would truly believe. And yet, the chief priests and Pharisees derive no benefit from the many signs and wonders they see Jesus work. Watching and studying him, they fail to come to know him. By contrast, the guards they charge with arresting him are changed by their encounter with him, though they have seen no miracle. When asked why they haven't done their job, they mention only Jesus' way of speaking, which they describe as unlike anything they have heard before. It is by his words to them that our Lord has changed them, and it is by their listening that they have been changed. Unafraid of the authorities who sent them, they bear witness to the one they have come to know.

This is how Christ converts us and works wonders in our lives. He could dazzle us easily enough with miraculous visions or events, but this wouldn't do us much good. We have been made for more than entertainment, and our lives have been given us for more than thrills. We have been created for communion, the interpersonal engagement of knowing and loving the Triune God and all others in God. It is by his words to us that our Lord draws us into true life. He has the words of eternal life because he *is* eternal life, God's Word made flesh. This is why his words are enough to transform our ways of thinking and desiring, engendering faith and love, if only we would listen.

Almighty Father, you know all things. Grant us the grace to listen to the words of your Son, that we may see ourselves and others clearly by the light of your wisdom and so discern your saving action in our world.

The Grace to Judge Rightly

Father Timothy Bellamah, O.P.

So the Pharisees answered [the guards], "Have you also been deceived? Have any of the authorities or the Pharisees believed in him? But this crowd, which does not know the law, is accursed." (Jn 7:47-49)

None of us enjoys being lied to, but that doesn't mean we necessarily want to face the truth. When confronted with some reality we would rather not see, we may find it easier to contradict those presenting it to us than to accept what they have to say. Disputing of this kind arises not from a desire to have the truth, but from a wish to hide it or hide from it, and this because of fear, the fear of correction. Quarreling is often easier and less painful than coming to terms with a personal failing we would rather not see.

Such is the problem Jesus presents the Pharisees. In him they are confronted with God's truth in the flesh, who demands of them honesty with respect to God, the law, and themselves. Bickering with the guards for their belief in him and cursing the crowds for theirs, they try to justify their unbelief by pointing to their knowledge of the law. How is it that those who have studied the law misjudge Jesus, while those who would seem to know nothing of it come to believe in him? Judging rightly is possible only for those who are just in their character and actions. This is a matter of obedience to the law, not mere study of it. Knowing the law, the Pharisees have ignored its greatest and first commandment, to love God with all one's heart, soul, and mind (see Mt 22:37), and so cannot judge Jesus aright and accept him (see Jn 5:42-45). Lacking formal knowledge of the law, the guards and crowds have better obeyed it and so make better judgments about the one who gave it.

Should we be wise enough to receive our Lord in faith, we will find that he is not only God's truth, but also God's mercy in the flesh, who casts our sins not in our faces, but behind his back.

Loving Father, help us to see the wonders of Christ's mercy in our daily lives, so that we may proclaim that same mercy to all your people.

True Friendship

Father Timothy Bellamah, O.P.

Nicodemus, one of their members who had come to him earlier,
said to [the Pharisees], "Does our law condemn a person
before it first hears him and finds out what he is doing?"
They answered and said to him, "You are not from Galilee
also, are you? Look and see that no prophet arises from Galilee."
(Jn 7:50-52)

Most of us know what it's like to be out of our element, surrounded by people of a different background or culture, who think and speak in ways different from ours. In such situations we are struck not only by the oddness of their ways, but also by how inevitably our own ways of thinking and speaking expose us as outsiders. Whenever we stray too far from our home turf, our accents give us away, whether we like it or not.

Such is the problem of Nicodemus amidst a crowd of Pharisees. Himself a Pharisee and ruler of the people, he would appear to be one of them. But he no longer really belongs in their company, and the change is starting to show. Recognizing Jesus as a teacher who has come from God, Nicodemus has previously approached him, at night, lest he be discovered as one of his disciples (see Jn 3:1-2). Though drawn to him and eager to listen to him, he is unwilling to sacrifice his standing with the Pharisees by acknowledging him openly. So he tries to bring them around to Christ discreetly, hoping that a legal proceeding will provide the occasion for them to be persuaded by his words. Knowing Jesus only as a Galilean, these sophisticates of Jerusalem think of his followers as Galileans, and seeing through Nicodemus' artifice, they suggest that he too is one of them. They are not entirely wrong. His belief in Christ has affected his ways of thinking and speaking. Perhaps without his noticing, Nicodemus has picked up a certain accent, and it is giving him away. He can no longer have it both ways.

Neither can we. If we have come to believe in Christ and have listened to his words, we will speak in ways that will give us away. We may even become strangers to those we once considered friends. But such is true friendship with God and the blessed.

Merciful Father, grant me the courage to renounce everything that
can block my path in following your Son our Lord Jesus Christ.

Speaking and Doing the Truth

Father Timothy Bellamah, O.P.

Then each went to his own house, while Jesus went to the Mount of Olives. But early in the morning he arrived again in the temple area, and all the people started coming to him, and he sat down and taught them.

(Jn 7:53–8:2)

Talk is cheap, or so they say. Saying we are going to do something and doing it are two different matters. It's one thing to promise something, and it's another to deliver what we have promised. It's one thing to talk about living rightly, and it's another to practice the preaching. Even small children are quick to spot differences between what their parents say should be done and what they actually do. However much smoking fathers or mothers may preach to their children of the evils of smoking, their children are far more likely to pick up the habit than the children of parents who don't smoke. Why is it that actions speak louder than words, even to children? Because they understand that what we say indicates what we want to matter to other people, while what we do shows what really matters to us.

Each of the Pharisees goes to his own house, with nothing more to say to anyone, because Jesus has shown them how dramatically their talk about the law differs from their practice of it. But Jesus comes to the Temple with much to teach anyone willing to listen, and all the people come to him, knowing that his words are not cheap.

There is no separation between the Lord's words and actions, between his promises and his fulfillment of those promises, because what he wants to matter to us is one and the same with what matters to him—his own goodness and his own life, which he offers to us by his words and deeds. Those who trust in Christ and allow his words to penetrate their minds and hearts come to think and act such that there is no separation between what they want to matter to others and what matters to themselves. They speak and do the truth of the one whose promises cannot fail.

Faithful Father, grant us the grace to trust in your promises and to serve you in drawing all people into the beatitude you have prepared for us.

Living Memory

Father Timothy Bellamah, O.P.

Then the scribes and the Pharisees brought a woman who had been caught in adultery and made her stand in the middle. They said to him, "Teacher, this woman was caught in the very act of committing adultery. Now in the law, Moses commanded us to stone such women. So what do you say?" They said this to test him, so that they could have some charge to bring against him.

(Jn 8:3-6a)

A mong the most basic precepts of the Old Testament is remembrance. Repeatedly Moses commands the people to remember, and forbids them to forget, the wonders God has worked for them. The annual Jewish celebration of Passover is a prolonged commemoration of their ancestors' deliverance from slavery in Egypt.

In condemning a woman caught in adultery, the scribes and Pharisees pretend to uphold the law of Moses, while showing themselves forgetful of its true meaning. Their true purpose in accusing her is to accuse Jesus. If he consents to the stoning, he contradicts his own preaching of mercy; if he doesn't, he contradicts the law of Moses. Forgetful of their own need for mercy, they are blinded to Jesus' identity and come to the absurdity of seeking to condemn God's mercy in the flesh, innocence itself.

Amnesia of this kind threatens Christians of all ages. It is too easy for us to forget that the battle lines between good and evil pass through our own hearts. Should we fail to recall our own need for God's mercy, we are apt to become more preoccupied with the failings of others than with our own; we risk becoming persecutors of Christ. But if we remember our need for mercy, we will have it.

Writing to Roman Christians more prone to correct others than themselves, Saint Paul tells them to recall their sins, so that, reflecting on the kindness and patience the Lord has shown them, they may be led not to presumption and judgment of others, but to repentance (see Rom 2:4). Saint Paul understands that Christ has given remembrance new meaning by his commanding his disciples at the Last Supper, "Do this in memory of me." When we take part in that sacred banquet we celebrate the memory of his Passion, as he makes present its saving effects, forgiving our sins, filling our souls with grace, and offering us a pledge of future glory.

Merciful Father, grant us the grace to keep ever in our minds the memory of Christ's Passion, that we may live in your grace and come to the glory you promise.

Words That Give Life

Father Timothy Bellamah, O.P.

Jesus bent down and began to write on the ground with his finger. But when [the scribes and the Pharisees] continued asking him, he straightened up and said to them, "Let the one among you who is without sin be the first to throw a stone at her." Again he bent down and wrote on the ground. And in response, they went away one by one, beginning with the elders.
(Jn 8:6b-9a)

It's not uncommon for Christ's teachings to be characterized as stifling and oppressive, but to those who heed them they never fail to give life and freedom. Who else has ever put forward a teaching as life-giving and liberating as his prohibition of judging and condemning, and this so that we may avoid being judged and condemned? (see Lk 6:37).

By making this teaching known to a crowd of would-be stone throwers, Jesus saves a woman's life and frees her from the deadly circle in which they have put her. But he also liberates us, setting us free from the fear of being judged by anyone other than God. Of course, police officers, magistrates, governors, and authorities of all kinds make judgments of people all the time, sometimes condemning them to harsh punishments. But they can judge only actions and never the state of anyone's soul. God alone looks into the soul because he alone has created it. And he alone recreates it, restoring the beauty of his image therein by forgiving sin with the outpouring of his grace. Knowing that the one who judges him is the Lord, Saint Paul can serenely tell his Corinthian audience that he is not in the least concerned that he be judged by them or any human tribunal (see 1 Cor 4:3). Such is the peace of those who have come to know Christ.

But this isn't the only respect in which his teaching liberates. It frees the would-be stone throwers from the guilt of a murder they would otherwise commit, and it frees us from spending our precious time and energy in this life judging and condemning others. We have countless far more worthwhile things to do, such as giving thanks for the wonder of creation, for our place in it, and especially for the surpassing wonder of the new life we share in Christ.

Loving Father, help us to hear the words of your Son and so come to share in the life he won for us on the cross.

Going with God

Father Timothy Bellamah, O.P.

So [Jesus] was left alone with the woman before him.
Then Jesus straightened up and said to her, "Woman, where are
they? Has no one condemned you?" She replied, "No one, sir."
Then Jesus said, "Neither do I condemn you. Go, [and]
from now on do not sin anymore."
(Jn 8:9b-11)

It is important for us to remember that unlike most people who know our faults, God loves us in spite of them, warts and all. It is all the more comforting to realize that God loves us in spite of our actual sins, that no evil deed of ours can cause him to stop loving us and place us beyond the reach of his mercy.

So it is understandable that people often say that God loves us just as we are. But this remark is often made to suggest that God would somehow love us less if he were to call us to change. On this way of thinking, any requirement on God's part for us to transform our ways of thinking and acting would suggest that he is insulting his own creative work. Taken for granted in this view is that the pursuit of our natural inclinations is justifiable and good, that we have no need for redemption.

After the woman's accusers leave, Jesus alone remains with her, as he alone is sinless. The only one there who could condemn her without injustice replaces a barbaric application of the Mosaic law with the logic of pardon. But his mercy takes the form of forgiving her sin, not of condoning it. Perhaps the latter course of action would have been more tactful, more polite. But it would have been no act of mercy. The logic of pardon, of forgiveness, presupposes acknowledgment of and contrition for a wrong done. Neither this woman nor any one of us can be forgiven unwillingly. To enjoy God's mercy, we must be willing to receive it by acknowledging our need for it. Christ loves this woman too much to leave her where she is, as he loves each one of us too much to leave us where we are. Why would anyone want to be left behind?

Merciful Father, whose will is for our good, allow us the grace to accept the healing you offer us in your beloved Son for a life more wonderful than all we ask or imagine.

Light in Darkness

J. David Franks

Jesus spoke to [the people] again, saying, "I am the light of the world. Whoever follows me will not walk in darkness, but will have the light of life." So the Pharisees said to him, "You testify on your own behalf, so your testimony cannot be verified."

(Jn 8:12-13)

Life is ambiguous, a play of shadow and light. We need mutual recognition, but status anxiety can interfere, concerns about what one has to show for one's life, routinized emotional response patterns from childhood. Think of the ambiguous emotions that are stirred up at funerals, weddings, at a dinner party held by friends who are more materially successful than we are, in friendships with members of the opposite sex.

That is why we read great poets, novelists, dramatists, and watch probing movies: to gain some clarity.

The goodness of God the Father is not ambiguous in any way. He IS good, and he means good to us. This is what John the Evangelist later says is the substance of the testimony Jesus gives: "God [the Father] is light, and in him there is no darkness at all" (1 Jn 1:5).

These are words every sophisticated modern person needs to hear. Behind our blasé approach to life and religion, there is a niggling terror that God is a dark force, out to get us. He doesn't care. He's cunning. This is simply a repetition of Satan's primal temptation—falling for which, Adam transferred man from the dimension of gift (the divine economy of gratuity) to the dimension of concupiscence (an economy of scarcity).

Now my heart is compromised. It has devious passages, fearful involutions. Vulnerability means shame. So I have to be on guard with you—and with God. Our hearts cannot be free as long as there is such fear, which strangles love and traps us in a death in life. I am the woman caught in adultery. I need the radiant countenance of love in order to rise.

Jesus is Light from Light, the splendor of the Father, "the visible reminder of Invisible Light" (as T. S. Eliot would affirm). Becoming flesh, the Word of life shines in the darkness of anxious ambiguity. His perfect love exorcises fear; he raises us up to new life.

Beneficent Father, who shower upon us grace upon grace: thank you for your inexhaustible goodness. Make me ever more free to love in the truth, leaving all anxiety behind.

Fluid Dynamics

J. David Franks

Jesus answered and said to [the Pharisees], "Even if I do testify on my own behalf, my testimony can be verified, because I know where I came from and where I am going. But you do not know where I come from or where I am going. You judge by appearances, but I do not judge anyone." (Jn 8:14-15)

Where does this prophet come from? How will it all end? Jesus shows a glimpse of the heaven of divine love whence he comes, and therefore what possibilities are open to our sluggish spirits. He promises an elemental reforging of our spirit, which will make our appearances on the world stage trustworthy.

Jesus comes in the Spirit of love, who is the secret of all animating, of all flowing—who is water, air, fire.

The Spirit hovers over the womb of Mary, so that the Word becomes flesh in the maternal water and blood. The Spirit hovers again over the Jordan. Jesus will tell Nicodemus of the need to be born from above through water and the Spirit. The water of the Spirit flows on, from the stone jars of Cana to the woman of Samaria, the living water that will satisfy all thirst, that will flow out to the world from those who drink of Jesus.

Then we hear that the water becomes something more than wine: the flesh of Jesus is true food and his blood true drink. The flow of self-expenditure continues to the baptism of blood, the crucifixion, when the Word spoken to the end is eloquent in death, in his final liquefaction. From his pierced heart come water and blood, the sacramental life of the Church: the baptism which unites us to the Son, and the Eucharist that, received worthily, intensifies that intimate union.

The water and blood of divine mercy flow down the ages. So we are enwombed in our spiritual mother, Mary-Church. Water, blood, Spirit. Our rigidity gives way slowly under sacramental sculpting. We are liquefied as self-giving love. Through the channels of everyday life, we witness to a higher way of being—like wind, like fire, like love.

Spill your heart, and you communicate the Spirit of life: the life from above, a cataract flowing into history from the throne of God and of the Lamb.

Father, who give us the Spirit of your Son so freely, make us ever more faithful and powerful witnesses in our daily lives of the golden city of heaven, the city of divine love and total intimacy.

An Avowal of True Love

J. David Franks

"And even if I should judge, my judgment is valid, because I am not alone, but it is I and the Father who sent me. Even in your law it is written that the testimony of two men can be verified. I testify on my behalf and so does the Father who sent me."

(Jn 8:16-18)

Romantic love comes out of nowhere. It gusts up in the human heart, like doves swooping and climbing, and everything changes. Beauty causes you to gasp, strength of character makes you sigh: one is charmed, captivated, enraptured. Love breaks in, heals, upsets the venal tables of the soul.

So love can be daunting. Where does love come from? Where will it lead? What solidity is there to love? Who can attest to it? Love is the joining of spirits, so the testimony of love must be from at least two. Their shared spirit testifies.

Jesus is the Son, whose life is the eternal rhythm of coming forth from the Father and returning thanks to his Father for generating him, in their shared Spirit of love. The Father sends his Son into history to bear witness to the boundless love he has for every single human being. So the One through whom all things were made enters into the world as an actor on the world stage, to make invisible love visible.

The Evangelist will later describe this mission of the Word coming in the flesh, his giving himself to us without defense or limit, as a Trinitarian testament of love: "This is the one who came through water and blood, Jesus Christ, not by water alone, but by water and blood. The Spirit is the one that testifies, and the Spirit is truth. So there are three that testify, the Spirit, the water, and the blood, and the three are of one accord" (1 Jn 5:6-8). The Spirit hovering—always enfleshing love: Nazareth, Bethlehem, Jordan, Golgotha, Pentecost, font, altar, liturgy, holy life, martyrdom.

In the consummation of his passionate love for us, revealing at the same time the Father's love for us, Jesus gives us everything: he gives us the Spirit, who *is* in his Person the love union of the Father and Son. "And bowing his head, he handed over the spirit" (Jn 19:30).

Loving Father, who love us so totally and unaccountably, thank you for the Spirit of love toward us that you share with your Son. Make us trust that love more and more.

Storm's a-Comin'

J. David Franks

So [the Pharisees] said to [Jesus], "Where is your father?" Jesus answered, "You know neither me nor my Father. If you knew me, you would know my Father also." He spoke these words while teaching in the treasury in the temple area. But no one arrested him, because his hour had not yet come.

(Jn 8:19-20)

In New England, the first bands of a nor'easter make one take a deep breath. You're in for a siege. The beauty of the seasons comes at a cost: there are times when just carrying out what Denise Levertov calls the "dear tasks of continuance" becomes burdened by the atmosphere. So it is with the bitter cold, and snowfall. What you want to get done during your day becomes less a matter of course. Concentrated effort is called for to accomplish the desires that get you out of bed in the morning. Time slows down. But paying attention to the fine contours of life thereby becomes easier.

Jesus lives his earthly life measured by the "hour" of the Father, a storm to come dwarfing any hurricane or Great Red Spot. Jesus is to be the lightning rod to absorb all the energy of the maelstrom of evil engulfing human history. This is the consummation of the Father's plan of loving goodness: to expose his Beloved Son, his heart's treasure, on the high rock of the world, till he be carrion. That harrowing moment of darkness is in fact the hour of utmost glory, for it is the hour of love to the end. No more eloquent avowal of love has there been than the Word of the Father silent in his love death, his heart open to each of us.

Jesus' current Temple discourse concludes his time at the feast of Tabernacles, the feast of water and light. We glimpse the fluid dynamics of the Spirit: water, air, and fire are coalescing in a storm of infinite love. Evil will swallow Jesus whole, but from the belly of the beast, after a moment of silence, light will explode and shake the foundations of the world.

Our culture has for a long time sought to denigrate fatherhood: we do not trust that the Father really loves us. Jesus is back in the Temple. He must be about his Father's business.

Almighty Father, heal the wounds of our heart, the ones that keep us from fully trusting in your infinite love for us. Give us zeal to radiate your love to hearts that thirst.

Depth Charge

J. David Franks

[Jesus] said to [the Pharisees] again, "I am going away and you will look for me, but you will die in your sin. Where I am going you cannot come." So the Jews said, "He is not going to kill himself, is he, because he said, 'Where I am going you cannot come'?" (Jn 8:21-22)

Participating in prison ministry, you have to empty your pockets, including that smartphone so recently become indispensable. You are divested—not exactly bare, unaccommodated man, but close. You go behind the walls, and though you are a free man among the unfree, there is still the brute fact: you're in prison.

Jesus comes to set us free: from sin and suffering, futility and death. To break us out, though, he has to enter into our prison. The world as such is not a prison, but my secularized heart with its selfish desires most certainly is. We have built hardened bunkers of the spirit. To rescue us, Jesus has to assume the flesh of our death in life. The crowd gets it almost right: though it will be utter surrender, not suicide—at our hands, not his—the result will be Jesus' death.

The monster of the deep whose threatening presence makes our days unquiet is death itself. It spreads poison, with a reek of vanity: why bother? The ones I love suffer and die, and I will suffer and die.

Through the shaft, into the maw, Jesus drops, down and down. But he is a depth charge, and the gates of hell will not withstand the megatonnage of an innocent love utterly divested—yet infinite.

We cannot follow? What could Jesus mean? We do die after all, though we can't descend as deep, for love suffers more. The question is death as return to the Father. If we believe in Jesus, that he is the Son of the Father, and cling to him by the power of his Spirit, we can follow him. And we don't have to wait until death to begin eternal life: Jesus opens the way for us in baptism. In Christ we break through the center of hell—and find ourselves rising on the other side of the world. The new Exodus ends above the stars, before the face of the Father.

Father of all freedom, free us from the unreasonable attachments to the goods of this world that hinder us from loving to the full. Make us shine with a love irresistible to our friends and neighbors.

Lose Farther, Lose Faster

J. David Franks

[Jesus] said to [the Jews], "You belong to what is below, I belong to what is above. You belong to this world, but I do not belong to this world. That is why I told you that you will die in your sins. For if you do not believe that I AM, you will die in your sins."

(Jn 8:23-24)

Jesus is in the midst of an incipient riot, and he's the reason they're riled up. As he keeps talking, more and more want to see him dead. It is the last night of the feast of Tabernacles, and he stands in the Court of the Women, the large outer court of the Temple. The full harvest moon shines benignly in the clear autumnal sky. Jesus declares *himself* to be the light of the world as he stands amidst the four massive menorahs with their bonfires roaring seventy-five feet high in the air. They are the symbols; he is the substance.

He has exposed, perhaps earlier that very day, the hypocrisy and misogyny of a lynch mob, and shown his forgiving, gallant, and paternal love for the woman caught in adultery.

Jesus' cousins had wanted him to go to the feast to consolidate his popularity (Jn 7:3-4). But Jesus starts saying offensively hard truths instead. Jesus isn't here to be acclaimed king. No normal campaign has a bumper sticker that says, "You will die in your sins."

This is Life according to the Spirit of true love confronting "life" according to consumerist desire, which battens on the good world the Father creates, yet leaves us ever more diminished. Jesus prosecutes a relentless campaign against the traitor in our own breasts, against the self-destructive negation of our truth as saints the Father long ago dreamed up.

Jesus is infinite Being from infinite Being. Our resistances before love, our flight from love: this is not. Jesus is the Word dividing soul from spirit, joints from marrow, drawing signal from noise.

This being divested is shattering in its pain, but is the only way to draw off the poison of secularized desire. "Then practice losing farther, losing faster," writes the poet Elizabeth Bishop. Our Physician, who wields the scalpel, is the same God who freed the Israelites from Egypt. And he goes under the knife first.

Faithful Father, do not leave us to pursue our reckless will apart from your wise and loving will. Show us the mercy of interrupting our sinful patterns, as gently as can be, but as surely as necessary.

A Beginning without End

J. David Franks

So [the Jews] said to [Jesus], "Who are you?" Jesus said to them, "What I told you from the beginning. I have much to say about you in condemnation. But the one who sent me is true, and what I heard from him I tell the world." They did not realize that he was speaking to them of the Father. (Jn 8:25-27)

Who are you? Our eldest daughter is just entering adolescence, and the grace with which she has been dealing with the changes has been most heartening. She has always been thoughtful, and we were there right when she really had the question about sex. The mechanics seem obvious once one describes them, so what she really had questions about was the drama of love. We made clear that she can ask us any question, and so she has the confidence to move into the obscure horizon of the future.

As we emerge from the enwombment that is childhood, we start to struggle in earnest with the question, "Who am I?" Negotiating how much to identify with, and set ourselves off from, parents and peers and celebrities, with the dawning knowledge about all the currencies of human interaction, tinged with sexual energies: it's tough work being a teenager!

And it doesn't usually get much easier. As John Prine sings, "The years just flow by, like a broken-down dam." Tomorrow becomes today so quickly, we hardly have time to assess the social script we've been handed, telling us what makes a successful life. Thirty, midlife, empty nest, evening of life: the question of my identity becomes electric again for a time, but who is there to guide us?

Jesus is in his very Person the Word told "from the beginning." The crowd asks his identity, but his identity is precisely to be the one spoken to us by the Father, answering our identity crisis. Each of us is a song sung by the Father before every molecular cloud collapsed into flame in the first stars: his Word gives the lyrics, and their Spirit of love the melody.

We shrink a little: we know deep down there are things we have done to compromise our identity, which deserve condemnation. But that's not the point. When Jesus comes close to us, the Father is whispering our name, in infinite gentleness.

Eternal Father, fill me with the Spirit of your Word, so that all my words and all my actions may utter one thing and one thing alone to those you place on my path: that you love each with an eternal love.

Falling Upwards

J. David Franks

So Jesus said [to (the Jews)], "When you lift up the Son of Man, then you will realize that I AM, and that I do nothing on my own, but I say only what the Father taught me. The one who sent me is with me. He has not left me alone, because I always do what is pleasing to him." Because he spoke this way, many came to believe in him. (Jn 8:28-30)

How do we evangelize? We have the greatest treasure in the world, Jesus Christ in the Eucharist, and the rest of the sacramental system, and the teaching authority and liturgy and devotions of the Church, and Mary: Jesus englobing us and filling our days with his tangible love. How can I keep from singing? But if the song is to touch the human heart, the sometimes screaming agony of human existence must be included. We must proclaim "Christ, and him crucified" (1 Cor 2:2).

Love is a beginning with no end. "In the beginning" God created the heavens and the earth. "In the beginning" was the Word: not a "beginning" 13.7 billion years ago when the space-time continuum exploded into existence, but a beginning that perdures, the eternal fontal source of all time and space. In the beginning, love goes on and on, which is why Jesus is so emphatic with the Pharisees in refuting divorce (see Mt 19:1-12).

Before the mountains were formed, the Son proceeds eternally from the Father in their shared Spirit of love. This Trinitarian dynamism of loving understanding is what being is. The secret of reality is infinite True Love.

This secret is revealed in its full glory on the cross, for hanging between heaven and earth is the Father's Word of Love, faithful to the end because he is endless. Through him all the holy energy of being itself flows out to us.

Love *is*, always. Before the foundation of the world, the Father has chosen every human being to be holy and immaculate in Christ (see Eph 1:4). The call to holiness issues from the Lamb slain.

There he hangs, Christ crucified. He opens his arms for all of us. We obscure the fabric of reality with our rationalizations and ideologies. The pierced Heart exposes all that. Reality is a vortex of love. Will we let go? Will we abandon ourselves, and fall upwards, into the hands of a loving God?

Eternal Father, blessed for ever, thank you for calling us into existence to share your eternal joy, that festival of light and love that is communion with your Son in the Spirit. Break our fatal self-assertion; do not give up on us.

The Liberating Power of Truth
Douglas Bushman

Jesus then said to those Jews who believed in him,
"If you remain in my word, you will truly be my disciples,
and you will know the truth, and the truth will set you free."
(Jn 8:31-32)

Common experiences confirm that truth sets free. Coaches unleash athletes' potential. Physicians employ their medical knowledge to set people free from illness, and financial planners free their clients to fund their children's education and retirement. Because people take sports so seriously, successful coaches are well-rewarded. Lawsuits over medical malpractice and financial misrepresentations prove that people highly value health and wealth, and have a sense of objective truth. Coaches, doctors, and financial planners only serve us when the truth guides them. These examples show that in a culture considered to be fundamentally relativistic people still have an irrepressible sense of objective truth. Man is made for the truth, and he knows that it has the power to set us free in many ways. Jesus appeals to this innate sense of truth. He is the truth about God and about man. He is the ultimate life coach training us for lasting happiness, the consummate physician healing our souls, the supreme advisor guiding us in storing up treasure for eternal life. Yet, a double standard exists. Why do people value coaches, doctors, and financial advisors more than Jesus?

When it comes to the truth about life—the truth about moral principles and religion—many seem to wonder whether objective truth exists, and if it does, whether it can be ascertained. What sports, finances, and health have in common is that people care deeply about them. Relativism ends as soon as there is passionate involvement, intense concern, or commitment. In a word, the antidote to relativism is deep and ardent love. Once love is set into motion, matters of truth are everything. The reason is that love desires what is good for oneself or another. Knowing what the true good is for those we love, and what must be done to make it a reality, sets love free from the frustration of having an ineffective desire. Jesus reveals the truth that sets us free to love.

Father of faithful love, I thank you for revealing the truth in your Son, Jesus Christ. Let me always love you in the truth; never let me take your saving truth for granted.

God's Truth Is Habitat for Humanity

Douglas Bushman

[The Jews] answered [Jesus], "We are descendants of Abraham and have never been enslaved to anyone. How can you say, 'You will become free'?" Jesus answered them, "Amen, amen, I say to you, everyone who commits sin is a slave of sin. A slave does not remain in a household forever, but a son always remains. So if a son frees you, then you will truly be free."
(Jn 8:33-36)

In a large enough cage, animals do not feel restricted. We can think of ecosystems as nature's cages, God's zoo for various species, providing all they need to thrive, but also imposing limits on their range to roam. A giraffe resentful over being bound to a grassland, or a whale annoyed at being confined to the sea are absurdities. But if it happened, their spiritual director might say: Get a grip. God has provided well for you. The grassland and ocean are sufficient. You flourish here. There is no happiness for you elsewhere. You are not made for other habitats. If you use your freedom to try to break out, you will lose it. It's suicide.

God's truth is the habitat for humanity. There our freedom roams without restriction, and there we flourish. Any thought of a fulfillment outside of God's truth is illusory. Sin begins with resentment that we have a habitat at all. Rather than thanking God for creating an ecosystem of truth in which we can thrive, sin takes umbrage over being dependent on any ecosystem. This is to resent being a creature and to be envious of God. The result is a fundamental conflict with the truth of our own being. The garden of Eden is humanity's first, pristine habitat of truth. There Adam and Eve are free to enjoy every fruit except one. That forbidden fruit symbolizes the limit that comes with being a creature, like a border around the original habitat for humanity. Their sin is to trespass into the space reserved for God. The result is the loss of the perfect freedom enjoyed within the God-given ecosystem. It would not take our imaginary giraffe and whale very long to figure out that they were better off in their natural habitat and to return to it. We can learn from them the wisdom of conversion, which is to return to the habitat of truth and lasting freedom.

Merciful Father, when I have trespassed the border of my freedom, help me to return, like the Prodigal Son, to your house, the Church, my true habitat of truth, freedom, and love.

Showing Jesus Hospitality

Douglas Bushman

"I know that you are descendants of Abraham. But you are trying to kill me, because my word has no room among you. I tell you what I have seen in the Father's presence; then do what you have heard from the Father."
[The Jews] answered and said to [Jesus], "Our father is Abraham." (Jn 8:37-39a)

The pain of not being believed is familiar to all. "So, you don't believe me" means: You have shut me out. Such words reveal the realization that one is not trusted, and thus that there is no foundation for communicating the truth. One might as well say: "So, we are not really friends after all, are we." Jesus phrases it differently, but it comes to the same thing: "My word finds no room among you." His word is everything. Because he is the eternal Word of God all of his words are so many expressions of his very being. To reject his words is to reject him. This is why Jesus links his death to the refusal to receive his word.

The Bible highly esteems hospitality. Abraham insists that three men be his guests. Jesus' friends (Mary, Martha, Peter, Matthew) and others (Zacchaeus, Simon the Pharisee) welcome him into their homes. But what God desires most is that we welcome his words in faith, like Abraham, Mary, and the Centurion. At Mass, we show this hospitality first by welcoming the bread of God's saving Word. Then, we receive "under our roof" the Eucharistic Bread of Life. Without this Bread of Life we have no life within us. But to close our hearts to him is also death for Jesus. His death on the cross is inseparable from the death that happens in people's hearts. Words serve to carry truth from one person to another and thereby to unite them in the truth. Rejection of another's word is rejection of the one who speaks it, and this effectively kills any relationship. Jesus' love is already crucified when his word is not welcomed. Thus, the drama of the Paschal Mystery occurs in each moment of truth in a human heart. As he offers his word to us his life hangs in the balance. To show him or not to show him hospitality, that is the question.

Forgive me, Father of infinite compassion, for the times I have failed to welcome the saving words of your Son. Make my heart an abode of welcome to his words of saving truth.

True Descendants of Abraham

Douglas Bushman

Jesus said to [the Jews], "If you were Abraham's children, you would be doing the works of Abraham. But now you are trying to kill me, a man who has told you the truth that I heard from God; Abraham did not do this. You are doing the works of your father!" (Jn 8:39b-41a)

An integral element of knowing oneself is to know one's lineage. Websites helping people discover their ancestry attest to the natural desire to know one's origins. And it's not just about genetic inheritance. The family transmits cultural, moral, and religious tenets that shape our personalities by giving us a vision for our fulfillment. In this way they give direction to our freedom. Certainly, at a particular point of maturity everyone must reflect on his cultural, moral, and religious inheritance, either to make it his own, to amend it, or to reject it. Jesus provokes such a moment of truth for the family of his disciples when he asks: "Do you also want to leave?" (Jn 6:67).

Something similar happens when Jesus confronts his audience about their ancestry. As Abraham's offspring, they are heirs to his faith. They are blessed to know the true and living God. This blessing entails the responsibility to acknowledge God by acknowledging the truth, every truth they encounter, because he is the source of all truth. Their encounter with Jesus is the occasion for the sons of Abraham to affirm their ancestry by acknowledging the truth in him and by placing their faith in him.

In baptism we become adopted children of the heavenly Father, Christ becomes our brother, the Church is our mother, and the saints are our elder siblings. We enjoy all the blessings of our new, supernatural family. The question is: Do we make the effort to know our family tree and the values of our forefathers in faith? Like the Jews of Christ's time, these family values are constantly on the line as our freedom is put to the test. We encounter Jesus in every moment of truth, since he is the truth. Every day we draw on our inheritance, the values of our family of faith, by putting the truth, that is, Jesus, first in every thought, word, and deed.

Father of eternal truth, may your kingdom come and your will be done on earth as it is in heaven by my earnestly searching for your truth and by my faith in your Son.

Love, the DNA of God's Family

Douglas Bushman

[So] [the Jews] said to [Jesus], "We are not illegitimate. We have one Father, God." Jesus said to them, "If God were your Father, you would love me, for I came from God and am here; I did not come on my own, but he sent me. Why do you not understand what I am saying? Because you cannot bear to hear my word."

(Jn 8:41b-43)

In this passage, the issue of ancestry moves from Abraham to Abraham's God. This move is decisive because, as we know, Jesus is the Only Begotten Son of God, whom the Father sends to speak the truth about him. So, only he can reveal what it means for God to be Father. The Father and Son are so profoundly one that Jesus could say: "Whoever has seen me has seen the Father" (Jn 14:9). Seeing Jesus we see the Father's merciful love, disclosed in the figure of the father of the Prodigal Son and definitively revealed when Jesus loves us "to the end" (Jn 13:1). The love of which none is greater (see Jn 15:13) is the love between the Father and Son, made visible in Christ's sacrifice of love.

The Father "destined us for adoption to himself through Jesus Christ" (Eph 1:5). By baptism, we are born anew, adopted in God's love. In the memorable words of Blessed John Paul II, love is the DNA of God's children. Adopted children often strive to meet their biological parents. Deep down, is this not symptomatic of a need to know that their origin is love, that their existence is fundamentally good because they are conceived in love? For God's children, this drive leads to the Eucharist. There, in faith, we see divine love poured out in sacrifice. We see the Son in his supreme act of love, and thereby we also see the Father. This is why it is profoundly fitting that we say the Our Father immediately following the Eucharistic Prayer. In the Son's sacrifice we see the Father and know the full truth about his love. Formed by this divine doctrine, we can address the Father in full knowledge of who he really is: the Father of the Only Begotten Son, Jesus Christ, who rejoices over the conversion of his children as the father of the Prodigal Son rejoiced over his return.

All praise and thanks to you, eternal Father, for revealing your love in Jesus. May every Eucharist be for me a celebration of praise and thanksgiving for your love.

The First and Greatest Lie

Douglas Bushman

"You belong to your father the devil and you willingly carry out your father's desires. He was a murderer from the beginning and does not stand in truth, because there is no truth in him. When he tells a lie, he speaks in character, because he is a liar and the father of lies. But because I speak the truth, you do not believe me." (Jn 8:44-45)

A standard category for trivia questions is "Firsts": first to run a sub-four-minute mile? Roger Bannister; first American to orbit earth? John Glenn; first billionaire? John D. Rockefeller; first to transplant a human heart? Christiaan Barnard. "Firsts" like these are benchmarks of history. Jesus measures history differently. His key categories are truth and lie, life and death. He knows, and wants us to know, that the first lie is linked to death. This link goes back to "the beginning," to the Garden, where the first battle between the culture of truth and life and the culture of lie and death occurs. By the first of God's graces, the first couple enjoys the gift of immortality, but they lose that gift by believing the devil's first lie. The lie is that they will not die if they disobey God's commandment. This directly contradicts God's warning that disobedience will bring death, and implies that the commandment is not rooted in God's love. The devil's lie brings disobedience, disobedience brings death, and death confirms that God spoke the truth.

The drama continues: "Woe to those who call evil good, and good evil" (Is 5:20). The battle between truth and lie, life and death occurs in every decision whether to obey God's commandments. The truth is that the commandments are at the service of a full, meaningful, and happy life because they come from God's love. The lie is that they prevent man from living a fully meaningful and happy life because he is jealous. The truth that God is love sets us free to obey his commandments. Our hope for victory over the lie, disobedience, and death is as certain as Christ's witness to the truth that God is love. The victory is his, yet through him, with him, and in him we crush the serpent's head by every act of obedience rooted in the truth that God is love.

Through the intercession of Saint John, grant me, Father of truth and life, the grace to use the great gift of freedom to join with Christ in his victory of truth, obedience, and life.

The Art and Risk of Listening

Douglas Bushman

"Can any of you charge me with sin? If I am telling the truth, why do you not believe me? Whoever belongs to God hears the words of God; for this reason you do not listen, because you do not belong to God." (Jn 8:46-47)

It's a familiar scene. Just as I am about to order a steak dinner, my Catholic friend reminds me it's a Friday in Lent. An inconvenient truth registers, and I say: "I wish you hadn't said that!" I find myself torn between the truth and what my heart is set on doing. Listening, taking in words, is risky because words convey truth, and truth makes demands on us. Really listening requires being receptive to the truth that words convey. Sometimes the truth that words carry surprises us and reveals inclinations that need amendment.

To belong to God is to seek the truth. Seekers of the truth believe that truth sets free (see Jn 8:32). This is why they listen to others, who can be a source of truth. Openness to someone known to be a person of truth—a saint, a Father or Doctor of the Church, the Magisterium—is a sure sign of belonging to God. It is an act of humility, which for Saint Thomas Aquinas means submitting to what is of God in another. Nothing is more "of God" than the truth. The most common opportunity to be humble comes with being receptive to the truth in what others say or write. It is a form of worship since, again for Saint Thomas, worship of God consists in receiving and giving his gifts. Certainly truth is one of God's greatest gifts. Those who seek the truth and turn to Jesus and his Church worship God and give him glory.

These considerations should make us pause to reflect on the quality of our conversations. If the words of others can bring the truth to me, then my words can be truth-bearing for them. The premise of the New Evangelization is the twofold risk of being open to the truth when others speak to us, and of being the occasion for a moment of truth for others by what we do and say.

Gracious Father, give me the humility to love your truth more than I love myself and to receive saving truth from your Son and his Church, so that I may bring the truth to others.

Jesus Fulfills the Fourth Commandment

Douglas Bushman

The Jews answered and said to [Jesus], "Are we not right in saying that you are a Samaritan and are possessed?" Jesus answered, "I am not possessed; I honor my Father, but you dishonor me. I do not seek my own glory; there is one who seeks it and he is the one who judges."

(Jn 8:48-50)

To tweak a phrase, imitation is the best way to honor someone. We're talking about something deeper than physical imitation. "You have your mother's faith, or your father's courage" honors parents in a way that "You have your mother's eyes, or your father's nose" cannot. The greatest honor children can show to their parents is to become everything genuine, true, and good that their parents desire them to be. Children's virtues bear witness to good parenting, the work of grace, and the piety and wisdom of someone that recognizes the blessing of such parents and makes their values his own. John the Baptist, Thérèse of Lisieux, and the Blessed Virgin Mary honor their parents by living in faith. What begins as the honor of obedience, as children, culminates in the honor of virtue. Their parents could say of them what Jesus says of his disciples: "I have been glorified in them" (Jn 17:10). We, the Church, are Christ's glory! It is perhaps more conspicuous in the saints and martyrs, but we all honor him by imitating his virtues. Because he imitates the Father, this honor rises through him to the Father: "Through him, and with him, and in him, O God, almighty Father, in the unity of the Holy Spirit, all glory and honor is yours, for ever and ever."

Jesus reveals the full meaning of the fourth commandment: he honors the Father by receiving from him all that the Father gives—his very self—and by faithfully being and doing everything the Father wants him to be and to do. Because the Father's love for the Son is perfect, in Jesus, the honor of obedience and the honor of imitation are one and the same. He obeys the Father by imitating him: "A son cannot do anything on his own, but only what he sees his father doing; for what he does, his son will do also" (Jn 5:19).

Holy Father, fulfill the desire you have placed in my heart—to imitate your Son, so that your glory may shine in the world and all may come to hallow your holy Name.

The Right Question about Jesus

Douglas Bushman

*"Amen, amen, I say to you, whoever keeps my word will never
see death." [So] the Jews said to [Jesus], "Now we are sure that
you are possessed. Abraham died, as did the prophets, yet you
say, 'Whoever keeps my word will never taste death.' Are you
greater than our father Abraham, who died? Or the prophets,
who died? Who do you make yourself out to be?"*

(Jn 8:51-53)

The TV game show *Jeopardy* starts with answers and moves to
questions. Perhaps that is the secret of its popularity, for we
are accustomed to the opposite movement, from questions
to answers. Questions provoke a spontaneous search for an answer.
Jesus builds on this truth-seeking dynamism. "Bring your questions
about the purpose and meaning of life to me," he says. But, not all
questions lead to him. To those whose main questions concern
material comfort—health, wealth, and the like—Jesus can only say:
"Why do you not ask the big questions? You are made for more;
you are made for love. Ask me about love."

When people ask who he is, Jesus can be evasive. Similar to today's
passage, in another context, when asked if he is the Messiah, he
replies: "If I tell you, you will not believe" (Lk 22:67). Jesus wants
us to answer the question about his identity. As with Saint Peter,
he asks us: "Who do you say that I am?" (Mt 16:15). At the right
time, Jesus expects us to answer this question of questions: Who
do I make Jesus out to be? Who is Jesus for me? It is a grace to
realize that to evade this question is to dodge the fundamental
responsibility that accompanies our dignity as God's image. God
wants our faith to be light for our living, truth that sets free, a
life-transforming discovery of the meaning of our existence. This
happens when we discover that Jesus is the answer to our search.
But, who is engaged in the search for love? Where are those restless
hearts that Saint Augustine describes? For, what value is an answer
without a question? The challenge in coming to mature faith, then,
is to formulate the questions corresponding to the answer that Jesus
gives, the questions to which only his answer is adequate: What is
love? Am I loveable? Where can I find real love?

*Gracious Father, by revealing your love in your Son and in the
gift of the Holy Spirit, you have granted rest to my restless heart.
I love you with my whole heart, mind, soul, and strength.*

The True Measure of Joy

Douglas Bushman

*Jesus answered, "If I glorify myself, my glory is worth nothing;
but it is my Father who glorifies me, of whom you say, 'He is
our God.' You do not know him, but I know him. And if I should
say that I do not know him, I would be like you a liar. But I do
know him and I keep his word. Abraham your father rejoiced
to see my day; he saw it and was glad." (Jn 8:54-56)*

To promote self-knowledge, a spiritual director assigns periodic reviews of life to identify the times when a person recalls being filled with joy. Joy is an indicator of priorities. If the sports team's success triggers joy, you're a sports enthusiast. If joy accompanies sharp rises in the stock market, you're into prosperity. To adapt a saying: where your joy is, there also will be your love (see Lk 12:34). The priority of God's love is communion with men through conversion, as we see in the exuberant joy of the Prodigal Son's father.

Jesus is the cause of Abraham's joy. By faith, his priorities are the same as God's priorities. His one desire is that God be recognized as God and honored and obeyed by all. Jesus fulfills this desire, thus Abraham rejoices, and so should his descendants—if they have his faith priorities. Jesus plays on the Jews' reverence for Abraham to provoke a moment of truth: where is their joy? Why do they not respond to him as Abraham did? His goal is their conversion to faith in him. Then their joy would be the same as Abraham's.

God's people rejoice when he fulfills his promises. God's blessings—bountiful harvests, answered prayers, peace in Jerusalem, return from exile—cause joy in the Lord's faithful love. Since this love culminates in God sending his Son, Jesus should be our greatest joy. But this requires faith. Jesus is a sign of contradiction. His demands are great. His answer to suffering and sin is shocking: his own death and Resurrection. His question to everyone is: "Am I the measure of your joy? If not, your priorities are not God's priorities." His invitation to joy is universal: "Come to me and you will know the joy of God's love, the joy of forgiveness." Jesus' joy is the Father. He comes to reveal him so that his joy may be in us and our joy may be complete (see Jn 15:11).

*Eternal Father, I believe in your love, I hope in your love, I love
your love. May every celebration of your love in the Eucharist be
for me and for all the world the source of abiding joy.*

Speaking the Truth about God

Douglas Bushman

So the Jews said to [Jesus], "You are not yet fifty years old and you have seen Abraham?" Jesus said to them, "Amen, amen, I say to you, before Abraham came to be, I AM." So they picked up stones to throw at him; but Jesus hid and went out of the temple area. (Jn 8:57-59)

High-profile trials—O. J. Simpson, Casey Anthony—grip the nation. They remind us that matters of truth are important. We easily relate to the members of the jury, whose lives are profoundly interrupted as they weigh weeks of testimony to reach a verdict bearing on life and death. Everything hinges on the credibility and coherence of the words of witnesses. Words count even more when they concern God. God's advocate is his own Word, Jesus, who presents the evidence that God is love. He alone speaks the full truth about God. His own life is the evidence, on it he rests his case before each of us: Do I speak truthfully about God? God summons everyone as juror to examine Jesus' life and teachings: Is he guilty or acquitted of blasphemy? Once Jesus claims to be divine, there is no middle ground. He is either the Lord of the universe or deserving of a blasphemer's death: "Whoever blasphemes the name of the LORD shall be put to death. The whole community shall stone him" (Lv 24:16). "We are not stoning you for a good work but for blasphemy. You, a man, are making yourself God" (see Jn 10:33).

Before his conversion, Saint Paul similarly judged Christ's followers, commending the stoning of Saint Stephen (see Acts 8:1). After his conversion he reverses himself; he is the blasphemer (see 1 Tm 1:13), who forced Christians to blaspheme by denying their faith in Jesus (Acts 26:11). This teaches us that in the trial of Jesus we too are on trial. Reaching a verdict about Jesus necessitates reaching a verdict about ourselves. To take sides with the truth means to acquit Jesus and to convict oneself. Every moment of conscience is a summons to jury duty. Far from interrupting life, such moments are the soul of life. And, we are not alone. We have another advocate, the Spirit of truth, who convinces the world concerning sin, righteousness, and condemnation (see Jn 16:8).

All thanks to you, most gracious Father, for providing me, through your Church, the truth and grace to make my conscience a holy sanctuary where you are worshiped in Spirit and in truth.

Seeing Means Believing

Father Herald Joseph Brock, c.f.r.

As [Jesus] passed by he saw a man blind from birth. His disciples asked him, "Rabbi, who sinned, this man or his parents, that he was born blind?" Jesus answered, "Neither he nor his parents sinned; it is so that the works of God might be made visible through him." (Jn 9:1-3)

Chapter 9 of John's Gospel has a privileged place in the Church's liturgy. It is used in full as the Gospel for the Fourth Sunday of Lent during Year A of the three-year cycle of readings. The Sunday Lenten Gospels for Year A are specially chosen to help prepare catechumens for baptism at Easter. The theme of sight dominates the chapter, and is symbolic in John's Gospel for faith, an essential quality in the life of any Christian. Believing means being able to see and recognize Jesus.

While the story revolves around a man born blind who receives his sight from Jesus, it quickly becomes clear that he's not the only one with impaired vision. The opening verses disclose the disciples' myopic presumption that the man's blindness is a punishment for sin. It's their short-sightedness, as much as the man's blindness (and the Pharisee's self-righteousness), that Jesus wants to heal. In fact, Jesus wants to transform completely the way they look at situations like this from a cause and effect blame-oriented analysis, to recognition of an opportunity for the works of God to be made visible.

It was Servant of God Luigi Giussani's "chance" encounter with a few woefully uncatechized youths that redirected his life from teaching graduate theology to high school religion, a shift that eventually led to establishing the movement Communion and Liberation. What could have been an occasion for blaming and bemoaning became instead an opportunity to make visible the works of God.

Preconceptions and tunnel vision distort our perspective and blind us to unexpected possibilities, resulting in wasted words and missed opportunities. The gift of faith transforms and expands our perception, enabling us to see even in challenging circumstances a chance to allow God to work, and to recognize the presence of Christ who surprises us by what "might be."

Father, open the eyes of my mind, expand my vision and increase my faith, so that I may recognize and respond to the countless opportunities you give me to allow you to work.

Here's Mud in Your Eye!

Father Herald Joseph Brock, c.f.r.

"We have to do the works of the one who sent me while it is day. Night is coming when no one can work. While I am in the world, I am the light of the world." When [Jesus] had said this, he spat on the ground and made clay with the saliva, and smeared the clay on [the blind man's] eyes, and said to him, "Go wash in the Pool of Siloam" (which means Sent). So he went and washed, and came back able to see. (Jn 9:4-7)

Jesus is "the light of the world" (Jn 9:5), "the true light which enlightens everyone" (Jn 1:9). When we are close to him, suffused by his radiance, we see clearly, life has purpose, and we can labor productively, imitating Jesus as he does the work of his Father (see Jn 5:19). The further we are from him, the murkier and more meaningless life becomes, rendering us incapable of doing anything but destructive deeds of darkness (see Rom 13:12 and Eph 5:11). No one can work constructively at night.

Jesus does something startling in this passage that evokes the primordial work of creation. He exerts himself by taking some of the same clay of the earth from which we were formed (see Gn 2:7), made life-giving and restorative by the saliva from his mouth, and smears it on the eyes of the blind man. It's like the effort he expends in the Gospel of Mark to pray repeatedly in order to overcome the stubborn blindness of the man at Bethsaida (see Mk 8:22-26), and to insert his fingers and groan "*Ephphatha!*" in order to open the blocked ears of the deaf-mute (see Mk 7:31-37)—in both cases also using his own saliva as healing salve. He is the "potter" (see Jer 18:1-6) working to refashion us in the original image of God— a work set in motion at baptism ("Go wash").

When Jesus is working on us, it can be a painful and confusing experience, like clay being pounded and squeezed. His methods and means can be as disconcerting and messy as spit and mud. Once when traveling, Saint Teresa of Ávila was thrown from her mount— into the mud!—and told by the Lord that's how he treats his friends. But his goal is clear and worth whatever the discomfort. He desires our complete transformation, and continues to labor until that is complete. He works on us, so we can work with him, in the light.

Father, keep working on me and don't stop, despite my groans and complaints, until your image is completely restored in me and I can labor together with your Son to do your works.

The Same But Different

Father Herald Joseph Brock, C.F.R.

[The healed man's] neighbors and those who had seen him earlier as a beggar said, "Isn't this the one who used to sit and beg?" Some said, "It is," but others said, "No, he just looks like him." He said, "I am." (Jn 9:8-9)

A new detail now emerges for the first time, a direct consequence of the man's blindness: he was a beggar. Unable to work to sustain himself because of his condition, he was forced into demeaning dependence on the condescending generosity of others. It's not difficult to imagine how having to plead and cajole daily for donations eventually eroded the man's sense of his own dignity in a way that affected every aspect of his appearance.

Jesus' miracles and healings always go far beyond the physical manipulation of matter or curing of illness. Their aim is the restoration of the humanity of the person in the fullest sense, both in terms of their individual existence and in the way they stand before others. By taking the time in such a personal and attentive way to give this man his sight, Jesus not only opens his eyes, but restores his sense of self-worth, enabling him to stand up straight and face with confidence the opposition and accusations that will ensue.

The man's neighbors and acquaintances recognize the physical traits of the former blind beggar, but are confused by his altered appearance as much as by his ability to see. Is it really he? For his part the man states plainly: I'm the one. The same yet different, not only in terms of the physical ability to see, but changed in the way I look at myself and you.

After the Resurrection, Peter and John were recognized as men who had been with Jesus (see Acts 4:13); many saints would emerge from prayer with changed countenances and radiant faces. The encounter with Jesus alters us, and begins to bring about in us a different humanity, the new humanity of the Gospel. Our personal identity is not destroyed; instead we become fully ourselves in a way that was never possible before: the same but different and new in a noticeable way.

Father, I want to be able to look at myself and others in a different way, from your own perspective. Help me to live fully the new humanity revealed and made possible by your Son.

From Eternity to Infinity

Father Herald Joseph Brock, C.F.R..

*So [the healed man's neighbors] said to [the healed man], "[So]
how were your eyes opened?" He replied, "The man called Jesus
made clay and anointed my eyes and told me, 'Go to Siloam
and wash.' So I went there and washed and was able to see."
And they said to him, "Where is he?" He said, "I don't know."*
(Jn 9:10-12)

There's a fascinating substratum that underlies these verses.
Responding to a query from his neighbors, the man states
the simple facts: *The same Jesus who made clay and anointed
my eyes told me to go wash. I went and washed and now see.* We've
already noted the baptismal context of this chapter, reinforced by
the imagery of washing and anointing, and how sight is a metaphor
for faith. We've also seen how the use of clay evokes the primordial
act of creating man. Here those two actions, creation and baptism,
are brought together and identified with the same author: Jesus.

The same God who created me is the God who rescues and
recreates me in baptism. The logic of creation and baptism is
identical. I am not an afterthought, and my salvation is not a last
minute invention. In homilies he preached for the Easter Vigil,
Pope Benedict XVI pointed out the profound link between creation
and the Resurrection. The Resurrection ratifies and restores God's
original purpose in creating the universe. It puts everything back
on track and assures its final consummation. My own creation is
revindicated by my baptism, my insertion into the Paschal Mystery
of Jesus.

I remember distinctly as a young man praying on my college dorm
roof in the middle of the night, and being suddenly overwhelmed
by the awareness that the thought of me delighted God so much
that he was moved to create me, and the thought of losing me was
so intolerable to him that he sent his Son to ransom me. Servant of
God Luigi Giussani, founder of the ecclesial movement Communion
and Liberation, used to paraphrase Jeremiah 31:3 as: "I have loved
you with an eternal love and I have had pity on your nothingness."
God's love and plan for us reaches from eternity to infinity (and
beyond!) and hinges on the death and Resurrection of his Son into
which we are baptized.

*Loving Father, you are the author of my creation and my re-creation!
Help me to glimpse your eternal and infinite love for me, and make
it the foundation of my life.*

Equal Opportunity

Father Herald Joseph Brock, C.F.R.

[The people] brought the one who was once blind to the Pharisees. Now Jesus had made clay and opened his eyes on a sabbath. So then the Pharisees also asked him how he was able to see. He said to them, "He put clay on my eyes, and I washed, and now I can see." (Jn 9:13-15)

Apparently not satisfied with the evident meaning of simple facts, the crowd of uncertain onlookers turns to the religious experts for an authoritative interpretation. The Pharisees were an extremely rigorous sect of first-century Judaism that emphasized ultra ritual purity. Because of the number and complexity of religious regulations, practically speaking, such observance was reserved to the wealthy who had the luxury of not becoming too involved in the messier aspects of day-to-day survival. This combination of riches and rigor established them as a class of religious elite with a strong tendency toward spiritual snobbery.

While there is certainly a need for experts in theology, their contributions can never substitute for the indispensable role of authentic religious experience in the life of ordinary believers. No one is exempt from the privilege and necessity of examining the facts, verifying the proposals, and probing the path pointed out by Christ. Others can accompany me in this process, but no one can do it for me, otherwise my faith remains at best a fragile superficial religious affiliation—if it remains at all. The true authority is one who helps me to see the facts more clearly, recognize their meaning more easily, and undergo this process of personal verification more effectively.

Part of the wonderful newness of Christianity is that it offers everyone an equal opportunity to encounter Christ and grow in holiness. Simple Franciscan Blessed Brother Giles once asked the erudite doctor Saint Bonaventure if an uneducated person could love God as much as a scholar. When Bonaventure replied that such a person could love him even more, Giles ran out, grabbed a startled old woman and told her that if she loved God she could be greater than a doctor of theology. That message should grab and startle us, too.

Father, give me a profound awareness of the opportunity I have to encounter personally and respond directly to your Son at every moment and juncture of my life.

Observing the Sabbath Faithfully

Father Herald Joseph Brock, C.F.R.

*So some of the Pharisees said, "This man is not from God,
because he does not keep the sabbath." [But] others said,
"How can a sinful man do such signs?" And there was a division
among them. So they said to the blind man again, "What do
you have to say about him, since he opened your eyes?"
He said, "He is a prophet." (Jn 9:16-17)*

The Pharisees had a tragically impoverished understanding of the faith of Israel, one they enforced with fierce fidelity. Religion ended up reduced to a kind of empty shell, leaving only the strictures of the law without the hope of the Promise or the intimacy of the Covenant, making exaggerated legal observance the exclusive criterion of faithfulness. This faulty premise leads to flawed conclusions, especially in the case of Jesus' supposed violation of the sabbath by healing the man born blind. It reaches the extreme of reasoning in reverse.

For the Pharisees the demands of the sabbath rest are apparently absolute and unyielding. Though Jesus exposes their inconsistency when it comes to caring for livestock (cf. Lk 13:15 and Mt 12:11-12), they refuse to accept that it's lawful to do good to people and save human life (cf. Mk 3:4) on that day. They seem to have forgotten the origin of the sabbath in the safeguarding of creation, and the fact that the injunction to keep it holy is part of what Pope Benedict XVI called the law of liberty, the commandments given to Israel to preserve their freedom after their exodus from slavery. The sabbath was meant to protect us from becoming slaves to work, not to prevent us from doing good. Restoring God's intent for creation, especially in the lives of the children who bear his image, is absolutely consistent with the meaning of the sabbath.

The Pharisees are easy targets, and there's a kind of smug satisfaction in denouncing them that can blind us to the danger of a peculiarly Catholic version of their mistake. Dostoevsky's description of the Grand Inquisitor in *The Brothers Karamazov* bears an eerie resemblance to the way the Pharisees treat Jesus. Let's be wary of reducing religion to a complicated game with intricate rules that ends up betraying what it pretends to protect.

Father, help me live the law of freedom that protects me from slavery to sin, and joyfully do good and safeguard life on the Sabbath and on every other day!

Mounting Evidence

Father Herald Joseph Brock, C.F.R.

*Now the Jews did not believe that he had been blind and gained
his sight until they summoned the parents of the one who had
gained his sight. They asked them, "Is this your son, who you say
was born blind? How does he now see?" His parents answered
and said, "We know that this is our son and that he was born
blind. We do not know how he sees now, nor do we know who
opened his eyes. Ask him, he is of age; he can speak for himself."*
(Jn 9:18-21)

I t is an unfortunate tendency in human nature that when facts
don't fit into our preconceived schema of understanding, we
are more likely to try to alter the facts than revise our way
of thinking. As the story of the healing of the man born blind
unfolds, the increasing strain of the Jewish authorities to try to fit
the round peg of the mounting evidence into the square hole of
their prepackaged interpretation stretches the dramatic tension of
the narrative almost to the breaking point. And others are inevitably
drawn into this conflicted dynamic and provoked into making some
kind of response.

Once it becomes clear that the man's straightforward statement of
what took place can't be contradicted, and the somewhat inescapable
conclusion that it was done by "a prophet" can't be refuted, the
authorities seek to undermine the man's credibility by calling into
question the reality of his blindness in the first place. In this they
try to intimidate the man's parents by underscoring the supposed
impossibility of what in fact has occurred and demanding an
explanation. To their credit they identify the man as their son and
reaffirm his blindness from birth. To their disgrace they avoid taking
a stand on the central question, and put their son back in the hot
seat—a mixed scorecard.

Scientists and social theorists speak of "paradigm shifts" that take
place when new evidence acquires the "critical mass" necessary to
overthrow an existing theory that no longer adequately explains
reality, and forces new conclusions. Perhaps this helps explain what
happens when the imposing presence of Jesus and the proportions of
his person cause our prejudices to collapse, leaving us with the only
adequate explanation of his identity. The vain efforts to suppress this
truth and alter these facts is like trying to hold back a tidal wave.

*Father, help me to allow the truth and reality of who your Son Jesus
is to overthrow my mind and heart. Give me the honesty and the
courage to recognize and bear witness to him.*

Courage Contrasted by Fear

Father Herald Joseph Brock, C.F.R.

[The healed man's] parents said this because they were afraid
of the Jews, for the Jews had already agreed that if anyone
acknowledged [Jesus] as the Messiah, he would be expelled
from the synagogue. For this reason his parents said,
"He is of age; question him."
(Jn 9:22-23)

S cholars say that at least part of the reason this story was included in the Gospel was to encourage later Christians who were facing similar expulsion from the synagogue because they acknowledged Jesus as the Messiah. If that's so, the narrative also subtly touches on another challenge that many later believers would face: the wedge that is driven into a family because of the willingness (or unwillingness) of some to take a stand for Christ.

Though it's impossible to know for sure, there is reason to hope— because of the force of his encounter with Jesus and the courage and confidence it gave him—that the man healed of blindness was ultimately able to forgive his parents for abandoning him in the midst of the ordeal with the authorities. Clearly they were overcome by fear. And there would be the later example of Jesus himself, betrayed and abandoned by—and yet forgiving—his closest friends.

Perhaps the shadow of the doubts and denials of some becomes the backdrop against which the even more heroic witness of a few shines with greater intensity and vividness. And perhaps the even more magnified testimony of the few somehow becomes the forgiveness and redemption of the many who faltered. There is a quite moving and dramatic prayer attributed to an anonymous concentration camp prisoner that reads:

> O Lord, remember not only the men and women of good will, but also those of ill will. But do not remember all the suffering they have inflicted on us; remember the fruits we have brought, thanks to this suffering—our comradeship, our loyalty, our humility, our courage, our generosity, the greatness of heart which has grown out of all this, and when they come to judgment, let all the fruits which we have borne be their forgiveness.

Father, help me to recognize even in the failures and betrayals of
others that affect me an opportunity to love you even more, and
give me the greatness and freedom of heart to forgive.

181

Assuming Too Much

Father Herald Joseph Brock, C.F.R.

So a second time [the Jews] called the man who had been blind and said to him, "Give God the praise! We know that this man is a sinner." He replied, "If he is a sinner, I do not know. One thing I do know is that I was blind and now I see."
(Jn 9:24-25)

The assumptive close is a sales technique in which the seller acts as if the open question of whether the shopper will indeed make a purchase or not has already been settled, and moves on to other secondary questions that depend upon and specify (how many? what color?) the implied decision to buy. It is a variation of the broader strategy of treating an unverified proposition as established fact, putting anyone who might disagree in the uncomfortable position of seeming to contradict commonly agreed upon knowledge. The way this technique works is to distract us from the essential question and get us to focus on what is secondary. If the secondary can be established as already settled, we are coerced out of consistency to reason backward to the assumed essential.

The once blind man in John chapter 9 may have known little about sales techniques, but perhaps his former lack of sight made him more attentive and astute with regard to verbal communication. In any case, in light of the attempted manipulation by the authorities, his lucid testimony emerges as all the more remarkable. He remains steadfastly fixed on the fact that is most evident to him ("I was blind before, but now I see") and refuses to accept assumptions or jump to conclusions about which he is not certain and which might call into question the fundamental fact about which he is certain.

Perhaps there's something we can learn from this man about how to navigate in the marketplace of ideas and information in which we live. We have to be very clear concerning that about which we are certain and that about which we are not, and very careful about not allowing that which is secondary and peripheral to dictate and determine what is primary and essential. This is true most of all regarding our experience of Christ and our life in the Church.

Father, give me the clarity of mind and purity of heart to remain always fixed on that which is fundamental, and never be distracted from your Son, who is Truth and Life in Person.

Why Are You Asking?

Father Herald Joseph Brock, C.F.R.

So [the Jews] said to [the healed man], "What did he do to you? How did he open your eyes?" He answered them, "I told you already and you did not listen. Why do you want to hear it again? Do you want to become his disciples, too?"
(Jn 9:26-27)

B adgering the witness. It's a tactic that's been around as long as there have been trials and courts of law: asking the same questions with slight variations repeatedly and antagonistically in order to confuse the person under scrutiny and cause him to contradict himself. It's hard to tell whether the man's questions in response ("Why do you want to hear it again? Do you want to become his disciples, too?") are innocent or tongue-in-cheek, but the effect is the same. It highlights the fact that the prosecutors are not really interested in learning the truth. Their questions are not sincere but manipulative, and are aimed at gaining the advantage and bringing about a predetermined outcome.

This man's interrogation by the Jewish authorities bears striking similarity to Jesus' adversarial encounters with the same crowd. On several occasions, both during his trial and before, Jesus refuses to reply to their questions because he knows the real answers don't matter to them. At other times, like the man in this passage, he challenges them on the real motivation behind their inquiries. Other men and women in the course of Christian history, mostly martyrs, have likewise been put on the witness stand in proceedings with purposes other than the search for truth. Saint Thomas More and Saint Joan of Arc are two that come to mind.

These examples help to distinguish the unique quality of Christian witness from political campaigns, public relations strategies, legal maneuvers, and marketing schemes. The latter all have a pragmatic goal of how to succeed and be effective in winning votes, opinions, arguments, sales. Christian testimony is different and focuses instead on substance and meaning, the *what* and the *why*, seeking to disclose the truth, above all, the truth about Jesus, that sets free and gives life. That should be our aim, too.

Father, please help me to be more concerned about truth than tactics, and more intent on bearing witness to truth than winning arguments.

Evasive Maneuvers

Father Herald Joseph Brock, C.F.R.

[The Jews] ridiculed [the healed man] and said, "You are that
man's disciple; we are disciples of Moses! We know that God
spoke to Moses, but we do not know where this one is from." The
man answered and said to them, "This is what is so amazing,
that you do not know where he is from, yet he opened my eyes."
(Jn 9:28-30)

When manipulation and intimidation don't achieve the desired effect of getting the healed man to change his testimony, the authorities turn to insult and ridicule to tarnish his reputation and undermine his stature. Beside the unquestioned divine origin of the authority of Moses, whom they claim to follow, they place the "dubious" authority of Jesus, the origin of which they assert is unknown. Clearly what is doubtful should give way before what is certain, right?

This deliberate doubt, this intentional uncertainty on the part of those who claim to be well-educated and well-informed (and so should know better) shocks the man. He's astonished because there's a clear signpost that points to the answer: the fact that Jesus opened his eyes—a point which the interrogators continually evade. The obvious implication is that the power to perform that extraordinary deed came from God. But the officials can't see that, won't see that. There's a difference between not knowing and refusing to know, and this is a case of willful ignorance.

In this era of heightened psychological awareness, most of us are familiar with the concept of a defense mechanism. It's a consistent subconscious pattern of distorted perception and response that "protects" us from facing a reality that is regarded as a threat. The most common of these is denial of a painful truth. While defense mechanisms per se operate subconsciously, if we're honest we can recognize that there are times when we consciously cooperate with the evasion and deliberately activate the defenses, both as individuals and as groups. The problem is that the costs are high and the results are disastrous.

Let's never be afraid of welcoming a truth that can set us free, above all the Truth that is a Person. It would be foolish and tragic to "protect" ourselves from Jesus.

Father, help me to drop all my defenses, objections, and excuses to
be able to welcome your Son with open arms and an open heart,
and allow him to lead me into truth, life, and freedom.

The Absolute Exceptionality of Jesus

Father Herald Joseph Brock, c.f.r.

"We know that God does not listen to sinners, but if one is devout and does his will, he listens to him. It is unheard of that anyone ever opened the eyes of a person born blind. If this man were not from God, he would not be able to do anything."

(Jn 9:31-33)

Pushed over the edge by the authorities' outrageous refusal to admit the obvious, our man goes on the offensive and drives his point home: *Opening the eyes of someone born blind is something no one ever did anywhere at any time, until now.* And those eyes happen to be mine! It's completely unheard of, something totally new and surprising, unquestionably a miracle from God, something the Lord would never do through someone who was unfaithful to him. To say anything else just doesn't square with the facts.

This kind of singular event and superlative language isn't restricted to this passage. It's something that punctuates all the Gospel narratives. "Never before has anyone spoken like this one" (Jn 7:46). "Nothing like this has ever been seen in Israel" (Mt 9:33). "Who then is this whom even wind and sea obey?" (Mk 4:41). "A great prophet has arisen in our midst,…God has visited his people" (Lk 7:16).

Perhaps the most compelling evidence as to the uniqueness and identity of Jesus is not found in events that take place outside of us, but rather in the response that Jesus evokes from within us, the internal earthquake he provokes, the enduring fascination he generates, the overpowering attraction he radiates. Albert Einstein once said that he was "enthralled by the luminous figure of the Nazarene…. No one can read the Gospels without feeling the actual presence of Jesus. His personality pulsates in every word. No myth is filled with such life."

The Mystery standing before me in Christ corresponds like nothing else to the "criteria" within me: the needs and longings of my heart, my desire, my destiny, what I've been looking for and waiting for and created for. Saint Francis of Assisi once spent a whole night in prayer repeating two questions: "Who are you, O Lord? And who am I?" The answers are related.

Who are you, Father, and who am I? Help me to discover the only complete and satisfying answer to those questions revealed in your Son, Jesus.

185

Expanding Freedom Predisposed to Goodness

Father Herald Joseph Brock, C.F.R.

[The Jews] answered and said to [the healed man],
"You were born totally in sin, and are you trying to teach us?"
Then they threw him out.
When Jesus heard that they had thrown him out, he found him
and said, "Do you believe in the Son of Man?" He answered and
said, "Who is he, sir, that I may believe in him?" (Jn 9:34-36)

The now-seeing man's last reproach pops the blister of the Pharisees' phony piety, and out oozes all the venom of their arrogance and contempt for this "ordinary" man. Their arsenal of intimidation depleted, they take the one remaining step of expelling him.

It's clear by now, though, that this man is anything but ordinary, and it's worthwhile considering two of his exceptional qualities. The first is the amazing (and expanding) freedom he displays in adhering to the truth despite the escalating animosity of the authorities. The more hostile they become, the more adamantly he asserts the truth. This is a very real, though quite different, kind of freedom. Freedom is often conceived of as an absence of constraint or the ability to pursue one's preferences. Here we see it as the inner strength to face without collapsing whatever "powers" may threaten our humanity—like William Wallace in the last scene of the film *Braveheart*, who would rather endure prolonged torture than contradict his convictions. His final cry: "Freedom!"

The other is a predisposition in the heart of this man to welcome truth and affirm goodness. So many of our responses to life depend on this preexisting quality of heart. We tend to face reality either from a jaundiced perspective as something to dominate, control, or protect ourselves from (because it's overwhelmingly negative). Or we approach it as something fundamentally positive, to be welcomed with openness and simplicity of heart. This is what Jesus means by becoming childlike in order to enter the Kingdom of God.

This man's use of his reason and freedom to adhere to the truth, and his heart's predilection for goodness that enables him to recognize the exceptionality of Jesus, lead him to the very threshold of faith: "Do you believe in the Son of Man?" "Who is he, sir, that I may believe in him?"

Father, give me courage and freedom to adhere to the truth, and openness and simplicity of heart to welcome goodness, especially as they are revealed in the face and heart of your Son.

Faith: Reason Transcending Itself

Father Herald Joseph Brock, C.F.R.

Jesus said to [the healed man], "You have seen him and the one speaking with you is he." He said, "I do believe, Lord," and he worshiped him. Then Jesus said, "I came into this world for judgment, so that those who do not see might see, and those who do see might become blind."
(Jn 9:37-39)

The interplay between faith and the metaphor of sight comes to the fore in a pointedly paradoxical way in the final verses of this chapter: Do you believe? Who is he that I may believe? You are seeing him. I believe! The "judgment" of Jesus seems to consist in flip-flopping the status of the blind and the seeing, and is part of the larger theme of the "great reversal" that permeates the Gospels.

Seeing is a way of knowing, something that puts us in direct contact with the reality it enables us to perceive, or at least it's meant to be. Although faith is often misrepresented as a kind of subjective sentimentality, the Church's intellectual tradition has always insisted that it, too, is a way of knowing. Faith is not an irrational leap into the absurd; rather, it is reason at its apex, reason transcending itself. Reason brings us to the threshold of mystery. It enables us to perceive our life and reality as something good given to us, originating from a source beyond us. Faith enables us to "see" that source not as a "what" but a "who," and to give it a name. It also enables us to recognize in Jesus that Source stepping onto the stage of human history as one of us. That is how the blind man's sight becomes sight in this story. Tragically, it's also how the Pharisees' sight terminates in blindness, by aborting this process and not allowing reason and knowledge to come to fruition in faith.

Perhaps an analogy will help. Reason is a road that brings us to the edge of a cliff that opens onto a canyon of immense majesty. Faith is a bridge that meets that road and enables us to cross over, enter into, and touch the breathtaking beauty on the other side. Together they form a single route leading to the same destination.

Father, I too want to believe and see. Help me to use all the gifts you have given me, above all my mind and the virtue of faith, to profess and worship your Son, Jesus Christ.

Seeing Our Blindness, Receiving Mercy

Father Herald Joseph Brock, C.F.R.

Some of the Pharisees who were with [Jesus] heard this and said to him, "Surely we are not also blind, are we?" Jesus said to them, "If you were blind, you would have no sin; but now you are saying, 'We see,' so your sin remains."

(Jn 9:40-41)

You would have thought that Jesus' solemn declaration at the end of the previous verse ("I came into this world for judgment, so that those who do not see might see, and those who do see might become blind," 9:39) would have been the perfect conclusion to the story, it packs such a punch. Yet—to our surprise—the story continues with a brief epilogue similar to the one that follows the conversation between Jesus and Peter in Jn 21:20-22. It's kind of like one of those bonus scenes that suddenly appear during the credits at the end of a film, and it enables John to make one last point.

A glint of hope flickers in the Pharisees' assertion of their non-blindness—not in the assertion itself, but in the "Surely" with which it begins and the "are we?" with which it ends. Those two tiny details hint at an uncertainty on their part, and transform their rebuttal into a semi-sincere question that represents a crack in the façade of their stubborn resistance. And there's much more than a glint of hope in the statement of Jesus that follows.

In our desire to be supermen and superwomen, to be "like gods" (Gn 3:5), we unwittingly condemn ourselves to unending internal turmoil. Pope Benedict XVI repeatedly warned that utopian ideologies lead to tyranny, and this is as true for the individual as it is for the state. The one advantage of original sin is that we are born needing Christ, needing him desperately. Our need is our greatest asset because it drives us to Christ, the only one who can fulfill it. The problem is not our blindness, but rather our blindness to our blindness. Once we acknowledge it, the remedy is close at hand.

Jesus has reminded us of this through the revelations of Divine Mercy to Saint Faustina: the greater my misery, the more abundant his mercy.

Father, help me not to be afraid of my need and my weakness, but rather let it be an occasion for me to cry out—in the name of your Son, Jesus—for your unfailing mercy.

The Name He Calls Is Mine

Monsignor Gregory E. S. Malovetz

"Amen, amen, I say to you, whoever does not enter a sheepfold through the gate but climbs over elsewhere is a thief and a robber. But whoever enters through the gate is the shepherd of the sheep. The gatekeeper opens it for him, and the sheep hear his voice, as he calls his own sheep by name and leads them out."
(Jn 10:1-3)

The small café was filled with customers, most of whom were tourists catching a quick lunch before the matinee. As I finished my lunch, my eyes met a woman with a tray looking for a seat. I told her I was leaving and the seat next to mine was free. Elated to have found two seats in the crowded room, she called to a friend also searching for a seat. The woman kept calling "Joyce," but could not be heard above the noise. Several more attempts were in vain. Realizing her frustration, I joined the effort. "Yo, Joyce," I yelled across the room. "We're over here." Making her way through the crowd, a grateful Joyce came over, but with a puzzled look asked, "Do I know you?" "Nope," I replied, "but here's your seat."

It is touching to think that biblical shepherds had names for their sheep. Often the name was based on some physical attribute. More than identifying the animal, a shepherd grew to understand the characteristics and needs of each member of the flock. Jesus uses this beautiful image to explain his relationship with his followers. Disciples are not a nameless group or a faceless flock. He knows not only our name, but also our hopes, our struggles, and the desire to find our place in the world. No matter where they are on the journey of life, Jesus wants his followers to believe he sees them and is calling them.

In our daily life, there are many things that can rob us of hope, joy, and peace. All around us there are voices that distract from what really matters. Daily stress and our own failures might make us doubt that there is a place for us in the flock that Jesus has gathered. In those moments, the first step is to stop, be quiet, and listen. He knows us and is calling our name.

Loving Father, give me the grace to be still and listen to the voice of your Son reminding me that my life is precious to him.

The Choice Is Yours

Monsignor Gregory E. S. Malovetz

"When [the shepherd] has driven out all his own, he walks ahead of them, and the sheep follow him, because they recognize his voice. But they will not follow a stranger; they will run away from him, because they do not recognize the voice of strangers."
(Jn 10:4-5)

They lay on their sides, sighing occasionally while their paws rapidly move as they dream. Several times a week, I watch two golden retrievers that belong to a friend. I have watched them grow from frisky puppies into the beautiful, intelligent, and active dogs they are today. After a day of walks and play, they can often be found in late afternoon asleep in my office. When it's time to take them home, I call them. But one of the dogs, who thoroughly enjoys the afternoon nap, only opens her eyes and wags her tail. Sometimes no amount of coaxing can convince her to leave her spot. But when she hears my voice say, "We're going home to see your dad," she bolts for the door.

It's easy to get stuck in life. Maybe our job is unfulfilling or a relationship is stale. There are times when it is hard to rouse ourselves from a resentment, an anger, or a disappointment. It can seem easier to stay where we are and dream of how things might be rather than change an attitude or make a new choice.

The truth of our faith is that Jesus comes to change our lives. He desires to lead us from our complacency and show us a new vision of the people we can be. The power of the Resurrection is not confined to the end of our lives when the Shepherd promises to lead us home. Every day the power of the Resurrection can move us from our tired, distorted view of life to seeing new possibilities.

None of this means that life will be without challenges. There will be many days when we prefer to nap rather than hear the call of Jesus to get up and take a chance. To get up and follow is a daily choice. The challenge is this: what would rouse you enough to take that chance?

Loving God, rouse me with your loving Spirit so that every day my choice will be to follow Jesus.

Listen to My Voice

Monsignor Gregory E. S. Malovetz

Although Jesus used this figure of speech, [the Pharisees]
did not realize what he was trying to tell them.
So Jesus said again, "Amen, amen, I say to you, I am the gate
for the sheep. All who came [before me] are thieves and robbers,
but the sheep did not listen to them. I am the gate. Whoever
enters through me will be saved, and will come in
and go out and find pasture." (Jn 10:6-9)

I am a peaceful person, but I am fighting a huge battle these days. The enemy is fierce, cunning, and deceptively cute. Groundhogs. They destroyed my carefully planted and arranged flowers. In replanting, I have read about every product that keeps them away. The new phase of the battle began on Friday. Before I went to sleep I checked my garden. I then woke up every hour on the hour, and looked out my bedroom window. By the time 4 AM came, I reminded myself that it is a sickness when you can't stop.

I am sure that more than a few of you have some good advice from your experience about how to deal with groundhogs. I know all about the traps, the sprays, and the organic pellets. But what advice would you give me if I were losing a more important battle? Jesus tells his followers that in life there will be things that rob our spirit and steal our hope. He knows there will be moments of chaos and confusion in the pasture of life. The doctor tells us the news is bad, a relative tries our patience, or our work is unfulfilling. Often it is a daily battle to keep focused, to realize some things are not in our control. It is a challenge to be attentive, but not obsessed. The promise of the Shepherd is that he stands with us in all those moments.

How has your experience as a follower of Christ helped you in the battles and struggles of life? What advice would you give me? You could give me a spiritual book, tell me a story, or offer to pray for me. Sometimes our first impulse is to do or say something. Or you could sit with me in the pasture, and listen to my voice.

Loving Father, give me the courage each day to stand with those
who are losing the battle and need my listening heart.

Refreshing the Flock

Monsignor Gregory E. S. Malovetz

"A thief comes only to steal and slaughter and destroy; I came so that they might have life and have it more abundantly. I am the good shepherd. A good shepherd lays down his life for the sheep."
(Jn 10:10-11)

"Wait," he said, "I'll buy it for you." I heard those words while waiting to buy lemonade from a street vendor. A man with a child in a stroller was attempting to buy drinks with a credit card. Since the vendor only took cash, the man began to walk away, until the person behind him offered to buy the drinks. The man said it was not necessary, but the stranger behind him insisted. Pressed for what he wanted, the man replied he just wanted water. But the stranger looked at him and said, "But what were you *really* going to get." The reply, "A smoothie for my daughter and lemonade for me." The stranger took out some cash and smiled, "Then that, my friend, is what we are going to get."

At night, a shepherd would lie down at the opening of the pen where the sheep were kept. Lying there assured the flock's protection. No one could go in or out without first encountering the shepherd. Jesus has this image in mind when he says he will lay down his life for the sheep. Of course, we understand the cross as that key moment. Yet, throughout his ministry, there are countless moments when Jesus lays his life to protect, to encourage, and to refresh the parched lives of his sheep. A word he speaks, a glance he gives, where he eats, and a choice he makes. So many of those moments put Jesus in peril with those who do not understand. But to his flock, they are moments as refreshing as a cool drink.

We too are called to lay down our lives. Too often we misunderstand this call, thinking we are meant to do something big or challenging. Many times it is as simple as responding to the hopes and needs of a person standing in front of us.

Loving Father, open my eyes to the needs of those around me, and let my listening heart respond in love.

Embracing the Work

Monsignor Gregory E. S. Malovetz

"A hired man, who is not a shepherd and whose sheep are not his own, sees a wolf coming and leaves the sheep and runs away, and the wolf catches and scatters them. This is because he works for pay and has no concern for the sheep." (Jn 10:12-13)

E very afternoon at five I would log on, hold my breath, and—dare I admit it—cross my fingers. Having received a summons for jury duty, my instructions were to check each day if my number had been called. Of course, I wanted to do my civic duty, but was glad each day when I found my number was not chosen. This continued until the end of the week when the website thanked me for my time and availability. It concluded with this message: *This means your term of service is over.*

For most people, a job involves a certain amount of hours for a particular number of days. Some jobs are salaried positions, while others work for an hourly wage. While some people may take work home, there are many others for whom work is over at the end of the day.

Jesus uses the image of the hired man and the shepherd to emphasize his total commitment to his followers. Jesus never withholds mercy and forgiveness because he is "off the clock." Serving others is not a job, but rather a way of life. Every human encounter is an opportunity to reveal the presence of God and the power of God's love.

We often confuse being a volunteer with being a disciple. There is a clear beginning, middle, and end to the work of a volunteer. Discipleship is a way to live every hour of every day. Disciples realize that when we put limits on our service and love, we scatter and do harm to the flock.

The flock of Jesus will never get the message I received. Our term of service is never over. No matter how difficult the moment, how lazy or distracted we become, there are people in our life needing to be led to Jesus. It is hard and it is a challenge, but we do the work, because we have heard his voice.

Loving Father, in my work today—at home, at work, or at school— let me see the moment you are calling me to do the work of Jesus.

The Flock We Do Not See

Monsignor Gregory E. S. Malovetz

"I am the good shepherd, and I know mine and mine know me, just as the Father knows me and I know the Father; and I will lay down my life for the sheep. I have other sheep that do not belong to this fold. These also I must lead, and they will hear my voice, and there will be one flock, one shepherd."

(Jn 10:14-16)

Sitting in the back of a cab, the businessmen took in the sights of the city as they made their way to dinner. Several homeless people were spotted on the streets, some quite young while others appeared bizarre in behavior. A conversation began about the world we live in, these lazy homeless on the street, how they live off others and are unwilling to get a job. As the animated talk continued in a disparaging way, one man—a relative of mine—stayed quiet. The men noticed and asked why he was silent. He explained that he did not want them to feel bad, but they should know his son is an addict and is homeless. "I don't know where he is," he told them, "and I was thinking one of those young people could be him."

When Jesus says he has other sheep, he is not referring to cute animals grazing in another field. He is thinking about the poor, the misunderstood, and those who had chosen so badly there seemed to be no hope. For Jesus, it does not matter where they are or how they got there. What matters is that they know he is looking for them and cares for them.

As the flock of Jesus, we must extend our hearts to the other sheep. Sometimes they are the homeless and the addict. And at times it is your child, too focused on Facebook and who needs to see a bigger world. It's the family member who doesn't come to church and needs you to ask "will you come with me," even if every week the answer is no. It's people complaining at the cocktail party about the Church, who need you to acknowledge the complaints but speak about the grace. The other sheep will not come to Jesus because of program or policy. But they might just come if we're willing to go to them.

Loving Father, I pray this day for those I do not understand, and ask you to give me the grace to remember they belong to the one flock.

The Power We Need

Monsignor Gregory E. S. Malovetz

"This is why the Father loves me, because I lay down my life in order to take it up again. No one takes it from me, but I lay it down on my own. I have power to lay it down, and power to take it up again. This command I have received from my Father."
(Jn 10:17-18)

I looked at the calendar and then looked out the window. It was indeed October and a major snowstorm was falling outside. As I saw the tree limbs bend close to electric lines, it happened: the power went out. There is that moment when you freeze, wondering what to do next. Then came the moment of relief: my generator in the garage. A previous power outage of several days prompted that purchase. As night began to fall, I quickly connected the generator to two lights, the microwave, and a radio. In the middle of the night I was awakened by the power returning as lights came on, the computer rebooted, and the furnace resumed its work. I remember lying on my bed and thinking: How much power do we have and how much power do we need?

Jesus knows that the power he needs to be the shepherd has nothing to do with wealth, social status, or academics. The power he needs is the grace of God—the power of the Spirit—that enables him to be a light in the darkness of the world. He will lead his followers to understand that God's grace is the power that will help them forgive when it is difficult, or stand firm when their heart is broken. It is always tempting to think that having more money, a better job, or a family who is more cooperative will get us through. Jesus assures us grace is the only power that can truly help us rise after we have fallen.

I get out of bed and start shutting off lights, wondering why I had so many on. As I lie back down I realize there will be future outages. But more importantly there will be other kinds of darkness. I am grateful for the power of Christ's light, realizing it is the only power I need.

Loving Father, in times of darkness, let me turn to you, confident that your powerful grace will lead me.

Getting It Right

Monsignor Gregory E. S. Malovetz

*Again there was a division among the Jews because of [Jesus']
words. Many of them said, "He is possessed and out of his mind;
why listen to him?" Others said, "These are not the words of one
possessed; surely a demon cannot open the eyes of the blind,
can he?" (Jn 10:19-21)*

Shortly after Christmas I stopped in a department store to buy
a small item. As I went to check out, I was stunned at the
long line. I soon realized the line was not for purchases, but
for exchanges and returns. The area became crowded with people
getting in the wrong lines, so one of the customers began to direct
traffic. At one point she looked at the long line, looked at me, and
asked, "Can you believe that many people got it wrong?"

You may have the talent to pick out just the right gift. The challenge
of life, however, is whether we understand and live the gift that
Jesus offers us each day. Many people in his time cannot believe
this message Jesus lives. All this talk of God's care and a flock that
includes even the most unloved is too much for them. Rather than
embrace the message Jesus offers, they rigidly hold on to what is
safe and predictable. It is easier to dismiss Jesus as crazy instead of
looking at how his message could change them.

The work of a disciple is to embrace the message and live it. It is
our life's work to try and get it right. That does not mean we have
to become theological giants. It does mean we have to open our
hearts to Jesus who says that he desires to be your shepherd, even
when you are possessed by other things.

Sometimes we are possessed by anger or disappointment. We
get busy and distracted. Those are the moments when Jesus will
be found with his gifts of love and grace. Sometimes we may want
to return those gifts, thinking there may be something better. Our
eyes are opened when we realize these are the gifts that are worth
keeping, because the shepherd we follow is that good.

*Loving Father, open my eyes to your presence so that I will always
be possessed by your love.*

The Walk of Winter

Monsignor Gregory E. S. Malovetz

The feast of the Dedication was then taking place in Jerusalem.
It was winter. And Jesus walked about in the temple area on
the Portico of Solomon. So the Jews gathered around him
and said to him, "How long are you going to keep us
in suspense? If you are the Messiah, tell us plainly."
(Jn 10:22-24)

Walking a dog is a spiritual ritual, if your eyes are open. I learned this years ago when I would walk my dog down the same street every morning. Over the years our path would be the same, but the change of seasons always gave a new vision. While the budding of spring, the warmth of summer, and the brilliant leaves of fall were all beautiful, it was in the winter that you could see most clearly. With the trees bare and crisp, white snow on the ground, winter offered a clear vision, even on a gloomy day. Deer usually hidden by the blooming trees would appear in the distance, reminding us that we were not alone.

The feast of the Dedication took place in winter. Some believe John includes this detail not to tell us the time of year, but that the weather is gloomy. It is in the midst of rainy weather that Jesus walks in the Temple area and is hounded by his detractors. They want to know who he really is.

As we walk through life, we too want to know who Jesus really is. Not the holy card or the image in Scripture. Who is Jesus for me right now? No matter how profound our faith, there are those moments of questioning. It's not just when something bad happens or life seems to be out of control. It's the gloomy days, when life is boring or we feel no energy. Those days when nothing seems new and the daily grind exhausts us. It is the moments when we work hard and try harder, and still wonder what's the point?

When those gloomy moments come, when it's a spiritual winter in May, I find the need to get up and walk. The walking reminds me that I am called to follow the Shepherd. The walking helps me to see he is there.

Loving Father, nudge me in those dull moments of life to get up
and believe I will be shown the way.

The Voice He Desires to Hear

Monsignor Gregory E. S. Malovetz

Jesus answered [the Jews], "I told you and you do not believe. The works I do in my Father's name testify to me. But you do not believe, because you are not among my sheep. My sheep hear my voice; I know them, and they follow me."

(Jn 10:25-27)

"Of course you know who she is." He is always insistent and somewhat perplexed that I do not remember. Over the years my twin brother has attended our high school reunions. I have never attended any. When he returns he calls and reports who was there, what they are doing, and how they look. Having gone to several schools and lived in a number of places, my remembrance of people from high school is sketchy. My brother is usually undeterred from giving me all the details even after my usual response, "I have no idea of whom you are talking about."

Does Jesus remember me and does Jesus know me? And more importantly, what exactly does he know about me? I think about those questions when faced with the words of Jesus saying he knows the sheep of his flock. It is curious that many will often think first of their failings and sins when considering what Jesus remembers about them. Perhaps that is understandable. But if the shepherd we follow is good, then I believe he knows and hears much more. He hears my voice.

The works that Jesus does are more than turning water into wine or making the lame walk. The true miracles are when he listens to others. He hears their fears and worries, their hopes and their dreams. The more he listens, the more people believe they can rise above their fears and worries and follow a Jesus who will lead them to their hopes and their dreams. This is the work that shows he is the true shepherd of the flock.

It is the work Jesus will do in our life today. It is the miracle he wants to perform. We always have a choice. Believing Jesus knows me can lead to worry, or it can bring relief. You can only follow if you believe he wants to hear your voice.

Loving Father, let me always trust that your Son hears my voice, and believe that he loves the person I am.

We Make the Journey Together

Monsignor Gregory E. S. Malovetz

"I give [my sheep] eternal life, and they shall never perish.
No one can take them out of my hand. My Father, who has
given them to me, is greater than all, and no one can take
them out of the Father's hand. The Father and I are one."
(Jn 10:28-30)

You see them on the street. Sometimes they are on a class trip visiting a museum or a park. I have seen them twenty strong, often wearing the same T-shirt or school uniform. They are usually younger children whose eyes are wide as they take in all the sights around them. And they are holding hands, linked together, not only to protect one from getting lost. Their hands together seem to say *we are on this journey together*. Guided by a few teachers, they are frequently reminded to watch where they are going and not to let go.

I watch this army of children moving up the avenue, playful, laughing, and full of grace. As they disappear from view, I wonder, when does it happen? When is the moment that we "grow up," keep our eyes on our own paper, and let go? When do we let go of our hands and forget we are on this journey together?

Jesus assures us that God's hand is lovingly placed on our lives. Nothing in life will ever cause God to let go. Not our poor choices or our bad attitude. Nothing. We, however, let go because other things seem more important or attractive. We are reaching for many things, and our hands get full of stuff. We forget the hand of God who wants to give us life. We fail to notice the hands of others reaching out to us. The promise of the shepherd is that God's hand is always extended to us, ready to grasp our life in forgiveness and love.

Look for a moment at your hands. What are you holding on to these days? If your life were to end this day, would you be glad you held on to those things. What could you drop from your hands today, so that your hand might grasp another who is reaching out to you?

Loving Father, with open hands I pray, grateful that you will always hold me in your care.

The Dent We Can Heal

Monsignor Gregory E. S. Malovetz

The Jews again picked up rocks to stone [Jesus]. Jesus answered them, "I have shown you many good works from my Father. For which of these are you trying to stone me?" The Jews answered him, "We are not stoning you for a good work but for blasphemy. You, a man, are making yourself God."

(Jn 10:31-33)

I notice him as I put my groceries in the trunk. A man was sitting in a car parked next to mine. His window was down and he looked annoyed. I didn't at first realize his glare meant he had been waiting for me. As I moved to open my door, I said hello. In an accusing voice he asks me, "Did you put the dink in my car?" Not understanding, I replied, "Excuse me?" He repeated the question and pointed to a small scratch toward the back of his car. Apparently he thought I hit his car when I opened my door. I assured him I did not, but his look said he thought I was lying. Noticing the location of the scratch, I opened my door, proving that I could not have scratched his car. He was still annoyed, and before I drove away he said unconvincingly, "I guess I didn't think of that."

The need to be right. As I go through life, I have come to believe this attitude is the cause of so many relationship problems. I am sure your intentions were bad; I know this is the only way to do things; you are the one with the problem. Slowly this attitude chips away at others and us. It creates more than a little dink or scratch. It can kill our spirit.

When the people pick up rocks to throw at Jesus, they want to silence him. They want to punish him for saying things they think are blasphemy. But it all comes from the need to be right. They cannot accept that God might have another way of acting in the world and the works of Jesus might just be that way.

What dink or scratch or dent could you heal with the Spirit's help, because you let go of the need to be right?

Loving Father, help me to let go; give me patience and understanding; use my life to heal the spirit of others.

The Clarity We Seek

Monsignor Gregory E. S. Malovetz

Jesus answered [the Jews], "Is it not written in your law, 'I said,
"You are gods"'? If it calls them gods to whom the word of God
came, and scripture cannot be set aside, can you say that the
one whom the Father has consecrated and sent into the world
blasphemes because I said, 'I am the Son of God'?"
(Jn 10:34-36)

Checking into the hotel, the woman at the reception desk began to explain all the amenities. She pointed out the restaurants, the location of the gym, and some special features of my room. She then moved to the subject of the minibar. Taking her time, she carefully explained that the minibar was weight activated and sensitive to motion. Picking up a bottle of soda and putting it back would mean it would appear on your bill. Putting the candy back after you decided you wanted pretzels would find both on the bill. Her long explanation seemed to indicate that she had dealt with many angry guests who were billed for items they did not consume. She asked me if I clearly understood. I replied, "All you had to say was, 'You move it, you bought it.'"

We all like clarity. We like people to say what they mean. No long or detailed explanations. Just tell us clearly and simply. The three verses for this reflection contain a statement from Jesus that is hard to understand. Many long articles have been written about the possible meaning and explanation of Jesus' words. None gave me greater clarity.

But the words that stood out for me were these: "Scripture cannot be set aside." The opponents of Jesus used Scripture to try and discredit him. They failed to see the bigger picture of the Scripture, as well as Jesus' message. If they really moved the Scripture and held it close, they would not only buy it, but would embrace the powerful message Jesus insisted it contained.

If we are the flock of Jesus, then the daily challenge is to embrace the Scriptures. It is not enough to hear it proclaimed at Mass. Every day, we must reach into the Scripture and ask what it is saying to me. The more we move toward the Scripture, the more it will clearly move us.

Loving Father, open my heart this day to the Word; let it move me to follow your Son.

Experience on the Journey

Monsignor Gregory E. S. Malovetz

"If I do not perform my Father's works, do not believe me; but if I perform them, even if you do not believe me, believe the works, so that you may realize [and understand] that the Father is in me and I am in the Father." [Then] [the Jews] tried again to arrest [Jesus]; but he escaped from their power.

(Jn 10:37-39)

It was a brilliant summer morning, just the kind of day to stroll through a street fair in Manhattan. There is laughing, and eating, and occasionally you hear snippets of conversation in many different languages. I stopped to look at some art, and heard one sentence that stayed with me for the rest of the day: "You are ruining this experience for me, so I think I will leave you here and go back to the hotel."

The places and names are different, but throughout the Gospels the experience people have of Jesus is always the same. The work of Jesus is to transform lives, transform institutions, and transform the world with love, forgiveness, and a burning heart for justice. When people have an experience of Jesus, they see before them a choice. They can follow in this new way and be part of his transforming kingdom, or they can walk away.

In all of these verses from chapter 10, the adversaries of Jesus have a troubling experience with him. In their eyes, he is ruining their understanding and experience of faith. They want physically to go after him, but in their hearts they walk away. These people have no power over Jesus because anger and arrogance change nothing.

My thoughts keep returning to that moment on the street and those words I heard from a person I could not see. I will never know what ruined the experience, but I suspect most of us could guess. The greater challenge is not what happened then, but what is happening now in your life. What is the experience people have of you in the place where you work, the school where you study, or the street where you live? How different would those places be if you entered realizing you may be the only experience of Jesus someone will have this day?

Loving Father, let me hear your voice calling me to let others see the saving and loving presence of Jesus in me.

Looking for Wonder

Monsignor Gregory E. S. Malovetz

[Jesus] went back across the Jordan to the place where John first baptized, and there he remained. Many came to him and said, "John performed no sign, but everything John said about this man was true." And many there began to believe in him.

(Jn 10:40-42)

I squinted my eyes and looked at my watch. It was 2:30 AM and my friend was at the door of the bedroom. "What's wrong?" I asked. The reply, "Nothing. Perseid Meteor Shower." Spending a few days at the beach, I had forgotten the news story that a great meteor shower would be visible in the early morning hours. My friend had not. Armed with towels, cushions, and binoculars, we headed down to the beach. Lying on the dunes, we looked up at the sky and waited for the show. Unfortunately, there was considerable cloud cover. While I didn't see a shower of meteors, I was rewarded with seeing at least five.

In those early morning hours, I thought: you can call it prayer or you can call it looking for wonder. The disciple of Jesus has to take time each day to be looking for the signs of grace and goodness. There is a lot of cloud cover in our lives. There may be economic challenges, health issues, or world news that make us wonder if God has lost control of the world. What is required of a disciple is to be willing to stop and look around at our life. Where are the signs of God's presence, even if they are as fleeting as a meteor in the sky?

Like a flock of sheep, the people follow Jesus across the Jordan. They follow him because in the midst of a dark and uncertain world, they see a glimpse of hope in Jesus. Opening their eyes, they begin to see in him the promise made by the Baptist: God will come, bringing a new light.

We fool ourselves into thinking that we could be saved from our problems if we were smarter or had more time. But it is the willingness to stop, look, and wonder at God's presence that will save our lives.

Loving Father, let me never be so busy or distracted that I do not take the time each day to wonder at the signs of your love.

Looking for Lazarus

Regis Martin

Now a man was ill, Lazarus from Bethany, the village of Mary and her sister Martha. Mary was the one who had anointed the Lord with perfumed oil and dried his feet with her hair; it was her brother Lazarus who was ill. So the sisters sent word to him, saying, "Master, the one you love is ill." (Jn 11:1-3)

Asked once by an interviewer what bothered him most about life, the poet Robert Lowell answered ruefully, "That people die." What else have we to weep for but that, living in a fallen world, we are fated to die? "It is the blight man was born for," says the narrator of Gerard Manley Hopkins' haunting poem "Spring and Fall," to the young child who, wandering into the forest full of dying leaves, is suddenly moved to tears. "Margaret," he asks, "are you grieving/ Over Goldengrove unleaving?" And with brutal finality he tells her: "It is Margaret you mourn for."

If death awaits us in the end, sickness will be the road on which most of us travel. "All my life," Flannery O'Connor was wont to say, "death and suffering have been brothers to my imagination." She had never been anywhere but sick, a place, she said, "more instructive than a long trip to Europe…a place where nobody can follow."

Isn't this what strikes us on opening chapter 11 of John's Gospel? Not just that Lazarus is ill, but that he is *Everyman*. With repeated hammer blows, John hits us head-on with the news of our shared brokenness. And who is this fellow for whom two sisters will mobilize to summon Jesus? A single feature defines his life: silence. Like Joseph, spouse of Mary, he does not speak. Yet he is loved by Jesus, which greatly distinguishes him. That and the blessing of these remarkable women, the practical Martha, the prayerful Mary, whose company Jesus often came to Bethany to share. Especially now, of course, when word having gone out to him, Jesus must surely come to comfort and heal his friend. How can he refuse so blithe, so beguiling a request? Here are the two sides of the Church, active and contemplative, combining their gifts to urge Jesus to bring solace and healing to his friend. Indeed, to all who, like Lazarus, are sick.

Loving Father, solace of all who suffer, come quickly, we pray, to comfort and restore a broken and fallen world which only you can make whole.

The Languishing of Lazarus

Regis Martin

When Jesus heard this he said, "This illness is not to end in death, but is for the glory of God, that the Son of God may be glorified through it." Now Jesus loved Martha and her sister and Lazarus. So when he heard that he was ill, he remained for two days in the place where he was. (Jn 11:4-6)

Amid the raging winds of the storm that caused the wreck of the *Deutschland*, its last hours immortalized in thirty-five stanzas of harrowing, heart-stopping verse by Gerard Manley Hopkins, stood a tall, gaunt Franciscan nun, her voice rising above the storm's tumult, above even the cries of terrified passengers and crew, calling, "O Christ, Christ, come quickly!"

But did he come? Not, it seems, between the hours of midnight and dawn when the ship, wave upon wave having "rolled on her beam with ruinous shock," at last broke apart off the coast of England, pitching hundreds into the sea to die, including five Franciscan nuns exiled from their native land.

How startlingly reminiscent this is of the last hours spent by poor Lazarus! Who awaited Jesus no less longingly than did these doomed souls lost at sea. And why didn't he come sooner? What prevented him from leaving at once on hearing the news? Lazarus, after all, was his dearest friend. To delay coming seems strange, even heartless. A kind of death sentence. In his great work, *The Lord*, Romano Guardini tells us that in allowing Lazarus to die, "Jesus does something that seems monstrous." How could he abandon one whom he very much loved?

But hadn't he announced in advance that this illness would not end in death, but rather redound to his own glory? That here would be foreshadowing of a death toward which Jesus himself is moving, so that the delay along the way prefigures the time he too must spend in the nether world? So Lazarus' sickness unto death becomes a signpost pointing us to an ultimate vindication. The two days spent before leaving for Bethany, during which death appears victorious, become thus emblematic of the time of Christ's own entombment, utterly vanquished in Easter joy. As von Balthasar reminds us, Christ is so intensely alive he can afford to be dead.

Come, Father of unending life! May we receive in joy your saving presence in our lives, lest sickness and death leave us forsaken and alone.

Light of the World

Regis Martin

Then after this [Jesus] said to his disciples, "Let us go back to Judea." The disciples said to him, "Rabbi, the Jews were just trying to stone you, and you want to go back there?" Jesus answered, "Are there not twelve hours in a day? If one walks during the day, he does not stumble, because he sees the light of this world. But if one walks at night, he stumbles, because the light is not in him." (Jn 11:7-10)

If human life is a question that can only finally be answered in Christ, then what is the answer to the question that is *his* life? Can he look to himself for the meaning of his being? Since both his identity and mission stand in relation to the Father, everything proceeds from above. From all eternity he is the Word spoken by Another, who has no other Word to speak. And because he dwells in light unapproachable, there can be no end to the mystery of trying to parse his ways. The exercise of God's freedom, wholly impenetrable to the world, is revealed only through the life of the Son. Decisions made by Jesus, therefore, who comes to us out of the fullness of the Father, simply cannot be encompassed by the mind of the creature. "If all things were within our grasp," warns Gregory of Nyssa, "the Higher Power would not be beyond us." Intelligible, yes, but not the least comprehensible.

So when Jesus tells his disciples, "Let us go back to Judea," they are utterly baffled. Wasn't he nearly killed there? Surely it would be madness to return. But the counsels of human prudence are not for him; his purposes entirely transcend the calculations of men. Besides, does he not walk while the day is still light? How then can he stumble? Indeed, he is the light of the world. An intensity of light and life, no less, whose source and duration are eternal. Nothing can put out this light. And those who walk with him in the light, however strewn with suffering and death the path may be, will neither stumble nor fall. For bathed in this light, the radiance of God shall stream forth continuously, quickening the courage of those who choose to follow him back to Judea where "his hour," the ultimate triumph of the Father, awaits him.

Heavenly Father, give us the light of your Son, that we may have the clarity to see and the courage to follow, in faith, the path he first blazed through the world.

Life Vanquishes Death
Regis Martin

[Jesus] said this, and then told [his disciples], "Our friend Lazarus is asleep, but I am going to awaken him." So the disciples said to him, "Master, if he is asleep, he will be saved." But Jesus was talking about his death, while they thought that he meant ordinary sleep. (Jn 11:11-13)

"Beautifully Janet slept/ Till it was deeply morning." So begins a poem by John Crowe Ransom about a little girl who, upon awakening, goes in search of her beloved brown hen, only to find that "poor old Chucky" has died in the night, victim of "a transmogrifying bee." Stricken with grief, she turns to those whom she childishly imagines have the power to wake the dead, imploring them to bring him back to life. "And would not be instructed in how deep/ Was the forgetful kingdom of death."

If life is a journey, then at some point it comes to an end. There are no exemptions, no loopholes for the lucky few. "Like as the waves make for the pebbled shore," says Shakespeare, "So do our minutes hasten to their end." With each rise and fall of the sea, we are drawn nearer and nearer to death. Unless, that is, Christ were to reach in and rescue us from that dread, implacable sea. He whose capacity to lay hold of death, and thus turn it back to life, is foundational to his being God. He knows that death can have no claim upon him; neither dust nor sin can put him in harm's way. So in telling his disciples, "Our friend Lazarus is asleep, but I am going to awaken him," Jesus is putting them on notice that not only does he stand superior to the forces of darkness and death, but that he is free to return to life those whom it pleases him to raise. And, to be sure, standing in the shadow of poor Lazarus, a whole universe has fallen asleep, separated from a light that it simply hasn't the power to turn on. We are all waiting for *Someone* to bring us light and life.

Yet the disciples remain completely clueless, thus confirming in their very obtuseness the great darkness in which we all share. Jesus will soon put an end to such nonsense.

All-powerful Father, you who sent your Son to those who have fallen asleep in sin, grant us the grace to receive this healing Word and so awaken to a life that will never die.

Jesus the Ever-Greater God

Regis Martin

So then Jesus said to [his disciples] clearly, "Lazarus has died.
And I am glad for you that I was not there, that you may
believe. Let us go to him." So Thomas, called Didymus,
said to his fellow disciples, "Let us also go to die with him."
(Jn 11:14-16)

"Do tell me what you think of life," someone asked Henry James. "I think," replied the master, "it is a predicament which precedes death." Well, Lazarus has certainly had his predicament and, failing to survive it, he is now dead. Meanwhile, the news of his passing is announced by Christ, who appears determined to go to him. Why now? For what purpose if Christ, had he only gone to him in the first place, his friend might have been spared? And what does he mean when he tells his disciples that he is glad for their sake that he wasn't there?

These are questions that, as Pascal would say, take us by the throat. Because they turn on the whole matter of faith, of which neither the disciples nor ourselves have much to show. In fact, it was precisely for the grace of that faith, awaiting them (and us) in the future, that Jesus put off going to Lazarus. But in going to him now, Jesus is able all the more convincingly to demonstrate his capacity, owing to his being God, to destroy death. This will move them to place their confidence in him. Like children, they need to see in order to believe. And if Lazarus had been prevented from actually dying because Jesus was already there, how would they ever know Jesus has the power to break the kingdom of death in two?

Of course, they understand nothing of this at the moment. Constrained to see things in earthly terms only, they would sooner force the Lord of the universe onto a Procrustean bed, in which the "always greater" aspect disappears altogether, than to submit in nakedness of faith to the designs of a God beyond their capacity to know. Jesus will need to stretch them so that, while he will for ever exceed their reach, they may at least learn that an ever-greater God is a mystery worth every effort to grasp.

Loving Father, in sending your Son to Lazarus our brother, we glimpse the always-greater glory of your Mystery. Enlarge our faith so that, like Lazarus, we too may recognize the signs of your coming.

Giving Death Its Due

Regis Martin

When Jesus arrived, he found that Lazarus had already been in the tomb for four days. Now Bethany was near Jerusalem, only about two miles away. And many of the Jews had come to Martha and Mary to comfort them about their brother.
(Jn 11:17-19)

I once knew a fellow who, anytime he was asked how he was doing, would instantly reply, "I am decomposing." He lived a heap of years. Perhaps it was hyperbole that finally killed him. Nevertheless, the point survives his exaggeration of it. We are all decomposing. "Flesh fade and mortal trash/ Fall to the residuary worm," warns Gerard Manley Hopkins. "Man," he exclaims, "how fast his firedint, his mark on mind, is gone!" Nobody gets out alive. "We all are falling," writes Rainer Maria Rilke in the final stanza of "Autumn," a poem full of moving lament. "This hand falls./ And look at others: it is in them all." The unraveling that leads to the great Nightfall begins fairly soon, too. The moment we begin to be we are old enough to die. It is a point about which we have often and morosely been reminded. That spellbinder John Donne, for instance, in a sermon preached before the king, drew an image of "a winding sheet in our mother's womb," around which our lives are tightly, inexorably wrapped. "We come into the world wound up in that winding sheet; for we come to seek a grave." It is with the same tears that we observe both events, too: first birth, then death.

So when Jesus arrives four days after the body of Lazarus had first entered the tomb, the course of corruption will certainly have taken matters in hand. Signs of decay are not so easily disguised in a desert land. In fact, the situation appears quite hopeless. Isn't this why so many of the Jews have come to offer the usual funeral comforts to the family? But the gesture will prove both hollow, because they do not really believe, and ineffectual, because only the Lord can bring the kind of consolation that transforms sorrow into joy. At the least, however, their being there will furnish witnesses for the miracle Christ has come to perform.

All-powerful and ever-living Father, death can lay no claim on you. Grant, we beseech you, the grace so to overcome the curse of our mortality, that the sting of death shall leave no lasting hurt.

Martha's Moxie

Regis Martin

When Martha heard that Jesus was coming, she went to meet him; but Mary sat at home. Martha said to Jesus, "Lord, if you had been here, my brother would not have died. [But] even now I know that whatever you ask of God, God will give you."
(Jn 11:20-22)

I t is said that there are three kinds of people. Those who make things happen. Those who watch things happen. Then there are those who wonder what happened. Nothing ever happens to them, save only that they are fated to wander haplessly to their graves, their souls sent to the netherworld where, according to Dante, they join the ranks of the Futile, condemned for ever to chase after a whirling standard symbolizing the choices they never made. "Heaven cast them forth," he tells us in the *Inferno*, "their presence there would dim the light;/ Deep Hell rejects so base a herd,/ Lest sin should boast itself because of them."

To be sure, the ever-practical, always active Martha, is not one of these. Whatever needs to be done, she is there to do it. Her kind are the ones who make things happen, whether it's food or a fuss. Which is why she does not hesitate an instant in going out to meet Jesus on the road, there to accost him about doing something that, in her mind, he could so easily have done before. "Lord," she speaks almost accusingly, "if you had been here, my brother would not have died." What an amazing admission of faith! Such resolute confidence! Of course she cannot be certain of this apart from the hope that springs eternal in her heart. Here is that wonderful "thing with feathers," as Emily Dickinson calls it, "That perches in the soul/ And sings the tune without the words/ And never stops at all." Convinced that God will give Jesus anything he asks for, she simply knows that "even now" it is possible to bring her brother back, retrieving the lost loved one from the dank grave of death. This is real and honest hope, because the outcome of her desire does not depend on her, but on God, the Father, who will not refuse his Son anything.

Father in heaven, give us the grace of Martha always to persist trustingly in the certainty that nothing is impossible to those who love God.

Resurrection Is Real

Regis Martin

Jesus said to [Martha], "Your brother will rise." Martha said to him, "I know he will rise, in the resurrection on the last day." Jesus told her, "I am the resurrection and the life; whoever believes in me, even if he dies, will live, and everyone who lives and believes in me will never die. Do you believe this?"

(Jn 11:23-26)

O f all creatures great and small, man alone knows that he must fall. And death, the last rung on the ladder of finitude, awaits us in the end. Each man carries his own death before him, seeing it as the final cancellation of all that he might have done or become. So what happens when those we love die? When the shell of the self we rejoiced so recently to know is lowered into the ground? "The houses are all gone under the sea," writes T. S. Eliot, sounding the elegiac note. "The dancers are all gone under the hill."

O dark dark dark. They all go into the dark...

And if God himself were to descend into those dark "interstellar spaces, the vacant into the vacant"? What then? How vastly different death would then be! To the dead, certainly. And what about the living who, with stabbing, heartbreaking loss, mourn their passing? Yes, Lazarus must die. And those who loved him must bear the pain of his absence. Even if they were to follow him into those deep cavernous regions where the dead dwell—"to lie in cold obstruction," says Shakespeare, "and to rot"—it would do them no good. Like Orpheus in search of Euridice, none may return from that place with the dead in tow. Only God can reach into the darkness and bring them back. "Your brother will rise," Jesus tells Martha. Followed by that blinding, heart-stopping affirmation revealing the absolute, sundering uniqueness of the Christian claim: "I am the resurrection and the life..." Here is the music we most long to hear. Here the chord of hope is struck with majestic finality. "One short sleep past," the poet Donne reminds us, "we wake eternally;/ And death shall be no more; death thou shalt die." It is a song only Christ can play, which means that without the tuning fork of faith our ears will not be moved to hear it.

All-powerful God and Father, you are the true giver of life. Keep us safe in your Son's keeping, whom you sent into Sheol to bring the dead to life.

The Promised One Has Come

Regis Martin

[Martha] said to him, "Yes, Lord. I have come to believe
that you are the Messiah, the Son of God, the one
who is coming into the world."
When she had said this, she went and called her sister Mary
secretly, saying, "The teacher is here and is asking for you."
(Jn 11:27-28)

If the desire for God is a drive so deep within the human heart as to be almost indestructible, then God's answering response becomes an event of revelation no greater than which can be imagined. It is the sending of the Son who, in breaking himself to become our bread, invites us to a life of unending love and communion. The eternal Word enters the human estate in order to reach right to the heart of its brokenness, setting all things straight. "Never," said J. R. R. Tolkien, "was a tale told men would rather find true." What a nice touch to have the practical-minded Martha be among the first to strike the incomparable chord that carries the sound of its music. Scripture has given her one of the best lines in the Gospel, thus enabling her to pay Jesus the highest possible compliment, namely, her admission that he is indeed the Christ, the Anointed One from Above.

Clearly he knows himself to be the Messiah, but wishing others to come to an acknowledgement as well, it must please him to hear Martha say it. "Yes, Lord...you are the Messiah...the one who is coming into the world." How does she know? Only the grace of God can account for a certainty of belief this adamantine. "Faith," writes von Balthasar, "is the surrender of the finite person in his entirety to the infinite person." It is a submission of love, he tells us, "which in the temporal structure of existence...reveals itself as hope." And where does Martha go with the faith and the hope and the love that move her so deeply? She goes off to fetch her sister Mary, letting her know that Jesus is here, "asking for you." Such is the office of those in the active life: to go and alert the contemplatives for the loftiest pursuit of all, communion with the Lord. Her sister will be grateful for the summons.

All-merciful and loving Father, in giving us the God-Man to be our Redeemer, you delivered on your promise to set us free. We praise and glorify you for your surpassing goodness.

Longing for God

Regis Martin

As soon as [Mary] heard this, she rose quickly and went to [Jesus]. For Jesus had not yet come into the village, but was still where Martha had met him. So when the Jews who were with her in the house comforting her saw Mary get up quickly and go out, they followed her, presuming that she was going to the tomb to weep there. (Jn 11:29-31)

Was it Oscar Wilde who, on first seeing Niagara Falls, pronounced it altogether perfect, save for the fact that the water, had it only flowed the other way, would then be still more perfect? What a spectacular illustration of the Law of Tropism that would have been! If the tendency of all living things is to search out the light, then surely we ought to be able to witness water thirsting to return to its own ultimate source. Isn't that why the sunflower is so tall?

When tourists go to Rome they often visit the Pantheon, which is among the glories of the ancient world. The odd thing about it, however, is that there's a hole in the ceiling, stretching hundreds of feet into the air; so high, in fact, that when it rains the water never reaches ground zero, having evaporated en route. Actually, there is nothing the least bit odd about that opening: it is a symbol of the sheer universality of man's thirst for God, his yearning finally to be free of the limitations of space and time. "Oh, I have slipped the surly bonds of earth," exults the poet John Gillespie Magee. "Oh, I have trod/ The high untrespassed sanctity of space,/ Put out my hand, and touched the face of God." Call it the Law of Theo-tropism.

How perfectly it applies to the figure of Mary, whose longing to be with the Lord is so ardent and uncomplicated that on hearing news of Jesus, she rises at once and goes to him. Even as he has yet to arrive, Mary goes unhesitatingly to meet him. As if her thirst for God were so great, so consuming, that an intimation of the Blessed Presence had already made itself felt, filling her heart with the foretaste of waters that will never run dry. "All the way to heaven," Catherine of Siena tells us, "is heaven, because Christ is the Way."

Heavenly Father, source of life-giving waters, we ask you to lead us always to springs that will never run dry.

Troubled by Her Tears

Regis Martin

When Mary came to where Jesus was and saw him, she fell at his feet and said to him, "Lord, if you had been here, my brother would not have died." When Jesus saw her weeping and the Jews who had come with her weeping, he became perturbed and deeply troubled. (Jn 11:32-33)

The way to the Father, to the place where perduring peace may be found, does not permit us to circumvent the Son, for he is the only road that will take us there, catapulting us into the arms of God. And while we can never know this with an exactitude absolutely arithmetic, nevertheless, as Augustine assures us, "we know that there must be something we do not know towards which we feel driven." We can no more abstain from ardently desiring it than we can jump out of our skins. It is the flywheel that turns the engine of hope.

Which is why we may not dispense with faith, either, since the two are joined at the hip. It is, to quote the Letter to the Hebrews, "the substance of things hoped for; the proof of things not seen" (cf. 11:1). So powerful is the pull of faith, Pope Benedict told us, that it "draws the future into the present," giving us "something of the reality we are waiting for," so that it is no longer a blind groping in the dark.

Isn't this the faith and the hope that, taking hold of Mary at a level deeper even than that of her sister, sends her fleeing to Christ, moved to make a total gift of self? It is the grace of the purest possible readiness to receive whatever Jesus is prepared to give. She entrusts everything to him, evincing such complete and childlike confidence that Jesus himself undergoes a perturbation of spirit. Seeing the face of grief, of depthless human misery for which there is no remedy in this world, Jesus is moved to pity, his whole being "deeply troubled" by the realization that it was for such as these that he came to suffer and to die. The way to the Father mustn't sidestep the Son; nor may it bypass the cross. Bethany is but a way station en route to Calvary.

O most compassionate Father, your Son Jesus opened the very Heart of God to those who suffer. May our tears move you to look with compassion on the sorrows of our own poor hearts.

Where God Weeps

Regis Martin

[Jesus] said, "Where have you laid him?"
[The Jews who had come with Mary] said to him,
"Sir, come and see." And Jesus wept.
(Jn 11:34-35)

Imagine, says Rabbi Abraham Heschel, two very disparate views of the world confronting the patriarch Abraham. In neither of which, he adds, will Abraham suffer God to be absent. He is first shown a vision of "infinity, beauty, and wisdom," which moves him to ask if it be possible for such grandeur to exist without God. Then, finding himself in a world "engulfed in the flames of evil and deceit," he asks if it be possible that there is no God "to take this misfortune to heart?"

However one parses the equation, the existence of a gracious and merciful God remains an axiom on which we absolutely depend. Which is why, as Heschel argues in his great work *The Prophets*, the sorrows of Israel become, quite literally, God's grief. "No words have ever gone further in offering comfort when the sick world cries," he says of Isaiah. For too long the voice of Yahweh kept silent. But now, *like a woman in travail*, he will cry out. It is, Heschel insists, "the boldest figure used by any prophet," striking a chord of deepest sympathy between Yahweh and the people he loves.

In his encyclical *On Christian Hope*, Pope Benedict, reflecting on the fact that God, while he cannot suffer in himself, is nevertheless free to *suffer with*, reminded us that so precious are we in God's sight that he became man precisely in order to prove it. "Hence in all human suffering we are joined by one who experiences and carries that suffering *with* us; hence *con-solatio* is present in all suffering, the consolation of God's compassionate love—and so the star of hope rises."

There is no greater sign of solidarity, of the sheer depth of divine kinship, than the tears of Jesus. Indeed, a God who will not weep for the children who are lost is no better than the god of Aristotle, an unmoved mover whom no one is moved to love.

Father of mercy and love, we thank you for the tears of Jesus, which he freely shed on behalf of all who undergo pain and death.

On the Wings of Hope

Regis Martin

*So the Jews said, "See how he loved him." But some of them said,
"Could not the one who opened the eyes of the blind man have
done something so that this man would not have died?"*
(Jn 11:36-37)

I t is certainly to their credit that the Jews, seeing how the death
of Lazarus moves Jesus to weep, assume that his tears testify
to the depth and sincerity of his love. Never mind that God
weeps wherever there is suffering, at least they have understood
that the two go together. "Love anything," writes C. S. Lewis, "and
your heart will certainly be wrung and possibly be broken. If you
want to make sure of keeping it intact, you must give your heart to
no one, not even to an animal." The heart of Jesus, broken on the
wheel of an unjust world, is given to all.

But they are mistaken on the matter of the miracle they imagine
Jesus might have performed had he only wished to avert the death
of his friend. Of course he could have spared him. How difficult
can it be if you are God's Son? So why *did* he stay his hand since
it could so easily have been used to prop up poor Lazarus? "They
are like pupils," writes Adrienne von Speyr, "who have understood
one principle of geometry and now try to apply it everywhere." If
he's done one already, what's keeping him from doing another?
They do not see that the dispositions of the Lord are not subject to
calculation. One imagines Dante in the *Paradiso*, gazing upon the
inner life of God and suddenly seeing the human face of Jesus. "Like
a geometer who sets himself/ To square the circle, and is unable
to think/ Of the formula he needs to solve the problem," so are we
left with a God whose timetable it is not our business to know. We
need to move in darkness here, toward that final *dazzling darkness*
of which the dying and rising of Lazarus is but a part. Jesus will
carry us there, and longs to do so, but only on the wings of hope.

*Almighty Father, in allowing your servant Lazarus to die, you
revealed the face of a compassionate Son with whom we had not
reckoned. Teach us to be patient in accepting your will even when
we do not understand your way.*

Dread of Death

Regis Martin

So Jesus, perturbed again, came to the tomb. It was a cave, and a stone lay across it. Jesus said, "Take away the stone." Martha, the dead man's sister, said to him, "Lord, by now there will be a stench; he has been dead for four days."
(Jn 11:38-39)

Why do we fear the dead? Clearly there is nothing, this side of a titmouse, less threatening. And as for death, who wouldn't prefer a brightly colored door thrown open upon great sun-swept vistas of joy? Who wants to fall haplessly into a black hole where neither light nor love awaits the soul? No wonder Homer exclaims, in speaking of Hades, fearful god of the underworld, "Men hate him most of all the gods." Yet it was into such a place as this that Jesus went in search of his dead friend. Note the fetid air amid the stench of decaying bodies. See how he trembles before the tomb. The sheer dread-inducing fact of death makes cowards of us all. The real horror, however, is not the rotting flesh; it is the soul's corruption of which the hideousness of death stands as expressive symbol. Thus Jesus insists on our seeing the evidence of four days' decomposition with our own eyes. What he's really after is stripping the soul naked, unmasking its disguise of flesh, beneath which the essence of sin lies hidden no more. So the Lord of light and life steps across the gate and grave of death, showing himself superior to the forces of death and darkness. He goes to bring Lazarus back, not just to a state of renewed bodily being, but to that risen condition in which flesh and spirit unite in a redeemed actuality purchased at the cost of his own life. It is the decisive sign, impressing upon his friend the image of what he aims to accomplish in himself.

"So death will come to fetch you?" asks Thérèse of Lisieux. "No, not death, but God himself." So do not fret if body and soul be separated for a time. It is a small price to pay for what "will unite me forever with God." Death holds no terror for those who cling to Jesus.

Heavenly Father, on whom death has no hold, you sent your Son into the tomb where death holds sway in order to deliver us from its terrors. We praise you for the hope you have given us in the midst of darkness.

217

Telling Lazarus to Get Up

Regis Martin

*Jesus said to [Martha], "Did I not tell you that if you believe
you will see the glory of God?" So they took away the stone.
And Jesus raised his eyes and said, "Father, I thank you for
hearing me. I know that you always hear me; but because of
the crowd here I have said this, that they may believe that
you sent me." And when he had said this, he cried out in
a loud voice, "Lazarus, come out!"* (Jn 11:40-43)

I n meditating on the meaning of the scriptural word, one sees
that here is no ordinary word, but rather the eternal Word made
visible in finite form. "The meaning of this word," writes von
Balthasar, "is inexhaustible and utterly profound…it can ultimately
be interpreted only by means of itself. It contains latent within itself
the fullness of the eternal life, the mysteries of heaven, the ocean of
Trinitarian truth and love."

From the moment God began to speak this Word, welling up
from the eternal depths of the Godhead, there was never another
word he had in mind to speak. "In the beginning was the Word,"
declares John's Gospel, scaling the heights of a Christology no
loftier than which can be imagined. It is this very exchange, this
dia-logos between Father and Son, God's innermost secret, that the
crowd actually hears. Eavesdropping on a conversation that has
neither beginning nor end, but is a relation of knowledge and love
so profound as to breathe forth the Spirit. Could the mere raising
of a dead man reveal a glory greater than this? Here is the Circle
Dance of the Trinity itself, in which the Son gives thanks to the
Father in the Spirit, whom together their love *spirates*. No mortal is
equal to an event of such magnitude. Who Christ is, the relation he
has from all eternity with the Father, whose commission he carries
in the Spirit, now determines everything Christ does, including
the miracle he is about to work. If faith comes from what is heard,
then the faith awakened by this miracle testifies to all that was
heard before, to that unending reciprocal exchange without which
nothing is possible. Jesus will tell Lazarus to get up because, from
all eternity, he knows the Father always hears him. "In this circle of
love," wrote Pope Benedict, "there is the highest degree of unity and
constancy," the animating source that sustains the entire universe.

*O Father of our Lord Jesus Christ, you speak the Word always, and
you allow his voice to resound everywhere. Let us hear this Word
that brings life and hope to the world.*

What the Dead Now Know

Regis Martin

The dead man came out, tied hand and foot with burial bands,
and his face was wrapped in a cloth. So Jesus said to them,
"Untie him and let him go."
Now many of the Jews who had come to Mary and seen what
he had done began to believe in him. But some of them went to
the Pharisees and told them what Jesus had done. (Jn 11:44-46)

When Alfred Delp, the German Jesuit priest martyred by the Nazis, was about to be hanged, he told the prison chaplain who accompanied him to the gallows, "In a half hour, I'll know more than you." What does he know? Can we too know what he knows? Only if he came back to tell us.

So why hasn't Lazarus told us? "What difference," asks Gerald Vann in *The Divine Pity*, "did his journey into eternity make to him?" We are left only a single scrap of information, to wit, a supper where he and the Lord are present during which Lazarus says nothing. Might he have been in a somewhat dreamy state? "You imagine," suggests Vann, "the practical, motherly Martha having to tell him repeatedly: 'Lazarus, do get on with your food.'"

But here we are shown the most riveting scene imaginable. Lazarus, responding to Christ's summons, suddenly appears wrapped in his winding sheet of death. "Untie him," Christ commands. All at once the dead man is returned to life. Brought forth from the tomb of darkness, Lazarus is ushered into the light of day, before whom stands the source of all light. One recalls the famous figure in bronze by Jacob Epstein, adorning the antechapel of New College, Oxford, in which the freshly resuscitated corpse is freed from all that had bound him. How powerfully it reminds us that death cannot be the last word. Christ, in freely assuming our death, vanquishes it utterly. Lazarus is his down payment on the victory to come.

How, in all seriousness, could anyone refuse an offer this wonderful? To reject it seems not just stupid, but suicidal. Still, many have come to believe, revealing the depth of their desire for a destiny which death cannot disturb. Leaving the others to remain bound by a darkness that, for all Christ came to free us from it, they would sooner have than him.

O God and Father of all the living, your Son brought Lazarus
back to life. Make us heirs of this same life so that in Jesus, in the
life of the Spirit he breathed into the world, death will never have
the last word.

Christ Fulfills Passover Spirituality

Douglas Bushman

So the chief priests and the Pharisees convened the Sanhedrin and said, "What are we going to do? This man is performing many signs. If we leave him alone, all will believe in him, and the Romans will come and take away both our land and our nation." (Jn 11:47-48)

Passover and July Fourth both celebrate the birth of a nation in freedom from a repressive rule. They differ regarding who gets credit for the emancipation. The liberation of Israel is God's work: ten plagues, parting of the sea, and ten commandments "inscribed by God's own finger" (Ex 31:18). The colonies' independence is the work of the Founding Fathers and their compatriots, who signed the Declaration of Independence and prosecuted the Revolutionary War. A man-made nation depends on the sustaining efforts of men, while a nation created by God depends on him.

Passover is an act of faith that the God who freed his people continues to protect and sustain them. In faith-solidarity with the slaves in Egypt, Israel acknowledges its total dependence upon God. This spiritual return to servitude produces the poverty and humility that assure divine intervention and protection. Jesus fulfills this Passover spirituality by making himself poor, abject, and utterly reliant on God, who is his only hope: "Look at my affliction and rescue me" (Ps 119:153). In contrast, the Jewish leaders reason as if the future of Israel depends on them. There is no turning to God, no prayer for guidance. Fearing that the religious zeal of Jesus' followers will bring Roman reprisals and the destruction of Judaism, they must take measures to prevent it. Their Passover spirituality falls short. This is why they cannot recognize God at work in Jesus.

The lesson for us? To avoid thinking the Church's future depends on our plans, and to trust it is assured by God's promise to rescue the afflicted. What we can do is to become poor, with Christ, in repentance, prayer, almsgiving, poverty, chastity, obedience, and above all, the Eucharist. With Saint Paul we can boast of being weak, for then we are strong in the strength of the Lord (see 2 Cor 12:10). "Our help is the name of the LORD,/ the maker of heaven and earth" (Ps 124:8).

Almighty Father, our refuge in time of need, you always hear the cry of the poor; bless your Church with the spirit of humility, that we might always turn to you to receive grace and mercy.

Receive the Future from God

Douglas Bushman

*But one of [the Sandedrin], Caiaphas, who was high priest that
year, said to them, "You know nothing, nor do you consider
that it is better for you that one man should die instead
of the people, so that the whole nation may not perish."*
(Jn 11:49-50)

People often grumble when God delays in answering their
prayers to know his will. Why does he wait so long to reveal
our future? Spiritual directors answer that people are not
as ready to embrace his will as they think they are. God's will is
unimaginable, so there is need for preparation. Otherwise they try
to evade it. Jonah runs away from his future, but does not succeed.
When Jesus prophesies his death, Peter rebukes him.

In the Gospels, three men make predictions related to Jesus' death.
Peter declares his readiness to be jailed and die with Jesus (see Lk
22:33). He is wrong; he wilts under pressure and denies Jesus. Yet, he
is right; after Pentecost, in the power of the Holy Spirit, he is arrested
and martyred. Caiaphas anticipates that Jesus' death will benefit the
nation. As a political calculation he is wrong; Jesus' death does not
prevent the eventual destruction of the Temple. Yet, in terms of God's
plan he is right; Jesus' sacrifice is the source of salvation for all the
nations. Finally, Jesus foretells his death and Resurrection, Judas'
betrayal, Peter's denials, and the Holy Spirit's coming. He is right,
with no qualifications, because he fully embraces the Father's will.

Peter and Caiaphas cling to a future according to their own
imaginings and expectations rather than God's. Jesus, too, is conscious
of a possible future according to his own desires. But, his love for
the Father causes him to pray: "Not my will but yours be done"
(Lk 22:42). By faith we participate in Jesus' act of total entrustment
to the Father. He alone can say with credibility: "Do not worry
about tomorrow; tomorrow will take care of itself" (Mt 6:34).
The tomorrow of his Resurrection makes our hope about the future
unshakeable, for God promises that no "future things...will be
able to separate us from the love of God in Christ Jesus our Lord"
(Rom 8:38-39).

*Father, I trust and hope in your promises. Heal my lack of hope,
that I might glorify your name by living free from all distress about
tomorrow while awaiting the blessed hope and coming of your Son.*

Nothing Takes God by Surprise
Douglas Bushman

[Caiaphas] did not say this on his own, but since he was high priest for that year, he prophesied that Jesus was going to die for the nation, and not only for the nation, but also to gather into one the dispersed children of God. So from that day on they planned to kill him. (Jn 11:51-53)

Evil and suffering test our faith. They seem incompatible with God's love and power. This is why times when suffering is unavoidable are opportune moments for catechesis. In the context of suffering, a father reminds his children, first, that nothing takes God by surprise. Everything fits into his plan of love: "All things work for good for those who love God" (Rom 8:28). Second, the instinct that evil and suffering conflict with God's love and power is correct. They do not have the last word. God's love does. There is no suffering in heaven.

Saint John records Caiaphas' words to show that nothing escapes God's plan. His support for killing Jesus is not hidden from Jesus' Father, who knows all thoughts and actions. As the Father's Son, Jesus too is aware of the treachery: "You are trying to kill me" (Jn 8:37, 40); "the Father loves me, because I lay down my life.... No one takes it from me, but I lay it down on my own. I have power to lay it down, and power to take it up again. This command I have received from my Father" (Jn 10:17-18).

As it unfolds, the Apostles do not see Jesus' arrest and crucifixion from God's perspective. It is darkness for them, an irreconcilable incompatibility between the goodness of Jesus and of God's love, and the evil that transpires. Then, on Easter, comes the light of faith: everything happens according to God's plan. Nothing takes God by surprise. Henceforth, the light of faith overcomes all darkness, and the Apostles see God's plan as it unfolds in their own trials, persecution, and martyrdom. They live, preach, and write this Good News so that we too may perceive the light of God's love when it appears that the powers of darkness are prevailing, taking comfort in the Lord's words: "In the world you will have trouble, but take courage, I have conquered the world" (Jn 16:33).

Glorious Father, through the intercession of Saint John, grant me the grace to believe that your "light shines in the darkness, and the darkness has not overcome it."

Contemplating Our Final Eucharist

Douglas Bushman

*So Jesus no longer walked about in public among the Jews,
but he left for the region near the desert, to a town called
Ephraim, and there he remained with his disciples.*
(Jn 11:54)

A chess master easily anticipates a novice's moves. In his wisdom, he can anticipate his opponent's reactions. Nothing is forced, freedom is safeguarded, but the novice's chess-freedom is limited by his lack of experience. The match is over before it begins. The Jewish leaders act as if they were controlling events, conspiring against Jesus and planning his death. In reality, he is the master. They must wait until the moment he has chosen. That moment coincides with the Passover, so that Jesus can bring to fulfillment what the Passover lamb signifies: God's saving love. It all must happen "according to the revelation of the mystery kept secret for long ages but now manifested... according to the command of the eternal God" (Rom 16:25-26).

"Jesus knew that his hour had come to pass from this world to the Father" (Jn 13:1). Though they are with him, his disciples do not know it is their final Passover with him. Why should this Passover be any different than the prior two? They cannot know that the Father's plan is about to be fulfilled. Yet, without realizing it, they are prepared for what is coming. Jesus has prepared them. He knows their trial, little faith, weakness, and fear. They will lose Jesus through his arrest, death, and burial, but they will regain him through faith in the Resurrection, the gift of the Holy Spirit, and the Eucharist. Their faith, celebration of the Eucharist, and martyrdom are proof that they were prepared for conversion.

We are like them. Through the Church's teaching and sacraments, and the support of the communion of saints, we are ready for a final Eucharist with Jesus on earth. Through our death we will lose him as he comes to us in the Eucharist, only to gain him in the glorious vision of heaven. Every Eucharist reminds us that Jesus has one final gift to make—the gift of heavenly glory.

*Most wise Father, make me ready for your final gift by keeping
me close to Jesus. May I celebrate every Mass as if it were my final
Eucharist, praying fervently: Come, Lord Jesus.*

223

Looking for Jesus

Douglas Bushman

Now the Passover of the Jews was near, and many went up from the country to Jerusalem before Passover to purify themselves. They looked for Jesus and said to one another as they were in the temple area, "What do you think? That he will not come to the feast?" For the chief priests and the Pharisees had given orders that if anyone knew where he was, he should inform them, so that they might arrest him. (Jn 11:55-57)

For a child, being lost triggers a sense of vulnerability and a desperate search. Nothing else matters, because separation from parents is to be cut off from the love and protection upon which life depends. The search for parents is a search for security and meaning in life. Today's reading depicts God's children in two overlapping movements. In their pilgrimage toward God's holy city, they are moving, in faith, toward God. He is their security and meaning. They are lost without him. Simultaneously, they are moving toward Jesus. His impact inspires a search for him as they reach Jerusalem. His teaching, way of life, and miracles so make God present and enliven their faith that the Passover, their most solemn feast, seems incomplete without him. Their zeal for God and the Passover merges with their zeal for Jesus. Jesus fulfills the meaning of life that they celebrate at Passover. This twofold movement sums up man's search for God. Every search for the meaning of life is a search for God, and every search for God is a search for Christ.

On God's part, there are also two intersecting movements. In Jesus, God too is moving toward Jerusalem, where Jesus will fulfill the Father's plan for our salvation by offering himself in sacrifice. His journey to the Father is simultaneously a search for man, for the Father sends him "to seek and to save what was lost" (Lk 19:10). In his final Passover, Jesus is the Paschal Lamb offered *to* the Father *for* man. Precisely here, in Jesus, who is true God and true man, man's search for God and God's search for man converge and reach their summit. Lost children do not know that their parents search for them more intensely than they search for their parents, because parents love more intensely. The Paschal Mystery reveals that God's search for us, that is, his love, far surpasses our search, our love, for him.

All praise and thanks to you, Father of perfect love, for sending your Only Begotten Son to seek me when I was lost.

Reclining with Jesus

Father Richard G. Smith

*Six days before Passover Jesus came to Bethany, where
Lazarus was, whom Jesus had raised from the dead.
They gave a dinner for him there, and Martha served,
while Lazarus was one of those reclining at table with him.*
(Jn 12:1-2)

The catacomb of Saint Priscilla in Rome contains a well-preserved fresco from the second century often called the *Fractio Panis* (Breaking of Bread). It is a striking image: seven people are reclining around a semicircular table, sharing a meal. At the far left, a bearded man extends his arm to break and share a loaf of bread with the other six. To the Christian eye this is no ordinary meal, but a very early depiction of the Eucharist in which the participants at table take the reclining position common in the time of Jesus.

Jesus shares a meal in Bethany with his close friends who are "reclining at table with him." There is a sense of peace and intimacy to the scene—it's difficult to imagine a person reclining at table and at the same time rushing through the meal to get it done. Instead, we find here a sense of leisure and a desire on the part of all to enjoy the meal and the good company of friends without being rushed. We can easily imagine the give-and-take of the conversation among friends taking place at this meal in Bethany—a scene that would have looked very much like the *Fractio Panis* depicted in the catacomb.

The Eucharist is our opportunity to recline at table with Jesus now. Although we don't physically "recline," we can embrace an attitude of reclining in our hearts, and enjoy the same sense of intimacy and leisure of the meal in Bethany. It is good for us simply to be with Jesus and to rest in Jesus' love when we celebrate the Eucharist, allowing for the unrushed and natural conversation between close friends.

Heavenly Father, thank you for calling me to the Eucharistic table of your Son; I ask the grace to rest simply in his love at the Eucharist as I listen to his words.

Holy Fools

Father Richard G. Smith

Mary took a liter of costly perfumed oil made from genuine aromatic nard and anointed the feet of Jesus and dried them with her hair; the house was filled with the fragrance of the oil.
(Jn 12:3)

Mary's actions are bold, even to the point of foolishness. In Jesus' time, a woman would never have touched a man in public and in such an intimate way—a woman would not even have touched her husband this way. Good, religious people in Jesus' time understood that a person could be made ritually impure when touched by a person who was already impure, and so people had a heightened sensitivity to being touched by someone else. Mary would have understood very well that Jesus was a faithful Jewish man and that she was calling both of their reputations into question by her bold, public act. Can you imagine the gossip this must have fueled?

Despite all that, Mary not only touches Jesus—she anoints his feet and dries them with her hair. It's a bold act of love on her part, and she seems to be fearless about possible consequences. Mary gives flesh to the words of Saint John: "There is no fear in love, but perfect love drives out fear" (1 Jn 4:18). There is a long and ancient Christian tradition of "holy fools" who, emboldened by the love of Jesus, are fearless and bold in their response to Jesus, even to the point of foolishness. Saint Francis of Assisi is perhaps the most striking and well-known example of a "holy fool" for Jesus. Francis never does anything by halves, never carefully evaluates the cost and consequences of taking the Gospel to heart—he casts his lot with Jesus entirely, with all his heart, and never looks back. He, too, gives flesh to Saint John's promise that perfect love casts out all fear.

Disciples like Mary, Francis, and countless others through the ages teach us that we need never fear making a bold, generous response to Jesus, even when the world thinks we're foolish for doing so. The love of Jesus is always far stronger than our fears!

Kind and generous Father, may your love cast out all fear from my heart, that I may always respond to the call of Jesus with an open, generous heart.

Active Love

Father Richard G. Smith

Then Judas the Iscariot, one [of] [Jesus'] disciples, and the one who would betray him, said, "Why was this oil not sold for three hundred days' wages and given to the poor?" He said this not because he cared about the poor but because he was a thief and held the money bag and used to steal the contributions.

(Jn 12:4-6)

In Dostoevsky's *The Brothers Karamazov*, the wise monk Zosima tells us active love is a harsh and fearful thing compared to love in dreams. It's true: when we love someone, when we're in it for the long haul, love asks difficult things of us sometimes, things we would never choose, things we thought we never could do. What seems extravagant or over-the-top from outside a loving relationship makes sense within the relationship.

I remember a wonderful woman in the Bronx who would never let her husband be alone during his increasingly frequent hospital stays, spending night after night in an uncomfortable chair at his bedside. A family in another parish spent decades visiting their father daily in a nursing care facility as the Lou Gehrig's Disease he contracted as a young man slowly progressed. Their actions might seem over-the-top: an adult man can learn to be alone at night in a hospital, and a man confined to a nursing home for so many years could not have expected family visits every day. It was enough for the wife to stay with her husband a few hours each day, or for the family to visit their father a few times a week. But when you love someone you never want to give just enough, you want to give more than enough.

Judas is completely insincere here, but he does have a point. What Mary does is extravagant and over-the-top, even senseless. That's how it looks from the outside. But, Mary has already been loved by Jesus. What she does here is a response to Jesus' love, an outward sign of what she feels in her heart. Mary has what Judas does not: a loving friendship with Jesus. Such signs of active love make complete sense within that friendship.

Loving Father, may I come to know more and more the active love Jesus has for me, and may I hold nothing back in my response to that love.

The Both/And of Saint Francis

Father Richard G. Smith

*So Jesus said, "Leave her alone. Let her keep this for the day
of my burial. You always have the poor with you,
but you do not always have me." (Jn 12:7-8)*

Few Christian disciples in the life of the Church embraced
Gospel poverty and love for the poorest of the poor better
than Saint Francis of Assisi. From his embrace of lepers, to his
renunciation of even legitimate comforts of life, to his death naked
on the bare ground, Francis embraced "Lady Poverty" as few others
have. In recent years, critical editions of the extant writings of Saint
Francis have been published in English, giving us new insights into
his life. In his authentic writings, again and again Francis exhorts
his brothers to provide the finest vessels and decorations possible
for the celebration of the Eucharist. The same man who disdained
even a second tunic or a bed will spare no expense in honoring Jesus
in the Eucharist. For Francis, this is not a matter of providing either
for the poor or for Jesus. He embraces the great Catholic principle
of "both/and"—choosing to serve and honor Jesus both in the poor
and in the Eucharist.

Jesus knows Judas' heart and the insincerity of his concern for the
poor. He also knows the heart of Mary, and the love that motivates
her extravagant gift. He responds to Judas by calling his bluff. Judas
has set up a false dichotomy, pitting the service to Jesus against
service to the poor. Judas suggests that, in spending her financial
resources on Jesus, Mary neglects the poor in some definitive way,
as though her resources had been entirely exhausted! In reality,
Mary draws from the *inexhaustible* resources of her love for Jesus. In
honoring Jesus and loving him in this way, her ability to recognize
and love him in the poor is not diminished but greatly strengthened.

We who know and love Jesus give of our time, talents, and money
to honor and serve him with the best we have, both in the Eucharistic
celebration and in the poor. After all, we are drawing from a deep
wellspring of love!

*Almighty Father, give me a heart so full and generous that I may
serve Jesus wherever I find him, without counting the cost.*

The Power of Love over Hate

Father Richard G. Smith

[The] large crowd of the Jews found out that [Jesus] was there and came, not only because of Jesus, but also to see Lazarus, whom he had raised from the dead. And the chief priests plotted to kill Lazarus too, because many of the Jews were turning away and believing in Jesus because of him. (Jn 12:9-11)

Hatred easily takes on a life of its own. The Polish poet Wisława Szymborska has a perceptive and haunting poem entitled *Hatred* in which she describes the power of hate. It's not an optimistic poem. Having lived through the Nazi oppression of Poland in the Second World War and the subsequent communist regime that oppressed her people for decades, Szymborska knew hate's power firsthand. In her poem, she describes the ways hatred can take hold of the human heart and fuel entire groups of people in a way that (she claims) compassion doesn't. She traces the many ways hatred grows and attracts crowds, creating a perverse sort of brotherhood.

By this point in the Gospel, hatred has taken on a life of its own. The hatred in the hearts of those who oppose Jesus has grown to the point that they not only want to kill Jesus, but also Jesus' friend, Lazarus. There's a growing evil in the hearts of these men that they've allowed to go unchecked. It's a hatred that begins to see everyone and everything as a threat. Now it is no longer enough merely to stop Jesus—even the friends of Jesus must also be stopped at whatever cost. This hatred will continue to grow and spread, drawing crowds and fueling the eventual murder of Jesus.

But that is not the end. Hatred can never be the end, because it always ends up as self-consuming. If the human heart has a deep capacity for hatred, we have a far deeper capacity for love. Jesus' cross and Resurrection reveal the love of God as far stronger than hatred and evil. Love is stronger than death. The love of Jesus also takes on a life of its own, guided by the Holy Spirit; it continues to grow and spread, drawing and fueling a community that even now brings life and salvation to a broken world.

Almighty Father, help me surrender anything in my heart that prevents me from being a loving person, so that I may more fully embrace Jesus Christ and become a means of his life and salvation to my brothers and sisters.

The Small Entrance of a Great King

Father Richard G. Smith

On the next day, when the great crowd that had come to the feast heard that Jesus was coming to Jerusalem, they took palm branches and went out to meet him, and cried out:/ "Hosanna!/ Blessed is he who comes in the name of the Lord,/ [even] the king of Israel." (Jn 12:12-13)

The Palm Sunday liturgy is one of the most visually striking celebrations of the Church year. In many places, the congregation gathers outside the church where the palms are blessed and the first Gospel is proclaimed. Then, with great enthusiasm, the people heed the priest's invitation: "Like the crowds who acclaimed Jesus in Jerusalem, let us go forth in peace!" All at once, a great crowd of people enters the church singing and waving palm branches.

The Palm Sunday liturgy shapes our imagination about this scene of Jesus' entry into Jerusalem. We imagine the triumphal entrance of a king into his city, surrounded by the loud praises of the people, as the rest of the city stops to take notice. However, on a recent pilgrimage to Jerusalem, a guide suggested the reality might have been very different. Passover was the busiest time of year for the ancient city of Jerusalem. We should imagine an overcrowded city streaming with pilgrims and priests. Large numbers of animals were constantly flowing into the city for Temple sacrifices. There also would have been the normal activity of life in the political center of the region. The entrance of Jesus on a humble animal, surrounded by a crowd of social outcasts, may very well have been just one little eddy of activity in a swirling, bustling city. It was likely such an insignificant event that most people in Jerusalem barely noticed it.

But isn't that the way Jesus so often chooses to act in the world and in our lives? Jesus frequently acts in quiet and seemingly small ways that can easily go unnoticed by people going about their daily hectic schedule. With all the surrounding drama in Jerusalem, there still were those who saw Jesus and the awesome events about to unfold in those days. When our eyes are firmly set on Jesus, we are likely to perceive his movement in our lives.

Loving Father, with eyes and heart always set on Jesus, may I never fail to perceive and to respond to his voice and movements in my life.

The Broad and Deep River of the Gospel

Father Richard G. Smith

Jesus found an ass and sat upon it, as is written:/ "Fear no more, O daughter Zion;/ see, your king comes, seated upon an ass's colt."/ His disciples did not understand this at first, but when Jesus had been glorified they remembered that these things were written about him and that they had done this for him.

(Jn 12:14-16)

The Fourth Gospel was the last to be written and so the words and actions of Jesus are related decades after the fact. For generations of biblical scholars, this has meant that the Gospel ought to be read with a grain of salt when it comes to historical facts. The analogy of a river is frequently used—just as the water of a river is purer the closer it is to the source, so too the earlier Gospels are more reliable when it comes to history since they are closer in time to the earthly life of Jesus. Those presuppositions have recently been called in question, and now many scholars assert that Saint John's Gospel is based on eyewitness testimony and should not be so quickly discounted when historical questions about the earthly life are raised.

While it may be true that the water of a river is pure near the source, it is also true that the river achieves new breadth and depth as it flows from that source. Rowan Williams, the former Anglican Archbishop of Canterbury, says that Saint John writes his Gospel as a disciple who has spent decades *praying through* every aspect of Jesus' life and words. Through prayer and reflection, Saint John has been led to a deep understanding of what he had seen and heard decades before.

We're told that Jesus' disciples did not understand "at first" but later come to understanding when they *remember* what Jesus said and did. Of course, by then they have seen the risen Jesus and have received the Holy Spirit. Although removed in time from the source of their experience of Jesus, the disciples understand Jesus with a new depth as they *pray through* the life and words of Jesus under the Spirit's guidance. In our prayerful *lectio* of Scripture, the Spirit guides us to a deeper knowledge and understanding than we may have had on first reading.

Father in heaven, send your Spirit upon me as I read and pray with your Word. Deepen my understanding of the Word so that I may follow Jesus with all my heart.

How Can I Keep from Singing?

Father Richard G. Smith

*So the crowd that was with [Jesus] when he called Lazarus
from the tomb and raised him from death continued to testify.
This was [also] why the crowd went to meet him, because they
heard that he had done this sign. So the Pharisees said to one
another, "You see that you are gaining nothing. Look,
the whole world has gone after him."*

(Jn 12:17-19)

There's a beautiful old Baptist hymn that starts, "My life flows on in endless song;/ Above earth's lamentation,/ I hear the sweet, though far-off hymn/ That hails a new creation;/ Through all the tumult and the strife/ I hear the music ringing;/ It finds an echo in my soul:/ *How can I keep from singing?*" You can almost hear those who have seen Lazarus raised from the dead singing those words in this scene. They continue to "testify" to this great thing they've seen Jesus do, even as the darkness grows in the hearts of those who oppose Jesus and are actively seeking his death. Jesus has allowed these people a glimpse of what he is able to do—of what he *will do* for us through his Passion, Death and Resurrection—and it is so awesome, so truly unexpected, that they cannot but testify to Jesus in a bold and joyful way, "singing" their testimony.

In his *Expositions on the Psalms*, Saint Augustine tells us that to sing is such a thing of joy and love that "only the lover sings." A grateful heart has a tendency to see more and more of the good things Jesus does in our lives. When we look back upon our lives with eyes of love, we discover how generous and good Jesus has been to us. We discover that we have been witnesses of God's goodness and grace in the world. We're invited, then, like those in the Gospel to continue to testify to Jesus and all he has done in and for us. That's not something we ought to do begrudgingly or halfheartedly. We are to *sing* our witness to Jesus Christ—in other words, to testify to him with great joy and gratitude, as a thing of love. When I see the loving presence and action of Jesus in my life, how can I keep from singing?

*Dear Father, give me a full and bold heart that I may sing of your
love and mercy, giving testimony to my brothers and sisters about
all Jesus has done for me.*

A Reminder for Aspiring Preachers

Father Richard G. Smith

Now there were some Greeks among those who had come up to worship at the feast. They came to Philip, who was from Bethsaida in Galilee, and asked him, "Sir, we would like to see Jesus." Philip went and told Andrew; then Andrew and Philip went and told Jesus.

(Jn 12:20-22)

A few summers ago, traveling through England, I came across a beautiful pulpit carved in stone in a countryside church. It is a true work of art. Detailed figures of prophets, evangelists, and great theologians and preachers from throughout the centuries surround the pulpit on all sides visible to the congregation. The pulpit itself is reached by a small staircase that is not visible to the congregation, but only to the preacher ascending to his task. Carved into the base of this staircase we read the touching words of the Greeks in Jerusalem: "Sir, we would like to see Jesus." It is a simple, powerful reminder to the preacher: the congregation in front of you has not come to be fascinated by *you* or to hear *your* agenda. They've come because they want to see Jesus.

We've all sat through some ho-hum homilies. Sometimes it's a matter of the preacher's poor preparation or rambling or an "off" day. But then there are homilies where the preacher seems to get in the way. We can feel as though the preacher is trying to entertain us, or relate his life story, or show off his education. As well-intentioned as the preacher may be, we come away missing something—or, better, missing some*one*: Jesus. We want to see Jesus!

The Greeks in the Gospel express the desire of every human heart. We want to see Jesus! We who have become friends of Jesus are called now to make him known and loved. Each Christian is called to preach the Gospel by his or her own life. The words on the pulpit are for all of us to remember: the people we encounter each day are looking for Jesus. We want to help them see Jesus and not get in the way!

Loving Father, thank you for letting me see Jesus. May I be an instrument through which my brothers and sisters see Jesus also.

Learning from Creation

Father Richard G. Smith

Jesus answered [Andrew and Philip], "The hour has come for the Son of Man to be glorified. Amen, amen, I say to you, unless a grain of wheat falls to the ground and dies, it remains just a grain of wheat; but if it dies, it produces much fruit."
(Jn 12:23-24)

With good reason, the Holy Land has been called the "Fifth Gospel." A visit to the Holy Land brings into focus elements of Jesus' earthly life that are not explicit in the written Gospels. For example it's surprising to find relatively long distances between one town and the next. It would have taken Jesus and his disciples many hours on foot to move from place to place—and, for the most part, we don't know what was said or done during those in-between times. But we can easily imagine Jesus taking in the beauty of the countryside, carefully observing creation.

The Gospels reveal clear evidence that Jesus is a keen observer of creation. Here is a man who truly sees the world around him. Many of the most striking images Jesus uses in his teaching come directly from nature. These images speak with power to people who live and work in rural areas, and so Jesus frequently chooses to call his hearers' attention to what they see each day in order to teach some profound truth.

The image of a grain of wheat falling to the ground and dying in order for new life to begin is a particularly powerful one, even for those of us with little or no firsthand knowledge of farming. Jesus invites us to see through his eyes, in order to discover how new life sprouts in places where there appears to be only death. Only days after he speaks these words, Jesus will be in a place where there appears to be only death. Even in that place, the Father, the Creator, brings new and abundant life in a way no one could have imagined. Jesus himself becomes the grain of wheat that dies to bring new life. He becomes our assurance that, for God's own sons and daughters, death does not have the final word—Life does.

Father of life, in the wonder of your good creation you reveal the truths of the kingdom. You desire to give me abundant life: help me trust in you as you bring new life even to those places of my life where there seems to be only death.

Serve the Lord with Joy!

Father Richard G. Smith

"Whoever loves his life loses it, and whoever hates his life in this world will preserve it for eternal life. Whoever serves me must follow me, and where I am, there also will my servant be. The Father will honor whoever serves me."

(Jn 12:25-26)

Sister Marie Assunta, my fourth grade teacher, introduced my class to the "Saint Dominic Savio Club." The club took its inspiration from Saint Dominic Savio, the teenage saint who had been a student of Don Bosco. Members studied the life of the saint and tried to imitate him in concrete ways in daily life as individuals and as a community. The program was conducted nationally by the Salesians of Don Bosco, and basically amounted to an introduction to Salesian spirituality, rooted in the practice and writings of Saint Francis de Sales. Salesian spirituality is decidedly optimistic and joyful. In that light, the motto of the Savio Club, taken from the Psalms, has a thoroughly Salesian tone: *Serve the Lord with joy!*

These verses of Saint John's Gospel might appear gloomy on first reading. There's talk of hating one's life in order to save it and of serving and following Jesus (who is heading toward the cross at this point in the Gospel) so that we will be "honored" by the Father. It all sounds so heavy, so difficult. But a Salesian reading of Saint John reveals the true spirit of Jesus' words. There is a joy in forgetting ourselves and our own needs, so that we become available to our brothers and sisters and their needs. Loosing our lives in this way opens us to the fullness of life we are created to experience. There is a joy in serving the Lord, and discovering that, no matter how generous we imagine ourselves to be, our God is never outdone in generosity. And, above all, there is an unsurpassable *joy* in following Jesus, who comes not to add to our burdens, but to lighten and share them. Even when following Jesus leads us to a share in his cross, we have the confident joy of knowing the cross is Jesus' place of triumph, not failure. All good reasons for us to serve the Lord with joy!

Eternal Father, when I find the words of Jesus challenging or difficult, help me to read and to hear them with a sense of Christian joy, that I may wholeheartedly serve Jesus and follow where he leads.

The Prayer of a Troubled Heart

Father Richard G. Smith

*"I am troubled now. Yet what should I say? 'Father, save me
from this hour'? But it was for this purpose that I came to
this hour. Father, glorify your name." Then a voice came
from heaven, "I have glorified it and will glorify it again."*
(Jn 12:27-28)

Saint John does not include an account of the agony in the
garden. Instead, we have this indication of Jesus' inner struggle
as he approached his death. While the agony in the garden
appears as an intimate prayer between Father and Son, Jesus' struggle
in this Gospel is very public. In a plain manner, Jesus says aloud
to the crowd, "I am troubled now." With the crowd, we are given
a window into the real humanity of Jesus. We shouldn't imagine
that Jesus doesn't want to follow the will of the Father, or that he's
questioning whether or not he should follow through to the cross.
Nevertheless, in his humanity, Jesus experiences a struggle, an
"agony" to remain faithful to the Father's call. These few words of
Jesus remind us that he fully shares our humanity in every way but
sin, and that our struggles are also his struggles.

There's another difference between the account of Jesus' struggle
here and that in the other Gospels—Jesus (and those around him)
hear the voice of the Father *respond* aloud to Jesus' words. Jesus will
tell the people the voice came for their sake, not his. Jesus speaks
from the depths of his heart, and a response comes from the depths
of the Father's heart. In this glimpse of the relationship between
Jesus and the Father, we are permitted to hear the Father's response
to Jesus as a sort of assurance that the Father *does* hear the cry of
a troubled heart!

We all face our own agonies and struggles in life. There are many
times when our hearts are troubled like the heart of Jesus is here.
Jesus himself instructs us to voice those struggles and to be honest
in prayer. And the Father assures us that he truly hears and responds
to those prayers.

*Loving Father, I give you thanks and praise for calling me your
own beloved child, confident to speak to you in a plain, honest
manner; I know you always hear the prayer of my heart. May I
have the wisdom to discern the sound of your voice in response.*

Perceiving God's Presence

Father Richard G. Smith

The crowd there heard [the voice from heaven] and said it was thunder; but others said, "An angel has spoken to him." Jesus answered and said, "This voice did not come for my sake but for yours." (Jn 12:29-30)

Blessed John Henry Newman wrote that it would be as strange and disconcerting for him to look out at the world and not see the reflection of God as it would be to look in a mirror and not see his own face! Like Jesus, Newman sees the whole of creation as a reflection of the Good Creator. The English Jesuit priest and poet, Gerard Manley Hopkins, shares this same sense of God's presence when he writes in his diary that a star-filled night sky opened his heart to praise God "to whom and in whom all beauty comes home." For those with open hearts and eyes, the world is, to cite Hopkins again, "charged with the grandeur of God."

The Father speaks clearly to the Son in the previous Gospel verse. But here the "crowd" hears only the sound of thunder. "Others," Saint John writes, discern the heavenly source of the voice. Both groups experience the same reality, but only one gets the message. There are always some people who are what Pope Benedict XVI described as "tone deaf" to God—people who do not seem to perceive the presence of God in the world and in their lives. There are also those "others" like Newman and Hopkins who have a deep ability to recognize God all around them.

Newman teaches that we bear responsibility for which group we fall into. Our attitudes toward and ideas about God, the world, and human nature help determine our ability to perceive God's presence. The person who accepts and trusts in the goodness of God, who studies and prays the Scriptures as a way of understanding God, and who recognizes the capacity of the human heart for God puts himself or herself in the right position to see and praise God reflected in creation.

Eternal Father, I thank and praise you for the many ways you speak and act in my life. Shape and guide my heart and mind so that I may see and hear you ever more clearly.

The Love Story of the Cross

Father Richard G. Smith

"Now is the time of judgment on this world; now the ruler of this world will be driven out. And when I am lifted up from the earth, I will draw everyone to myself." [Jesus] said this indicating the kind of death he would die.
(Jn 12:31-33)

Early Christian images of Jesus on the cross don't emphasize the humiliation and suffering of the crucifixion. Instead, the earliest depictions of Jesus on the cross show him alive and fully clothed, seemingly in control of all that is happening. In this way, these images are particularly faithful to Saint John's account of the crucifixion. Jesus describes his being "lifted up" in glory on the cross when he will actively "draw everyone" to himself. In all the Gospel accounts there's a strong sense that Jesus remains in control during his Passion, but this sense is heightened and made explicit in Saint John's Gospel. Everything unfolds according to a plan, and Jesus' every action is deliberate.

In the cathedral of the small Tuscan town of Sansepolcro, there is a striking example of an early depiction of the crucifixion. The figure of Jesus is so serene and beautiful that the locals do not refer to the image as a "crucifixion" at all, but rather as the *Santo Volto,* or "Holy Face." It is the face of Jesus that draws us toward him on the cross. His head is slightly bowed and his eyes are wide open as though he is lost in contemplation. In the dim light of the cathedral, it is easy for us in turn to get lost in contemplation of Jesus' face. We're reminded that the Passion and death of Jesus is not a horror story, but rather a love story in which Jesus is a willing and active participant.

At this point in the Gospel account, we are quickly approaching the Passion and crucifixion. Saint John repeatedly calls our attention to words and phrases of Jesus, like those we find here, in order to help us understand the Passion and death of Jesus more deeply. When we contemplate Jesus on the cross in Saint John's Gospel, we discover the depths of his love for us, as Jesus draws us into the full embrace of his outstretched arms.

Loving Father, guide my heart and mind as I look upon Jesus lifted up on the cross; draw me more and more into his embrace. May my every thought, word, and action flow from that embrace.

The God of Surprises

Father Richard G. Smith

So the crowd answered [Jesus], "We have heard from the law that the Messiah remains forever. Then how can you say that the Son of Man must be lifted up? Who is this Son of Man?"
(Jn 12:34)

One of the traps into which religious people frequently fall is imagining they have God all figured out. We can think (or act as though we think) we know God so well that we know not only what God will and will not do, but also what God can and cannot do. We put God into a tidy box—where he can no longer surprise us. But God is always far greater than the god-in-a-box created after our own image. God is a God of surprises.

It's surprising how frequently Jesus comes into conflict with religious people in the Gospels. In part, the tensions arise because the religious people have fallen into the trap—they imagine they've got God all figured out, and they're certain that God wouldn't say and do what Jesus says and does! In the time of Jesus, there were all sort of images of the coming Messiah floating around, ranging from an entirely political savior, to an entirely religious one, to everything in between. Most times, these images of the Messiah were more about serving an agenda than discerning the promises and actions of the living God. Jesus comes as the Messiah no one was expecting. In Jesus, the Father does something new and unexpected, so that old ways of thinking and acting will need to be set aside.

We see some tension in this verse. What Jesus says is different from what the crowd has heard in the past. Something new is happening, and the crowd's not sure they like it: "Who is this Son of Man?" Those who give their own answer to that question will remain in their lifeless and tired agendas. Those who allow Jesus to answer will discover abundant life and salvation; they will discover the true God, who is far more generous than they could ever have imagined.

Father of my life, I want to know you as you truly are: the God who offers me new life and salvation. Setting aside my own tired agendas, may I become more aware of the new ways you act in my life and in the world.

Saint John, Evangelist and Poet
Father Richard G. Smith

Jesus said to [the crowd], "The light will be among you only a little while. Walk while you have the light, so that darkness may not overcome you. Whoever walks in the dark does not know where he is going. While you have the light, believe in the light, so that you may become children of the light."
After he had said this, Jesus left and hid from them.
(Jn 12:35-36)

Saint John's Gospel can sometimes intimidate people. It's easy to see why—the Gospel begins with a profound theological reflection on the eternal existence of the Word, contains lengthy and involved discourses of Jesus, and uses enigmatic terms and phrases that can often leave you scratching your head. The other Gospels seem more straightforward and simple in comparison. We can feel more at ease praying with those Gospels rather than tackling the profound Fourth Gospel, which is best left to the more spiritually advanced.

That is truly a misreading of Saint John's Gospel. Saint John, inspired by the Holy Spirit, is not only a masterful theologian—he is also a masterful writer and poet! These two verses are an eloquent example of the way Saint John relates the very simple words and ideas of Jesus and, by gently repeating and intertwining them, draws us into a profound truth. Here, simple concepts of "light" and "darkness" almost dance with each other. In a gentle way, Jesus assures his little flock that the growing darkness will not ultimately triumph over him or them. He promises that he himself is Light in the darkness and that they can share in that Light by trusting and believing. At the same time, we are given to understand that Jesus himself is the Light who guides *us* through and is stronger than the darkness that enters into every human life.

The great biblical theologian Origen of Alexandria wrote that, in order to understand Saint John's Gospel, one must rest his or her head on the breast of Jesus in imitation of the Beloved Disciple at the Last Supper. This Gospel is not for spiritual elites, but for simple believers who are willing to rest in Jesus' love and spend time reading and rereading the poetry of the Gospel, allowing the Word slowly and gently to speak to the heart.

Kind Father, I come to your Word resting on the heart of Jesus; guide me and give me patience to stay with the words of Scripture, trusting that you desire to speak to my heart with these words.

To Believe or Not Believe

Father Jacob Restrick, O.P.

Although [Jesus] had performed so many signs in [the crowd's]
presence they did not believe in him, in order that the word
which Isaiah the prophet spoke might be fulfilled:/ "Lord,
who has believed our preaching,/ to whom has the might
of the Lord been revealed?" (Jn 12:37-38)

Father Isaiah is very depressed. He has a master's degree in New Testament studies; he reads biblical Greek fluently; he spends hours preparing his Sunday homilies; and he preaches what he humbly thinks is one of his finest, most inspiring homilies. He greets the parishioners at the door after Mass, and Father Isaiah waits for his most respected parishioner, the city's mayor, to comment on his erudite sermon. His Honor, the mayor, approaches. "Hey, Father, did you catch that game on TV last night?"

Josephine, the plumber's wife, went on a pilgrimage to a famous shrine, noted for its healing miracles. She came home full of faith and overflowing with devotion…for a week. Then it was back to her old routine; she hardly even thought about God during the day; she was too busy. She shook hands with Father Isaiah after Mass and commented: "Beautiful service, Father; looks like it'll be a nice afternoon; have a nice day."

Do people really believe? Father Isaiah sits at his kitchen table drinking coffee and wondering what he is doing wrong. Why do so many people not believe? He knows the parish population is down 65 percent from forty years ago. The bishop may have to close the church. Do people not believe because they don't need God anymore? What has deafened their souls so they can't even hear his preaching? Maybe it's not too different from the Lord's own day. If faith comes from hearing, is there something amiss with our hearing, or is it the message?

Another parishioner, who rarely speaks to Father Isaiah, but who listens attentively to the readings and homily at Mass, when asked why he is so happy, says that there are miracles all around him; every day is a miracle, just to be alive. Father Isaiah doesn't know his past, only that today, he's a daily communicant.

Loving and gracious Father, help me to see the miracles of grace in my life today; open my ears to hear your Word, for it is never far from me.

Far From the Maddening Crowd

Father Jacob Restrick, O.P.

For this reason [the crowd] could not believe, because again Isaiah said:/ "He blinded their eyes/ and hardened their heart,/ so that they might not see with their eyes/ and understand with their heart and be converted,/ and I would heal them."/ Isaiah said this because he saw [Jesus'] glory and spoke about him.

(Jn 12:39-41)

"The crowd could not believe." The year before our Lady appeared to the children at Fatima, they were visited by an angel who called himself "the Angel of Portugal." The angel taught them several prayers, which the children began to pray every day. One of the prayers says: *O Lord, I believe in you; I hope in you; I adore you; I love you.*

That's a beautiful prayer, beginning with a profession of belief: "*I believe in you.*" There's a second part to the prayer which prays for others, the "crowd" who over the centuries cannot believe. *I beg pardon for those who do not believe, do not hope, do not adore, and do not love you.*

When I pray this prayer, I think of the people I know who are "nonbelievers." They "crowd" into my heart, even if they are just a few. We all have our "crowd" of nonbelievers, sometimes right in our own families. And I catch myself adding to the prayer: those who do not and *cannot* believe in you.

Why are some people not able to believe? Why can some live without any faith in God or an eternal life to come? Saint John gives two reasons that he gets from Isaiah: spiritual blindness and hardness of heart. And it can be widespread; it can be said of a whole "crowd."

We don't have to go any further than the popular culture. Some of the television dramas are so well-written and marvelous in their storytelling that I'm easily hooked. But in every one of them, I've realized that the main characters do not have any faith in God. No one is shown praying or going to Mass, unless it's portrayed as a negative. How easily we can grow up with the crowd, and not believe in anything spiritual. Another prayer is most powerful: *Lord, I do believe, help my unbelief.*

Loving Father, you want us to know you and love you. Remove any spiritual blindness from my heart, that I may always see your face in others.

Got Milk-Toast?

Father Jacob Restrick, O.P.

Nevertheless, many, even among the authorities, believed in [Jesus], but because of the Pharisees they did not acknowledge it openly in order not to be expelled from the synagogue. For they preferred human praise to the glory of God.
(Jn 12:42-43)

My mother used to make up names for people, usually with a humorous spin to them. For example, "Mr. or Mrs. Milquetoast" was someone who didn't have much of a backbone when it came to standing up for what he believed.

Mr. Milquetoast would identify with the dilemma in today's reading: he believes, but he doesn't want to lose his standing in a particular circle. Ms. Milquetoast is a young attractive woman starting a new job in a prestigious firm. She is quickly swept under the wing of the popular set who are all very professional, sophisticated, and modern women. She's invited to a smart cocktail party after work. She believes that she has "arrived," and splurges on a new dress to come up to the standard of the other women.

The talk of the party is about a weekend away the women are planning for themselves, and Ms. Milquetoast is invited. Plans for Sunday morning are being discussed, and no one ever mentions Mass. Ms. Milquetoast is a good practicing Catholic who never misses Mass unless she's really sick. But she's afraid to mention it, lest she be excluded from this inner circle. She even hides a small gold crucifix she has worn for years.

She mentions all this to Father Milquetoast, expecting him to reproach her for being so timorous. But Father Milquetoast doesn't want to offend her because her parents are generous parishioners. It's best not to ruffle feathers. He learned that from Bishop Milquetoast who never speaks out on anything that will make him unpopular.

Ms. Milquetoast realizes she is surrounded by milquetoasts. This makes her very uncomfortable because she knows she is a timid people pleaser, living out of her fear of disapproval. She tells her co-workers that she can't go because it would mean missing Mass. There is a stunned silence. She eventually loses her job...and her name. She's "milquetoast" no more.

Loving Father, you know we live in a secular world, and you call us to believe in you and love you in our world today. Give us strength and courage to be for you, now and always and for ever and ever.

"Break a leg"

Father Jacob Restrick, O.P.

Jesus cried out and said, "Whoever believes in me believes not only in me but also in the one who sent me, and whoever sees me sees the one who sent me. I came into the world as light, so that everyone who believes in me might not remain in darkness. And if anyone hears my words and does not observe them, I do not condemn him, for I did not come to condemn the world but to save the world." (Jn 12:44-47)

There is a deep spiritual depth beneath most of our human actions, or there can be if we have eyes to see. The spirit of man is so manifestly different from the animating principle in animals. Animals do not sing, write poetry, relish words, think about abstract concepts; animals do not speculate or have imaginations that create fantastical worlds in music, dance, drama, and storytelling.

They do not play games and keep score; they do not laugh, not even the hyenas. We love stories—the animals don't sit around telling each other stories about their day. They do not text or email or twitter news about themselves.

To delight in the incongruities of life and human action because we can see them means that we have a sense of humor, which lifts up the human spirit and helps (I hope) to lighten our burdens. To smile and laugh and enjoy each other are all expressions of the "spiritual nature" in us and among us...and helps us to see things in their right perspective because we are not animals.

Human nature is so different from animal nature. Jesus is fully human, with a real human nature (except for sin), and he is fully God. He is one with the One who sent him, namely, God the Father. To see him is to see God with us. That is a light that frees us from darkness and ignorance and from the shackles of sin.

We believe in him, and it colors our whole wonderful world. Our human nature participates in what is supernatural, and we can see God's love and truth in a sad and agnostic world.

It's wonderful to read a little of John's Gospel each day. After all, it is the "greatest story ever told." We are not just spectators or "readers"—we are living characters as the drama unfolds and when we learn the script and make it our own. Break a leg.

Gracious Father, you are the Author of the Book of Life, for it is all written in your Word. Help us to hear the Word and embrace your story before our final curtain comes down.

Is It Desperation or Urgency?

Father Jacob Restrick, O.P.

"Whoever rejects me and does not accept my words has something to judge him: the word that I spoke, it will condemn him on the last day, because I did not speak on my own, but the Father who sent me commanded me what to say and speak. And I know that his commandment is eternal life. So what I say, I say as the Father told me."

(Jn 12:48-50)

These strong words of the Lord are not among his first, but his last. He has been about his Father's business for three years now, and his Passion and death are drawing near. Perhaps there is more urgency in his voice than desperation. His signs and miracles over the last three years have been to draw people to himself. He hasn't had a heartbeat apart from the will of his Father who art in heaven. Everything from his conception and birth to his Resurrection and Ascension is the will of God, his Father. *Thy will be done.*

How casual we can become about our spiritual lives. Merrily we roll along day after day, without much of an awareness of why we are here and where we are ultimately going. Eternal life doesn't move us any more than the sentiments of a sympathy card.

The Lord may do some rather dramatic things in our lives to wake up our spiritual consciousness. When my sister was diagnosed with breast cancer at the age of forty-three, her life took a dramatic about-face. The time she had left with her husband and three children became precious to her, and she never took it for granted. Her faith and faithfulness to God became real and more important than her membership in the country club.

The Lord loves us and does everything he can to get our attention so he can draw us to himself, because he was sent from God the Father to bring us back "home" to heaven with him. He doesn't punish us or condemn us, but loves us and saves us. And all we have to do is to let him do it. Is he doing something in your life right now to get your attention? I think about that when I pray the prayer he wants us to pray because he taught it to his Apostles: Our Father in heaven; thy will be done. Thy kingdom come…

Merciful and loving Father, may your holy will always be done in my life, even when I don't see it or understand it. I trust in your Word and believe you created me to be with you for ever in heaven.

245

The Love Story Never Ends

Father Jacob Restrick, O.P.

Before the feast of Passover, Jesus knew that his hour had come to pass from this world to the Father. He loved his own in the world and he loved them to the end. The devil had already induced Judas, son of Simon the Iscariot, to hand him over.

(Jn 13:1-2a)

The scene now changes to a "spiritual slow motion" as we climb the stairs to the Upper Room where the table has been set for a "last supper" with his Apostles. Saint Luke tells us that Jesus took his place at table and said to them: "I have eagerly desired to eat this Passover with you before I suffer" (Lk 22:15).

We climb the same stairs every time we gather for Mass. The beautiful words of Eucharistic Prayer IV remind us: "For when the hour had come for him to be glorified by you, Father most holy, having loved his own who were in the world, he loved them to the end."

It's all a love story, and it hasn't ended yet. We gather before the "table of the Lord." It may be a marble high altar in a glorious baroque basilica or the unadorned altar of a humble chapel; it may be a hospital table or the hood of an army jeep. But most often it is the altar of our parish church where the Lord desires to eat this meal with us every Sunday, and for many of us, every day. Every day in the Upper Room—how full of love is that!

From the sacrifices of Abraham and the high priest Melchizedek, to the first Passover meal eaten by the Hebrews awaiting the exodus from slavery, to every burnt offering and holocaust in the Temple of Jerusalem—all these come together tonight, on this Holy Thursday in the Upper Room, where the Lord will love us in a way that only God can. Only God could have thought of the Eucharist and made it possible.

John's Gospel is a love story from start to finish. But slow down and relish the next five chapters, for they take place in this Upper Room where a table is set for the Supper of the Lamb. Blessed are those called.

Most loving Father, look upon us with mercy, and help us to make our way up the steps to the Supper of your Son, who loves us to the end, for ever and ever.

Put on Your Glasses

Father Jacob Restrick, O.P.

So, during supper, fully aware that the Father had put everything into his power and that he had come from God and was returning to God, [Jesus] rose from supper and took off his outer garments. He took a towel and tied it around his waist. Then he poured water into a basin and began to wash the disciples' feet and dry them with the towel around his waist.

(Jn 13:2b-5)

I was excited to go to a 3D movie after decades had passed since the original 3D movies. Impressed for ever in my memory was the ball on a rubber band and paddle coming right at your face in *The House of Wax*. Taking off the 3D glasses, which were handed out for free, everything was two-dimensional and blurred. So, fifty years later, I'm excited to see what modern technology has done. The first surprise (after the extra cost) was that the glasses were almost like regular sunglasses with hard plastic frames. The depth of perception, thanks to these glasses, was a marvel to behold.

It's like that when we read Saint John's Gospel. There is a depth of perception not found in any other book of the Bible. If we have our glasses on, namely, our "eyes of faith," we are going to see things in a greater dimension than the most brilliant agnostic reading the book for its contribution to second-century literature. Put on your glasses now....

Jesus was fully aware that he had come from God the Father and was returning to him. The mystery of the Incarnation of God is the most profound event, the most profound truth we hold. Jesus rose from the supper and took off his outer garments. The Second Person of the Blessed Trinity took off the divine glory that is his as God, and became man, while remaining God. He took a towel and wrapped it around his waist. He wrapped himself up in a real human nature. And what does God-Made-Man do? He becomes a "servant boy" washing the feet of his disciples.

The scene, remember, is in the Upper Room. God is Love. And divine Love has become man and loves us with his Infinite love, even with our "dirty feet" that plod along the dusty road of life, and lifts up our hearts to the Upper Room.

Almighty and all-loving Father, you sent your beloved Son to us, that in him we may return to you. Cleanse us now and have mercy for ever and ever.

The Paradox of Love

Father Jacob Restrick, O.P.

[Jesus] came to Simon Peter, who said to him, "Master,
are you going to wash my feet?" Jesus answered and said
to him, "What I am doing, you do not understand now,
but you will understand later." Peter said to him,
"You will never wash my feet."

(Jn 13:6-8a)

People are quick to point out the human sinfulness of spiritual people, usually talked about in a gossiping tone, hoping to highlight the hypocrisy of the ones talked about. But rarely highlighted are the paradoxes woven into the fabric of the Christian faith. For example, the spiritual reality of the Lord's word that "the greatest among you is the one who serves the others" (cf. Mt 23:11). That exaltation comes from humility is a paradox.

I was new to Rosary Hill Home where the Hawthorne Dominican Sisters take care of incurable cancer patients, totally free of charge. The Mother General resides here as well, and I pictured her engrossed in a computer in an office far removed from the hustle and bustle of the patients' floors. I went into a two-man room to meet a new patient, and a sister was quietly feeding the other patient, fully attentive to his need at the moment. On my way out I turned to say goodbye to this sister, and it was the Mother General.

When one would visit the Mother House of the Missionaries of Charity in Calcutta, you would see the sisters doing the most menial of tasks, and comforting the sickest, smelliest, skinniest poor people on the brink of death. And the one holding the poorest of the poor was probably Mother Teresa herself.

Where does the paradox of love come from? Like Peter when the Lord approached on his knees to wash his grimy feet, we may not want the Lord to love us in this way. We feel we are not worthy, and surely we are not. But we do not yet understand the paradox of love. So the Lord will have to teach us by his example. Then we may begin to see the menial tasks, the humdrum routines of our lives as encounters with the living God. When we know our powerlessness, then we are strong. It's a paradox!

Loving and gracious Father, help me to let go of the need to be in
control, and to let you be the light in my darkness.

The Cost of Discipleship

Father Jacob Restrick, O.P.

Jesus answered [Simon Peter], "Unless I wash you,
you will have no inheritance with me." Simon Peter said
to him, "Master, then not only my feet, but my hands
and head as well." (Jn 13:8b-9)

Uncle Joe was a distant relative. He literally lived at a distance from us, and we rarely visited him. I was a "middle-aged teenager" when we spent a weekend at his house. To my surprise (and delight) he had something for me. He laid out five items: a collection of baseball cards, headed by Richie Ashburn, my favorite Phillies player; a man's silver and gold watch with all the paraphernalia my Mickey Mouse watch didn't have; a lovely black onyx man's rosary unlike any I had ever seen before; a live hamster hiding under a mound of shredded paper in a small cage; and, last but not least, a real leather wallet, with a new fifty dollar bill peeking out of the money fold. And he said: "Choose which one you want."

You can be sure, I scrutinized each gift like I was a contestant on *The Price is Right*. After much mental deliberation I blurted out: "I choose them all!" And Uncle Joe laughed and laughed, saying I was "like Saint Peter." I had no idea what he meant, until I heard Peter's response to the Lord—"Wash all of me, Lord." When the Lord draws us to himself, he wants us to give him our all. That's a lesson it may take a long time to learn.

Like my Uncle Joe, we want to pick and choose what we will give *or* receive from the Lord. Sometimes we even fall into the bargaining game: "Lord, if you will find me a job that pays well and fulfills me, I will go to Mass every Tuesday and Thursday, during my lunch hour." And sometimes, we bargain over more serious things like life and death and sickness and health. The Lord wants to be in every part of our life. He wants to give us many gifts, and wants us to choose all!

P.S. I named the hamster Uncle Joe.

Merciful Father, help me to love you with all my heart, all my mind, all my soul, and all my strength, for you are my Father, now and always and for ever.

Broken Heart of Jesus

Father Jacob Restrick, o.p.

Jesus said to [Simon Peter], "Whoever has bathed has no need
except to have his feet washed, for he is clean all over; so you
are clean, but not all." For he knew who would betray him;
for this reason, he said, "Not all of you are clean."
(Jn 13:10-11)

Molly was one of those people who are near and dear to God because she was so poor, at least in material things and social standing. She was what we call a "homeless person" who walked the streets of New York pushing all her worldly belongings in a shopping cart. She avoided shelters and chose to sleep on the street, sometimes in the side alcove of our church. And by day, if she wasn't panhandling or rummaging through the corner trash bins collecting empty cans and bottles, she'd be in church, sometimes praying on her knees very devoutly, and sometimes sound asleep in a back pew.

It took awhile, but Molly became my friend, and she was delighted (I think) to have someone willing to listen to her stories. Her early life was like a fairytale wedding with all the schmaltz of a television drama. Prince Charming, however, was not what she loved and believed in, and when he left her for another woman it broke her heart. She got all choked up telling me the story, thirty years after the fact. I always remember her words: "I was betrayed." Such a betrayal affected the rest of her life. She never let herself fall in love again because her trust in men disappeared.

It's a different story from today's reading, but the Lord knew what it was to be betrayed. It broke his heart in a way none of the other Apostles would. Peter denied him, and Jesus forgave him. The others all fled, except for John, the sole Apostle at the cross. Jesus didn't lose his love for mankind. It was for us—the homeless of his Father's house—that he came. Sometimes we're very devout and full of faith, and other times we're asleep in the back pew, and sometimes we have our hearts broken and we are betrayed. If that has happened to you, stay close to the Lord. He knows.

Merciful Father, we place our trust and our hope in you. Whatever
cross you may offer us, we embrace with confidence in your grace.

Cleaned and Pressed

Father Jacob Restrick, O.P.

So when [Jesus] had washed [the disciples'] feet [and] put his garments back on and reclined at table again, he said to them, "Do you realize what I have done for you? You call me 'teacher' and 'master,' and rightly so, for indeed I am. If I, therefore, the master and teacher, have washed your feet, you ought to wash one another's feet." (Jn 13:12-14)

Only Saint John tells us of this incident when Jesus washed his Apostles' feet. Earlier, John tells us that Jesus knew he was from God and was returning to God. John, of course, is writing after many years have gone by, and Jesus rose from the dead and ascended into heaven. In effect, he returned to the table of his Father and was again clothed in the divine glory, which is his as beloved Son. He returns with a glorified human nature, with a body of flesh and blood—risen from the dead to die no more.

He wants to bring us with him. And he "washes" us clean before we join him at his table. My mother had some weird ideas. She used to think, or so she would say, that I could grow potatoes in my ears. She'd say that as she was swirling a wet washcloth around my ear grooves. Then she'd attack my neck and hands, and once they were all clean, I could leave the kitchen and go sit at the table for supper. She stopped doing that when I was a certain age, like when I was old enough to know to do it on my own.

She and my father were wonderful "teachers" and neither one of them graduated from high school, but they taught by the example of their lives. The Lord left us not just his words to ponder and inspire us, not just a set of commandments and rules to live by, but the example of serving one another. And he left us a Mother.

If my mother "knew" I could grow potatoes in my ears, the Lord knows all the crops we can grow in our hearts. We are constantly bombarded by impure images and thoughts filling our hearts with all kinds of "dirt." Holy Mother Church washes out our ears in the kitchen and sends us with clean hearts into the Banquet table.

Eternal Father, open our ears and cleanse our hearts that we may always offer you praise and thanksgiving for all you have given to us.

Driving Lesson 101

Father Jacob Restrick, O.P.

"I have given you a model to follow, so that as I have done for you, you should also do. Amen, amen, I say to you, no slave is greater than his master nor any messenger greater than the one who sent him. If you understand this, blessed are you if you do it." (Jn 13:15-17)

When my father would get angry his voice would go up an octave. It rarely happened, but I can still hear him screeching: "Don't do as I do, do as I say!" That was after one of my adolescent challenges to his authority. It's not always easy to have a parent teach you how to drive...the family car.

The Lord didn't raise his voice an octave higher when he wanted to get a strong point across, but he would begin his sentence with: "Amen, amen, I say to you..." When that happens, we should stop in our tracks and listen.

We're with his disciple-Apostles in the Upper Room. It's their "ordination night," and he is preparing them for the awesomeness of their role in the unfolding of God's plan. They have become the foundation stones, and Christ himself is the cornerstone. They will be "other Christs" when they gather people around the Lord's table and "do" what he does with bread and wine. He wants to instill in them all a servant's heart; they should remember they are not the masters, but the slaves—the servants.

Everyone who is "washed clean" by baptism becomes "other Christs," other anointed ones, set apart to love and serve. The Lord doesn't want us to drive our cars on our own without learning how. Better still, he wants us to let him be in the driver's seat. The car is your body and soul making its way through the highways of life. We learn by experience that driving at night, in the dark, is different than in the light; that the freeway is crowded and fast and the single-lane streets are slower and have a nicer view.

The Lord has a lot to teach us about navigating through it all, but if we let him do the driving, and fasten our seat belts, we're in for a marvelous trip with a destiny beyond compare. Blessed are you if you do it!

Heavenly Father, when we are lost and do not know where we are going, send your Holy Spirit to light the way, and bring us safely home.

The Upper Room Shockwave

Father Jacob Restrick, O.P.

"I am not speaking of all of you. I know those whom I have chosen. But so that the scripture might be fulfilled, 'The one who ate my food has raised his heel against me.' From now on I am telling you before it happens, so that when it happens you may believe that I AM." (Jn 13:18-19)

My mom had a most delightful sense of humor. However, she could easily be shocked by things she would hear on television, like in the evening news, or in her soap operas, or a mystery drama. And when she was shocked, she would stomp her foot on the floor and say: "Mercy!" She's been gone now for thirty years, and I've often thought there would be a hole in the rug from her foot stomping were she alive today and watching television.

If any of the Apostles had her habit of stomping a foot and saying "Mercy," today's reading would be such a time. It would seem that the Lord has been shocking his poor Apostles all night. It began when he got up from the table and wrapped a towel around his waist and began to wash their feet. It was a shock when he told them that one of them would betray him this very night. Mercy! It had been a shocking week. They hadn't gotten over the raising of Lazarus from the dead, and now they were alone with him in this Upper Room and he tells them that he knows each of them in their very being; he knows whom he has chosen. He is eating this sacred meal with them, and one will "raise his heel against me." That is shocking enough, but then he says he is telling them this before it happens so that afterward they may believe that—are you ready?—that I AM!

This is the divine Name that God revealed to Moses from the burning bush; this is the Name still not uttered by devout Jews; this is the Name that would cause the scribes and Pharisees to rend their garments if someone spoke it. Jesus, in this sacred moment, says he is God!

We are not shocked. But may we sit with these words of his in utter silence and whisper: "Mercy."

Compassionate Father of our Lord Jesus Christ, have mercy on us in our complacency and awaken in us the awesomeness of your Truth.

Picture ID Required

Father Jacob Restrick, O.P.

*"Amen, amen, I say to you, whoever receives the one
I send receives me, and whoever receives me receives
the one who sent me."
When [Jesus] had said this, Jesus was deeply troubled and
testified, "Amen, amen, I say to you, one of you will betray me."*
(Jn 13:20-21)

I was rummaging through some old boxes and found my old high school class ring. There was an instant flood of memories just from holding the ring. How proud we were to be the Class of such and such a year. The ring gave us a class identification. I remembered when I had to take it off, not to "go steady" with a girlfriend, but to put on another sign of identification. I attended a college seminary, and on day one we handed over rings, jewelry, and car keys (if we had car keys!) and put on the simple black cassock of a diocesan seminarian.

Throughout all our lives we put on and take off signs and symbols of our "identity." A married couple exchange rings, more precious and significant than a high school ring for sure. Many of us put on "uniforms" that identify something that we do for a living: the flight attendant, the waitress, the auto mechanic, a religious sister or brother, to name only a few.

The Lord was giving his Apostles an identity which was not just symbolic but actual. *Whoever receives you whom I am sending, receives me!* This is as real and pertinent as when the Lord says, *Whatever you do to the least of my brothers or sisters, you do unto me.* There is no "ambassadorship" more intimate or divine than what the Lord gives us, and this is given to us first at baptism. This means every Christian is an "ambassador of Christ," and that is why our naughty words and bad actions can be scandalous or even sacrilegious.

After giving the Twelve this apostolic lesson, the Lord is deeply troubled and says words that must have cut to the quick: "one of you will betray me." This was not "graduation night" but "ordination night"; the night Jesus entered into his Passion; the night he was betrayed. No class rings or diplomas…he took bread and broke it.

Almighty and loving Father, you have made us your own, marked us with the sign of the cross of your Son, and sealed us with the Holy Spirit. May we never forget our dignity and our destiny.

Stay in the Curve

Father Jacob Restrick, O.P.

The disciples looked at one another, at a loss as to whom [Jesus]
meant. One of his disciples, the one whom Jesus loved, was
reclining at Jesus' side. So Simon Peter nodded to him
to find out whom he meant. (Jn 13:22-24)

The details John gives underline the deep significance of these moments. The Evangelist is almost painting a portrait with words. We are present there too, "looking at one another." Many of us, I presume, have our own image of the Last Supper. One of the most famous is Leonardo da Vinci's with the Lord and the Apostles seated at a long table, all on one side as if they were posing for the camera.

We know from history, however, that meals in the Mideast were eaten while reclining at a low table. One would rest on the left elbow and eat only with the right hand. A group setting table was probably U-shaped, and the host would recline at the center of the curve. Everyone would be on the outside so servants could move about the inside bringing and removing dishes. The guest of honor would be at the host's right, within the curve of his heart, or "close to his heart." The guest on the left would have the host close to his heart, and also be close to his ear. It is believed that John was on the right, and so Jesus had him in the curve of his heart. Judas was on his left, close to the Lord's ear. Judas thus had Jesus in the curve of his heart.

This "intercession" among the Apostles is an apostolic form of "social networking." If you want to know a secret, you wouldn't ask the secret keeper. So you ask his or her best friend. Peter nodded for John to ask.

We should also note that in a Semitic culture, eating together, especially "sharing bread," was an intimate event. It's called "table fellowship." That one of the Lord's most intimate disciples would betray him "from the table" is heart-wrenching. May we always place ourselves, like John, within the curve of the Lord's Sacred Heart, for there is no greater intimacy.

Gracious and loving Father, give us this day our daily bread, and keep us always in the curve of your heart, close to the heart of your Son, Jesus.

Bless Us, O Lord

Father Jacob Restrick, O.P.

[The disciple whom Jesus loved] leaned back against Jesus' chest and said to him, "Master, who is it?" Jesus answered, "It is the one to whom I hand the morsel after I have dipped it." So he dipped the morsel and [took it and] handed it to Judas, son of Simon the Iscariot. (Jn 13:25-26)

Father Peyton, the "Rosary Priest," used the slogan: "The family that prays together, stays together." Perhaps another one for our day and age, at least in our fast-paced American society, would be "the family that eats together, stays together." I remember when "supper time" was a family institution. We ate together every night, at the dining room table, and on Sundays, it was like a weekly feast day! This is even more true for Jewish families who observe the sabbath every week, not to mention the various ethnic customs and foods which make up American families.

This Last Supper is "super-charged" with significance, not only as it may have been a Passover Seder, but because of what the Lord is doing now within his "college of Apostles." Sharing a meal is intimate and exclusive; friends and families eat together. For the host to offer a morsel of food to a guest is a mark of extraordinary favor and love. We can easily imagine the Lord doing that often with these twelve men who left everything to follow him.

And on this night, as he quietly shared with John what he would do, he leaned back into the curve of Judas' heart, and handed him a morsel. Judas was much loved by the Lord.

Artists and film producers and directors have given us their visual version of this moment. The Apostle John himself remembers every detail and has written it down. The Gospel is not a history book about past events, but God's living Word in our hearing. Meditating on these moments of the Lord's Last Supper, we find ourselves at the table; we are there with the whole family of the faithful. If we receive the Lord in Holy Communion, we receive "a morsel" from his hand. We share in the deepest intimacy with him this side of heaven. May our poor hearts never betray him, but love him more each day. Amen.

Most loving and gracious Father, gather us together often at the Church's table of the Lord, for we are your family, now and always and for ever and ever.

Inside Secrets of a Traitor

Father Lawrence Donohoo

*After [Judas] took the morsel, Satan entered him. So Jesus said
to him, "What you are going to do, do quickly." [Now] none of
those reclining at table realized why he said this to him. Some
thought that since Judas kept the money bag, Jesus had told him,
"Buy what we need for the feast," or to give something to
the poor. So [Judas] took the morsel and left at once.
And it was night.* (Jn 13:27-30)

Why doesn't Jesus talk Judas out of his imminent act of
betrayal? Even if Jesus is ready to do the Father's will and
die for our sins, surely he should not do so at the price
of Judas' destruction. Instead, he surprises us by almost encouraging
the renegade to go do his dark deed. The Gospels have suggested here
and there that Judas has been showing patterns of evil behavior for
quite some time now, and that he has planned his betrayal of Jesus
with cold calculation. In fact, truth be told, he's already in execution
mode. Showing up at the Last Supper helps keep everything on
cue and above suspicion. Everything is working according to The
Plan except—Jesus blindsides him by calling him out, naming his
strategy, exposing the plot. But instead of preventing it, he allows it!
He lets Judas be Judas. For Jesus is now in passive mode: decreasing
so others might "increase," receding so others come to center stage
and act. More importantly, Jesus doesn't arrest Judas because he
can't without violating his freedom: it's already too late.

Centuries before Judas acted, Aristotle taught that the virtuous
person deliberates slowly, but executes quickly. The weak person,
on the other hand, does just the opposite. He deliberates in haste,
but then, seeing an action poorly planned and perhaps ill-advised,
dithers and dallies, hesitates and procrastinates. But surprisingly,
Judas shows us that a perpetrator of evil can possess the resolution
of the virtuous person. What a wonderful teaching, then, that the
Apostle of the night offers us. If even he can show a resolute capacity
to plan his dark deed meticulously and execute it with dispatch, even
with his cover blown and exposed to broad daylight by the Light
of the World, how much more should we be able to think through
to the Father's will and, once clear on his plan of action, just do it.

*Loving Father, your Son always proved decisive in word and action
because he spent long hours with you. Help me to pray deliberately
so I might act resolutely in service to your will.*

Make It Shine

Father Lawrence Donohoo

When [Judas] had left, Jesus said, "Now is the Son of Man glorified, and God is glorified in him. [If God is glorified in him,] God will also glorify him in himself, and he will glorify him at once. My children, I will be with you only a little while longer. You will look for me, and as I told the Jews, 'Where I go you cannot come,' so now I say it to you." (Jn 13:31-33)

"The Last Discourses" begin here and conclude with the High Priestly Prayer of chapter 17. Judas has left, and with him, the night. At once Jesus begins to speak of light—of radiance, glory, "shine." The Discourses begin with dialogues: with Peter, then Thomas, then Philip. But even these disciples soon lapse into awe-filled silence as Jesus' sublime teachings, unmatched in Scripture, lift us above the Upper Room into the presence of the risen Christ of all times and climes. The initial theme of glory is one of ten major themes found in the Discourses. The word of the Father, Son, and Spirit, the hour, the question of identity, Jesus' presence and absence, the Paraclete, life after Jesus is gone, the world and Satan, faith and love and obedience, and the unity and binding of God and the human person all make a carefully interwoven tapestry that seamlessly blends one theme into another.

After unity, glory is the second greatest of these themes. Introduced here, it will continue to show its face throughout the Discourses. And while it may appear as a high-sounding theological theme, we should first see it in terms of God's problem—a problem very much akin to ours: making a good impression, presenting a great image, doing basic PR work, marketing oneself. How God actually goes about this work in the Scriptures is a fascinating study, of course, for his appearances in salvation history show a remarkable agility and many-sided splendor. He shows himself in the wind, the earthquake, the fire, the tiny whispering sound. But how God shows up in Christ, particularly at Calvary, is the most remarkable of all shines: manifesting divinity in the face and body of a broken, naked, abandoned man dying on a God-forsaken hill on a tree of torture. But that is our sole entry through the stone wall to the glistening face of the risen One.

Almighty Father, the story of your divine showings in creation and history is a mystery beyond words. Help me to trace your revelations of love in creation and history, and then show myself to you.

Love's Labors Won

Father Lawrence Donohoo

*"I give you a new commandment: love one another. As I have
loved you, so you also should love one another. This is how
all will know that you are my disciples, if you have love
for one another." (Jn 13:34-35)*

Love may be a many splendored thing, but it can also be a
downright nuisance and a real cross. Why is this? When our
nature takes to something, it hardly needs instructions in
love. We don't have a problem in loving a warm fireplace on a cold
day, a cool breeze in a hot sun, a sympathetic ear in a cacophony of
disapproval, a hand lifting us up when the chips are down. It's when
our nature has other desires in mind that love becomes a burden.
But why isn't nature always excited about love?

Saint Thomas answers by defining true love as willing the good of
another. By this he doesn't mean my idle, good-natured wish from
my armchair that you stay warm and well fed, as the Letter of James
critiques. No, he means that I work, I labor for my neighbor's good.
And who is my neighbor? Jesus, pointing to the heap of humanity
lying in the ditch, says he's the one without a "next person," to
borrow the original sense of neighbor. And what precisely is his
good? Oil, bandages, a lift to the inn, medical help, three meals, a
bed, and cash to pay for this. The good of my neighbor is what's
not there yet, the need he's grasping for but not reaching. To love in
this way is to complete the other, to become another's completion.
And that's why this kind of love is hard work, why it's a labor of
love. For John, the high theme of unity is underwritten by faith,
obedience, and love—becoming one with God's thinking, God's
will, and God's heart. Divine love for us means God has chosen
to invest himself in his work—us. Since I'm his image who should
look like him by acting like him, he wants me to do the same, even
when my nature says no. And because I shun hard work, I need
this command of love.

*Eternal Father, there are laws against false kinds of love. In imitation
of your Son who worked so hard for you, give me a love of labor,
so that I might enjoy the labor of love.*

The Road Few Traveled

Father Lawrence Donohoo

Simon Peter said to [Jesus], "Master, where are you going?"
Jesus answered [him], "Where I am going, you cannot
follow me now, though you will follow later."
(Jn 13:36)

Peter is asking the right question, for ever since that first day when called from fishing to fishing, he has wanted to follow his Lord. As one of the chosen three, he even followed him to the raising of Jesus to glory and of Jairus' daughter from death. In a few moments he will accompany Christ to the Garden as Jesus raises his prayer to the Father. "We have given up everything and followed you," Peter once boasted, but then added, "What will there be for us?" (Mt 19:27). So he also followed his desires as well as his fears, and then boldly proposed to Jesus a better way than the cross.

Not only on land, but also on sea Peter followed Jesus. We chide him for sinking, yet he alone climbed from the boat and actually made some progress on the waves. For all we know, Peter was also alone in even thinking that someone besides Jesus could do this, so desperately did he want to follow his Master. He is censured for denying Christ, but he alone courted trouble by following Jesus all the way to the high priest's courtyard. In the end, he will be asked to follow Jesus one more time to a death like his by stretching his hands where they would rather not go.

If Peter's career of following follows a wayward line, at least he stayed with the program. After he wondered, he spoke; after falling, he rose; after chastisement, he repented; after denial, he wept. We too can expect a crooked path from the time we first said yes until the last time we say yes. Not only are we also weak and burdened, we follow One who keeps a brisk pace to places where we would rather not go. Yet we follow a King of the road who never asks us to climb where he has not already been to prepare the way for us.

Most merciful Father, I understand that life is a road that takes me through mountains and valleys. Your Son is my pathfinder, a lamp for my steps, a light for my path. Help me to keep pace.

Promises across the Miles

Father Lawrence Donohoo

*Peter said to [Jesus], "Master, why can't I follow you now?
I will lay down my life for you." Jesus answered, "Will you lay
down your life for me? Amen, amen, I say to you, the cock
will not crow before you deny me three times."*
(Jn 13:37-38)

The best laid schemes of mice and men often go awry, the poet reminds us, and we might think that Peter would be the first to confirm Robert Burns's adage. He would likely assent to the verse's sequel as well: "And leave us naught but grief and pain, for promised joy!" When the problem is ourselves, we say the road to hell is paved with good intentions. But then again, just to complicate matters, so is the road to heaven, since salvation is a gift that must be accepted. So the fork in the road comes later. Before that parting of ways, we construct for ourselves, as Peter does, an impressive network of good intentions, and when the moments are grand, with grand intentions. Yet when traveling down the way of decision that we have laid out, where wide is the gate and broad is the road, we discover before long that it's often the street from hell—and to there as well—when we fail our Lord and ourselves once again. So what's going on?

The fork is not only in the road that divides at the point where we encounter quicksand or drop-off, but also right here and now in our very hearts. For even in there at this very moment I discover a well-meaning will, ready to jump into resolute speech, really desiring to follow Jesus wherever he may go. But I also detect an ossified nature not easily convinced and long hardened by years of faithful obedience to self-inflicted waywardness, stubbornness, cowardice, and stupidity. To recognize this conflict within me here and now helps me to see that the future road problem is really a present heart ailment, that humbler promises are often the better ones, that I am weaker than I think, and above all, that I need divine help in forming the promises to keep as well as walking the miles to reach them before I sleep.

Heavenly Father, part of the mystery of being human is that our song is played out over time. With your Son's grace and example, show me that the seeds of my future lie in the present of your love.

Custom-Built

Father Lawrence Donohoo

"Do not let your hearts be troubled. You have faith in God; have faith also in me. In my Father's house there are many dwelling places. If there were not, would I have told you that I am going to prepare a place for you?" (Jn 14:1-2)

We've all heard stories of rags to riches, and, especially these days, of riches to rags. Biographies and news segments ratify Jesus' obvious teaching that treasures on earth succumb to moths and theft. Perhaps for this reason we're all the more tempted to store up treasures within our heart and memory. But the ravages of forgetfulness, dementia, and waning desire for remembrances of things past remind us that we can't bank even on maintaining our interior savings account. Clearly we're not up to the task of storage, with safeguarding treasures without or within. So when Jesus speaks of storing up treasures in heaven, he must be assuring us that it is he who will save us from the ravages of accident and time.

What a consolation to know then that he goes to prepare an individual place for each of us. For many dwellings can't only mean that heaven is big enough to fit us all in. We know that already. Rather, Jesus teaches that heaven is designed to receive all the treasures that I've made my own, or become. When all the dross is purged away, my loving acts, hidden sacrifices, and unrequited deeds that even I've forgotten will be remembered by God, for they are etched in the divine memory. The eternal dwelling we'll call home will save and welcome all that grace has enabled each of us to become: this matchless person we are. Eternal life will gather the various fragments of my being stretched over a lifetime so that nothing I've become will be lost. Jesus' work of saving the whole person comes to full fruition when my entire being is welcomed into his kingdom. There I can finally retrieve and enjoy the treasures he has given me that I have made my own. There will be my own dwelling place. So now I can be busy becoming rich in the sight of God, knowing my efforts won't be in vain.

Loving Father, like all your creatures I'm desperate to be saved on all fronts. Because of your Son's work, I'm confident that all that I am will escape destruction. Into your hands I commend my spirit.

Home Sweet Home

Father Lawrence Donohoo

"And if I go and prepare a place for you, I will come back again and take you to myself, so that where I am you also may be. Where [I] am going you know the way."
(Jn 14:3-4)

While enjoying dinner at a colleague's home, I tried to time my departure just right to avoid the affronts of premature exit or prolonged stay. Moments before I planned to announce my leave, my colleague's wife lost her composure, loudly asking when I would leave since she had to rise early and she was tired and it had been a long evening and I was staying rather long. Completely nonplussed, I quickly expressed my thanks for a wonderful evening and an excellent dinner, hastened to the door, and drove home as fast as possible. Wearing out one's welcome is always painful, whether it happens in a brief conversation when wandering eyes fasten on the watch or cell phone, or during a weeklong stay with a relative when the host's sullenness and forced smiles allow only one possible painful explanation. Wouldn't it be wonderful to be invited to where this could never happen, where my presence was never a burden?

This is what Jesus promises. He goes before us to prepare our lasting home. An antiphon on Saint Martin's feast day expresses this poignantly: "How happy is that man whose soul gains paradise! Angels rejoice, archangels sing praise, choirs of saints call out to him: Stay with us forever!" This is exactly what Jesus invites us to do. Right after predicting Peter's triple denial that he ever knew his Lord, Jesus assures him and the other disciples that he wants them in his eternal dwelling place for ever. This home differs from all other homes not only in never ending. It is also our only true home, because only there can our heart find ultimate rest and supreme joy. So when we find ourselves longing for home, often for one that is no more or no longer the way it was, Jesus invites us to look ahead rather than back—to a dwelling that he, with his Father and Spirit, calls home himself.

Most merciful Father, like all your poor images, I recognize the simple truth that here I'm really homeless—until I lift my eyes to the eternal dwelling places. Help me get ready to get home.

Land's End

Father Lawrence Donohoo

Thomas said to [Jesus], "Master, we do not know where you are going; how can we know the way?" Jesus said to him, "I am the way and the truth and the life. No one comes to the Father except through me. If you know me, then you will also know my Father. From now on you do know him and have seen him."

(Jn 14:5-7)

I tell you I'm heading out west by foot from Maine. You ask (among other things!) about my route and destination. It makes a big difference if I answer that I'm stopping at the eastern rim of Death Valley, or that I'm going all the way through Death Valley to reach the California shoreline. Not only does the destination shape the route we take (pausing to rest up north in Calgary wouldn't work), it also requires the traveler to go the whole length of the journey. So if human life ends at the rim of the valley of death, and that's all there is, a destination that stops just short of eternal life will mean a human life very differently lived.

The accent should be placed on "I": *Jesus* is the way and the truth and the life. As way, he is our companion on the road of life and in some sense the road we're traveling on. As life, he is the eternal destination we're aiming for. As truth, he is the continuity of way and destination. His word of truth assures me that I traverse across the continent of earthly life to the rim and through the valley of death, and beyond to the ocean of divine love. Many segments, one trip. So I will avoid the mistake of living a life that ignores death or views it as an insurmountable wall. I will also resist the error of avoiding life and waiting for God or Godot to arrive or fetch me. I will laugh and cry, but not excessively, because no story ends here. Embracing every leg of the journey, I will use my two legs to experience life "more abundantly" (Jn 10:10). And this in imitation of the Way who fully walked the way of life through death to the Resurrection, and the Life who rose to speak the Truth that ours is his journey and his journey ours.

Heavenly Father, there's a journey to be made, and it should be exciting. Good things are meant to happen along the way of life. Help me be a seasoned traveler who walks behind and with your Son.

Sight Unseen

Father Lawrence Donohoo

Philip said to [Jesus], "Master, show us the Father, and that will be enough for us." Jesus said to him, "Have I been with you for so long a time and you still do not know me, Philip? Whoever has seen me has seen the Father. How can you say, 'Show us the Father'?" (Jn 14:8-9)

Johnny always plays by the rules. So after agreeing that hide-and-seek is confined to Mr. Olson's property, I know when I'm "it" that Johnny, as one of the "hiders," is there but not seen. Because I'm hampered by adulthood, I can't tell him how metaphysically interesting hiddenness is. Darting here and there, I can't pause to explain that hiddenness is the presence of being and the absence of appearances. I "see" that Johnny has got to be here somewhere through the evidence of fair play, but I can't see where he is just yet.

The philosophers explain that God in a similar way is hiding behind and within his world. Those who trace back the ways of truth and being and beauty to ultimate origins should arrive at Saint Paul's "unknown God," who is only known by the marvelous works of his hands. And the believer, of course, may go further and read into creation the Lord who showed his face, seeing his blood in the rose and his eyes in the stars. In this way, with the eyes of faith, he or she illuminates creation in the colors of Scripture and engraves nature with the textures of revealed love.

Jesus, however, is expressing a truth still deeper. We see him with the eyes of faith, although differently from Philip who once walked beside him. And seeing Jesus, we see his Father. This sighting differs from the divine showings revealed in the flowers. Seeing with the eyes of faith in fact is often clearer when the earthly eyes are shut. It is firmly sighting him in an empty full gaze as invisible as the air and as palpable as the wind. Of course this isn't the vision of heavenly glory. When we see him that way later, we'll no longer see him this way now. But this is enough for us for now. Our journey is meant to lead us through different kinds of vision.

Almighty Father, I'm not now overcome by the vision of your beauty so that I might see you in the world you've made. Train my vision to see you with and beyond your creation through your Son.

A Reason to Reason

Father Lawrence Donohoo

"Do you not believe that I am in the Father and the Father is in me? The words that I speak to you I do not speak on my own. The Father who dwells in me is doing his works. Believe me that I am in the Father and the Father is in me, or else, believe because of the works themselves."
(Jn 14:10-11)

Likely the work of a malcontent or a prankster, my mail includes a letter from the American Association of Atheistic Academies inviting me to think. Their argument asks me to begin with common experience about the three Ss that religionists allegedly have so much trouble with: science, sickness, and suffering. From a correct interpretation of those universal phenomena, I'm to make the grand step to the conclusion that a God who lacks compassion is a far less attractive proposition than a God who lacks existence. In other words, I'm to move from rather certain realities, to specific interpretations about them, to a grand leap of faith about the nonexistence of God. A rather tall order.

Jesus is asking the inquirer to engage in an act of reasoning as well. For those who cannot take the more direct path from engaging him to belief in the Father, he opens to them another. They can train their reason on the Father's works, but this rather general term can span the range from Christ's deeds to the marvels of creation. If God is the creator of heaven and earth, how in the world can he require that we check our reason at the door of belief? Did he not also create the logical, inquiring human mind as well as a world that yields itself to human inquiry? Does he not also expect us to begin with the evidence around us, interpret it carefully, and then make this grand leap of faith—or rather, of reason—to conclude that he is alive and well? Can't he also enable reason to take a further step to affirm that it is reasonable that the Creator of heaven and earth might actually wish to reveal himself personally? And that God can reward the one who reasons through to faith with the further conviction that submitting one's reason to the Creator of knower and known is a most sensible thing to do?

Eternal Father, I thank you for the truth and my capacity to find it. You show me in faith that your creative love is the reason for any knowledge I possess. Help me to mind this gift with care.

Much to Be Humble About

Father Lawrence Donohoo

"Amen, amen, I say to you, whoever believes in me will do the works that I do, and will do greater ones than these, because I am going to the Father. And whatever you ask in my name, I will do, so that the Father may be glorified in the Son. If you ask anything of me in my name, I will do it."

(Jn 14:12-14)

Humility is perhaps the victim of more bad jokes than any other virtue. The reason for this is that virtues, like people, are expected to leave a good impression. As soon as humility tries to meet this demand, it is roundly reprimanded for presenting itself at all. How can this poor virtue win? By effacing itself; by not consorting with other virtues; by hiding under aliases. Humility does best when it remains true to its capacity to step aside in order to allow another to share some domain of being. It flourishes when it goes unnoticed. We see this illustrated clearly in Jesus' saying that his disciples' works will surpass his when he departs to the Father. By empowering them to outpower him, Jesus enables his followers to have their glorious day in the sun.

In fact, the mystery of divine humility shapes and penetrates our world. Creation is the act by which God willed to abandon solitude and share being with us. The very world he created often looks as if it's doing just fine without him. Hiding behind his world, God gives creatures a space to flourish without the presence of his blinding glory. By giving us free will, God humbly accepts the risk of being insulted, ignored, and denied. His humility allows atheists to flourish and profit richly from his "nonexistence." The supreme expression of divine humility is Jesus. In his Incarnation, God willed to look like a common human being. In his death, God consented to be confused for an uncommon criminal.

What we do without Jesus' earthly presence but with his heavenly support is greater than what he does alone. In this way God allows us to share in his riches by permitting us to claim them as well. By letting us share the limelight, the divine humility, which would otherwise remain hidden, appears. In this way we glorify God—and shine ourselves—by doing his work for him.

Loving Father, I thank you for making me all that I am. I ask forgiveness for diminishing myself, the work of your hands. Through your Son's grace make me great enough to help others become great.

A Rare Bird

Father Lawrence Donohoo

"If you love me, you will keep my commandments. And I will ask the Father, and he will give you another Advocate to be with you always, the Spirit of truth, which the world cannot accept, because it neither sees nor knows it. But you know it, because it remains with you, and will be in you."

(Jn 14:15-17)

Long before the rosy-fingered dawn stretched her hands toward us, we heard the distant calls of hooting owls alert the landscape. I had joined an Audubon Society bird count to help out—and see more of God's flighty creatures. I wasn't disappointed: before afternoon struck we had sighted seventy-eight species, blessed by a professor ornithologist as our leader and a wetland shoreline as our tract. As I lay half dozing in the returning car, I mused on all these creatures whom we so seldom see or hear.

Like these elusive birds, the Divine Dove too is often difficult to sight. And yet he is not very far from any one of us. The Holy Spirit is easily missed, then forgotten—the neglected Person of the Trinity. Why is this? Perhaps because he's humble, working behind the scenes. He's also hard to sight because he's hard to picture— a dove, tongues of fire only go so far. Maybe he's also shy, like those winged marvels that appear only to the patient. Yet he is present everywhere, even on Scripture's first and last pages. In the beginning he says: "Go!" Go forth, creation, become order and beauty! At the end he says: "Come!" Come into the New Jerusalem! Between beginning and end he says: "Renew!" Come back, creation, to the God who sends you forth!

"When you send forth your Spirit, they are created, and you renew the face of the earth." To renew is to take the old and transform it, to acknowledge that the old is good, but not good enough. If it weren't good, he would just start over. If it were good enough, he wouldn't change it. The Holy Spirit is a caring curator who specializes in restoring and perfecting. He is the Divine Steward who brings out of his storehouse things both old and new. He is the forger of desire who stirs the heart to rise early and wait for him in silence.

Heavenly Father, your Holy Spirit is my silent companion who teaches me how to fly. He is never satisfied until I have developed the wings of truth and love. Teach me to discover him.

The Present Indicative

Father Lawrence Donohoo

"I will not leave you orphans; I will come to you. In a little while the world will no longer see me, but you will see me, because I live and you will live. On that day you will realize that I am in my Father and you are in me and I in you."

(Jn 14:18-20)

According to the sacred myths, Lycurgus, founder of Sparta, secured an oath from its citizens that they would not alter the laws he promulgated until he returned from a long journey. He never did, disappearing into the mists of time and thus assuring an eternal fidelity to the laws he bequeathed his people. The great men of Scripture faced a similar task of preserving their legacy in farewell speeches. Moses poignantly exhorted the Chosen People to hold steadfast to the Law. Saint Paul charged the Ephesians to remain true to the Gospel he preached. And Revelation, providing a coda to the entire Scriptures, warns and invites believers to hold fast to God's Word.

We expect nothing less from Jesus, and so we read the Last Discourses as the farewell speech of God. And yet they differ from all the testaments—of Jacob, Moses, Joshua, David, Elijah, Stephen, Paul—for the one who leaves behind his words will take no final leave! Rather, the Last Discourses promise us that the one who speaks them will be right back—twice. But after he rises, and again, after he ascends, he's finished going. Now he is "with [us] always, until the end of the age" (Mt 28:20). Historically and visibly, Jesus goes before us; spiritually and mystically, he remains: "you are in me and I in you."

So we must be careful with our tenses. The Apostles' present is our past; their future is our present; Jesus' future is our past; his present is his presence. I resist the urge to conjure up the presence of one long gone. I read these words *with* Christ who is present within and before me. Indeed, his presence in me means he reads these words "out loud." I'm hearing him. Jesus does for me today what he did yesterday in Emmaus. This book, then, is different. We're reading this together. He's in the room here. The Last Discourses are my present guide.

Almighty Father, I need to keep clear on the simple fact that your Son who has gone before me is in my very presence. I am the one who is too often absent. Help me with your grace to show up and stay.

This One's For You

Father Lawrence Donohoo

"Whoever has my commandments and observes them is the one who loves me. And whoever loves me will be loved by my Father, and I will love him and reveal myself to him."

(Jn 14:21)

When communism ruled large swaths of mankind, the votes of their ruling bodies were usually almost unanimous. Why almost? Since there was no freedom of dissent, why 435-2, or 287-3, or 371-1? To give citizens of free nations the false impression that most were convinced by the wisdom of the "proposal" rather than coerced by the iron hand. The one or two naysayers were either stooges told to vote no or dissenters who would never vote again. Anyone over the age of two knows that no two people agree on everything. Not only is that impossible, it's also undesirable. Each of us has a unique take on life, seeing the true, the good, and the beautiful somewhat alike and somewhat differently. The reason we argue and debate and discuss is precisely to convince and be convinced. We recognize that the other person doesn't have the whole corner on truth, and neither do we.

Why should we expect God to require anything different? Just as we aspire to common ideals and shared visions and even unanimous decisions, so we recognize and affirm the goodness of *e pluribus unum*—out of many, one. Unity is not the lockstep of uniformity; it is the successful gathering of harmonious differences. Saint Paul, employing the body and its various parts as an image of unity in difference, expects distinctions to be maintained even as he reminds us of "one body and one Spirit...one hope of [our] call; one Lord, one faith, one baptism, one God and Father of all" (Eph 4:4-6).

What a consolation to learn that Jesus affirms for each believer a distinct revelation of himself and of his Father through him. Each of us is given a particular portrait of Christ, a special grasp of the Gospel, a unique experience of God. And with that in our possession, we have the joy of exchange as we give to and take from those likewise—and differently—blessed.

Eternal Father, I thank you for the distinct vision of you in your Son that my knowing, loving, conscience, and vocation reveal. Help me to treasure my grasp of you and to pass it on to others.

To Become Another

Father Lawrence Donohoo

*Judas, not the Iscariot, said to [Jesus], "Master, [then] what
happened that you will reveal yourself to us and not to the
world?" Jesus answered and said to him, "Whoever loves me
will keep my word, and my Father will love him, and we will
come to him and make our dwelling with him. Whoever does
not love me does not keep my words; yet the word you hear is
not mine but that of the Father who sent me." (Jn 14:22-24)*

Some forty-five years later, Alistair Horne returns to Verdun,
France, the site of the longest and perhaps bloodiest battle ever
waged. Entering a local bistro, the author of *The Price of Glory*
finds some French veterans at one table and some German veterans
at another. They nod respectfully to one another, and then wine
and dine with their comrades of old. After all those years these old
soldiers return to hell on earth, a place so grim that even today it
remains abandoned, untilled, desolate—a perpetual memorial to the
waste of war, the worship of power, the destruction of God's image.
After all those years, they return, not so much to commemorate the
nobility of sacrifice but to tighten the bonds of love. In the crucible
of battle, they learned that "stern as death is love,/ relentless as the
nether world is devotion" (Sg 8:6). They learned that even if the
battlefield is a foundry for love, love's essence is to form something
larger and greater than oneself. To love is to escape the confines of
self, to become owner and possessor of a larger world.

This is the promise of Jesus to his disciples as he invites them into
the most intimate and intense of all communities: the Blessed Trinity.
Indeed, the mystery of God's social life is that each divine person is
so completely the other that they form together a common nature.
When Pythagoras in ancient times noted that friends share all things
in common, he meant something more than goods, pleasures, or
even experiences. He meant we share our very selves, becoming
someone else. Not only are we one with another's good, we are
one with another's being. The true lover's "I" becomes "we." One
who understands this much will also grasp why God wills to share
all things in common, taking on our human nature at Nazareth,
our human lot at Bethlehem, and our human suffering at Calvary.

*Loving Father, when all is said and done, the language of love is
spelled with unity. You are the supreme expression of love with
your Son and Holy Spirit. Teach this world to follow your example.*

Next

Father Lawrence Donohoo

"I have told you this while I am with you. The Advocate, the holy Spirit that the Father will send in my name—he will teach you everything and remind you of all that [I] told you."
(Jn 14:25-26)

Once upon a death a soul was sent to the Waiting Room. Soon his number was called and was stamped with a *P*. "Thank God!" he exclaimed, delighted to be running to the Purgatory Express. Feeling sociable, he asked what it would be like. "Oh, just a basic review of your life," the conductor responded. Not bad at all, the soul mused. An hour later he was sobbing uncontrollably as a film of his life unwound. With the "Reveal Codes" function, a saint exposed the persons he wounded, the pleas he ignored, the qualms he despised, the prospects he missed, the graces he lost. "That's enough for today," the saint said, consoling the soul with a big spiritual hug. "Tomorrow's lesson is the Divine Fire of Love."

The Spirit of truth's task is to save us from self-deception. Always gentle with the budding saint, he still "tells it like it is" and "speaks the truth in love." But the other side of truth is consolation. The One who critiques consoles, reminding us that God is patient, kind, bears all things, endures all things. Between critique and consolation is challenge, so that we can be more consoled than critiqued. The Spirit moves us to accept the Mover within. He comes now because fire already should blaze in our hearts. No reason to fear he'll destroy; he takes what's there. Conversion means to "turn with." He turns with what we have. He turns with us, turning dross to gold, tested by fire. The Holy Spirit is fire. Turning needs oil to keep things smooth: the Oil of Gladness. Turning needs water; water makes churning. He hovers over the water. With the Spirit and the water we are born anew. Fire, oil, water. Let's take on the challenge now. The oil salves our wounds. It keeps us afloat in the water, though the waters rage and foam. We can't forget he once formed a world the same way.

Most merciful Father, I need not fear the truth of myself because your Holy Spirit's greatest lesson is that grace is stronger than my sins and follies. Teach me to trust his school of truth and love.

The Gift of Peace

Father Richard Veras

"Peace I leave with you; my peace I give to you.
Not as the world gives do I give it to you. Do not let
your hearts be troubled or afraid." (Jn 14:27)

How does the peace of Jesus compare to the peace that the world gives?

After many years of helping on a yearly high school vacation/retreat that takes place in my home state of New York or in nearby New England, I was informed on a month's notice that the annual trip would be changed to California because a beautiful mountain retreat house had a sudden cancellation.

I was stunned that some of the other teachers and priests were even considering the ambitious undertaking on such short notice. I had all my reasons not to go: the expense, the high altitudes for hiking, airport challenges, lack of time for preparation.

However, some teachers were certain that this was a God-given opportunity that we shouldn't fear. In the end, I begrudgingly agreed to participate.

The vacation/retreat was among the most fruitful that we have had, and perhaps the most personally fruitful for me thus far.

The students' appreciation of the beauty, their attentiveness and responsiveness to the content of the retreat, and the depth and creativity of their own contributions that week were astounding. Even airport personnel were amazed at how smoothly our group moved through security and connecting flights, and fellow hikers were amazed at the students' maturity and even more at their joy.

The peace of Jesus comes from following him even when he leads us outside of our categories of possibility and invites us to depend like little children. The worldly peace I was tempted by is a kind of self-satisfaction at being right, which is shallow and short-lived.

Jesus' peace is his presence. If we are open to his surprising action in our lives, and to the fact that he is God and we are not, his presence begins to speak to us. Through what happens in the events and encounters we experience, he says to us, "Do not let your hearts be troubled or afraid."

Almighty Father, grant me the humility to realize that I cannot give myself peace, but can only find it in following Christ with the wide-open eyes of a child.

The Son of the Father

Father Richard Veras

"You heard me tell you, 'I am going away and I will come back to you.' If you loved me, you would rejoice that I am going to the Father; for the Father is greater than I. And now I have told you this before it happens, so that when it happens you may believe."

(Jn 14:28-29)

When I used to invite my students at an all-boys high school to retreats, my invitation would invariably elicit the question "Will there be girls?" And in one class another student responded to the question by saying, "Forget it, any girl you're gonna meet on a retreat is a 'daddy's girl.'"

It turns out that boys with bad intentions know that if a girl's father is present in her life, i.e., if she knows that she is a "beloved daughter," then they can't take advantage of her. The embrace of their fathers enables these young women to become themselves and to flourish within a relationship of true love. It also makes them quick to recognize and to reject love's false and harmful impostor: possession.

If the disciples begrudge Jesus' going to the Father, they not only do not love Jesus, but they don't know who he is. Everything that Jesus is—his authority, his love, his mercy, his tender gaze, flows from his relationship with the Father. In fact, his way of looking at us is so attractive because he never looks at us apart from our relation to the Father who has loved us into existence. There is no such thing as Jesus abstracted from the Father. Recall that he told the Apostle Philip, "If you have seen me, you have seen the Father."

When Jesus was tempted in the desert, the devil tried repeatedly to separate Jesus from his Father, for the devil is the paragon of the boy with bad intentions.

We cannot possess Jesus. We cannot reduce him to what we want him to be. If we love him, we rejoice in who he is and whose he is. He is the revelation of the Father. He leads us to the Infinite Love who will never be possessed by us, and for that very reason continually stretches our capacity to receive and to give love toward infinity.

Eternal Father, may we rejoice in the unity of the Father, the Son, and the Holy Spirit, which has loved us into being and redeemed us into salvation, that we may be exalted within that unity now and for ever.

The Liberation of Following Christ

Father Richard Veras

"I will no longer speak much with you, for the ruler of the world is coming. He has no power over me, but the world must know that I love the Father and that I do just as the Father has commanded me. Get up, let us go." (Jn 14:30-31)

Nazism seemed powerful, but it couldn't stop Maximilian Kolbe from loving a relative stranger, even to the point of death. It couldn't stop Corrie and Betsie ten Boom from risking their lives to hide Jews, and from living their faith even in a concentration camp.

Communism seemed to be very powerful, but Servant of God Walter Ciszek, an imprisoned priest, remained a free man, full of faith and certainty and human dignity even in the most difficult moments of his confinement.

The culture of death seems extremely powerful, but Dr. Bernard Nathanson, who was responsible for thousands of abortions, recognized the human destruction it caused and, doing his best to speak to the truth, he eventually found his way to Jesus Christ and entered the Church.

The hatred caused by the aftermath of the genocide in Rwanda seemed too strong a force to resist for those who lost loved ones, but Immaculée Illibagiza found the freedom to forgive, and thus to live.

These are but a few witnesses to the truth that the ruler of this world has no power over Christ. Against the assertion of oppressive power that threatens our hope as much as anything else, what is Christ's secret weapon? The person! The person who knows that Christ is real and that Christ is present. That person cannot be stopped from begging for Christ's love and witnessing to it by overflowing with that same love for others. That person, in the midst of even the most horrendous difficulties, discovers by experience the promise of Saint Paul who tells us that nothing can separate us from the love of Christ.

The powers of this world are not ultimately vanquished by strategies or by a reactive show of power, but by Christian disciples who, wherever they find themselves, respond with a simple "yes" to Christ, just as Jesus saved the world by offering a "yes" to the Father at his most difficult moment.

God our Father, grant us the grace to let the world know that Christ loves you. May we follow Jesus with the same filial "yes" as he ever offers to you.

Loss and Gain

Father George William Rutler

"I am the true vine, and my Father is the vine grower.
He takes away every branch in me that does not bear fruit,
and everyone that does he prunes so that it bears more fruit."
(Jn 15:1-2)

When Christ comes into the world, he declares his divinity in the same harmonious pattern which holds the world together. As he made the world together with the Father and the Holy Spirit in seven stages, so he reveals in seven utterances that he is the "I AM" who spoke to Moses. He says I AM the Light of the World, the Way and the Truth and the Life, the Bread of Heaven, the Good Shepherd, the Gate of the Sheepfold, the Resurrection, and the Vine.

As the Father sends the Son into the world, so Jesus explains that he and the Father "are one" and so he is "never alone." As the Creed says, the Son is "true God from true God." The Son comes into the world to die for us out of love. Experience teaches that love grows the more it gives itself for others. That sacrifice of the self requires suffering because it is up against the selfish world that rejects selflessness. Growth in love is like "pruning" vine branches. To lose a little is to gain a lot, rather the way an athlete slims down to become stronger. Suffering for a purpose cures the misery of pleasure without a purpose.

Aristotle said that to get a message across convincingly, it takes three things: *ethos*, which is honesty of character; *sophos*, which is wisdom; and *pathos*, which is suffering endured to strengthen character and broaden wisdom. *Pathos* is God's pruning. Jesus says that if we try to save our life we shall lose it, but if we lose our life for his sake we shall gain it. That is his straightforward explanation of the pruning process. Fruitless vines contradict why they exist, but "less is more," as some architects say, when we are willing to trim our ego in order to fit into the heart of Jesus.

Heavenly Father, as you have given me my life, grant me the courage to lose what you want me to lose, so that I may not lose myself along the way.

Sent by Christ

Father George William Rutler

*"You are already pruned because of the word that I spoke to you.
Remain in me, as I remain in you. Just as a branch cannot bear
fruit on its own unless it remains on the vine, so neither
can you unless you remain in me."*
(Jn 15:3-4)

Jesus has been accustomed to people calling him Teacher, and his teaching has "pruned," or strengthened, his followers. But his teaching is not just a matter of words. He himself is the Word that made all things and that gives life to each of us. So he does not say simply that God's Word is true. He says more wonderfully that God's Word is truth (see Jn 17:17). The best of human teachers pass along truths, but they cannot pass along truth itself, for they can pass along information but they cannot pass along themselves. When a professor of some science dies, someone else takes his "chair" and may try to emulate or even improve upon what he had been taught by his predecessor. That old genius Saint Albert the Great may have hoped that the young genius Saint Thomas Aquinas sitting in his lecture hall might someday take up where he left off, but Thomas never said, "Albert lives in me." Saint Paul boasted that his teacher had been the great Gamaliel, but he never said, "Gamaliel lives in me." But after his conversion, Paul says, "I have been crucified with Christ; yet I live, no longer I, but Christ lives in me" (Gal 2:19-20).

More than giving the facts of life, Christ gives life itself, and once his followers accept that life, he is able to tell them, "Whoever receives you receives me" (Mt 10:40). To be cut off from the Word of Jesus would be to make our own words what Macbeth called "sound and fury, signifying nothing." The Apostles bring Christ the Living Word, and not Christ as a quotation, to the world. The Second Vatican Council says: "The Bishops, from divine institution, have taken the place of the Apostles, as the pastors of the Church, and he who hears them, hears Christ; he who spurns them, spurns Christ and him who sent Christ" (*Lumen Gentium*, 20).

Eternal Father, let me hear your voice through the prophets and saints, so that I may then answer by saying Amen.

Doing Nothing

Father George William Rutler

*"I am the vine, you are the branches. Whoever remains in me
and I in him will bear much fruit, because without me you can
do nothing. Anyone who does not remain in me will be thrown
out like a branch and wither; people will gather them
and throw them into a fire and they will be burned."*

(Jn 15:5-6)

Our Lord seems to be predicting the fate of Judas Iscariot who wanted to be the Vine rather than a branch. This is the original sin of pride which is the ego playing God: "You will be like gods" (Gn 3:5). So spoke "the Father of Lies" who tries to separate souls from the Vine through flattery one moment and intimidation the next, enticing with false pleasure and then frightening with real pain.

Judas tried to live as a Christian without Christ, and so he withered. His shriveled soul tried to return the money for which he sold the Master, but he was "thrown out like a branch" by the same people with whom he had conspired, rather like Benedict Arnold who, in exile in London, was shunned on the streets by the people for whom he had spied. Jesus does not say that he will burn the withered branch. He says "the people" will do that. The people are the cynics who love sin and hate the sinner, in a reversal of the divine mercy which hates the sin and loves the sinner.

Every time we delight in beauty and truth and goodness in their countless forms, we show in small human ways something of the delight God takes in the world he made. This is what Saint Irenaeus meant in saying, "The glory of God is man fully alive." To try to delight in creation without delighting in its Creator is to self-destruct as Judas did. No one hanged him. He hanged himself, and by so doing, he unmade what God had made. "Without me you can do nothing." Once separated from the Vine, we actually can "do" nothing, forming emptiness and framing futility. The True Vine warns us of this because he does not want it to happen, and it will not happen if we remain in him as he wants to remain in us.

*Merciful Father, grant through your Son and Holy Spirit that we
may always love you and never be separated from you.*

To What He Wants

Father George William Rutler

"If you remain in me and my words remain in you, ask for whatever you want and it will be done for you. By this is my Father glorified, that you bear much fruit and become my disciples." (Jn 15:7-8)

Which comes first: the chicken or the egg? That old puzzle is updated in the expression taken from the 1961 novel *Catch-22*, meaning a situation that is impossible to get out of because of its inherent contradictions. It would seem that the Lord presents us with a conundrum when he says that anything we ask for will be done for us, if we stay with him and keep his words. There is a catch in the "if" but not a catch-22 sort of catch. If we are morally united with Christ through the bond of love which is the Holy Spirit, that same Holy Spirit will inspire us to ask for what God wants for us, and not just for what we want. He says "if" because we have a free will to ask for anything. But since God only wills our good, he gives us only what will make us eternally happy, even if at the time it may seem harsh and even wrong.

A true disciple prays as Christ himself prayed the night before his death: "Not my will but yours be done" (Lk 22:42). It cannot be denied that those words produce much fruit: Christian civilization, and the salvation of souls. It is the most powerful prayer ever uttered. Prayer always produces results when it is what Christ would pray. But when that bond is broken, prayer becomes like a man just talking to himself. When a crowd walks away from Christ, he asks the Apostles if they are also going to leave him. When the three Apostles fall asleep as he prays in his agony, he wakes them up to ask if they could spare just one hour with him. Remain. To stay with Christ is our greatest prayer, needing no words. Saint Peter learns that from experience: "He who believes in him will not be disappointed" (cf. 1 Pt 2:6).

Heavenly Father, through the power of the Holy Spirit, grant that I may ask for what your Son would want me to ask for, desiring him first above all else.

Love and the Law

Father George William Rutler

"As the Father loves me, so I also love you. Remain in my love.
If you keep my commandments, you will remain in my love,
just as I have kept my Father's commandments and remain
in his love.
"I have told you this so that my joy might be in you
and your joy might be complete." (Jn 15:9-11)

Once in reply to a scribe who had asked which is the greatest of the commandments, Jesus says, "You shall love the Lord your God…" The venerable law was old as Moses, but the difference now is that the God of Moses is in Christ reciting it. That is why Jesus then says to the scribe: "You are not far from the kingdom of God" (Mk 12:34). The scribe is just a few feet from the Kingdom of God, since Christ is the King. Yet, it is possible to be close to someone physically and still be a world away mentally. An x-ray gives many details about a person, but a good portrait evokes the personality. As "the face of God," Jesus says, "Whoever has seen me has seen the Father" (Jn 14:9). Moral laws tell what God is, but who God is can only be known by loving him. If love were not a fact but a feeling, it would not be love at all but sentimentality, and it would make no moral demands. Jesus bids obedience to his commandments, which are the truths of life, in order to remain in love with him who is Truth itself. Love and law go together, and love is the highest law. Love is not forced on us, but it is required of us. Once we choose to love, we move from closeness to the kingdom, to citizenship in the kingdom.

Saint Catherine of Siena said, "All the way to heaven is heaven, because Jesus said, I am the way." And as heaven is joy, so love is the way to it. Mark Twain, who knew something about humor, said that if you want to be cheerful, make other people cheerful. Jesus tells us this by living it. He wants our joy to be "complete." Now as then, he enthralls many and infuriates others, but he depresses none.

Eternal Father, grant me the strength to obey your commandments
with a loving heart, so that I may come to know the joy of the Holy
Spirit who is the bond of love between you and your Son.

What a Friend We Have in Jesus

Father George William Rutler

"This is my commandment: love one another as I love you.
No one has greater love than this, to lay down one's life for one's
friends. You are my friends if you do what I command you."
(Jn 15:12-14)

There was a man according to one account who said, "If there is one thing I cannot stand, it is name-dropping. In fact, I recently said the same thing to Her Majesty the Queen and she perfectly agreed." Everyone likes to have important friends. All Christians are allowed, and even commanded, to drop the name that is above all other names, because the Holy Name himself says that those who keep his commandment are his friends. But that highest friendship in the world has the highest cost: my whole life. When our heavenly friend came to us from the unseen world, his feet were covered with the dust of this very visible world. In him was the love that made man himself from that dust. Man himself, and not God, complicates the definition of love. It is easy to fall into the trap of making love a sort of difficult calculus: a "feeling" or an "attraction" or a "commitment" or a "benevolence." But that kind of complicated calculus would make the lover a calculator with mixed motives. Our Lord makes it simple: to love is to lay down one's life for one's friends. That is the "greatest" love, and any other version of it is at worst an imitation and at best an approximation. Self-sacrifice is the simplest of all things and also the hardest of all things. While everyone knows the meaning of "falling in love," the soul has to climb up to the greatest love. Jesus does that as he carries his cross. So says an old hymn: "Can we find a friend so faithful, who will all our sorrows share?" He "falls in love" three times under the cross for us, but he gets up three times and is raised up on that cross as the world's greatest love.

Almighty God our heavenly Father, grant that I might love your Son as he loves me, and give my life to him as my Savior and friend.

Strangers No More

Father George William Rutler

"I no longer call you slaves, because a slave does not know what his master is doing. I have called you friends, because I have told you everything I have heard from my Father."
(Jn 15:15)

It is easy to arouse curiosity by whispering, "I've got a secret." That sort of manipulation is characteristic of mere mortals who start up false religions by pretending to know some arcane information that only a few will be told. Christ does the opposite. He does not manipulate human curiosity. He gives us all we need to know by letting us know him as a friend. Of course the great truths he reveals have to be explained gradually through miracles, which is why the Scriptures call them "signs," and through parables that are meant to illustrate. "For there is nothing hidden except to be made visible; nothing is secret except to come to light" (Mk 4:22). A false savior mystifies people in order to impress them. The true Savior reveals mysteries so that we will not be mystified. To accept this bright encounter with the truth is to move from the slavery of ignorance to friendship with the Truth himself. Friends do not withhold secrets from each other. Blessed John Henry Newman wrote for his epitaph: *Ex umbris et imaginibus in Veritatem*—Out of the shadows and images into the Truth. Among the different talents that saints have, all of them share a talent for friendship. It is because they see their friend Christ in others. They really practice the saying that, apart from Christ, would risk being a cliché: "A stranger is a friend you have not met." Christ wants no one to be a stranger to him. He is not a stranger to us. "He will bring to light what is hidden in darkness and will manifest the motives of our hearts" (1 Cor 4:5). Children who read *Winnie the Pooh* may remember the line: "If you live to be a hundred, I hope to live to be a hundred minus one day, so I never have to live without you." Happily, with Christ age does not matter.

May I desire your truth, heavenly Father, as you have given it through your Son, so that I may be his friend in words and deeds.

Jesus Puts Us in Our Place

Father George William Rutler

"It was not you who chose me, but I who chose you and appointed you to go and bear fruit that will remain, so that whatever you ask the Father in my name he may give you. This I command you: love one another."

(Jn 15:16-17)

C hrist puts us in our place when he says that he chose us, and not the other way around. He does not put us in our place to make us feel inferior. Quite the opposite, he shows us our place in his great plan for saving the human race. He who is "God from God" does not need anything, but as God is love, he wants us. To be wanted without being needed is a sublime dignity. Christianity is not a human invention. Each Christian has his place in it—to "bear fruit that will remain" as agents of Christ.

Christ makes an impression on those he chooses, and that impression forms their character. There is a parallel in art, for an artist paints the impression a scene has made on him, but the image was there before the artist recorded his impression of it. This is true even of the most realistic classical styles of art. The Spanish artist Joaquin Sorolla said, "All inspired painters are impressionists even though it be true that some impressionists are not inspired." There is another school of art which is expressionist rather than impressionist. It distorts the image in order to express the artist's emotional state. The expressionist in religion thinks that he has chosen Christ as a projection of his own feelings. Matthew Arnold defined religion as a "morality touched with emotion." That diminishes Christ and all those Christ chooses. Christ chose Saint Paul by surprise, and so the Apostle knew that he had not imagined him. He would say: "I received from the Lord what I also handed on to you" (1 Cor 11:23). Once I let God be God in me, instead of designing a god like myself, I may receive whatever I ask for, provided I pray "Through Jesus Christ our Lord."

May I ever be thankful, O Father, that you have chosen your unworthy servant to do your Son's glorious work in this world and to be with you in the full glory of heaven.

Uncomfortable Words

Father George William Rutler

"If the world hates you, realize that it hated me first. If you belonged to the world, the world would love its own; but because you do not belong to the world, and I have chosen you out of the world, the world hates you."

(Jn 15:18-19)

A journalist did a survey of various churches, rating them somewhat like a restaurant review. To get five stars, the pews had to be comfortable. Christ did not neglect people's comfort. Before he fed them he checked to see that there was grass for them to sit on. But what he said was unsettling. Those who want comfortable pews are not likely to want to hear uncomfortable words. In the Sermon on the Mount, the eighth and last beatitude is jarring, for it blesses those who are "persecuted for righteousness' sake." That is the bass clef to the treble clef of Christ's warning that the world will hate true Christians. The "world" does not mean people of good will who may be ignorant of Christ. It is those who find evil more comfortable than good. They are the opposite of those who punish the bearer of bad news, for they punish the bearer of the best news, which is the Gospel. It was so from the start: John was the only Apostle who did not die a violent death. When Christ promises them, and us, a hundred times more joy than this world offers, he adds almost nonchalantly, "and persecutions" (cf. Mk 10:30). Souls are not converted by the quality of pew cushions—which are bad for acoustics anyway. Nor are they converted by half a Gospel with the hard parts left out. The symbols of the Evangelists are a man, lion, ox, and eagle. No little kitten or timid mouse. Saint Paul boasted: "If I were still trying to please people, I would not be a slave of Christ" (Gal 1:10). In a comfortable village, nights are peaceful; but in a large city, the dwellers get suspicious when there is a sudden silence. Christians who do not cause a stir should be suspect. Chesterton said that he believed in getting into hot water; it keeps you clean.

Almighty Father, may I not take pleasure in pleasant words but in true words, and may I seek to please none but yourself, who made me for your delight.

Walking Targets

Father George William Rutler

"Remember the word I spoke to you, 'No slave is greater than his master.' If they persecuted me, they will also persecute you. If they kept my word, they will also keep yours. And they will do all these things to you on account of my name, because they do not know the one who sent me."

(Jn 15:20-21)

All that Jesus preaches to crowds large or small is spoken with a glance toward his Apostles as a form of instruction for these future heads of his Church. Here Jesus reminds them that they are his agents and he is the chief, and what will happen to him will happen to them. As no slave is greater than his master, the lower down should not expect to have things easier than the one who is higher up. Each would follow different paths, but all would be persecuted. He already gave the reason for this: "Everyone who does wicked things hates the light and does not come toward the light, so that his works might not be exposed" (Jn 3:20). Every true Christian is a walking target because Christ is the one aimed at by evildoers, and Christ is in them: "I have been crucified with Christ; yet I live, no longer I, but Christ lives in me" (Gal 2:19-20).

The English poet John Dryden converted to Catholicism in 1686, when the Church in his land still was persecuted in some ways. He knew that there is no real time of peace for Christians, for all of history is a spiritual battle: "Peace is war in masquerade." It is the common experience of honorable veterans of real battles that they do not boast of their bravery, for they know that the real heroes are those who did not survive, and they often feel a tinge of guilt that they are alive while others lie in war cemeteries. Yet even the graves without names are marked with the cross. The calendar of saints marks dates in red for the feast of martyrs. But all the saints, be they soldiers, teachers, evangelists, virgins, clergy, mothers and fathers, and even children, were wounded one way or another for daring to shed light in the darkened battlefield known as human history.

Father of glory, let me serve you without fear of the future or dread of the unknown, for your Son is the light of my path and the victor of every battle.

Ignorance Is Not Bliss

Father George William Rutler

"If I had not come and spoken to them, they would have no sin;
but as it is they have no excuse for their sin.
Whoever hates me also hates my Father."
(Jn 15:22-23)

A blind Italian girl was taken to Lourdes many years ago against her wishes. Proclaiming herself an atheist, she hated the God she claimed did not exist. Her eyes remained blind, but when she entered the baths the sudden surge of love she felt for God never left her. She now is buried near the grotto of the apparition of the Blessed Mother, and her epitaph is as she requested: "What is important is not to see but to understand." There in a nutshell is the contradiction of the bromide "Seeing is believing." Eyes often see illusions, and were that not so, magicians and special effects engineers would be out of business. Christ healed blind people as a parable of the true sight that he has come to give the world: the ability to see the truth of God. Blindness to the truth is ignorance. The "darkness of the intellect" is cured by the light of truth. Philip had seen Jesus daily since the time he was called to be an Apostle, but he did not perceive him until the Master's voice spoke: "Have I been with you for so long a time and you still do not know me, Philip? Whoever has seen me has seen the Father" (Jn 14:9). When a priest expressed surprise that one of his altar boys had never heard of the saint whose feast was being celebrated on a given day, the boy said, "Father, I guess you think I'm stupid." The priest replied, "You are not stupid at all. You are just ignorant." Because the youth did not know the difference, he did not feel reassured. Ignorance is just a matter of not knowing something and, unlike stupidity, it can be cured by knowledge. Once that knowledge is given, rejection of it is what Blessed John Henry Newman called a sin against the light.

Almighty Father, I thank you for the gift of your Son, who opens our eyes of faith so that we might know you, whom no one has ever seen.

No Excuse

Father George William Rutler

"If I had not done works among them that no one else ever did, they would not have sin; but as it is, they have seen and hated both me and my Father. But in order that the word written in their law might be fulfilled, 'They hated me without cause.'"
(Jn 15:24-25)

The "lost sheep of the house of Israel" were God's own people. He could say "we" when he spoke of them, but now the "we" becomes "they" because his own have rejected him. The most harrowing of all the Church's liturgical chants are the Good Friday "Reproaches" which imagine the thoughts of Christ on the cross with lines like, "I led you from slavery to freedom and drowned your captives in the sea, but you handed me over to your high priests. My people, what have I done to you? How have I offended you? Answer me!" The works he performs go back to the beginning of time. The creation of days out of light is his first great work, and yet to our own day, there are people who deny that he made all things out of nothing. Saint John records seven miracles, which parallel the seven stages of creation itself. But even if people are so obtuse as not to grasp this symmetry, or so ungrateful as to forget it, he does not cut himself off from them. "They" may hate him without cause, but he does not hate them. In his dying hours, he asks his Father to forgive "them," but they are still "my people."

If those who saw him in the flesh had no excuse for rejecting him, even less do we have excuse after two thousand years of saints to intercede, and doctrines to teach, as well as the reminder of millions of lives destroyed when social systems rejected God. People hate him "without cause" because Satan hates him through them. Shall I let God love through me, or let Satan hate through me? God has done great works among us, and so there is no avoiding accountability for the choice. Rudyard Kipling said, "We have forty million reasons for failure, but not a single excuse."

Merciful Father, worker of wonders, let me sing with all the Church your praise, for despite my weakness I am wonderfully made by your love that never fails those who love you.

Not a Theft But a Gift

Father George William Rutler

*"When the Advocate comes whom I will send you from the
Father, the Spirit of truth that proceeds from the Father,
he will testify to me. And you also testify, because you
have been with me from the beginning."*
(Jn 15:26-27)

Those who hesitate to sound "too religious" find it easier to use the ancient classical gods to illustrate points, than to mention God himself. It is rather like the way some people hesitate to call a clergyman "Father," but have no problem calling him "Padre" even if they do not know Spanish. Perhaps it is the thrill of things foreign, which is why the wag said that opera is sung in Italian all over the world except in Italy where it is sung in German. When New York's Rockefeller Center was built, everyone seemed satisfied with the statue chosen for the skating rink: a gilded Prometheus. It was a safe choice because no one believes in him anyway. Though grand in design, the model for it was an ordinary postal worker, and the sculptor, Paul Manship, seemed rather bored with the whole project. But Prometheus is there because an industrialized culture does believe in what he symbolizes, as described in the quotation from Aeschylus: "Prometheus, teacher in every art, brought the fire that hath proved to mortals a means to mighty ends." That mythic Titan stole fire from the gods, and gave it to mankind. Sometimes the Greeks had a right intuition of God, if backwards. Christ came into the world to give mankind an everlasting fire, the love between him and his Father: "I have come to set the earth on fire, and how I wish it were already blazing!" (Lk 12:49). The holy fire was a blessed gift and not a criminal theft. Christ said that the Father would send this fire, the "Advocate" or helper, who is the Holy Spirit (see Jn 14:16). Now he says that he will send the Advocate from the Father. This is not a contradiction. Because the Holy Spirit makes God ever present, each day Christians testify that he "proceeds from the Father and the Son."

*Almighty Father, kindle in us each day the fire of your love, which
you gave to your Church as your Son promised.*

Sincerity Is Not Enough

Father George William Rutler

"I have told you this so that you may not fall away. They will expel you from the synagogues; in fact, the hour is coming when everyone who kills you will think he is offering worship to God. They will do this because they have not known either the Father or me." (Jn 16:1-3)

Religious fanatics tend to be even more violent and intractable than political fanatics or any other kind of zealot. The reason is twofold. First, the religious fanatic is totally sincere to the extent that he makes sincerity a vice instead of a virtue. Fanatics for causes other than religious ones rarely claim that they have the powers of heaven behind them. Second, the religious fanatic is often haunted by insecurity in his own belief. For Aldous Huxley, such a person "consciously overcompensates a secret doubt." Those whose arguments are fragile make the loudest noise. There was a lot of shouting at the foot of the cross, even as the Master uttered words of peace in great pain. Christ explains this to his followers, so that they not be taken by surprise when religious people behave badly. Their problem is that while they are in the image of God, they act as though God were in their image. As Finley Peter Dunne said, they do what they do because they think "it is what the Lord would do if he knew the facts of the case." This led to history's ultimate absurdity, when on a dark day in Jerusalem, people accused God of blaspheming God. Informed by the wisdom of Christ and fortified with his grace, the saints are astonishingly free of any fanaticism while living the virtues to a degree more heroic than any bellicose propagandist. Holy martyrs embrace martyrdom but they do not seek it. To give one's life for one's own glory would be, as T. S. Eliot imagined Thomas Becket pondering, "the greatest treason: To do the right deed for the wrong reason." Fanatics are what they are "because they have not known either the Father or me." With those words ringing in their ears, the disciples serenely go out into the world to make the Father and the Son known.

Father of truth and grace, let me measure my words and deeds according to your counsel, that I may desire to win nothing but souls for you, and thus claim a share in your mercy.

The Heart That Truly Loves

Father George William Rutler

*"I have told you this so that when their hour comes
you may remember that I told you.
"I did not tell you this from the beginning, because I was with
you. But now I am going to the one who sent me, and not
one of you asks me, 'Where are you going?' But because
I told you this, grief has filled your hearts." (Jn 16:4-6)*

The Apostles are in shock when Jesus says that he is leaving them. He is eager to tell them where he is going, but they are too shaken to ask the question. They think only of the astonishing few years he has been with them along the way. He wants them to remember what he said, but then he prods them on to a future which, at this moment, they cannot imagine, as they grieve for what they think they are losing. One thinks of what the White Queen said to Alice in Wonderland: "It's a poor sort of memory that only works backwards." That is the sort of comment made in a topsy-turvy world, but it is not absurd from the perspective of eternity. The memory belongs to the imaginative part of the intellect that is part of the soul. The imagination thinks of both past and future. If you change "memory" to "imagination," then the White Queen makes sense. In fact, not fiction, Christ is the Beginning and the End. And by stirring up memories of what he has done, he opens the way to what he will do. The Bible is not a scrapbook of nostalgic vignettes of the past: it is an explanation of where we are heading. Mary Magdalene is able to walk with her Lord when she stops clinging to him. Love unites past and future. In 1808 the wife of the Irish poet Thomas Moore hid from him when she was disfigured by smallpox. She opened the door and returned to him when he recited: "No, the heart that has truly loved never forgets/ but as truly loves on to the close…" In the Eucharist, the Divine Love says: "Do this in memory of me." In that moment we are in the Upper Room, in our own church, and in heaven.

Eternal Father, through your Son you have explained the past, given the present, and prepared the future, and so may you forgive what I was, strengthen what I am, and make me what I should be.

The Finished Symphony

Father George William Rutler

"But I tell you the truth, it is better for you that I go.
For if I do not go, the Advocate will not come to you.
But if I go, I will send him to you."

(Jn 16:7)

At the Last Supper, Jesus mentions the Holy Spirit three times. First, he promises that the Spirit will be with us for ever. Then he says that the Spirit will reveal the truth of life. The third time, he explains that the Spirit will be sent after the Son of God ascends to the Father. The supper ends with singing. Our Lord must have sung some of the "Hallel Psalms" which we know as Psalms 113 to 118. Among the verses, in Psalm 116, he would have sung, "I felt agony and dread./ ... O LORD, save my life!" Then he leads the Apostles into the garden where he will agonize, as in the forty days in the wilderness when he began his work. Satan who makes pain hates the Holy Spirit who makes peace. Satan can tempt with all kinds of false pleasures, but he cannot give the peace that is for ever. A Wagnerian opera diva who loathed the Nazis was ordered to sing for Hitler, and she replied, "He can make me scream but he cannot make me sing." In every age in various ways, Satan has made people scream, but he has never been able to make them sing.

The Advocate restores the song of the first moment of creation. Saint Anselm, probably paraphrasing Saint Augustine, says, "To sing is the work of a lover." The Holy Spirit turns human agony into a harmony that lasts for ever. God composes no unfinished symphonies. In the Mass he completes what he began when he said, "Let there be light." Vatican II proclaims that in the Eucharist we "take part in a foretaste of that heavenly liturgy which is celebrated in the holy city of Jerusalem" (*Sacrosanctum Concilium*). By sending the Advocate, the Mass is no longer confined to the earthly city of Jerusalem, but can be offered everywhere until the end of time.

Holy Father, guide me in the steps of your Son along the path of peace, by your Holy Spirit whose love was given to the world so that the world might love you.

The Happy Life

Father Romanus Cessario, O.P.

"And when [the Advocate] comes he will convict the world in regard to sin and righteousness and condemnation: sin, because they do not believe in me; righteousness, because I am going to the Father and you will no longer see me; condemnation, because the ruler of this world has been condemned."

(Jn 16:8-11)

Do you know anyone who says, with a straight face, "I want to find unhappiness"? Although folks hold very different ideas about what makes them happy, they nonetheless agree that happiness, as even the ancient philosophers remarked, is that which all people seek. The Gospel of John may be described as the "Book of Happiness." The inspired author, however, keenly points out the antinomies that people face in their search for happiness. Sin or virtue. Righteousness or lawlessness. Condemnation or acquittal. In the above verses, the Lord reminds us that the pursuit of happiness does not proceed without the judgment of God. From the moment that Christ speaks these words, the search for happiness no longer remains open to each individual's fancy. We must choose a life of virtue rather than the way of sinners. We must embrace the way of righteousness rather than the dwellings of the ungodly. We must seek the acquittal that only Christ can pronounce rather than succumb to the condemnation that results from following the "ruler of this world."

It is difficult to follow these recommendations without the help of the Church. The Christian moral life does not come easy. Several reasons intimated in Christ's words account for this challenge. For instance, people forget that sin harms their character even when they do not know that a particular action is sinful. Further, many people easily justify themselves so that they consider righteous whatever seems right to them. Finally, almost everybody forgets the judgment that the cross of Christ imposes on the "ruler of this world." The truth of the matter is that once Jesus announces the one and true way to happiness, no one can find alternatives that enjoy legitimacy. Rather, all are called to share in the one happiness that lasts for ever as the blessed vision of the Trinity.

Heavenly Father, make me attentive to your plan for my salvation. Give me what I need to find true happiness.

Late Have I Loved You

Father Romanus Cessario, O.P.

*"I have much more to tell you, but you cannot bear it now.
But when he comes, the Spirit of truth, he will guide you
to all truth. He will not speak on his own, but he will speak
what he hears, and will declare to you the things
that are coming." (Jn 16:12-13)*

Truth supplies the only measure for the good. The truth about a good apple appears when the apple possesses the qualities one expects to find in a ripe and juicy apple. In other words, the apple is not bruised or rotten. The truth about a good house is that it possesses the things required for human habitation. For example, a roof covers the house, the doorways allow entry and exit, and so forth. The truth about a good friend is that a person shares with you the communication characteristic of friends. In a word, the person is not, for example, duplicitous. We even speak of a true friend. Truth, however, does not always prevail in human choosing. A grocer can stock rotten apples. A real estate agent can show four walls without a roof or a building where the dimensions of the doorways allow no one of normal stature to walk in or out. People, even our friends, can turn duplicitous. All these things can happen. Because they happen, however, does not make the rotten apple good, the defective house solid, or the erstwhile friend true.

Jesus promises to the members of his Church "the Spirit of truth." We know this promised Gift is one of the Blessed Trinity. The Holy Spirit comes into the world invisibly. Sometimes the third divine Person is called the "Guest of Our Souls." What is important and encouraging for us appears in the words of promise that Jesus speaks to his disciples and to us: the Holy Spirit "will guide you to all truth." These words are important. Why? Without the Spirit of truth, we would not discover the whole truth about God or ourselves. These words also are urgent. Why? Without the assistance of the One Jesus promises to send, we would succumb to the many falsehoods that are leftovers from a world without Christ.

Merciful Father, keep me true. Send the Holy Spirit of truth to abide as the hidden guest of my soul.

The Praise of His Glory

Father Romanus Cessario, O.P.

"[The Spirit] will glorify me, because he will take from what is mine and declare it to you. Everything that the Father has is mine; for this reason I told you that he will take from what is mine and declare it to you."

(Jn 16:14-15)

There is something majestic about the words that Christ speaks to his disciples. We do not come away with the impression that Christ intends the Apostles to set up a small sectarian association of like-minded believers. Instead, Christ reveals something about the inner life of God. He tells us that God is a Trinity of Persons, Father, Son, and Holy Spirit. He speaks to his disciples as the Incarnate Son, while at the same time he identifies himself with the eternal Son of the Father. This is not academic or technical information that should concern only experts. The Trinitarian life of God stands at the origin and end of all that exists. We are born in the image of the Trinity. We bear the image of the Trinity. Nothing we do can erase the image of the Trinity. All this means that God stands supreme over the world and over those who dwell in it. Atheism is really an illusion. Agnosticism, an escape. Religious remains the only posture that reasonable people may adopt.

What is best, though, is to discover the true religion. So when Christ assures us that "everything that the Father has is mine," we find consolation in knowing that we receive from the Holy Spirit what is true. This is what the Church sings at Pentecost when she invokes the Holy Spirit as the Light of life: "O blessed Light of life Thou art." In order to establish ourselves firmly in the gift that the Holy Spirit communicates, Catholics should develop a devotion to the Light of life. The expression of this devotion can begin as easily as making the sign of the cross with reverence and attention: "In the name of the Father, and of the Son, and of the Holy Spirit." Devotion to the Holy Spirit develops as we come to appreciate deeply the power of the gift that he brings.

Omnipotent God, your wisdom governs all that exists. Make flourish in my soul the image of the adorable Trinity, Father, Son, and Holy Spirit.

The "Little While"

Father Romanus Cessario, O.P.

"A little while and you will no longer see me, and again a little while later and you will see me." So some of [Jesus'] disciples said to one another, "What does this mean that he is saying to us, 'A little while and you will not see me, and again a little while and you will see me,' and 'Because I am going to the Father'?" So they said, "What is this 'little while' [of which he speaks]? We do not know what he means." (Jn 16:16-18)

We cannot read the sixteenth chapter of Saint John's Gospel and conclude that Catholic life remains one option among many. At the same time, the practice of the Catholic religion requires that each believer recognize the darkness of faith. No one can figure everything out. True enough, sound catechetical and theological instruction can illumine the minds of those who believe. Good preaching ensures that the Christian people are drawn to divine truth and not human fables. In short, it is possible to make sense out of the Christian faith.

It is not possible, however, to penetrate the mysteries that God intends for us to assent to without seeing or without requiring apodictic proof. So the Good Lord prepares his disciples for the life of faith by speaking about the "Little While." They appear first to have interpreted Christ's remarks as indicating a calendar of events to come. In fact, Christ was preparing them to live in a whole new way. For once his earthly ministry is accomplished, they would no longer behold, that is, "see," Christ in the way to which they had become accustomed. Once Christ returns to the Father, the disciples will live by faith. It also will befall them, as the first bishops of the Church, to instruct others to live by faith. This instruction requires lessons about the dynamic of Christian living. Their instruction also includes how to live the faith through the sacraments and in the moral life. The darkness of faith sets up a stumbling block for many persons. People prefer their own thoughts and reasons to God's. They also prefer what satisfies their sensibilities to the darkness that surrounds sacred signs. So we behold in these words of Christ, words that his disciples initially find enigmatic, a foreshadowing of the Eucharist. There we do see Christ, though within the darkness of signs.

Loving Father, grant me the gift of faith. Steady my life in the practice of the Catholic religion so that after a little while I may behold your face for ever.

Mourning and Rejoicing

Father Romanus Cessario, O.P.

Jesus knew that [some of his disciples] wanted to ask him, so he said to them, "Are you discussing with one another what I said, 'A little while and you will not see me, and again a little while and you will see me'? Amen, amen, I say to you, you will weep and mourn, while the world rejoices; you will grieve, but your grief will become joy." (Jn 16:19-20)

Faith remains in the darkness. Christ however abides as the Light of the World. So we discover at this juncture, in the Discourse that the Catholic tradition calls the "Last" (Jn 14–17), an image of the Christ as the compassionate teacher. Christ knew that his disciples had failed to understand his meaning, and so he proceeds to explain to them further to what the "little while" refers. The bewilderment of the disciples affords Christ the occasion to speak specifically about the primordial rhythm of the life that divine grace introduces into the world—dying and rising.

Christ of course refers to his own forthcoming death and alludes to his Resurrection: "your grief will become joy." We usually limit the usage of the verb "to mourn" to times of loss, especially at death. Traditionally, those who assist at funerals are called "mourners." Death creates its own darkness. Burial customs are transcultural and universal features of human life. This fact suggests that no one in the history of human reflection has managed to persuade everybody that the death of a fellow human being is the same as the death of an animal. No one disposes of human bodies in the same way that they dispose of ordinary refuse. While philosophers and therefore human reasoning can gain some understanding of the immortality of the human soul, no philosopher can provide assurances about the lot of the soul after death.

What Christ announces to his disciples then comes as Good News: "You will grieve, but your grief will become joy." He announces a new pattern in the human reaction to death. He promises his disciples that what will transpire within the next days of their earthly time will establish a pattern that applies not only to the crucified Lord but to all those whom they draw to belief in his death and Resurrection.

Benevolent Father, you abide as the Lord of life and of death. Comfort me at the hour of my death with the sacraments of your Son's Church and the presence of his priest.

Spiritual Birth Pangs

Father Romanus Cessario, O.P.

"When a woman is in labor, she is in anguish because her hour has arrived; but when she has given birth to a child, she no longer remembers the pain because of her joy that a child has been born into the world. So you also are now in anguish. But I will see you again, and your hearts will rejoice, and no one will take your joy away from you." (Jn 16:21-22)

The English word "pang" denotes a sudden sharp pain. A woman who has gone into labor experiences these pangs. Christ makes use of this indispensable rhythm of human life. No one (except as a result of a special grace) is born without his or her mother experiencing birth pangs. Christ uses the birth process to illustrate what is characteristic about Christian living. The spiritual authors of yesteryear were accustomed to remind their readers of the phrase "No cross, no crown." This expression captures the spiritual instruction that Christ communicates to his disciples as he approaches his Passion and death. Bear in mind that the Christ of the "Last Discourse" soon will appear on Pilate's balcony as the *Ecce Homo*, "wearing the crown of thorns" (Jn 19:5).

Does this instruction tell us that the Christian life engages us in a perpetual anguish to which only our deaths bring surcease? By no means. Instead, Christ, by using the metaphor of a woman in labor, instructs the disciples that the Christian life always and inevitably entails two moments of grace. One is called the moment of restoration. No one turns away from sin, especially those sins to which one has become accustomed, without some pangs. Like the pangs of a woman in labor, these pangs are the necessary condition for arriving at joy. The other moment in the Christian life follows upon that of restoration. It is the moment of perfection. In other words, the Christian having worn the crown achieves a moment of glory. This moment of glory or rejoicing, as Christ himself promises, is not a fleeting moment. This moment represents the stability in the good that divine grace creates in us. So the Lord compares the perfection of the Christian life, which all people are called to receive, to a newborn child. The child brings rejoicing to the parents. The gifts of divine grace rejoice the Church.

Kind Father, watch over my steps. Ready me to accept whatever you send for my spiritual profit. Help me to embrace the cross of your Son.

Ask for Joy!

Father Romanus Cessario, O.P.

"On that day you will not question me about anything. Amen, amen, I say to you, whatever you ask the Father in my name he will give you. Until now you have not asked anything in my name; ask and you will receive, so that your joy may be complete." (Jn 16:23-24)

No more encouraging instruction exists than the one that Jesus gives to his disciples at this juncture in the Last Discourse: "whatever you ask the Father in my name he will give you." The words that Christ speaks provide a certain spiritual guarantee that we can have recourse to God for those things we need both for our temporal and spiritual well-being. Why then do we oftentimes find ourselves slow to ask Jesus for what we need? Why are we even loath at times to turn to him?

One reason stems from a serious misunderstanding that affects many persons about how God gives gifts. In a word, God does not give as human beings tend to give. God gives not out of a need to receive something back, nor to those who have something to give back. Rather, God bestows his gifts on account of the surplus of goodness that belongs to him. To express it simply, the human race is not accustomed to receiving from this kind of Giver. Who, for instance, would hope to receive a benefaction from someone whom he or she had grievously hurt? Because we are not accustomed to receive in the way that God gives, we need to learn the lesson that Christ teaches, "whatever you ask the Father in my name he will give you."

There is another reason, however, that ill disposes the human person to ask for something in Christ's name. Our sins. We find it difficult to invoke Christ's name when we find ourselves acting against Christ's law. The Last Discourse gives no warrant for this reaction. However, given the strong pulls that keep us from believing Christ's promise, we can learn this lesson best when someone who already takes Christ at his word teaches us about confidence.

Merciful Father, instill in me a strong love for the name of your Son. Make me ready to say the name of Jesus at any moment.

God Is Our Father

Father Romanus Cessario, O.P.

"I have told you this in figures of speech. The hour is coming when I will no longer speak to you in figures but I will tell you clearly about the Father. On that day you will ask in my name, and I do not tell you that I will ask the Father for you. For the Father himself loves you, because you have loved me and have come to believe that I came from God." (Jn 16:25-27)

After more than half a century of priestly life and formation, I still remember with great clarity the day when my spiritual father instructed me about the implications of this solemn declaration that Christ makes to his disciples. In principle, the instruction is not difficult to grasp. Because God the Father loves us, he will grant what we ask in his Son's name. Christianity does not depend on patriarchy. The Christian Gospel, however, does require that one appreciate paternity. Why? God has revealed himself as "Father." No one may lightly pass over this divine revelation.

The fact of the matter is that the Christian believer spends the whole of his or her life coming to appreciate what the divine paternity means. The implications of God's fatherhood for Christian living are far-reaching. We discover the relationship of justice and mercy as it exists in God. We come to realize that God does not fade into anonymity. We learn that the One who created us establishes not only the pattern of human existence but the conditions of our spiritual sonship. Because these lessons of the divine paternity affect directly our relationship with God and with one another, they are not lessons that one can teach oneself. True enough, scholars can write about these matters. Only those to whom it has been given can teach about them. It is significant, then, that Christ addresses the Last Discourse to his disciples. This chosen band Christ ordains on Holy Thursday as the first priests of the Church. Because of their sacramental bond with Christ—a bond that remains unique to the ordained man—priests find themselves in the best position to instruct the Church about the divine paternity. This divine instruction will proceed smoothly to the extent that those who receive it have experienced some form of natural paternity. So we need good human fathers and good spiritual ones too.

Father in heaven, hallowed be your name. Keep me close to your only beloved Son so that I may never abandon your gracious love.

Plain Talking

Father Romanus Cessario, O.P.

*"I came from the Father and have come into the world.
Now I am leaving the world and going back to the Father."
[Jesus'] disciples said, "Now you are talking plainly, and not in
any figure of speech. Now we realize that you know everything
and that you do not need to have anyone question you. Because
of this we believe that you came from God." (Jn 16:28-30)*

No plainer example of human speech exists than what the Bible records. The reason for this assertion is easy to see. "God is the author of Sacred Scripture," as the *Catechism of the Catholic Church* attests (105). Just because God is the author of Sacred Scripture does not mean that one may read the Sacred Scriptures without help from the Church. As anyone who picks up the Book of Leviticus or the Song of Songs will discover, Sacred Scripture is not self-explanatory. The plain talk of Sacred Scripture requires interpretation. The exchange that we read in this excerpt from the Last Discourse illustrates Christ accomplishing in person for his disciples what he, through the Holy Spirit, gives believers when they read Scripture. Christ opens our minds to understand the Scriptures. Each baptized believer enjoys the privilege of saying with the disciples, "Now you are talking plainly..."

It is traditional in the Church to read the Last Discourse of John's Gospel on solemn occasions, for example, during the main meal on Holy Thursday and even at the deathbed of a Christian. With all its rich teaching, the Last Discourse also impresses on the one who hears it the personal union that Christ establishes with those whom he draws to himself. No one can ponder these chapters of the Fourth Gospel and not realize that Christ invites us to share in an intimacy that one can only describe as beatifying. We frequently hear that Christian life requires commitment. What we do not hear enough is that the commitment issues forth from a gift of self that the Incarnate Son enacted with his disciples on the night before he died. The right understanding of the Scriptures does not ordinarily take possession of believers without their partaking of the Eucharist. Only the One who has come from God can give the gift that leads men back to God.

Loving Father, grant me the gift of your Truth. Keep me steadfast in pursuing your ways.

You Are Not Alone!

Father Romanus Cessario, O.P.

Jesus answered [the disciples], "Do you believe now? Behold, the hour is coming and has arrived when each of you will be scattered to his own home and you will leave me alone. But I am not alone, because the Father is with me."
(Jn 16:31-32)

No more exacting vocation exists within the Church than that of the hermit. One eremitical order, the Carthusians, explains to their new arrivals that getting used to the life takes a while. I have a friend who spent time in a Charterhouse. He wrote that his superior "likes to say that it takes about fifteen years for a Carthusian monk just to settle, to calm down a little bit." Even when the solitude is sanctioned by the Church, remaining separated from one's brothers and sisters requires special graces and fortitude.

When Christ predicts that his disciples will abandon him, we should not conclude that since he is God, their scattering, each to his own home, brought our Lord consolation. In his human nature, he experienced the isolation that being left alone entails. The affective solitude that Christ knows he will face does not conquer him, however. The Lord tells his disciples and us that, in fact, he is not alone: "I am not alone, because the Father is with me." When Christ makes this revelation, he signals that no amount of isolation from family and friends results in abandonment or final separation. For those who believe in Christ know that the Father is also with them, even in those moments when they suffer physical separation or emotional isolation. Those who choose a life of solitude within the Church bear witness to this fundamental truth of Christian living, even if it does take fifteen years for them to calm down a bit.

Truth to tell, every Christian vocation entails some unique form of solitude. Family life may seem exempt. However, the widow and widower recognize that marriage also leads to solitude. The priest, by reason of his promise of celibacy, faces an affective solitude. So everyone in the Church needs to take seriously what the Lord teaches when he says, "I am not alone."

Father of the universe, preserve me in the designs of your providence. Keep me always close to you, even when I find myself separated from the company of others.

Take Courage!

Father Romanus Cessario, O.P.

"I have told you this so that you might have peace in me.
In the world you will have trouble, but take courage,
I have conquered the world."
(Jn 16:33)

Some contemporary Christian outlooks tend to make the world more favorable to conversion than experience shows to be the case. Of course people are converted, not the world. Still, when Christ speaks about "the world," he refers to whatever exists that has not surrendered to the light and power of God. Throughout the Gospel of John, we encounter episodes where Christ brings his divine power and light to bear on human situations that otherwise would prove intractable. We find encouragement, for example, in the account of the marriage feast at Cana when Jesus miraculously supplies for the needs of an embarrassed bride and groom (see Jn 2:1-12). We take consolation from the way that Christ lovingly addresses the Samaritan Woman (see Jn 4:4-42). We derive comfort from the multiplication of the loaves (see Jn 6:1-15). And perhaps more than any other divine intervention made by Christ, we marvel at his reaction to the woman caught in adultery (see Jn 8:2-11): "Neither do I condemn you" (Jn 8:11). What more proof could one desire in order to realize that Jesus wants us to live in his peace? Again and again, he demonstrates peace.

At the same time, we observe that in each of the above mentioned instances where Christ introduces his peace, some trouble has gone before. Trouble is what "the world" brings. As long as we dwell here below, that is, as long as we brush up against the world, we can expect—on the Lord's own word—our share of trouble. Then too, we cannot forget the sins that we commit. These sins bring their own sorrows into our lives. So whether we are embarrassed newlyweds or hungry pilgrims or culturally confused bystanders or caught red-handed, we all need the peace that only Christ brings. What is great, Jesus himself assures us that this peace is ours. For he has "conquered the world."

Loving Father, grant me the gift of your peace. Lead me always in the path of your Son and sustain me by his conquest.

Belonging to Jesus

Father Romanus Cessario, O.P.

When Jesus had said this, he raised his eyes to heaven and said, "Father, the hour has come. Give glory to your son, so that your son may glorify you, just as you gave him authority over all people, so that he may give eternal life to all you gave him."
(Jn 17:1-2)

The chapters of Saint John's Gospel that contain the Last Discourse sometimes are designated as "The Book of Glory." Throughout these verses, Christ refers to his glory. Slowly we come to realize that Christ identifies his glory with our salvation. It is natural for us to attend to this element of Christ's glory, even as we also recognize that the glory of which Christ speaks encompasses a mystery that ultimately remains hidden in God. If we are destined to behold the fullness of Christ's glory, then we may reasonably expect this beholding to happen after death. Catholic teaching stresses, however, that Christ's glory takes hold of the created world here and now. Each Catholic sacrament displays through the means of created things or acts the glory of Christ.

The Gospel of John assures us that Christ enters into the final moment of his mission, that is, his "hour." At Cana, Christ tells his mother who asked of him a miracle to supply some more wine for the festivity, "My hour has not yet come" (Jn 2:4). Now Christ announces to his disciples and to the world that his "hour has come." The hour refers to the moment when by his death on the cross, Christ saves the world. From the pierced side of Christ, we learn that blood and water flows. Baptism and the Eucharist. The Eucharist remains the signal moment when Christ's glory appears before the world in a circle of gold. Catholic artists have expressed this mystery in the design of the monstrance or ostensory, the sacred vessel which exhibits the Sacred Host. The golden rays that stream from the center (oftentimes adorned with precious jewels) remind the worshiper that this memorial of Christ's Passion also radiates his glory. No wonder the Catholic tradition hails the Blessed Eucharist as a "pledge of future glory."

Almighty Father, keep me safe through the Passion of your Son. Protect the Eucharist throughout the world from all harm and desecration.

To Know the True God

Father Romanus Cessario, O.P.

"Now this is eternal life, that they should know you, the only true God, and the one whom you sent, Jesus Christ. I glorified you on earth by accomplishing the work that you gave me to do. Now glorify me, Father, with you, with the glory that I had with you before the world began."

(Jn 17:3-5)

As Christ draws close to the hour of his Passion, he tells his disciples that eternal life consists in possessing knowledge of "the only true God." This text is one of several places in the Fourth Gospel that help us to grasp why the Church describes eternal life as the happy possession of a vision of God, a "beatific vision." The *Catechism of the Catholic Church* reflects this practice when it reminds us that "faith makes us taste in advance the light of the beatific vision, the goal of our journey here below" (163). The virtue of faith then directs the Christian life. When the Church identifies knowledge as the essence of eternal life, she of course does not exclude love. Rather, she informs us that without a knowledge of the one and true God, we would discover nothing beatific to love.

There is special significance in the fact that the Gospel of John emphasizes the blessed vision of God. For the Beloved Disciple is the one who remains with Christ at the foot of the cross, and the one to whom the dying Christ confides his Mother. We should note the places where our Lady appears in the Fourth Gospel, especially at the foot of the cross (see Jn 19:25-27). There Christ gives her to us as our spiritual Mother. Mary helps us to live by faith. Blessed Pope John Paul II made this observation explicitly in his encyclical letter, *Mother of the Redeemer*: "Mary figured profoundly in the history of salvation and in a certain way unites and mirrors within herself the central truths of the faith" (25). In order to appreciate as much as possible on earth Christ's glory, we need to remain—like the Beloved Disciple—close to Mary. The saints exclaim on how dark life's journey would be for the Christian who walks without Mary as his or her companion.

Most merciful Father, save me by the death of your Son. Give me the heart of Mary to love Christ as I should.

The Words You Gave Me

Father Romanus Cessario, O.P.

"I revealed your name to those whom you gave me out of the world. They belonged to you, and you gave them to me, and they have kept your word. Now they know that everything you gave me is from you, because the words you gave to me I have given to them, and they accepted them and truly understood that I came from you, and they have believed that you sent me."

(Jn 17:6-8)

Each day at Mass, the priest repeats the words that Christ himself spoke at the Last Supper, "This is the chalice of my Blood...which will be poured out for you and for many for the forgiveness of sins." These words of consecration alert us to the fact that Christ's death on the cross reaches those whom God the Father gave him "out of the world." These chosen ones remain the privileged beneficiaries of a divine gift that Christ has gained for us. The gift follows faith. Those who eat Christ's Body and drink Christ's Blood must believe all that the Church teaches, especially about the Blessed Sacrament of the Altar. Otherwise the Holy Communion that represents our sharing in the Eucharist suffers depreciation. To accept what the Church teaches as God's own truth is ordered intrinsically to loving the realities that these truths enshrine. Christ sums up this mystery of the Christian life when he proclaims before the Father, "I revealed your name to those whom you gave me out of the world." To speak about "the many" does not contradict the truth that Christ died for all men. When we receive Holy Communion, we also take up the task of evangelization. Whether we are clergy, laity, or consecrated, each member of the Church bears the responsibility to draw more and more people into "the many."

The Gospel of John illustrates the sacramental life of the Church. Signs and glory especially point toward the Eucharist. Catholic life flourishes only under the signs of the sacraments. As we have seen in the Gospel of John, the sacraments bring us the light of truth and the new life of grace. No wonder Christian art has often portrayed Saint John the Evangelist giving Holy Communion to the Blessed Virgin Mary. We find in this image the depiction of the perfect communion on earth of God and man.

Loving Father, keep me in communion with the holy Catholic Church. Preserve my life from the destructive power of the Evil One. Mary, Mother of the Church, envelop me.

Jesus Prays for Us

Father Joseph T. Lienhard, s.j.

"I pray for them. I do not pray for the world but for the ones you have given me, because they are yours, and everything of mine is yours and everything of yours is mine, and I have been glorified in them."
(Jn 17:9-10)

The seventeenth chapter of Saint John's Gospel is often called the high-priestly prayer, and many understand it as the Eucharistic prayer that accompanies the one perfect sacrifice of the cross.

In each of the Eucharistic prayers that we use at Mass, we pray for the living and the dead, a moment we should not pass over lightly. At this most solemn moment of the Mass, we recall others—the pope and the bishop, surely; but also our closest family and friends, and then those who have gone before us in faith. So too, Jesus prays for us in the course of this solemn prayer that he addresses to the Father.

What do we mean by prayer? Saint John of Damascus wrote that "prayer is the raising of one's mind and heart to God or the requesting of good things from God." So prayer has two elements. We raise our minds and hearts to God, and leave other things behind, below. For a few minutes, we leave the lesser things of life behind. And then, we ask for good things from God, things that only God can give: grace, strength, peace, and so many other things, too.

Jesus prays for us because we are God's, and God has given us to Jesus. Jesus claims us as his own; his love for us is unending. Of course, what he describes is an ideal. We need to ask ourselves, do we fully belong to Jesus?

We might also ask ourselves the question, what did Jesus pray for, specifically for me, on that night? Could it have been only a general prayer, or did he somehow foresee every one of us who would someday be members of the Church? Can we ask ourselves: when Jesus prayed for me, what did he most want for me?—a question each of us might try to answer. Do I want the same thing for myself?

Almighty God and Father, Jesus Christ our Savior offered himself on the cross for our salvation; by the power of his sacrifice give us, we pray, what, in your infinite wisdom, is best for us.

The World and the Name

Father Joseph T. Lienhard, S.J.

"And now I will no longer be in the world, but they are in the world, while I am coming to you. Holy Father, keep them in your name that you have given me, so that they may be one just as we are." (Jn 17:11)

The phrases "in the world" and "in your name" offer an intriguing contrast. In Saint John's Gospel, "world" represents what is dark and evil, what is opposed to Christ, what must be left behind.

To some readers, this use of "world" could be confusing. The Book of Genesis tells us that God created the world and saw that it was good. The Old Testament continues this theme. God gives his people a good place in the world, a beautiful land, a land of mountains and rivers, of fruitful fields and orchards, of safe cities and a glorious Temple.

Does Saint John depart from this vision? Does Saint John's use of the word "world" introduce a kind of dualism, a view that suggests a cosmic tension between "world" and an escape from the world, or deliverance from it?

Such a view takes into account the first chapter of Genesis, but not the third—creation but not sin. God's creation has been corrupted by sin and cries out for deliverance.

Here is where "in your name" enters the picture. In Hebrew thought, we often read that knowing someone's name means having power over that person. In the Book of Exodus, God both reveals his name to Moses and conceals it. In the New Testament, God reveals his name fully; his name is Father, and that name gives us power—not to command God, but to invoke him as our deliverer. The tension between "world" and "name" is the tension we live our lives in. We are "in the world," but we live and act "in his name." Sin has not yet been fully conquered. We possess the name that gives us power over sin, if we will to use it. John does not offer a dualism but a way forward, a way toward the conquest of sin and the triumph of grace.

Eternal, ever-living God, you have revealed yourself to us in Jesus Christ your Son; grant us, we pray, the strength to overcome the power of sin in your name and to live in your grace.

The Scriptures Fulfilled

Father Joseph T. Lienhard, S.J.

"When I was with them I protected them in your name that you gave me, and I guarded them, and none of them was lost except the son of destruction, in order that the scripture might be fulfilled."

(Jn 17:12)

We often hear in the Gospel the phrase "that the Scriptures might be fulfilled." The phrase is worth reflecting on. It provokes two thoughts. One is that the Old Testament is God's authentic revelation. The other is that this revelation is incomplete until the coming of Christ.

In the second century, the Church rigorously rejected the teaching of Marcion, who believed that the God of the Old Testament was a lower god, a god of justice, while the God of the New Testament was the higher God, the God of love. As a result, Marcion rejected the Old Testament and wanted to banish it from the Church.

In rejecting Marcion, the Church affirmed that there is only one God, and that the same God who gave the law to Moses and spoke through the prophets is also the God whom Jesus Christ called his Father. The Scriptures, which God inspired, spoke the truth to those who heard and read them. But they also looked to the future, "through a glass, darkly," as Saint Paul says—they looked forward to Jesus Christ.

The New Testament writers, and Jesus Christ himself, understood this fact. They understood that the Old Testament was unfulfilled, and, in a mysterious way, it pointed ahead, through the mists of time, to Jesus Christ: to his Incarnation and birth, to his cross and Resurrection.

When the liturgy was reformed after the Second Vatican Council, a reading from the Old Testament was introduced for most Sundays and many weekdays. The Church recognizes these Scriptures as God's true and abiding Word. But also, especially on Sunday, the Old Testament passage that is read is chosen so that it can be understood through the Gospel, or throw further light on the Gospel. Jesus Christ is the key that unlocks the treasures of the Old Testament.

God our Father, God of Abraham, Isaac, and Jacob, who spoke in the law and the prophets: grant us, we pray, the grace to understand the Holy Scriptures in the light of Jesus Christ our Lord.

Hatred

Father Joseph T. Lienhard, s.j.

"But now I am coming to you. I speak this in the world so that
they may share my joy completely. I gave them your word,
and the world hated them, because they do not belong
to the world any more than I belong to the world."
(Jn 17:13-14)

Hatred is an ugly word and an ugly concept. We hear, "I hate this sort of breakfast cereal," but the speaker really means, "I dislike," "it doesn't please my taste."

To hate is much more than to dislike; to hate is to wish evil for another person, to want another person to suffer pain or loss. The *Catechism of the Catholic Church* teaches that the root of hatred is envy, which is sadness at the sight of someone else's good and the desire to acquire those goods for oneself, in an unjust manner.

What did our Lord mean when he said, "the world hated them"? He gave us God's word, and God's word set us apart from the world. The world envies us, because we have something good and beautiful and true; and because the world envies us, it hates us and wishes us evil. In a twisted way, the world wants what we have, because the world sees that it is good. At the same time, the world wants us to be deprived of that good.

Is there a contradiction here? Those who hate us want the good that we have, but they also want to see it taken away from us. The scholastic philosophers taught that good tends to diffuse itself, to spread itself out; in a sort of reverse move, evil tends to corrupt and destroy the good that is near it.

Most of us do not have enemies who want to kill us for our Christian faith, or to destroy our churches; but Christians in some parts of the world are indeed the objects of such hatred and envy. Many Christians have had their churches and homes destroyed, and more than a few have been killed. We should never forget those who, in our own day, suffer so greatly for the faith. It is wrong to brush over our Lord's words, "the world hated them"—it still hates them.

Almighty and eternal God, pour out your grace into our hearts,
we implore you; banish hatred from the world and let all peoples
live in your justice and your peace.

Consecrated in Truth

Father Joseph T. Lienhard, S.J.

"I do not ask that you take them out of the world but that you keep them from the evil one. They do not belong to the world any more than I belong to the world. Consecrate them in the truth. Your word is truth. As you sent me into the world, so I sent them into the world. And I consecrate myself for them, so that they also may be consecrated in truth." (Jn 17:15-19)

"Truth" is a beautiful word. The English word "truth" comes from the same root as "trust," and, surprisingly enough, so does "tree." Perhaps the people who spoke the language that English comes from, and who lived in the forests of Europe, knew certain great trees that marked a fixed point, something that they could rely on or trust.

Sometimes, of course, truth and trust get separated. In a famous incident when he was a student in Carthage in North Africa, Saint Augustine of Hippo was approached by some Manichees, religious sectarians who tried to convert him to their sect (and succeeded, at least for nine years). The Manichees were always saying, "Truth, truth," as they tried to convert Augustine. But they were not to be trusted; they did not really offer truth.

We might ask: whom can we trust? How do we know whom to trust?

The question is not easily answered. But at least this is true: trust is always in a person. I recognize someone who is sincere, honest, and has my interests at heart; I say, "I can trust that person." And one I trust will surely speak the truth.

Then we encounter the mysterious phrase "consecrate them in the truth." To consecrate means to make holy; and holiness is, before all else, the quality that distinguishes God from all else. We can share in God's holiness. "Be holy, for I am holy," the Scripture teaches often. Saint John Chrysostom, in a homily on this passage, teaches that the source of this consecration is right teaching, right doctrine; it is the word, the right word, that consecrates us and makes us holy.

And so, truth and trust coincide. I trust the Church because she teaches right doctrine, the truth. And trust and truth finally both go back to a tree—the tree of the cross.

God our Father, source of all light and truth, we place our trust in you; guide us by your grace, we pray, and consecrate us in the truth that you have revealed through Jesus Christ your Son.

Believe through the Word

Father Joseph T. Lienhard, s.j.

"I pray not only for them, but also for those who will believe in me through their word, so that they may all be one, as you, Father, are in me and I in you, that they also may be in us, that the world may believe that you sent me."

(Jn 17:20-21)

Those of us who are cradle Catholics can remember how we learned the faith. Perhaps our parents taught us to make the sign of the cross, and then the Our Father and the Hail Mary. At three or four, our parents began to take us to Mass on Sunday. At six or seven, we were instructed about the sacraments—First Communion, confirmation. And as we grew older, our knowledge of the faith also grew richer and deeper. But always, we learned from someone else—parents, or teachers, or Catholic authors.

And where did our parents and teachers learn the faith? From their parents and teachers. It is easy to imagine a great chain of believers, reaching back through the centuries to the Apostles themselves. Our thoughts can stretch back to that first act of passing on the faith, when someone said, "The Lord has been raised and he has appeared to Peter."

The work of the twelve Apostles is a powerful symbol. Legend has it that they went to every land of the ancient world, from Spain to India. This legend teaches an important truth and confirms our Lord's words: "I pray...for those who will believe in me through their word." The Apostles' word leads to faith. And each Sunday at Mass, we hear the Apostles' word: Paul and John and Matthew and James, our fathers in the faith.

And what is that faith? "That the world may believe that you sent me." When Jesus Christ proclaimed the saving Gospel, and when he offered himself in sacrifice on the cross, he was not acting on his own; he was not a self-appointed prophet. He was carrying out the mission that the Father had given him. So too, our call to faith is not our decision; we believe because God called us. God sent the Son and calls us to faith in him—and so we are one, as our Lord prayed.

Eternal Lord and God, you have constituted your Church in the truth revealed through your Son; confirm us, we humbly pray, in the faith of our fathers, and keep us true to it always.

Father, Son, and Holy Spirit

Father Joseph T. Lienhard, S.J.

"And I have given them the glory you gave me, so that they may be one, as we are one, I in them and you in me, that they may be brought to perfection as one, that the world may know that you sent me, and that you loved them even as you loved me."

(Jn 17:22-23)

"We are one…you in me…you sent me…you loved me." These few phrases turn our minds to God the Blessed Trinity.

The Trinity is often on our lips and in our hearts: when we bless ourselves in the name of the Father and of the Son and of the Holy Spirit; when we give glory to the Father and to the Son and to the Holy Spirit; when we pray to God the Father through our Lord Jesus Christ his Son in the unity of the Holy Spirit.

Our faith can be stated simply: we believe in one God, and this God has a name: his name is Father, Son, and Holy Spirit. The Father is true God, the Son is true God, and the Holy Spirit is true God, and yet there are not three gods but one God. This great mystery transcends arithmetic: only in God does one plus one plus one equal one.

But the three Persons are not three distinct entities, side by side. "You sent me," Jesus says. The Creed phrases it differently: the Father begets the Son, in an eternal act of generation, so that the Son's being proceeds from the Father's. And the Holy Spirit proceeds from the Father and the Son, as from one principle.

This is our faith: "firmly I believe and truly," as a hymn has it. "We are one," Jesus says, the Father and I, one God. "You sent me"; the Son receives his mission from the Father, who sends him into the world as our Redeemer. "You loved me," with an everlasting love, "unto the end," as Saint John says elsewhere. This faith needs to nourish our spiritual lives—in prayer, we need to enter into the mystery of the Trinity, to unite our person in love with the three divine Persons, till we can say with Jesus, "We are one."

Almighty, ever-living God, you are one God in three Persons, Father, Son, and Holy Spirit; strengthen our faith, we pray, and deepen our love for you each day of our lives.

Before the Foundation

Father Joseph T. Lienhard, S.J.

"Father, they are your gift to me. I wish that where I am they also may be with me, that they may see my glory that you gave me, because you loved me before the foundation of the world."
(Jn 17:24)

One of the most basic questions that philosophers ask concerns the intelligibility of the universe. Does the world make sense? Some would answer, no; the world is the product of pure chance, atoms bumping into each other. Any meaning that exists is one that we impose on our world.

Others see the world as the battleground between two opposing principles or forces—light and darkness, good and evil, spirit and matter. The name one gives them is not important; what is important is that these systems inevitably see the human person as the battlefield where these opposing forces contend with each other. Salvation may mean escape or deliverance from the dark or evil force; but that force will always remain a part of reality.

Christians see things differently. There is one God, and one God only. God created the world out of nothing, simply by his will: "Let there be light." And all that God made participates in his goodness; God cannot make anything evil because there is no evil in him. But more: God not only creates, but he cares for his creation and loves it, by what we call divine providence.

And so we come to Jesus' words: "You loved me before the foundation of the world." These words are not a passing sentiment; they give us insight into all of reality; they are the foundation of the great Christian vision.

Christians have the widest vision of all. They can see from eternity to eternity, from before the foundation of the world to the final triumph, when Christ the King will reign over all, in his kingdom, "a kingdom of truth and life," as the liturgy says, "a kingdom of holiness and grace, a kingdom of justice, love, and peace"—a kingdom we can fervently hope for. God loved Christ; God loves us. God has a plan, a destiny for us; and we are secure in his love.

God our Father, before the foundation of the world you called us and destined us to be your adopted children; give us, we pray, the gift of perseverance, and keep us always faithful to you.

Knowing God

Father Joseph T. Lienhard, s.j.

"Righteous Father, the world also does not know you, but I know you, and they know that you sent me. I made known to them your name and I will make it known, that the love with which you loved me may be in them and I in them."

(Jn 17:25-26)

How do we get to know someone? One way is by personal acquaintance. A man comes to know a woman by talking with her, spending time with her, showing interest in her. He asks her to marry him, and they start a family. As parents they discover their children's personalities, their unique traits.

Another way of getting to know someone is by what others tell us about him. None of us ever conversed with George Washington, for example; but we can read about him and study his writings.

But how do we get to know God? Our Lord says, "I know you... I made known to them your name." Our Lord knows God in a unique way; but he also reveals God to us. And our Lord's revelation is preserved, first of all, in the Scriptures. If we want to know God, we need to know the Scriptures; by listening attentively at Mass, by meditating on a chapter from the Gospel each day, by praying the psalms. Such reading and meditating should lead us to prayer of the heart, speaking directly to God in our hearts and minds. Sometimes prayer is discursive, as we speak to God of our needs. At other times we rest in the awareness that God is near, that God cares for us.

We might, perhaps, also have a mystical experience of God. A mystical experience is a moment of direct, unmediated awareness of God, awareness of his beauty, his love, his mercy. The great saints tried to describe these moments of mystical union; their words are rich and beautiful, but they always fall short of the reality. If we are granted such an experience, we will remember it all our lives. But whether we ever have such an experience or not, our Lord has prayed "that the love with which you loved me may be in them and I in them."

Eternal Lord and God, I long with all my heart to know you more deeply and to serve you more faithfully; give me the strength, I pray, to live in your grace all the days of my life.

There Was a Garden

Father Joseph T. Lienhard, S.J.

*When [Jesus] had said this, Jesus went out with his disciples
across the Kidron valley to where there was a garden, into which
he and his disciples entered. Judas his betrayer also knew the
place, because Jesus had often met there with his disciples.
So Judas got a band of soldiers and guards from the chief
priests and the Pharisees and went there with
lanterns, torches, and weapons. (Jn 18:1-3)*

The thought of a garden is almost always pleasant. "Garden" invokes images of sunlight, fresh air, and breezes. Gardens offer rich colors, the colors of flowers and fruit. Gardens provide food: vegetables that grow in the ground, fruit that hangs on trees and ripens in the sun.

As we study the Scriptures, the deeper significance of gardens emerges. The beginning of the Book of Genesis tells us that God planted a garden in the east of Eden and put the first man into that garden. Elsewhere in the Scriptures, we read that Jerusalem included the King's Garden. In the Song of Songs, the lovers speak of a fragrant garden enclosed, where they find spices and honey.

But the most memorable garden in the Scriptures is the garden of Gethsemane. The first sorrowful mystery of the rosary is the agony in the garden, an ironic title. A garden should be a place of beauty, quiet, and peace. But for Jesus, it is the place where he is arrested. Yet in this garden, just as in the garden of Eden, the destiny of mankind is changed for ever. In that first garden, sin entered the world and, with it, death; in this latter garden, the reversal of the effects of sin begins, and death is to be overcome in Jesus' Resurrection.

When Scripture sets these two great events of human history in gardens, it invites us to reflect on nature, its corruption, and its restoration. God established man in a state of elevated nature—that is, with the gift of supernatural grace, symbolized by the garden that God himself had planted. When they sinned, Adam and Eve were banished from the garden. Christ suffers agony in the garden and is taken from it by force. After his death he is buried in a garden. And when he is raised and appears to Mary Magdalene, she mistakes him for the gardener—but the divine gardener has restored what sin lost.

*God our Father, you created the world in beauty and in truth;
as we behold all that you have made, inspire us, we pray, to see in
all of creation a reflection of the beauty that you are.*

315

He Said, "I AM"

Father Joseph T. Lienhard, s.j.

Jesus, knowing everything that was going to happen to him, went out and said to [the soldiers and guards], "Whom are you looking for?" They answered him, "Jesus the Nazorean." He said to them, "I AM." Judas his betrayer was also with them. When he said to them, "I AM," they turned away and fell to the ground. (Jn 18:4-6)

A noteworthy feature of Saint John's Gospel is his report that Jesus used the phrase "I AM" of himself—not "I am he," or "I am here," or "I am the one," but simply "I AM." John notes the power of the phrase: when Jesus' enemies heard it, they turned away and fell to the ground. They turned away, because they stood for the opposite of what Jesus was: good and evil cannot face each other. They also fell to the ground: evil cannot stand up to good.

But what of Jesus' statement, "I AM"? Our translation prints it in capital letters, because Jesus is making an astounding claim. In the Book of Exodus, God appeared to Moses in the burning bush. When Moses asked God for his name, God replied, "I am who am." This name has puzzled and intrigued interpreters ever since it was recorded. Was God refusing to reveal his name? Was he saying that he is being itself, existence itself? Is some other mystery hidden here? In any case, God's proper name in the Old Testament, a form of "I AM," came to be regarded by the Jews as so sacred that they did not pronounce it.

Thus Jesus' pronunciation of "I AM" is deeply significant. Once, when he pronounced it, the bystanders picked up stones to cast at him, because they believed he had blasphemed. In the garden, the soldiers and guards fell to the ground in fear. But Jesus did not blaspheme. As our faith tells us, he is true God and true man. When he said, "I AM," he simply spoke the truth. Saying "I AM" is saying, "I and the Father are one."

When we look upon the face of Jesus, we look upon the face of God. Only, we do not turn away and fall to the ground; rather, we fix our gaze upon him and kneel down in adoration.

Almighty and ever-living God, you sent your Only Begotten Son to be our Lord and Savior; confirm our faith, we implore you, in him as true God, and deepen our love for him as true man.

Jesus the Nazorean

Father Joseph T. Lienhard, s.j.

*So [Jesus] again asked [the soldiers and guards], "Whom
are you looking for?" They said, "Jesus the Nazorean." Jesus
answered, "I told you that I AM. So if you are looking for me,
let these men go." This was to fulfill what he had said,
"I have not lost any of those you gave me."*
(Jn 18:7-9)

All of Christian theology is the answer to one question that
Jesus asked Peter in Caesarea Philippi: "Who do you say
that I am?"

In Caesarea Philippi, Peter confessed Jesus as Messiah and Son
of God. In the fifth century the ecumenical Council of Chalcedon
promulgated the most significant statement the Church has ever
made about Christ: the one Christ is true God and true man, one
person in two natures, a divine nature and a human nature. As God,
Jesus is divine just as the Father is; as man, Jesus is man just as we
are. He is not a demigod or a superman, not some third sort of being.

We encounter this teaching, veiled from unbelievers, in the deeply
moving words quoted from Saint John's Gospel. The soldiers and
the guards assume that they are searching for a human being; they
designate him by his proper name and by the town he came from:
Jesus the Nazorean. This is the sort of name they might use for
any suspect they were trying to find and take prisoner. And Jesus
answers with beautiful ambiguity: "I told you that I AM." The soldiers
and the guards take it with one obvious meaning: "I am Jesus of
Nazareth—that is my name, my identity." The Christian readers,
the Christian believers, grasp a second, far deeper sense: "Yes,
I am Jesus the Nazorean; but I am also the Second Person of the
Blessed Trinity."

What should this teaching mean to us? Our Lord Jesus Christ is
far more than a wise teacher or a courageous martyr. His words are
the words of God, his acts are the deeds of God. The soldiers and
the guards are right; he is "Jesus the Nazorean." And Jesus is right;
he may take the divine name to himself: "I AM."

As we pray in the Divine Praises, "Blessed be Jesus Christ, true
God and true man."

*Eternal, ever-living God, you sent your Son to ransom us from the
power of sin and death and to bring us to the fullness of life; keep
us, we implore you, faithful to him, and increase our love for him.*

His Name Was Malchus

Father Joseph T. Lienhard, s.j.

Then Simon Peter, who had a sword, drew it, struck the high priest's slave, and cut off his right ear. The slave's name was Malchus. Jesus said to Peter, "Put your sword into its scabbard. Shall I not drink the cup that the Father gave me?"

(Jn 18:10-11)

When the Evangelists recount the events of our Lord's Passion, they include a few details that are both vivid and unexpected.

One such detail is the way our Lord's clothing is dispersed. The soldiers tear up most of his garments, and each one takes a piece—a pathetic witness to their low pay and their simplicity. When they get to his tunic, they do not tear it up but gamble for it. Those cloths and that tunic might be taken as symbols of Jesus' two natures—his human nature could be destroyed, but his divine nature is intact.

Saint Mark records another such detail. As Jesus is being arrested, the soldiers find a young man sleeping out in the garden. It must have been a warm spring evening; he wears only a sheet. When the soldiers try to restrain him, he lets go of the sheet and runs away naked. Who but Saint Mark, later in his life, would have told such a story—about himself?

A third such detail is Peter's attempt at resistance. Mark tells us only that one of the bystanders draws a sword and cuts off the slave's ear. Luke adds that it is the right ear, and that Jesus touches it and heals it. John names the two men involved: Simon Peter and Malchus.

To pass off the incident with a remark about Peter's poor swordsmanship is to miss the point. The incident is part of our Lord's plan. Jesus had told the disciples to bring a sword or two with them. Peter's blow, aimed at the high priest's slave, is an act of resistance—the only one in all the accounts of the Passion. As such, it is a key symbol: evil is not to be accepted passively, even if our efforts to resist it are, in themselves, feeble.

Perhaps Malchus later became a Christian, and would delight in showing his ear when Christ's Passion was narrated.

God our Father, as we contemplate the mystery of Christ your Son's Passion, Death, and Resurrection, confirm us, we implore you, in faith and in fidelity to him, and bring us one day to the fullness of the life that is his.

One Man Should Die

Father Joseph T. Lienhard, S.J.

*So the band of soldiers, the tribune, and the Jewish guards
seized Jesus, bound him, and brought him to Annas first.
He was the father-in-law of Caiaphas, who was high priest that
year. It was Caiaphas who had counseled the Jews that it was
better that one man should die rather than the people.*

(Jn 18:12-14)

To balance a lesser evil against a greater evil: is that what is at stake here?

Let's step back for a moment. The first and most basic principle of morality is: good is to be done, and evil avoided. The two phrases are not exactly parallel. There are countless good acts that I might carry out; I cannot do all of them. The good presents itself as to be done, but not every good act is obligatory. Evil, however, presents itself as to be avoided, and it is never right or good to do evil; evil must always be avoided.

Of course, this basic principle does not answer all the questions that might arise. If one is forced to choose between two evils, may one rightly choose the lesser of the two?

Or—is that statement too abstract to apply to the Gospel passage we are pondering?

As Caiaphas phrases it, the Jews face a moral dilemma. But a Christian reader sees things differently. And the key word is "for" (as many translations have it). Caiaphas, it would seem, uses "for" to mean "in place of" or "instead of." But a Christian reader can easily understand it as "on behalf of" or "for the sake of." That is, Christians do not understand Christ's death as a politically expedient move but as an expiatory sacrifice. This Christian sense of "for" is the same one that we recognize in the words of consecration over the chalice: "for this is the chalice of my Blood,…which will be poured out for you and for many." And these words bring us to the very heart of the Christian mystery: the atoning death of Jesus Christ, carried out in the one perfect sacrifice of Calvary and made present and efficacious in every Mass that is celebrated on every altar in the world, even to the end of time.

Eternal God and Father, by the blood of Christ, offered on the cross for the redemption of the world, deliver us, we pray, from all that is old and sinful and make us new in the fullness of the Paschal Mystery.

The Gatekeeper

Father John Dominic Corbett, O.P.

Simon Peter and another disciple followed Jesus. Now the other disciple was known to the high priest, and he entered the courtyard of the high priest with Jesus. But Peter stood at the gate outside. So the other disciple, the acquaintance of the high priest, went out and spoke to the gatekeeper and brought Peter in. (Jn 18:15-16)

Simon received another name from Jesus. He was named "Peter," the rock on which he would build his Church. Of course, receiving one name did not mean the other went out of use. Just as we sometimes use one or another form of our friend's names to signal pleasure or displeasure, so Jesus uses "Peter" when he is approving of him—*You are Peter and on this rock I will build my Church*, and sometimes uses "Simon," the old name for the old man, when failure is in view—*Simon, Simon, Satan has asked to sift you as wheat.*

The curious and overlooked thing about this passage is that although both names are used, the name "Peter" is used more often. This is strange because failure certainly seems to be looming large on the horizon. Peter had boasted that he would face death rather than deny his Lord. This night would make short work of that boast. And yet even on the brink of betrayal he is called "Peter." Why?

Perhaps he is called "Peter" because even then someone was leading him "where he would not go." After all, Peter was at first excluded from the courtyard and was standing at the gate outside. He was excluded from the unfolding action and therefore from the danger of betrayal. But then John "brought Peter in."

Where did John bring Peter? John brought Peter into his place of maximum moral danger, into the place where he would be led into temptation, where he would in fact fall. But he was also bringing him to the place were Jesus was and was therefore helping him follow Jesus.

Jesus calls himself the true gatekeeper and the good shepherd. It isn't hard to imagine Jesus as the invisible gatekeeper that cold night, keeping watch over the soul of frail Simon, knowing him all the while as "Peter," for ever standing guard as the shepherd of his embattled and perpetually endangered flock.

Father, you know us by name. You know that if we are left to ourselves we will betray that name. Please remain with us and grant us the grace of fidelity.

The Dark and Cold

Father John Dominic Corbett, O.P.

Then the maid who was the gatekeeper said to Peter, "You are not one of this man's disciples, are you?" He said, "I am not." Now the slaves and the guards were standing around a charcoal fire that they had made, because it was cold, and were warming themselves. Peter was also standing there keeping warm.

(Jn 18:17-18)

There are two trials going on this evening. One is of Jesus and the other is of Peter. Peter is on trial as a disciple of Jesus. The gatekeeper maid asks him if he follows Jesus. Peter must now testify.

Is it possible to lie about these matters? Is it possible to deny that one is a disciple and nevertheless be one in truth? It seems not. The very fact that you deny following Jesus seems to show that you do not follow Jesus. Peter says, "I am not," and by the very fact that he says these words he seems to destroy his relationship with Christ.

Where Peter is situated is important. He is standing with the slaves and the guards. His position calls to mind the position of Judas when the crowd came to arrest Jesus. The night was dark and cold. Judas came with a crowd of guards and slaves armed and with torches and lanterns. They could not see except by their own lights. They were in darkness, and the Gospel makes a special point of saying that Judas was standing with them. When Jesus said, "I am he," those who came to arrest him fell down as though dead. Judas was standing with them, and with them Judas fell.

Peter, John tells us, was "standing there" with them in the cold. He was with them in the dark. Cold with the cold of this world, far from the fire of God's love, his path lighted by the feeble rays of his own resources, Peter was fated, with Judas and the crowd of the world formed by the way of the world, to fall.

Nevertheless, he was not to remain fallen. By the grace of God, by the Spirit of truth, when he denied that he was Jesus' disciple, he lied. By the Spirit of truth, he would finally testify to the truth. "Lord, you know everything; you know that I love you."

Father, grant that we may always confess to being your followers, and grant that in so doing we may be speaking in the Spirit of truth.

Open Secret

Father John Dominic Corbett, O.P.

The high priest questioned Jesus about his disciples and about his doctrine. Jesus answered him, "I have spoken publicly to the world. I have always taught in a synagogue or in the temple area where all the Jews gather, and in secret I have said nothing. Why ask me? Ask those who heard me what I said to them. They know what I said." (Jn 18:19-21)

Jesus is on trial and is treated as one with much to hide. The high priest questioned Jesus about his disciples. Why? Perhaps he feared they were abroad that very night, hiding in the shadows, heading up secret cells of religious and political revolutionaries, conspiring against both their own authority and the authority of the Roman Empire. He questioned Jesus about his teaching. Why? Most likely he thought Jesus had a secret and dangerous teaching delivered only to his closest collaborators. And so he imagined his role as bringing what was hidden into public view.

But it was these same authorities who, for fear of the crowds who held Jesus to be a prophet, did not dare arrest Jesus publicly. It was these same authorities who met secretly with Judas and conspired together with him to hand Jesus over.

Jesus draws a contrast between himself and the Jewish authorities. They fear a conspiracy from Jesus and his disciples, and yet they are the source of the conspiracy which has resulted in the arrest of Jesus. Jesus, on the contrary, has said and done everything in the full light of day. He can do this "because he has said nothing in secret."

Yet his teaching is both public and hidden. It is spoken openly to the world, but it is hidden because it is only understood when accompanied by the interior testifying action of the Holy Spirit. His hearers knew indeed what he said but could not have known what he meant "because the Holy Spirit had not yet been given."

We are always on trial with and before Jesus. We are often asked what he said, and sometimes we are not sure what he meant. The promise of the sending of the Spirit is that we will grow in our knowledge of God's secrets, of what God has intended for us from the beginning.

Father, help us to grow in the knowledge of your plan for our salvation. Help us to appreciate what you have confided to our hearts and to share it with others.

Rules of Evidence

Father John Dominic Corbett, o.p.

*When [Jesus] had said this, one of the temple guards standing
there struck Jesus and said, "Is this the way you answer the high
priest?" Jesus answered him, "If I have spoken wrongly, testify to
the wrong; but if I have spoken rightly, why do you strike me?"
Then Annas sent him bound to Caiaphas the high priest.*
(Jn 18:22-24)

In television dramas about the criminal justice system, the script
often centers on the admissibility of evidence and the fallibility
of law. The law is sometimes shown to block the admission
of evidence which would prove guilt or innocence. It seems that
keeping the letter of the law corrupts justice.

This passage is about law and evidence. But the operating
assumption in this drama, as opposed to our own, is that the law
in question is God's law, and that as such it cannot be mistaken
in its prescriptions or wrongheaded in its requirements. Keeping
the law always brings justice. As Jesus is on trial and as he is being
judged by the standards of God's law, Jesus insists that the standards
of law apply to him above all. That is why he asks, "Why ask me?
Ask those who heard me speak. They know what I said." The point
being made is that it is against rabbinical law to require a witness
to testify against himself. All evidence must come from witnesses
other than the defendant. There are no such visible witnesses on
offer. Jesus makes this clear and therefore makes clear that according
to the justice of the law he should be released. Unable to respond
verbally, they respond physically. He is struck by the police, and
bound and sent on to Caiaphas.

Obedience and disobedience, justice and injustice, truth and lies
sometimes are not spoken. Sometimes they can only be carried out
in an action. Sometimes the truth is too close to us to be verbalized.
Sometimes the evil clings too closely to us to be dissected and
analyzed. Only the Holy Spirit can serve as witness for us in those
moments of trial when it is a matter of spiritual life or death to do
the truth.

*Father, help us to see the inner truth of the Law you have given us
and give us confidence that in following it we shall see the triumph
of your justice and mercy.*

Promise Keeper

Father John Dominic Corbett, O.P.

Now Simon Peter was standing there keeping warm. And [the guards and slaves] said to him, "You are not one of his disciples, are you?" He denied it and said, "I am not." One of the slaves of the high priest, a relative of the one whose ear Peter had cut off, said, "Didn't I see you in the garden with him?" Again Peter denied it. And immediately the cock crowed. (Jn 18:25-27)

As is well known, names in the Bible are more than convenient ways to label or differentiate one person from another. When Adam was given the task of naming the animals of the earth, he was given a sort of creative freedom to name what each of these beasts would mean to him. A name reveals an essence or a given mission. According to the Scriptures, at least, Shakespeare's Juliet was wrong. There is much in a name.

God reveals his name throughout the Scriptures. He gives his name to Moses as he says, "I am who am." A fuller translation would be "I am always with you and I will always be with you." God's name reveals he is faithful promise. Indeed everything he says is a promise.

Peter got his name from a promise: "You are Peter and on this rock I will build my Church." He would be rock-solid ground for the other Apostles. Peter responded with a promise of his own: "I will give up my life for you." He wasted no time in breaking it. He was asked a direct question: "You are not one of that man's disciples are you?" The words he chooses undo his own identity. He says, "I am…not," which is a sacrilegious parody of the divine name. In unsaying his name, he unsays God's name and loses everything.

But Jesus has called and named Peter, and Peter is not allowed to undo that. Peter may deny his discipleship and his promise to the Lord, but Jesus can never and will never go back on his promise to Peter. The rock may crumble, but the rock will be restored. Jesus' own claim, "I am the good shepherd," and his decision to rehabilitate Peter, and to share with him the office of good shepherd, remind us that everything he says to us is a promise.

Father, you have fulfilled all of your promises to us in Jesus. Give us such confidence in your fidelity that we never cease to hope in the power of your will to save.

Purifying Blood

Father John Dominic Corbett, O.P.

Then [the Jews] brought Jesus from Caiaphas to the praetorium. It was morning. And they themselves did not enter the praetorium, in order not to be defiled so that they could eat the Passover. So Pilate came out to them and said, "What charge do you bring [against] this man?" They answered and said to him, "If he were not a criminal, we would not have handed him over to you." (Jn 18:28-30)

There is an easily appreciated irony in the fact that the Jewish leaders will not go in to see Pilate. They cannot enter his house without becoming "defiled" and therefore incapable of celebrating the Passover feast that night. Hence they take care to be ritually "pure." Nevertheless, their intent that morning is to deal death to one supremely undeserving of death, and this, of itself, and according to their own Scriptures, would render them far more profoundly incapable of participating in the worship of God than any contact with the unsanctified world of the Gentiles. After all, it is from the heart that defilement comes into the world and not from the world into the heart.

It is as though the leaders are somehow aware that no ceremonial bath could effect the purification needed to allow them to participate in this Passover supper. They feared a sort of ritual defilement caused by contact with a Gentile ruler but did not fear the purifying danger caused by a direct and unrecognized contact with God himself.

In his play *Macbeth*, Shakespeare shows us Lady Macbeth driven mad with guilt over her share in the murder of King Duncan. She wanders the halls washing her hands again and again murmuring, "Out, out, damned spot." She did not know that water was powerless on its own to wash away blood. Only blood could wash the stain of blood away.

The true Passover lamb was to be slaughtered that day. According to Exodus, the blood of the Passover lamb kept the angel of death from destroying God's own children. In the same way, the blood of Jesus was to protect and guard these "guardians and shepherds" of the people, allowing them, after the conclusion of these terrible days, in their acceptance of and belief in the good news, truly and worthily to "eat the Passover supper."

Father, help us truly to believe that the blood of your Son washes our sins away and gives us access to your presence in true worship.

Joint Responsibility

Father John Dominic Corbett, O.P.

At this, Pilate said to [the Jews], "Take him yourselves, and judge him according to your law." The Jews answered him, "We do not have the right to execute anyone," in order that the word of Jesus might be fulfilled that he said indicating the kind of death he would die. (Jn 18:31-32)

What sort of death did Jesus say he was going to die? You could distinguish between the physical cause of the death of Jesus, the persons responsible for the death of Jesus, and the effect of the death of Jesus. Each has its importance.

The physical cause of the death of Jesus was, of course, his crucifixion. Crucifixion was a vile sort of death reserved for especially reviled people. The feet of the condemned were fastened by nails to a wooden stake planted in the ground. The arms were stretched out and likewise fastened. The condemned could only breathe by lifting his torso upwards while supporting it by tearing his feet against the cursed nails. The condemned would collapse and then could only breathe by repeating the process. Death, when it mercifully came (sometimes days later), was caused by suffocation. What sort of death did Jesus die? He was tortured to death on a cross.

Who were the persons responsible for Jesus' death? The Jewish leaders wanted him killed. They told Pilate that they could not put any man to death. If Jesus was to die a death of capital punishment, it could only be by the decree of the Roman governor. So both the rulers of Jews and the rulers of the Gentiles were directly implicated. Who condemned Jesus? Everyone condemned Jesus.

What sort of death did Jesus die? His death was caused by the whole world. Therefore his death could effect the healing of the whole world. Jesus said, "If I am lifted up I will draw all people to myself."

Have you ever wondered how you would have behaved if the life of Jesus had somehow been in your hands that fateful day? Have you ever imagined that you would have been blameless? That would have been to your loss. If you could somehow absolve yourself from involvement in his death, you would also cut yourself off from its saving effect.

Father, help us to face our own responsibility for the death of your Son, and to rejoice in the share this gives us in his salvation.

Résumé

Father John Dominic Corbett, O.P.

*So Pilate went back into the praetorium and summoned Jesus
and said to him, "Are you the King of the Jews?" Jesus answered,
"Do you say this on your own or have others told you about
me?" Pilate answered, "I am not a Jew, am I? Your own nation
and the chief priests handed you over to me.
What have you done?"* (Jn 18:33-35)

We Americans now have some experience with trying to exercise political rule in a land and culture not our own. In Vietnam and in Afghanistan and in Iraq we have tried to control events and have found that an exceedingly difficult and dangerous project indeed. Control is hard to come by when you are a stranger in a strange land.

It should not be too hard to put ourselves in Pilate's shoes. His world is Rome and Roman politics. He has dreamed great dreams but has come up short. He has been saddled with the thankless task of governing a dangerous and explosive backwater. Just this morning a group of religious fanatics are dragging in another religious fanatic, and are baying for his blood. Why? It's not clear. This Friday morning Pilate would like to make this man and this problem and all these people simply disappear, and go back home to bed.

Poor Pilate. He asks Jesus, "What have you done?" when he himself has acknowledged his incapacity to understand any answer Jesus might give. He asks, "I am not a Jew, am I?" underscoring the fact that he could never understand what Jesus did with the wine at the wedding feast of Cana, or with the loaves and fishes, or with the faith of the centurion, or with the spittle that cured the blind man. He could never have understood the signs that Jesus performed. He would never understand the meaning of his own question, "Are you the King of the Jews?"

Sometimes we are like Pilate. We just want to go along and get along. Nevertheless, every once in a while a crisis of grace comes our way, and then it's vital that we recognize it for what it is. May God always give us the grace to meet those moments when the truth of our lives is in the balance on our own judgment day.

*Father, we belong to your people. Help us to recognize the signs you
send us of your presence, and to respond according to your will.*

Where He Rules

Father John Dominic Corbett, O.P.

Jesus answered, "My kingdom does not belong to this world.
If my kingdom did belong to this world, my attendants [would]
be fighting to keep me from being handed over to the Jews.
But as it is, my kingdom is not here." So Pilate said to him,
"Then you are a king?" Jesus answered, "You say I am a king."
(Jn 18: 36-37a)

Americans are often smitten by royalty. Whenever there is a wedding in Westminster Abbey the television ratings go through the roof. The pageantry of the ceremonies of coronation seems to point to a gracious and beautiful fairy tale at last come to life which is a crowning not only of an individual but of a whole political and cultural way of life, the legitimacy of which is placed beyond question or struggle.

The truth is that monarchies and royal dynasties find their foundations in blood and strife. The Houses of York and Lancaster, for instance, fought murderous wars in order to stage their respective coronations, and the price of keeping their crowns as well as keeping their heads was the lives of their adversaries.

For this reason Jesus says that his kingdom does not belong to this world. It does not run according to this world's rule, which is to say that it does not rest on a final foundation of violence. If it did rest on that foundation then more swords than Peter's would have flashed, and the final proof would have been given that even the rule of Jesus pays homage to the law of brute force.

But his kingdom is not here. He knows our wars but refuses to engage in them as a contestant or partisan. He does not condescend to struggle with us as a rival or a peer. Instead he reveals his majesty and his Father's glory by his decision to embrace his "hour" of glory on the cross.

Pilate asks, "Then you are a king?" and receives a reply which, while undercutting Pilate's idea of kingship, still conveys Jesus' assertion of royal authority. This authority does not rest on violence. It rests on the finally incontestable and irresistibly beautiful wood of the cross from which Jesus calls all people to himself.

Father, although you have sent us your Son to be our King, he has never left your side. Give us an ever-deepening thirst to be where he is now and ever shall be.

What Is Truth?

Father John Dominic Corbett, O.P.

"For this I was born and for this I came into the world, to testify to the truth. Everyone who belongs to the truth listens to my voice." Pilate said to him, "What is truth?"
(Jn 18:37b-38a)

Every so often we meet someone with whom it is difficult to communicate. We might be speaking the same language and using the same words, but we still can't seem to connect. Perhaps what is happening is that, although we are using the same words, these same words have very different meanings for us. Although we appear to be talking about the same thing, in reality we are worlds apart.

The encounter here between Jesus and Pilate is an encounter between people who use the same words to mean entirely different things. Jesus says that the reason he was born was to testify to the truth. Pilate asks, "What is truth?" Pilate is thinking like a Roman, like a pragmatist, like an engineer, like a practical man, like someone who at most expects "truth" to demarcate an arena of temporary utility.

On the other hand, Jesus is the Son of his Father and also the son of his people. The Jewish people knew truth not as abstract but as concrete. They knew it not as the conformity of mind to reality but as the faithful relationship between person and person. So for Jesus to speak about *the truth* is really to speak about *the relationship*. What relationship? The truth is the relationship between him and his Father, where the Son does the will of the Father and thereby glorifies the Father. And the will of the Father is nothing less than the salvation of the whole human race. The truth is the face of the Father turned in mercy to save his wayward children. Jesus shows us this face of the Father on the cross. All who are called to know the Father in this way are called by the voice of Jesus who is the very voice of truth.

Father, no one can come to Jesus unless you call, and no one can see your face unless he sees it reflected in the face of your Son. Let us see your face in his.

Mistaken Identity

Father John Dominic Corbett, O.P.

When [Pilate] had said this, he went out again to the Jews and said to them, "I find no guilt in [Jesus]. But you have a custom that I release one prisoner to you at Passover. Do you want me to release to you the King of the Jews?" They cried out again, "Not this one but Barabbas!" Now Barabbas was a revolutionary. (Jn 18:38b-40)

Pilate went out and faced the crowd and referred to Jesus not by his name but by his title. "Do you want me to release to you the King of the Jews?" Now the response of the crowd is precise: "Not this one but Barabbas." It is as though they were saying, "Not this man but Barabbas is the true King of the Jews." When we remember that names in the Bible are not just labels but are revelatory of the inner truth of the person, then Barabbas as a name is terribly significant. Barabbas means "son of the father." So the leaders were saying that this revolutionary and man of violence was the true son of the father and the true King of Israel.

Why would they say this? Could they have really meant it? If so, then the scribes and Pharisees were themselves revolutionaries looking to overthrow the rule of Rome "by any means necessary," including violence. Nothing that we know about them suggests this. If anything, they were more likely to turn a rebel in to Rome than support him.

Perhaps they were under a certain sort of pressure themselves, surrounded as they were by the partisans and allies of Barabbas filling the square all shouting his name. But it is more likely that they were so set on destroying Jesus that they would embrace any alternative at all to him and his claims. Later on they would shout to Pilate, "We have no king but Caesar." Caesar? Barabbas? It didn't matter in the end, so long as Jesus could be rejected.

We humans are odd. We can be trapped into saying things we don't really think are true and shouting for things we don't really want. The crowd was driven to shout for Barabbas that day, "son of the father" of lies, by the father of lies himself. What would we say, what would we shout for, to avoid letting God have his way with us?

Father, give us the inner calm and discipline we need in order to reject the bellowing babble which would drown out your own voice.

Despising the Shame

Father John Dominic Corbett, O.P.

*Then Pilate took Jesus and had him scourged. And the soldiers
wove a crown out of thorns and placed it on his head, and
clothed him in a purple cloak, and they came to him and said,
"Hail, King of the Jews!" And they struck him repeatedly.*

(Jn 19:1-3)

It would not be in keeping with the spirit of John's Gospel to emphasize the scourging. Scourging with leather straps and attached lead balls and fish hooks would tear flesh off bone, would break bone, would sever arteries, would cause concussion, and would certainly kill. Scourging was normally the beginning phase of the execution of a capital sentence, and it was not required that the victim survive.

The physical nightmare is only noted in passing. It is the mockery of Jesus which receives attention. A crown is placed on his head, but it is a crown of thorns. A cloak of royal purple is given him, but the cloak is soaked in his blood and covers a body torn by punishment reserved for slaves. The translation says the soldiers "came up" to him, but a closer translation would be "processed" to him, which catches the reverential manner one uses to approach a monarch. They "came up" to him in this fashion precisely to mock his Kingship with the back of their hands.

Anger is our normal human response to derision. It is normally exacerbated by the secret fear that we are indeed of little worth or substance. But Jesus displays not the slightest anger or impatience. In fact, Jesus retains a majestic silence throughout these proceedings. It would be a mistake to ascribe this to supreme self-control, as though Jesus violently had to suppress his violence. He knows who he is. He knows that he rules. He knows that as the heavens are higher than the earth so his way of rule is higher, infinitely higher than ours. He does not prove his majesty in this scene. He displays it in all the untroubled serenity of the Godhead.

We sometimes feel that we need to prove our worth. We need to react with violence to those who demean us. May we learn differently from our King—our truest, noblest, and only King.

*Father, we are so quick to detect any slighting of our own persons
and to respond in wrath. Help us to see that our own dignity rests
in yours, and is for ever safe.*

Ecce Homo

Father John Dominic Corbett, O.P.

Once more Pilate went out and said to [the Jews], "Look, I am bringing him out to you, so that you may know that I find no guilt in him." So Jesus came out, wearing the crown of thorns and the purple cloak. And he said to them, "Behold, the man!"

(Jn 19:4-5)

Pilate was a hard man. He was an unsentimental man. He had to be. Ruling in Rome's name over a conquered but restless and subversive people was no task for a man who fainted at the sight of blood.

Pilate was nonetheless human. The sight of Jesus torn from head to toe clearly moved him. Perhaps he saw in the figure before him an emblem of suffering, suffering beyond anything this man could have deserved. "Look, I am bringing him out to you. Look at the man and see. I find in him no guilt. At least I find no guilt that could possibly have deserved this. Look at the man!"

If Pilate had been versed in the Hebrew Scriptures he might have recognized in the crown of thorns an eerie reprise of the curse of waste and sweat and futility placed on Adam's brow, the curse of seed planted in hope and yielding nothing but thorns. Jesus' work, which was doing the will of the Father and therefore doing the work of the Good Shepherd, the crown of his labor, seemed to yield nothing but a crown of thorns, a love's labor truly lost.

Once someone asked Freud to sum up what it meant really to live a life and really to be a man. He said that life came down to two things. The first was love. The other was work. Freud overlooked something important. He overlooked suffering.

Suffering is often the price of both love and work. Sometimes suffering accompanies the work that we do for the sake of those we love. Sometimes suffering is the work that we do for those we love. Sometimes suffering is the real reason the work we do and the love we have finds its crown and reward.

Pilate sees and we see the Christ suffering in labor, suffering in love, crowned with the majesty of a King. Behold the man.

Father, may we understand and emulate the labor and the love and the suffering which formed your Son into the most human of men.

Finding of Guilt

Father John Dominic Corbett, O.P.

When the chief priests and the guards saw [Jesus] they cried out, "Crucify him, crucify him!" Pilate said to them, "Take him yourselves and crucify him. I find no guilt in him."
(Jn 19:6)

When Pilate told the chief priests and guards to crucify Jesus themselves, he was perfectly aware that they had not the power to do this. The law of Moses prescribed stoning for blasphemy, but not crucifixion. Even stoning had been withdrawn from their legal competence by the Romans. As for crucifixion, it was administered solely by the Romans, and solely for the crime of sedition.

Why then did the chief priests and the guards cry out for crucifixion? Most probably they did so in order to shift responsibility for the crucifixion onto Pilate and so evade this responsibility before their own people, many of whom were still potential followers of Jesus.

There is probably another reason they shout so specifically for crucifixion. In much popular piety a particularly gruesome event is often taken for a divine judgment. The Book of Deuteronomy reflects this when it declares, "Cursed be he who hangs on a tree." The fact that someone has met this cruel end could be interpreted to mean that this person has been publicly condemned and cursed by God himself. Given the unrest in Jerusalem and the risk these leaders were taking in trying to destroy someone spoken of as the King of the Jews, they probably reckoned that the sheer and ugly fact of crucifixion would, of itself, confirm the justice of the sentence to the people.

We tend to believe that history is written by the winners. This belief can motivate us to do anything to win because we believe that the win is its own proof of the righteousness of the cause. The Gospel here allows the truth, "I find no guilt in him," to be uttered by a pagan, and to be submerged and lost in surrender to political expediency. Yet this loss is not final, and the truth, not to be found in Pilate or priest, is set forth in relief by the revealing act of God, preached by the Apostles and embraced by faith.

Father, give us the confidence that this world's verdicts are provisional and that we may never be moved by the fear that our holding onto your truth is in vain.

Man of the World

Father John Dominic Corbett, O.P.

The Jews answered, "We have a law, and according to that law
he ought to die, because he made himself the Son of God."
Now when Pilate heard this statement, he became even more
afraid, and went back into the praetorium and said to Jesus,
"Where are you from?" Jesus did not answer him.
(Jn 19:7-9)

P ilate is pictured in these exchanges as a man in flux. He is inside the praetorium. Then he moves outside to face the chief priests and scribes. Then he retreats from them to the sanctuary of his praetorium to face his enigmatic prisoner. When the encounter with this man proves mysterious and troubling, he goes out again to face the crowd. In the face of the crowd's unyielding hostility and determination to secure his prisoner's death, he retreats once more to question and, more searchingly and tellingly, to be put into question. Men of the world find it difficult to position themselves within a world that is at once so sensible of power's advent and so unforgiving of its departure.

Pilate begins to sense that it is not he who is in charge that day. He hears that Jesus has made himself the Son of God. He does not know what that means but it suggests the presence of a power the likes of which he has never seen and whose range and punishing scope he begins to fear. Political winds are blowing strongly enough to threaten Pilate's rule. Religious passion he does not share or understand is being unleashed. There is more than a hint of the hidden action of angry gods stirring the crowds, this prisoner, and Pilate himself. No wonder Pilate "became even more afraid."

"Where are you from?" Pilate asks. Jesus does not reply, but an alert reader of the Gospel will recall Jesus' words to Nicodemus: "The wind blows where it wills,…but you do not know where it comes from or where it goes; so it is with everyone who is born of the Spirit" (Jn 3:8).

Pilate would not have understood. So Jesus remained silent. But the Wind blowing forth from Jesus as he breathed out his Spirit on the cross would henceforth bring life and light to any beleaguered man of the world humble enough to ask.

Father, you and your Son send the Holy Spirit into the world. May
this Spirit free us from worldly fear, teach us the fear of the Lord,
and bring us life.

Power Plant

Father William M. Joensen

*So Pilate said to [Jesus], "Do you not speak to me? Do you not
know that I have power to release you and I have power to
crucify you?" Jesus answered [him], "You would have no power
over me if it had not been given to you from above. For this
reason the one who handed me over to you has the greater sin."*

(Jn 19:10-11)

The gravity of sin is only partly determined by the matter at
hand. The "greatness" of Judas' sin stems from being the
one who sets this terminal chain of events in motion. He
has heeded the voice of the Tempter, succumbing to the seductive
belief that power possessed should be power put in play. The rulers
of this world are quick to make their power over others known.
They impress upon us their capacity to make us toe the line they
have drawn in their God-emptied domain. When someone acts
on temptation, the trend becomes malignant; we are tempted to
think we must respond in kind, trying to assert ourselves and make
others dance our dance.

Jesus adopts a different mode of acting. He extends mercy in the
face of contempt, and is selflessly silent in the presence of inquisitors
such as Pilate. Pilate seems to be more like a ventriloquist trying
to orchestrate responses than interested in the truth of what his
subjects have to say. Yet he is both fascinated and perplexed by the
Jesus whom he interrogates. If Jesus' authority is borrowed from
the Jewish people who have already been subjected to the power
of Caesar, then there is no problem—Jesus is but a diversion to be
dealt with and dismissed. But if his origin is from somewhere else,
then he is not so easily categorized or controlled.

Jesus keeps his wits about him: he knows who he is, and who
his Father is. He redirects Pilate's inquiry back to him. He bears a
different form of power and authority: one that listens, that testifies,
that fashions a richer, regal, and far-reaching form of belonging. His
authority is not to be feared, but found worthy of trust. Dependence
on God is the freedom of humans from the overt control of other
humans. The foundation of freedom is relationship with the Infinite.

*You have given us your Son from above, all-powerful Father, to
show us how to hand ourselves over in loving service to one another.
May Jesus' authority rule over my words and way of being.*

Catch of the Day

Father William M. Joensen

Consequently, Pilate tried to release [Jesus]; but the Jews cried out, "If you release him, you are not a Friend of Caesar. Everyone who makes himself a king opposes Caesar."
(Jn 19:12)

A last-minute getaway weekend with some family: I called my brother who frequently visits the city on business, and asked him to get us a dinner reservation at a good restaurant—no easy request on short notice. He succeeded, with one catch: the reservation was in a friend's name. So when we presented ourselves to the maître'd, I inquired, "Reservation for Peter King?" and we were promptly escorted to a choice table. I thought to myself, "It's good to be King."

Jesus does not make himself king. He is not like those who impose their wills by flexing connections with parties more powerful than anyone they're dealing with at the moment. We recognize times when it's "who you know," but this precept is perverted by those who exploit others without allowing their own true allegiances to be known. Even scoundrels have no shortage of useful friends, but they are fickle and fleeting until a better offer comes along.

Pilate prefers to play catch and release with Jesus. But he hesitates when his loyalty to Caesar is called into question. True enough: he is no genuine Friend of Caesar, but merely an upper-level employee fearful of his boss—more slave than citizen. Robert Spaemann observes that a slave cannot be truly obedient, attending to one's owner with genuine freedom whether to respond; hence, a slave owes nothing to the master.

Jesus is not interested in slaves or sycophants. He honors servants who relate to him not because they are coerced, but because they are more interested in him as a person than for the perks he supplies. He seeks to lead others to his Father's house where a feast of friendship is available, where Jesus not only supplies but becomes the Eucharistic meal, for he is a good and kindly king. If we release our fears of being associated with him, he will not flinch at being called our friend.

Father always for us: release me from my tendency to please only those who will help me get what I want, so that I may be free to cultivate true friendship with your Son.

Judge and Jury

Father William M. Joensen

When Pilate heard these words he brought Jesus out and seated him on the judge's bench in the place called Stone Pavement, in Hebrew, Gabbatha. It was preparation day for Passover, and it was about noon. (Jn 19:13-14a)

Some colleagues and I were called for jury duty. At the courtroom, I concluded I would be excluded since I had witnessed the wedding and baptized children of the prosecutor. When he posed a hypothetical situation of a child having stolen from a cookie jar, no amount of evidence besides actually witnessing the actual theft would convince a life science colleague "beyond a reasonable doubt" that the child had committed the theft. He claimed that the need for scientific certitude would preclude his rendering judgment. Needless to say, he was not selected to be on the jury.

Pilate places Jesus himself on the judge's bench. Jesus does not say a word; his presence evokes the accumulated evidence of his teaching and preaching, his healings and other acts of power. The people have observed Jesus and formed their own opinions. Now each woman and man must deliver a judgment on who Jesus is, and whether any actual crime was committed. To cling to doubt is to decide. No one can opt out of the "jury" pool and return home to one's former life. The guilty may withdraw, but guilt will not dissolve.

Jesus exposes our preference for a vague, noncommittal way of life. He compels us to look and not blink. We are obliged to act as jury and judge—on Christ's behalf and our own. We can declare his innocence and acknowledge our sin; this naked truth helps tip the scales in our favor as Jesus gazes mercifully upon us. We can cry, "Crucify him" again, and let the pretense live on. Or—and perhaps more grievous than other options—we can willfully suspend judgment so as not to have to call sin by its proper name. A rigorous scientist may merit respect and be excused; a dogged skeptic who refuses even to behold the man laid bare in the glare of the noonday sun deserves to be held contemptible in the court of his peers.

Father of lights, in the stark presence of your Son, all my life is laid bare. Help me not to shrink from acknowledging my sin, so that, duly convicted, I may be with him in all that lies ahead.

Royally Flushed

Father William M. Joensen

*And [Pilate] said to the Jews, "Behold, your king!" [The Jews]
cried out, "Take him away, take him away! Crucify him!"
Pilate said to them, "Shall I crucify your king?" The chief priests
answered, "We have no king but Caesar." Then he handed
him over to them to be crucified. (Jn 19:14b-16a)*

Citizens in democratic societies have an inordinate fascination
with royalty. We count on the press to supply us with the
latest escapades of today's princes and princesses. But the
attraction soon fades when accounts of ceremony and revelry recede
and genuine rule over our personal affairs is asserted. We like to
keep our kings and queens at a safe remove from real life.

Pilate is more bailiff than kingmaker when he presents Jesus to the
crowd. His declaration, "Behold, your king!" is neither confession
of faith nor the verdict he will soon ratify. In this forum, we come
face-to-face with God's incarnate wisdom, with the rule of law both
natural and divine exposed without the trappings to soften the blows
we will deliver by our words, our contempt. We behold the man
whom we can scarcely resist trying to make into our own image. Our
response pronounces judgment on ourselves. In our declaration of
who Jesus is, we reinforce the maxim that we usually get the leaders
we deserve—whether scofflaws or saints.

We are tempted to scorn those who would lead us primarily by
example, who show us that we are not only called to more, but
obliged to it. One neuralgic point connected with this reading is
the reference to "the Jews" as participants in this tragic tableau,
and sadly implicated in history as the primary culprits responsible
for Christ's death. But this is a mistake made only by those foolish
enough to reinforce the tendency to blame leaders and impute guilt
by association to those who surround them as a way of excusing
our own rebellious complicity in Christ's condemnation. Those who
say they have no king but Caesar are proxies for those of us who
regard kings as amusing diversions, but who would rather distance
ourselves from God's dominion and dwell in a realm where anarchy,
rather than law, rules.

*The words "Crucify him!" catch in my throat, though I know I have
failed to confess your Son or help others behold him, O just God.
In your mercy, afford me again the chance to show that Christ is
my true King.*

Buried Treasure

Father William M. Joensen

So they took Jesus, and carrying the cross himself he went out to what is called the Place of the Skull, in Hebrew, Golgotha. There they crucified him, and with him two others, one on either side, with Jesus in the middle.

(Jn 19:16b-18)

In my region, any builder has to check for not only buried gas or electrical lines, but to make sure that the parcel of land was not previously used as a burial plot. Respect for human remains has a way of thwarting the best laid plans of developers.

John the Evangelist does not mention others pressed into service to help Jesus carry the cross. Jesus alone is capable of excavating all that has preceded him on this Place of the Skull. Jesus will unearth all the evidence of human contempt, disobedience, and estrangement from God. Past artists set a skull and crossbones at the base of the crucifix, the vestige of the old man Adam (or Eve?) intended to be a stark sign to us of our plight were this site of countless crucifixions to remain territory foreign to the God-man.

The sentence of sin far surpasses any human punishment, even corporal. Death as ultimate separation from God disarticulates the skeleton that supports life in the flesh; our bodies rot, our bones sag aimlessly into the soil of oblivion. Our human project is quickly arrested if we do not heed the signs of our own mortality, if we do not pause before the mementos of death that surround us and refuse to become buried by preoccupations and plans meant to shift our gaze away from the fact that sin kills, while Christ alone and the power of his cross saves.

Archaeologists are capable of taking decrepit human skulls and making a digital reconstruction based on their contours and crevices, presenting us with a visage of the living person. Yet these skilled imagers or even prophets such as Ezekiel cannot achieve what Jesus alone is equipped to do (cf. Ez 37): to reconnect bone with bone, to layer flesh and draw us forth from the refuse pile of human corruption and make us stand upright before the tribunal of God, whose Son soon pirates life from death.

Author of life, instill in me a graced awareness of my own mortality, so that I may more and more resemble the new Adam, Jesus Christ, who died in the flesh so that I might live.

Encryption Software

Father William M. Joensen

Pilate also had an inscription written and put on the cross. It read, "Jesus the Nazorean, the King of the Jews." Now many of the Jews read this inscription, because the place where Jesus was crucified was near the city, and it was written in Hebrew, Latin, and Greek. (Jn 19:19-20)

Pilate is not trying to be politically correct for Christ's sake, but has his micro-billboard composed in three languages to raise awareness that the Roman Empire encompasses many tongues in the modern world. Yet to focus solely on comprehending the inscription is to fall prey to the flaws posed by some language translation software: one cannot simply translate words literally on their own terms, but must decipher their meaning by referring to the context in which they appear—in this case, the cross on which they are posted.

Once while looking for a gift, I flipped through one of those mail-order catalogues from which one rarely buys anything. I came across some beautifully bejeweled crosses to be used as pendants or necklaces. The adjoining caption read: "Ancient cosmic mark of the forces of nature and other consciousness, the cross is also revered as a Christian symbol." Also?! For the casual buyer, the cross may be interpreted to mean whatever you want it to be—Christians borrowed it, and others are free to appropriate it for their own purposes.

The cross is the intersection of all that is, all that has been, and is to come. The cross is where justice and mercy meet. The cross is the point at which human arrogance and divine humility converge. The cross is where the weak and the strong encounter one another and fathom what sense God makes of it all. For these agonizing hours, we see where things stand because we draw near with those who love Jesus to the intersection of the universe. Jesus shows us to ourselves and more. He shows us God—purifying appearances, if we dare to look—and in the communion of hearts we come to recognize what God has accomplished through "Jesus the Nazorean, the King of the Jews." We behold the encrypted cross and make it our own, worthy of our attachment and adoration.

Father of every race and tongue, you do not leave me to fend for myself. Fix my sights on your Son's cross, so that I recognize your immense love for us. May I be oriented to Jesus in all I do.

Embossed Truth

Father William M. Joensen

So the chief priests of the Jews said to Pilate, "Do not write 'The King of the Jews,' but that he said, 'I am the King of the Jews.'" Pilate answered, "What I have written, I have written."
(Jn 19:21-22)

I drive toward what seems to be yet another big, black, ugly crow standing over a road-killed carcass, but realize as I draw closer that instead it is trying to wrest a piece of printed cardboard from the ground. It furiously flaps its wings and tries to ascend ahead of my rapidly gaining vehicle. Finally self-preservation takes precedence over the paper product; the crow releases it and soars out of harm's way. As I look in the rearview mirror, the bird circles around for another attempt.

The priests, disgusted by Pilate's epitaph, think that he himself has committed a misdemeanor tantamount to spraying graffiti on public property. They are like crows trying to wrest a piece of parchment from its perch on the cross. From Pilate's perspective, "The King of the Jews" is not a public confession that Jesus is in fact what others have accused him of claiming. But by refusing to add words, Pilate opts out of the "he said, she said" dynamic that drowns all ultimate truth claims in the sea of subjective opinion. If the written word does not stand at some point, then persons of whatever political persuasion have no reason to argue in the first place.

It is not necessary to add the preface "He said, 'I am.'" Jesus declared these words on numerous occasions in the synagogue, market squares, and mountain slopes. They bear an authority that is eminently personal because it is rooted in the paternal. The Father of our Lord Jesus Christ has embossed his Son onto the tablet of our flesh. The blood of Christ bears meaning more powerful than words. Yet we do not discount the truth that what Pilate has written is more than a matter of interpretation; it is an article of faith ultimately dictated by God's merciful "I am": God's Son dies for all who confess him with their lives and not merely their lips.

Father of the Word made flesh, I want all my words to give honor and praise to you, and not steal from the splendor of his name which is above all others.

Bet the House

Father William M. Joensen

When the soldiers had crucified Jesus, they took his clothes and divided them into four shares, a share for each soldier. They also took his tunic, but the tunic was seamless, woven in one piece from the top down. So they said to one another, "Let's not tear it, but cast lots for it to see whose it will be," in order that the passage of scripture might be fulfilled [that says]:/ "They divided my garments among them,/ and for my vesture they cast lots." This is what the soldiers did. (Jn 19:23-24)

Accompanying another priest onto a gambling boat (he wanted to "win a farm" rather than "bet the farm" for a family at risk), I crossed paths with a blackjack dealer to whom I had previously ministered. "Father," he whispered, "take these five numbers and go bet them at the roulette table. Whatever you win, give to the Church." Soon stacks of chips were piled in front of me, and men with suits and earpieces were milling around the table. I cashed out and gave the money to the Church—minus ten percent for my "labor," since, after all, the worker is worth his wage.

The men in suits nail Jesus to the cross and then try to claim his tunic. They lend a certain symmetry to John's drama in which they assume bit parts by their treatment of their prisoner, and thus take full share in culpability for Christ's crucifixion. Their collective wager is an all-or-nothing personal affair for something more precious than an expensive piece of cloth; they "bet the house" of the heavenly Father of Jesus and gamble away the unlimited grace that is still available if they will look, see, ask for mercy from the one whom they have pierced.

The same odds apply to us. How readily we wager with God, indulging our appetite for sport that flaunts propriety, that suspends respect for persons in grievous fashion. How easily we parse our share in the suffering inflicted on others. How glibly we help ourselves to a tawdry tithe by rationalizing that we deserve something for our trouble, when it is our troubled neighbor's well-being—including her reputation—that is at stake. And yet, despite all these occult offenses, how steadily our long-suffering Jesus waits for us to look at him from top to bottom, to weave our own pathetic behavior into the seamless fabric of his love.

If I wager with your mercy, heavenly Father, I am sure to lose all. Yet countless times you extend to me a share in your Son's royal dignity. To labor for you is worth more than gold.

Sacred Solidarity

Father William M. Joensen

Standing by the cross of Jesus were his mother and his mother's sister, Mary the wife of Clopas, and Mary of Magdala.
(*Jn 19:25*)

The sorority of women who stand by Jesus crucified do not add to or subtract from Jesus' immense suffering. Their solidarity with Jesus when nearly everyone else has abandoned him composes a very different sort of *Magnificat* without words. Souls who do not shrink from God's invitation to be drawn more intimately into the mystery of death participate with God in conceiving meaning where before there was only a void. They magnify God's own steadfast love by refusing to let evil scatter their line of sight, even as their hearts are torn asunder.

A beloved priest of my archdiocese, Monsignor Leon Connolly, observed before he succumbed to cancer, "I'm not afraid of death, but I must confess to being afraid of dying." It is a privileged secret shared by the Father and the Son and these spiritual women to what extent Jesus' mortal fear of dying was quieted by their intrepid constancy and compassion. But we know from our own experiences that without a circle of faithful ones who stand by us in our hour of suffocating darkness, loneliness is lethally debilitating.

The sacramental encounter with Jesus transmitted through community frees us to hold dear and not fear what lies in store. As Jean Vanier relates, life is a journey home, a journey toward finding our deepest identity and gradually opening ourselves to others.

I was called to the bedside of one middle-aged woman dying of cancer as she entered her last days. After I offered her the sacraments of anointing and Eucharist, surrounded by her family and friends, she stirred and mouthed the words, "What should I do?" My response: "Be. Be Kathy. Be love. Say 'yes' when Christ says: 'Come, take your place.'" And she could finally close her eyes and rest. Through fidelity to those who are about to pass over, we reveal enduring communion with others and with God.

The places where people suffer and approach death are your sanctuaries, holy Father. With your Spirit burning within me, I desire to reflect your compassion to them in the night watches of fear and loneliness.

Adoption Agreement

Father William M. Joensen

When Jesus saw his mother and the disciple there whom he loved, he said to his mother, "Woman, behold, your son." Then he said to the disciple, "Behold, your mother." And from that hour the disciple took her into his home.
(Jn 19:26-27)

In 1895 the young man Maurice Bellière wrote to Sister Thérèse Martin's older sister Pauline at their Lisieux Carmelite convent requesting a pen pal who would be both spiritual sister and mother to him. He was looking for more than someone to "friend" on Facebook; he sought someone to call "mine," to encourage and challenge him to become all Christ willed. We might trace some of his "clinginess" to the fact that as an infant he was given away in adoption to his godmother aunt and her husband, but was not told of his adoptive status until he was nearly eleven years old. Providentially, Pauline passed on Maurice's letter to her blood sister, Thérèse, who readily embraced Maurice's desire without pretense or dissembling. Her openly disclosed spiritual adoption helped heal the wounds of his distrust.

Jesus spoke in the Upper Room of the thorough exchange of Spirit between the Father and himself: "Everything that the Father has is mine; for this reason I told you that he will take from what is mine and declare it to you" (Jn 16:15). God says "mine" and does not disturb or diminish the other. And the same is true when God says "you" and "your"—"your mother," "your son"—and begets relations among the Body he forms by Christ's death.

This is not the default state of affairs among humans prone to mistrust. We must welcome the "you" to whom we offer and receive more than nature dictates. Jesus initiates the reorientation of earthly persons who mean the world to him—his mother and the disciple he dearly loves—to one another. The woman gains a new son—and the son, a mother. Jointly, they gain a Mother beyond mothers: the Church. Together, by Christ's conferral, the distinction between "yours" and "mine" dissolves, so that a new bond that is familial and nuptial in its very essence might be generated.

Loving Father, your Son is not steeped in his own suffering, but takes his mother and his beloved disciple to heart. They are drawn into a new relation in your Church, the home where we draw Spirit and life.

Finishing Touches
Father William M. Joensen

After this, aware that everything was now finished,
in order that the scripture might be fulfilled, Jesus said,
"I thirst." (Jn 19:28)

My ninety-year-old friend Ollie and I occasionally reminisce about the time we went canoeing together, and once we arrived at our anticipated stopping point, I jumped off the canoe so violently that I plunged him into the drink. He thrashed and sputtered for a moment before hauling himself out of the river, shivering and glaring at me. In reparation, the least I could do was offer him a dry shirt—and buy him a drink—mindful of the fact that he is a longstanding diabetic. As the tension between us softened, we could both joke about his "second baptism," courtesy of yours truly.

Jesus has plunged into his Passion, experiencing the bath of suffering foreshadowed in his own baptism, and is about to be drawn to the shores of death. But first he pauses before calling for a last sip. He expresses his thirst one final time—the same thirst that was evident with the Samaritan woman (see Jn 4), the thirst which must have been temporarily slaked in his friendship with Martha and Mary and Lazarus, and now stands unrequited as his longing to relieve people of their self-imposed dehydration goes unheeded.

We humans often resemble gargoyles, plying our throats with the food and drink tendered by the world, longing for a fulfillment that eludes us and what the protagonist of John's Gospel alone can provide. We can be likened to spiritual diabetics who ply ourselves with the sustenance that is meant to ease our discomfort, but in the end results in a form of self-inflicted harm if we do not drink from the Source.

No shallow remedy is forthcoming, no shot of medicine or alcohol can avert this kind of crisis. At this point, the only thing we can do is to honor his thirst, so as to surface our own.

Though he can barely speak, Jesus your beloved Son blesses you,
Father of the heavens above and the waters below, for in his thirst
he reveals that your love alone is sufficient—for him, for me.

A Final Bow

Father William M. Joensen

There was a vessel filled with common wine. So they put a sponge soaked in wine on a sprig of hyssop and put it up to his mouth. When Jesus had taken the wine, he said, "It is finished." And bowing his head, he handed over the spirit. (Jn 19:29-30)

I once referred to a priest peer as a "sponge for popular culture." I meant it as a compliment: his familiarity with various genres of music, with movie references and sports figures all represented different flasks from which he could draw and offer others a sip of the familiar—and then proceed to share the choicer vintage of the Gospel. But over time, unfortunately, my sponge metaphor fell flat as it was squeezed once too often.

Jesus drinks the wine meant to be shared among commoners and declares, "It is finished." He reveals his ultimate commitment to us, a love that is meant to be uncontainable, poured into the world. His desire to complete the mission appointed him by his Father is fulfilled but not terminated, for he inaugurates a new form of longing that flows beyond death.

In Jesus' person our desire for love has met its proper match. Jesus wants to instill his desire in us—the desire to pour ourselves out for love's sake, even to the point of abject thirst, where nothing the world places before us will satisfy. The Christ who drinks in death releases a reservoir of spirit meant to permeate our palate and sink deep into our souls. He who first captured people's attention by changing water into wine at Cana now consummates his sacred calling by becoming the new wine that, once tasted, must be fully consumed, especially when we find ourselves numbered among the dregs of humanity.

There are many persons who do not interpret even their own desires as evidence that the spirit of Jesus courses within them. They remain to be convinced that God is love, and this love is life. When we take the wine reconstituted by Spirit as sacramental blood, we become ever more capable of extending evangelical hope and healing to those ensconced in their own private Calvaries, squeezed by life to the point of death.

How moved you must have been, tender and merciful Father, by the death of your Son. As I ponder what he has accomplished, may I be moved to fill others with the Spirit that together you have handed over to us.

Breaking a Way

Father William M. Joensen

Now since it was preparation day, in order that the bodies might not remain on the cross on the sabbath, for the sabbath day of that week was a solemn one, the Jews asked Pilate that their legs be broken and they be taken down. So the soldiers came and broke the legs of the first and then of the other one who was crucified with Jesus. (Jn 19:31-32)

A favored boyhood sledding run for my brothers and me involved scooting through some narrowly spaced small trees at the base of a hill. Our competitive instincts spurred us to race one another to see who could make it through the gap first; a neck-and-neck run turned nasty as I rammed my brother Dave into a tree, causing him to break his arm.

In the haste to avoid ritual impurity by having to tend to the expired Jesus, let alone leave a crime scene with evidence of their lethal handiwork hanging around on a high holy day, the Jewish leaders try to accelerate the death of Christ—and by default, those who frame their gruesome machinations like some tragic tableau—by breaking their long bones. They induce the Roman mop-up crew to wreak further havoc upon the bodies of those who may not have been Jesus' brothers in life, but who accompany him in death. The two criminals' failure to die as quickly as the Lord posed between them suggests that distinct dynamics are at work: Christ infinitely suffers and resolutely abandons himself entirely to pass over unto death. He neither hastens toward death in itself nor does he resist it. Hence, there is no need to break his bones, for he offers himself along the entire way to Calvary without reluctance or rivalry.

We, renegade brothers and sisters of Cain and Abel that we too often are, wrestle with death as our greatest antagonist amidst the complex of opposing forces and conflicts we generate. We pit ourselves against death as much as we wrestle with life, with each other. We end up broken because we are prone to breaking relationships, even or especially with our blood relations. Only the God first to die in this fashion, as one totally innocent of sin and thus undeserving of death, can knit our bones and our relations together again into one body, healed of all divisions.

I am broken, Father. And your Son alone can heal me. I do not want to wrestle with you, but to allow you gracefully to heal me within and without, so that I might take my place in the Body of Christ.

No Shell Game

Father William M. Joensen

But when [the soldiers] came to Jesus and saw that he was already dead, they did not break his legs, but one soldier thrust his lance into his side, and immediately blood and water flowed out. (Jn 19:33-34)

My friend—let's call him Guy—was dying of brain cancer. Anticipating the funeral Mass he asked me to celebrate on his behalf, he indicated his preferences, but he also consented to allow his body to be waked and viewed by loved ones before being cremated. After his death, his wife had second thoughts, and wanted to proceed with cremation before the Mass. She proposed a compromise: my instincts regarding the sacramentality of Guy's body would be respected by placing the cremains inside a rented casket, unbeknownst to most persons present. I counseled that it was more appropriate to place the cremains in a dignified container in the church, and not create an impression where appearances were divorced from reality.

Jesus appears dead. Some have claimed he is the Son of God come in the flesh. If this is the case, then for some the flesh was merely an accidental accessory. Given the mythic sensibilities of Romans and others who would follow with claims that the humanity of Jesus was a mere shell, his death a virtual appearance conjured by an omnipotent divinity, the postmortem details supplied in John's account are significant. The integrity of Christ's body is preserved not simply by refusing to break his bones. Those who pierce his side enable his blood and water to pour forth, becoming, as we publicly pray, "the wellspring of the Church's Sacraments." The integrity of Christ's body recounted by John means that when we baptize and celebrate the Eucharist—including a funeral Mass—and all the sacraments, we are not merely going through ritualized motions absent a truly human core. We enlist the power of Jesus' blood and water to become truly united with his wholly divine person, including his humanity, whose pierced side reveals the reality of his death—without which any hope of eternal life is mere illusion.

Death must be seen for what it is, revealed and not concealed, God who is. I could not live without the sacraments; inspire me to live, Father, as a person whose faith and outward actions are gracefully wedded.

Witness Protection Program

Father William M. Joensen

An eyewitness has testified, and his testimony is true; he knows that he is speaking the truth, so that you also may [come to] believe. For this happened so that the scripture passage might be fulfilled:/ "Not a bone of it will be broken."/ And again another passage says:/ "They will look upon him whom they have pierced." (Jn 19:35-37)

Just off the shores of Lake Superior lie the Apostle Islands. Each island has been sculpted by relentless waves from the often angry lake, creating ledges overlying caves and crevasses that are strikingly beautiful, if haunting. The more tranquil waters between the islands and mainland serve as refuge for the massive ore-bearing ships that risk being caught on stormy, open waters and broken to bits. The ships wait out the weather, and then proceed to deliver their cargo to their destination. The "Apostles" serve as safe harbor for vessels that draw from them protection in order to fulfill their appointed mission.

John's fellow Apostles may have left the stormy scene surrounding Calvary, but they have not drowned. Along with them, we are captivated by his account of standing close to the cross as the centerpiece of Good Friday. Unlike Pilate, who gets stuck posing the rhetorical question, "What is truth?" John knows his testimony is true. His apostolic brothers are the first to take heart in his eyewitness testimony. They may have been temporarily dispersed into "islands," but by the word of John's testimony, they are prompted to pool their own vivid encounters with Christ, even as their own shame buffets them.

John's Gospel buoys us up when we experience burdens and crosses too heavy to bear; his lofty vision elevates our belief in the indomitable, unsinkable love of Jesus Christ for us. We press on in our mission of sharing apostolic faith with others as witnesses in our own right. The mortician and man of letters Thomas Lynch has captured the sentiment that, as each of us approaches death, we come to terms with the deepest desire that, in life and death, all we "really wanted was a witness." Jesus wants a witness, and has found a worthy one in John—and in every one of us who takes his Gospel to heart.

You buoy me up, Father of energy and Spirit, with the Gospel of your Son whom you have begotten. I want to live a true life that witnesses to you to the end.

Revealing Dangerous Secrets

Father Anthony Giambrone, O.P.

After this, Joseph of Arimathea, secretly a disciple of Jesus for fear of the Jews, asked Pilate if he could remove the body of Jesus. And Pilate permitted it. So he came and took his body.
(Jn 19:38)

There is a theme in ancient literature pitting political authorities against the sacred duty of proper burial. In the biblical Book of Tobit, as in Euripedes' *Antigone*, the titular hero (or heroine) invites personal tragedy by burying the enemies of the state. When we consider, then, that victims of Roman crucifixion were conventionally left to rot and feed the carrion birds, it is remarkable to find the cowardly Joseph of Arimathea approaching the procurator with this bold request. He would honor the body of an executed revolutionary.

The Lord's more "courageous" disciples have, of course, fled—and with good reason. They fear they might share their master's fate. What is it that emboldens this rich member of the Sanhedrin, this too discrete counselor and wary tactician—a man with so much to lose and surely with nothing to gain—to risk all his standing (possibly even his life) and choose this inauspicious moment to emerge from hiding? The answer can only be the cross.

Made a witness in spite of himself (to run would betray his secret sympathy), the disciple is transformed. The death of the Lord works something powerful in Joseph, who is shamed to good by beholding Christ's austere glory. The counselor thus acts with open piety, disregarding all dignified propriety and political likelihood.

The cross of Christ refuses to countenance our well-meaning complacency; it will not permit us simply to stay *secret disciples*. Discipleship is not a private affair, for discipleship means sharing the public fate of Christ. Profession of our faith thus requires risking shame for the Lord's honor. It means that we risk being indicted with him as dangerous "fanatics." May we not fear to stand boldly, even before the power of the state, when we see Christ's body, the Church, exposed to become food for the vultures of our day.

Father in heaven, whoever denies your Son before men will be denied by him before you. Give me the courage to be a public disciple, working for the honor of the Church.

Christening the King

Father Anthony Giambrone, O.P.

Nicodemus, the one who had first come to [Jesus] at night, also came bringing a mixture of myrrh and aloes weighing about one hundred pounds. They took the body of Jesus and bound it with burial cloths along with the spices, according to the Jewish burial custom. (Jn 19:39-40)

The art of undertaking cannot hold off the onset of death's decay. We may stuff a corpse and plug it with nard, but our best taxidermy and cosmetics will never cure the dark disease of Adam's sons. To dust we all return.

Why then this extravagant offering by Nicodemus? One hundred heavy pounds of myrrh and aloes! A great bulk of ointments, wasted, poured out as rich perfume for devouring worms. In part, Nicodemus' mixture measures the depth of the disciples' mourning. "They shall mourn for him as one mourns for an only son" (Zec 12:10). We see here a regal oblation, a sacrifice of great lamentation. These unguents moan with high extravagance that all wealth is spent in the loss of David's Son (cf. 2 Sm 19:5). Yet the kingly proportions of this precious salve also tell a deeper tale. This is, at last, the festal unction of Israel's King. Unrecognized in life but glorified in death, the nation's Messiah is anointed in his tomb. During this night of his death, Christ is christened by the hand of Nicodemus, a leader of the people, "the teacher of Israel" (Jn 3:10) and "a ruler of the Jews" (Jn 3:1).

The hundred pounds thus answers for the Spirit, God's living Unction smeared on Christ at his mystic death. Just as Jesus entered the tomb of the Jordan's waters to rise resplendent and gleaming with the light of glory, so this humbler oil foretells Christ's preservation— not by the undertaker's art, but by the power of God's Holy Spirit. For as David prophesied in Psalm 16, "The Lord will not let his anointed undergo corruption."

We, too, as Christians, are liberally smeared with that same sacred chrism poured out over Christ our King. For us, as well, this oil marks our rare election. We, too, will reign with him *if we die with him* (see 2 Tm 2:11-12)—for the Spirit alone can preserve us from the corruption of Adam's sin.

Gracious Father, you will not deny your children when they ask. Generously anoint us with the sweet perfume of your Spirit to saturate our sinful flesh and make us holy.

The Holy Seed

Father Anthony Giambrone, O.P.

Now in the place where [Jesus] had been crucified there was a garden, and in the garden a new tomb, in which no one had yet been buried. So they laid Jesus there because of the Jewish preparation day; for the tomb was close by.
(Jn 19:41-42)

Only John reveals that Jesus was buried in a garden. The subtle implication is pregnant and poetic. Christ is planted like a seed. He is sown in expectation of a harvest. His burial is not his dumping in a biological landfill. He is not disposed of as some by-product in a plot of sullied ground. In Israel cemeteries are bedded in gravel, so that graveyards are stark and sterile. They house the lifeless dust turned back to dust. But in a garden, the earth glories to bud and flower; it blossoms with the richness of new life.

"Unless a grain of wheat falls to the ground and dies, it remains just a grain of wheat; but if it dies, it produces much fruit" (Jn 12:24). Christ is that grain which fell to the earth to be the living bread come down from heaven. He lays down his life to take it up again, sprouting from the earth to become supernatural food. Thus the yield of Christ's Passion is true fruit, meant to be replanted in us.

In a real way, then, our hearts must be either a garden or a graveyard; for we are the soil where the Body of Christ is sown. In Holy Communion, our soul receives Abraham's "Seed"—and we recall the parable of the Sower. If we would bring forth an abundant harvest—thirty, or sixty, or a hundredfold—our soil must nourish this holy seed.

Mary is the model of good soil. She is the "enclosed garden" (Sg 4:12), the virgin land unspoiled and never wasted on unfruitful, rotten seed. Her virgin womb prefigures the Lord's new tomb: an inner sanctum reserved for him, where life bursts in miraculous fertility. The question, then, is this: Does God's seed enter us as "whitened sepulchers" (cf. Mt 23:27), filled with filth and dead men's bones? Or do we make our hearts a new garden for his Passion, good ground softened by his precious Blood?

Father in heaven, clean my heart of all the filth of dead works. Make me new. Prepare me to welcome the Body of your Son, so that his new life will come to flower in mine.

"This is the night"

Father Anthony Giambrone, O.P.

On the first day of the week, Mary of Magdala came to the tomb early in the morning, while it was still dark, and saw the stone removed from the tomb. So she ran and went to Simon Peter and to the other disciple whom Jesus loved, and told them, "They have taken the Lord from the tomb, and we don't know where they put him." (Jn 20:1-2)

The Church pays special reverence to this darkness wrapped around Mary Magdalene. "*This is the night!*" "This is the night," the Church sings at her solemn Easter Vigil. For in this very darkness, before the sun, before the earliest riser, in the absolute darkness of death Christ awakes: he is first to rise, the firstborn from the dead. The sleep of death which holds the whole world under its spell is in that moment broken. Jesus himself becomes the Dawn who shatters the rule of the night.

This beautiful image of the breaking dawn allows for a world which has decisively turned—yet remains shrouded under cover of night. So it is in this age. Darkness still appears to reign over us—in all disorder, confusion, and suffering. But a crack of light has split open the black dominion, and the darkness cannot anymore overcome it. So Paul rings out the wake-up call: "The night is advanced, the day is at hand. Let us then throw off the works of darkness and [put] on the armor of light" (Rom 13:12). "Awake, O sleeper,/ and arise from the dead,/ and Christ will give you light" (Eph 5:14).

Mary Magdalene wakes first in answer to the call. She rises early as if to say that repentant sinners, dead in the deeds of darkness, are the first to taste the light of life in the new creation. She does not yet understand this strange morning, though. Her eyes must adjust to the supernatural glow of faith.

Faith itself is truly the morning light, a mixture of light and darkness. For us, still groggy with earthly thoughts, it pains the intellect's eye. But as we move toward the radiance of full day, heavenly vision can flood even our earthly life. Indeed, the sun of the Resurrection is good to stare at, like "a lamp shining in a dark place, until day dawns and the morning star rises in your hearts" (2 Pt 1:19).

Almighty Father, you called into being the first morning light by the power of your Word. Flood me with that radiance to make me a new creation and awaken me from the darkness of my sins.

Buried with Christ

Father Anthony Giambrone, O.P.

So Peter and the other disciple [whom Jesus loved] went out and came to the tomb. They both ran, but the other disciple ran faster than Peter and arrived at the tomb first; he bent down and saw the burial cloths there, but did not go in.

(Jn 20:3-5)

In Jewish law, entering a tomb would bring defilement. In fact, the impurity of touching a grave lasted seven whole days (see Nm 19:16). Was this taboo part of the reason John stopped short and did not enter? Did he pause to peer from the threshold in respect of some pious scruple?

Whatever the other disciple's reasons for halting, Peter goes barreling in. He arrives last, but enters first, disregarding the limits of the law. It is not so crazy, then, when Saint Thomas Aquinas compares Peter here to the Gentiles. They are the latecomers, but they pass by those who were privileged as the first to see. Unburdened by the yoke of Moses, which bends down John at the entrance, they enter the grave like Peter, and are mystically buried with Christ.

It is important to see entering the tomb here as a mystical image of baptism (see Rom 6:4), for this shows the divine irony of God's plan. The place of purification is that very place of deepest impurity—which is another way to say every impurity has now been made pure. Death is turned to life. Christ's "grave" holds no source of defilement (because it holds no corpse). It is pure inside, a place of life. It is even purifying. For the rite prescribed by Moses for the cleansing of corpse impurity was washing with spring water mixed with the sin offering's ashes. This is a type of the New Testament's sacred baptismal bath, that laver of true living water sanctified by Christ's one sacrifice for sin.

So, for those of us who have (however slowly) come to faith through water and the Spirit, death should not halt us like a precipice to be feared. Buried with Christ in baptism, we can enter every grave without worry. Like Peter, may we pass untroubled into that life-giving pit of death, whenever we have the chance to die again to ourselves.

Eternal Father, darkness is not dark for you. If I go down to Sheol, you are there. Give me courage to join your Son in his death, that I might know the glory of his Resurrection.

Folding Up the Tent

Father Anthony Giambrone, O.P.

When Simon Peter arrived after [the other disciple whom Jesus loved], he went into the tomb and saw the burial cloths there, and the cloth that had covered his head, not with the burial cloths but rolled up in a separate place. (Jn 20:6-7)

John's attention to Jesus' head cloth conceals a mystery. The burial bands are an image of this mortal flesh, the "earthly tent" Saint Paul says will be replaced by "God's building" (cf. 2 Cor 5:1). The Gospel here thus reveals the order of the Resurrection. In the rising of the Christ from the dead, the Head sloughs off this perishable skin apart from the rest of his mystical Body. Jesus rises first, by himself; and he will raise us up, as the head pulls up the body rising from bed.

John's careful mention of Jesus' head cloth directs us to recall the same *sudarion* wrapped around the face of Lazarus coming out from the grave (see Jn 11:44). But what still clings to the face of Lazarus, shrouding his vision with a mortal veil, is left behind by Jesus in the tomb. In Lazarus, then, we see the image of every Christian born to new life in baptism. By water and the Spirit, we live a new life, rising from the font as from a tomb. But we bear this new life *still clothed in death*. Where Christ emerges from the grave fully remade, a temple not built by human hands, we, like Lazarus, still wear the bands of corruptible bodies, natures born of "blood [and]...carnal desire" (cf. Jn 1:13). These must be stripped away by the ascetical pains of mortification and the sting of death.

Our lives, then, belong to that pile of disordered bandages—for this created garment still waits to be "rolled up". Like the burial Shroud of Turin we manifest the new life of the Lord, but our witness to his risen Body appears imprinted on the ragged cloths of this humble "tent." Accordingly, we all await the one who "will change our lowly body to conform with his glorified body" (Phil 3:21), so that we might "grow in every way into him who is the head" (Eph 4:15).

Almighty Father, in your Son you have begun to create a new heaven and a new earth. Unwrap the bands of death that bind me and begin to reveal in my life the face of the new creation.

Quick to Believe

Father Anthony Giambrone, O.P.

*Then the other disciple [whom Jesus loved] also went in, the one
who had arrived at the tomb first, and he saw and believed.
For they did not yet understand the scripture that he had
to rise from the dead. Then the disciples returned home.*
(Jn 20:8-10)

John is swift afoot and swift to faith. After racing ahead of Peter and reaching the tomb before him, the young disciple now passes his senior on the path of understanding. "He saw and believed." Like the nimble mind of Sherlock Holmes penetrating the evidence more quickly than steady Watson, John scans the scene and puts the pieces together before his friend.

The deduction is not elementary, however. Mary Magdalene sensibly concluded that there had been a crime. (Saint John Chrysostom observes that had the body in fact been stolen, the thieves would hardly have taken the time to unwrap it and fold the head cloth. We can only wonder if there were first-century Darwin Awards.) John's agile insight, of course, comes not from native wits but from the Spirit. It is Scripture's clue that now finally falls into place, revealing to him the mystery.

Our own advance in faith should run the same course as John's. He sees and directly believes; but what he sees is only indirect, the merest fingerprints of God. Mary and Peter and the other disciples— notoriously Thomas—will all need to see the Lord himself. For John it is enough to have the Scriptures to understand God's plan. But if our minds would be so swift to perceive through Scripture the saving meaning of events around us, our spirits must be as eager as John's to find the Lord.

Saint John's symbol is the eagle, and this certainly suggests his sharp spiritual sight. The eagle is also an image of tireless hope, however, which will put our heart on wings: "They that hope in the LORD will renew their strength,/ they will soar as with eagle's wings;/ They will run and not grow weary,/ walk and not grow faint" (Is 40:31). Expectant hope ultimately hastens the Beloved Disciple. The same hope will speed us too, truly blessed not to see yet to believe (see Jn 20:29).

Loving Father, with the help of the Scriptures, make me prompt to recognize your presence and plan in my life. May faith quicken my hope, and hope speed me to love.

A Time to Weep

Father Anthony Giambrone, O.P.

But Mary stayed outside the tomb weeping. And as she wept, she bent over into the tomb and saw two angels in white sitting there, one at the head and one at the feet where the body of Jesus had been. And they said to her, "Woman, why are you weeping?" She said to them, "They have taken my Lord, and I don't know where they laid him." (Jn 20:11-13)

At the heart of all Christian experience the Lord erects a paradox and provocation. "Blessed are those who mourn!" If this beatitude belongs to anyone, it belongs to Mary Magdalene.

Peter and John have now gone their merry way, one baffled, one believing—but neither disconsolate as Mary. She remains utterly immoveable in her grief. Hagar once found comfort in distress, when the Lord's angel addressed her in the desert, "Why are you troubled?" (cf. Gn 21:17). Yet two angels from heaven are not enough to dislodge the sorrowing Mary from her graveside mourning: "Woman, why are you weeping?"

Why does Mary weep? According to tradition, it was the Magdalene who once washed Jesus' feet with her tears. She is the sinful woman who loved much and was much forgiven. Her tears fall in drops of love mixed with sorrow; and here at the tomb, her special sorrow is that her love is so painfully helpless. She cannot even give her proper respect to the beloved dead. She weeps, it seems, not only in grief, but for that debt of love she cannot anymore repay.

But the beatitude of Mary is that her singular weeping wins her a singular joy. She is the first to see the Lord, and her happiness mounts in proportion to her sorrow. Peter, too, who knew bitter tears, will also know a special vision of the Lord. The invitation to us, from the example of these saints, paves the way for comfort by contrition. May we, then, learn to feel sorrow at our separation from the Lord. For once we can mourn the shortfall of our love, we will welcome the blessed paradox of Christian tears. We will even pray God that our hearts would rain more in mingled tears of sorrow and of love. "Oh, that my head were a spring of water,/ my eyes a fountain of tears,/ That I might weep day and night" (Jer 8:23).

Heavenly Father, protector of the poor, remember those who weep in this world. Give me the grace to welcome tears as a promise that I will know your comfort.

God's Green Thumb

Father Anthony Giambrone, O.P.

When [Mary] had said this, she turned around and saw Jesus there, but did not know it was Jesus. Jesus said to her, "Woman, why are you weeping? Whom are you looking for?" She thought it was the gardener and said to him, "Sir, if you carried him away, tell me where you laid him, and I will take him."

(Jn 20:14-15)

Rembrandt painted a wonderful image of Jesus, risen from the dead and standing behind Mary Magdalene. Jesus holds a gardening trowel and sports a deliciously oversized sunhat. John says nothing of this cap, but what a wonderful invention! The huge round brim of Jesus' bonnet serves as a kind of humble halo—less shading Christ from the sun than it from him. How else could Mary fail to know the Lord? His hat covered the radiant countenance of his divine humanity.

If God often wears disguises in our lives and dampens his proper glory, this getup Christ dons for Mary is beautifully chosen. In the beginning, God the Gardener planted a paradise in Eden. Gardening is the first thing he does after fashioning man and breathing life into his nostrils (see Gn 2:7-8). For God is the one who plants all life into the dust; fruitfulness follows his footsteps (see Ps 65:12). But God gives to Adam the task of tending this garden—and Adam trades the fruit for thorns and thistles (see Gn 3:17-19). He brings a curse upon the very earth from which he was made, and by sinning betrays God's gracious green thumb. So, when Jesus shows himself in this guise of a gardener, the message is subtle but clear. He shows himself the restorer of creation's paradise. The Godly Gardener comes hence to bless Adam's cursed clay, sowing with life his dust turned to dust and making this graveyard a garden.

Many times our own black thumb kills the life around us, and we find ourselves weeping in a graveyard. So, when our charity dries up and we parch the earth of blessing, we should look for the appearance of Christ with his trowel and hat. He will come at our tears of deep love and true sorrow to irrigate our gardens, watering with his Spirit our dried-up hearts. "You visit the earth and water it,/ make it abundantly fertile" (Ps 65:10).

Father, you bring all things to life. Make my soul a garden and fructify me with all the rich fruits of the Spirit: love, joy, peace, patience, kindness, generosity, faithfulness, gentleness, and self-control.

The Scandal of Glory

Father Anthony Giambrone, O.P.

Jesus said to her, "Mary!" She turned and said to him in Hebrew, "Rabbouni," which means Teacher. Jesus said to her, "Stop holding on to me, for I have not yet ascended to the Father. But go to my brothers and tell them, 'I am going to my Father and your Father, to my God and your God.'"
(Jn 20:16-17)

One of the most intriguing features of John's Gospel is that in it Jesus speaks more about his Ascension than in any of the other Gospels; yet we never actually behold the Lord lifted up into the cloud. In some sense, John understands that this mystery is more glory than we can bear. The Son's return to his Father is the final, supreme exaltation of the humanity of Christ. In this way the Ascension is the unrivaled scandal, a challenge simply to digest. "Does this shock you?" Jesus asks when the disciples murmur at his teaching. "What if you were to see the Son of Man ascending to where he was before?" (Jn 6:61-62).

We are accustomed to think of the scandal of *descent*, of the Incarnation or of the cross. How could God become so small or be so terribly dishonored? John confronts us rather with the scandal of Jesus' glory. How can God so glorify a man?

The challenge to let our minds soar in bold belief of what "eye has not seen, nor ear heard, nor the heart of man conceived" (cf. 1 Cor 2:9) is exactly what Mary struggles with in this passage. Jesus is not raised from the dead to go on as before. His rising passes far beyond the heights our minds can mount to from this world. Saint Augustine thus said that Mary's attempt to cling to Jesus was a failure in her faith and thinking. She tried to hold Christ down. She called him merely "Teacher"—unable to let him be fully equal with the Father.

Like Mary, we must let Jesus go abide in heaven. Truly, it is better that he does go, because when he goes he sends us the Spirit to give us adoption as sons. The higher we let Jesus rise in the glory of our affection, the more glorious our own destiny becomes. For that exalted Father he goes to is both his Father and ours.

Father in heaven, you have exalted your Son's human nature to sit at your own right hand. Broaden my mind to contemplate the heavenly glory you wish to show me.

Apostle to the Apostles

Father Anthony Giambrone, O.P.

Mary of Magdala went and announced to the disciples,
"I have seen the Lord," and what he told her.
(Jn 20:18)

I t is remarkable that Mary leaves the Lord so easily. After her hysterics, all her confusion and vain chattering, her disconsolate sobbing and grasping at Jesus, she who could not pull herself even to leave the tomb now at the briefest word departs from him in peace. What explains this transformation? Is she so quickly sated with her lost Lord's newfound company?

There is elegant simplicity in the report of Mary Magdalene. "I have seen the Lord." Somehow the vision of Jesus and the charge to preach his message remakes Mary. It fills and renews her with his presence. She who had wildly wanted to "take" Jesus' dead body from the "gardener," bears away instead Christ's living Word. By bearing his awesome revelation, Mary carries the vital likeness of the Lord. She is here made the "apostle to the apostles": the first to be sent, the one sent to the sent—a rare image of that true "Apostle" (see Heb 3:1) who was first sent from the Father.

Looking *upon Christ* thus makes Mary start to look *like Christ*. This happens through her obedience. "Stop holding on to me," the risen Lord commands; and Mary does not protest. Just as the Son did not cling to equality with God (see Phil 2:6), Mary does not cling to Christ her Lord. By preaching she foregoes his presence to execute his will.

Our own commission to proclaim the Gospel resembles Mary Magdalene's. The Lord finds us an embarrassing mess—and he knows us before we ever recognize him. But when he calls our name and invests us with a mission, he sends us out to be remade by obedience. With Saint Paul we agree, it would be better to be with Christ (see Phil 1:23); but, if we bear his Word, we will not need to cling. Like Mary we will be freed to be sent on Christ-like service once our hearts can also testify, "I have seen the Lord."

Eternal Father, you sent your Son into the world, that he might send us in your name. Transform me so that others may see in me the power of your grace to remake us in your image.

Opening the Door

Father Anthony Giambrone, O.P.

On the evening of that first day of the week, when the doors were locked, where the disciples were, for fear of the Jews, Jesus came and stood in their midst and said to them, "Peace be with you." When he had said this, he showed them his hands and his side. The disciples rejoiced when they saw the Lord.

(Jn 20:19-20)

All of us put up barricades. At some point, inevitably, like those scenes in the movies, we find ourselves cornered, robbed of defense, and desperately grabbing all the furniture in sight to bolt and bolster the door. The only question is what we are fleeing.

The disciples lock themselves in "for fear of the Jews." We might better say they feared the fate of Christ. In the end, indeed, all fear is fear of death; and in the spiritual life this means fear of mortification. We all crouch in terror to think what crucifying our passions might actually mean.

So, we make our unholy hearts into a strongbox. We safeguard ourselves, and lock up our sins, deciding that it is too risky to open the door to who knows what. What will happen, I ask, if I open my life to welcome the enemies of my guarded vices? What pain will ensue? What if I let in public shame to assault my entrenched vainglory? What if I invite the visits of injustice, so disagreeable to my dormant anger? What will happen if I throw open the doors and let my life be overrun by all that suffering which is so disagreeable and threatening?

In the Book of Revelation, Jesus says, "Behold, I stand at the door and knock" (3:20). Sadly, I fear, he often hears us turning the bolt. If we do our best to lock out the death that leads to life, however, the risen Lord is not so easily deterred. He picks the locks of our fear and conceit and penetrates through the closed doors of our hearts. "Peace be with you," he says, standing in our midst. His gift of peace comes from seeing his hands and his side. He shows us that the wounds he suffered are not mortal—that death itself is not mortal. This is true cause to rejoice, for it means finally we can fearlessly open our doors to the world.

Father, break down the bars I've raised to block your grace. Enter me with your Spirit. Let me live without fear, confident that your Son's presence will gift me with peace.

The Breath of Life

Father Anthony Giambrone, O.P.

[Jesus] said to [the disciples] again, "Peace be with you. As the Father has sent me, so I send you." And when he had said this, he breathed on them and said to them, "Receive the holy Spirit. Whose sins you forgive are forgiven them, and whose sins you retain are retained." (Jn 20:21-23)

Being breathed on can be remarkably unpleasant. I remember once spending an interminable hour in the very small office of a man with devastating Cheeto breath. I soon lost awareness of everything but his heaving chest as it pumped over me waves of withering, orange, powdery, fetid air. My end seemed very near.

Though chastened by such discomfort, it is not clear to me that mouthwash is always an asset. With due concern for gingivitis, our respiratory cosmetics can hide a basic truth. Breath, which is life, can yet be deadly. It is interesting, in this connection, how often God's breath in the Scriptures is an instrument of death. "He unleashed against them his fiery breath" (Ps 78:49); "By the breath of God they perish" (Jb 4:9); "His breath…will winnow the nations" (Is 30:28); "The grass withers, the flower wilts,/ when the breath of the LORD blows upon it" (Is 40:7).

The issue, of course, is not too many Cheetos. No, the Lord's breath, which is the wind of his Spirit, is life-giving freshness itself. But just as chaff cannot stand before the fan, so wickedness will not endure the winds of holiness. Thus it is with the Sacred Wind which the living Lord breathes upon his Apostles. "Receive the holy Spirit." This gust of the Spirit drives away sins and becomes the gift Jesus hands to those he sends. Holding this fan, they can blow forth true judgment to separate wheat from chaff on the threshing floor of human hearts. "Whose sins you forgive are forgiven them."

The Lord Jesus, Paul says, will with the breath of his mouth kill the "lawless one" who rebels against God (2 Thes 2:8). So, whenever this lawless one starts to rule over us, we know where we should go: the uncomfortably small quarters of the confessional, where a priest can pump into us the death-dealing and life-giving breath of the Spirit.

Almighty Father, the gentlest breeze from your lips can scatter the presence of evil. Send forth your Spirit to drive out the wickedness from my heart. Help me draw new breath from the air of sacramental absolution.

Blind Doubt

Father Anthony Giambrone, O.P.

Thomas, called Didymus, one of the Twelve, was not with them when Jesus came. So the other disciples said to him, "We have seen the Lord." But he said to them, "Unless I see the mark of the nails in his hands and put my finger into the nailmarks and put my hand into his side, I will not believe."
(Jn 20:24-25)

Gullibility is no virtue, but it is dangerous to set criteria for our faith. Thomas says, "Unless I see the mark of the nails... I will not believe." He controls the on-off switch. He sets the limits of how far he will walk in trust. The difficulty with this posture is that it stubbornly makes of "faith" a human judgment—capable of going no farther than human imagination can already go. What, then, if God is pleased to do something interesting or extraordinary?

In truth, faith's assent is given *to us* before it is ever given *by us*. In this sense, we can only resist the grace of faith. God determines what is worthy of belief: those deeds which are worthy of him. He, then, is the ultimate measure of miracles—whether these be big or small. When we look for verification, therefore, we must not determine in advance how our assent and worship might be won. This means that a trigger-happy faith, over-anxious to find miracles, is problematic, just like a faith that is too slow on the draw. Saint John Chrysostom says: "As to believe directly...is the mark of too easy a mind, so is too much inquiring of a gross one: and this is Thomas' fault." We should thus stand in simple readiness, expecting that the good God will visit us, poised to be surprised and unsurprised all at once. In this stance we will ever capitulate to God with pleasing faith.

The resolute disbelief of Thomas could not be more determined. He will not even trust his own eyes, but prefers to poke and prod around like a blind man. In this way, the poor doubter wretchedly robs himself of all light. Truly, doubt is blind, not faith. Faith is true vision, sight beyond the senses, but Didymus chooses to sit in double darkness. May we always be ready to believe, and never shut our eyes to the works of God.

Merciful Father, save me from the blindness of doubt. Open my eyes in faith that I may see. Never let me grope about, lost in darkness, as the result of my own stubborn disbelief.

"Behold the pierced one"

Father Anthony Giambrone, O.P.

Now a week later his disciples were again inside and Thomas was with them. Jesus came, although the doors were locked, and stood in their midst and said, "Peace be with you." Then he said to Thomas, "Put your finger here and see my hands, and bring your hand and put it into my side, and do not be unbelieving, but believe." (Jn 20:26-27)

I was amused recently when reading a Greek marriage contract from AD 66 (I recognize this as abnormal). All the signatories were listed by name, age, and *identifying scars*. Thus, the groom had a scar on the middle of his nose, the bride's father one on the left eyebrow, and the scribe one on the right side of his head. (The bride didn't have to sign.)

For our age of social security numbers, this is comically graphic and fleshy, yet a remarkably human way of knowing who's who. Scars, of course, even more than names, always reveal something of a person's own story. There is a famous scene in Homer, for instance, where Odysseus is suddenly recognized from the scar on his thigh—launching the poet on the tale of how the hero was wounded as a boy hunting boar with his grandfather.

The glorified scars of Christ share something of this nature. They identify this man as the only Jesus of Nazareth, crucified under Pontius Pilate and then pierced by a lance, revealing him as "truly the Son of God" (cf. Mk 15:39). The wounds of Christ thus bear in themselves the saving story of the Gospel. They are tokens of the Lord's true manhood and trophies of his victory over death. Like Prince Hal's proud heroes of Agincourt, Jesus thus takes the high initiative, displaying his scars to Thomas without ever being asked: "He will strip his sleeve and show his scars./ And say 'these wounds I had on Crispin's day'" (*Henry V*, Act IV, Scene III).

Scarred in his human nature and raised by his divinity, Christ's wounds reveal that he is both God and man. If Jesus flashes Thomas this marvelous ID, it is not identity theft to want noble scars of our own. Indeed, it is the glorified wounds of our own suffering that will manifest us as who we truly are when by his wounds we too are finally raised.

Righteous Father, the wounds of your Son are ever present before you, moving your heart with compassion. Give me humble obedience to bear the wounds of the world and so discover who you've made me to be.

Hearing Is Believing

Father Anthony Giambrone, O.P.

Thomas answered and said to [Jesus], "My Lord and my God!"
Jesus said to him, "Have you come to believe because you
have seen me? Blessed are those who have not seen and
have believed." (Jn 20:28-29)

The Old Testament saints longed in vain to see God's face. Even Moses was only granted a vision from behind (see Ex 33:19-23). Saint Peter says the ancient prophets "searched and investigated…things into which angels longed to look" (1 Pt 1:10, 12)—for even the six-winged seraphs were bound to cover their eyes before God's presence (see Is 6:2). With reason, David said the Lord makes his dwelling in darkness (see Ps 18:12).

Yet, in Christ "the veil…is taken away" (2 Cor 3:14). "Whoever has seen me has seen the Father," Christ declares (Jn 14:9); and Thomas now proclaims Jesus, "My Lord and my God!" Thomas thus knows the great blessing denied to Moses. "Blessed are your eyes, because they see… Many prophets and righteous people longed to see what you see but did not see it" (Mt 13:16-17).

Why then, at this high moment, does Jesus bless those who do not see? "Blessed are those who have not seen and have believed." The reason is found in the essential nature of faith. Paul says, "Faith comes from what is heard" (Rom 10:17); and, indeed, we believe what others' eyes have seen. As a result, our faith is in our ears, not in our eyes. This is a better place to hold faith, for the nature of God, who is spirit, has not changed. He remains invisible and immaterial, pure mind on the wavelength of intelligent hearing more than sight.

John affirms, "No one has ever seen God." Yet, "The only Son, God…has revealed him" (Jn 1:18). The Son alone has seen the Father (see Jn 6:46), and it is the witness of *his* eyes that we finally trust. The mystery, then, is that Thomas sees Christ's humanity, but confesses his unseen divinity. Saint Thomas Aquinas says, "He saw one thing and believed another." For to peer truly into the face of Jesus Christ we must apprehend him as the Word—and this means opening our ears to see what God has spoken.

Immortal, invisible Father, you dwell in unapproachable light.
We see now as through a glass darkly. Morning after morning, open
my ears, that I may one day know as I am known.

The Last Word

Fatther Anthony Giambrone, O.P.

Now Jesus did many other signs in the presence of [his] disciples that are not written in this book. But these are written that you may [come to] believe that Jesus is the Messiah, the Son of God, and that through this belief you may have life in his name.
(Jn 20:30-31)

Rumor has it that a recent survey found 70 percent of Swedish Lutherans think Jesus never laughed. Whether this statistic is fair to Swedish Lutherans, it is most certainly unfair to Jesus Christ. It is true, we never find him laughing in the Gospels. But this is where *sola scriptura* reveals its deep and implausible morbidity. We might as well say, as Dorothy Sayers once quipped, that Jesus also never said, "Please" or "Thank you."

The fact is, there are many things that are not written in this book—and it is alluring to wonder what might have escaped the sacred page. Pop fascination with "lost gospels" (like the Gospels of Judas or Thomas) addresses this curiosity, but such interest to see those "many other signs" is not without danger. Indeed, John records Jesus' displeased warning: "Unless you people see signs and wonders, you will not believe" (Jn 4:48). No, for John one should see *just enough* to believe. Yes, for him less is more—"Blessed are those who have not seen and yet believe." To want or need to see more than stands revealed shows the weakness or bad faith of our belief. It makes us the sad rivals of doubting Thomas.

John's reference to "many other signs" corresponds to Luke's mention of "many proofs" (Acts 1:3)—Jesus' demonstrations that he was alive after he had suffered. Despite the formal note of closure and the suggestion that he has said all he plans to say, John will nonetheless recount for us one more beautiful "sign": Christ's appearance on the shores of the Sea of Galilee (Jn 21:1-23), the third time the risen Lord makes himself known. In this sublime epilogue our faith is presupposed, for the last word will take another tone entirely. John will not speak any more to convince us, for faith is not the final word. With Peter, we will be asked to love.

Father in heaven, the world cannot contain all the glory of your Son. May I be prompt to believe him, that my heart might grow in grace, not struggling for signs, but eager to show my love.

Christ in Their Midst

Father Richard Veras

After this, Jesus revealed himself again to his disciples at the Sea of Tiberias. He revealed himself in this way. Together were Simon Peter, Thomas called Didymus, Nathanael from Cana in Galilee, Zebedee's sons, and two others of his disciples. Simon Peter said to them, "I am going fishing." They said to him, "We also will come with you." So they went out and got into the boat, but that night they caught nothing. (Jn 21:1-3)

I t was the end of a difficult day and I was having dinner with a group of very close friends. During that dinner, the companionship of my friends drew me out of myself and my myopic assessment of my problems. How? They laughed at my jokes, they spoke seriously of serious things and lightly of light things, their affection for me and for each other was evident in a thousand little clues of courtesy and generosity. Their gaze upon me was tender and somehow wide open, and it opened up my gaze upon myself which in the past few hours had been full of suffocating measure. As I drove home I thought, "Wow, these friends love me more than I thought even Jesus could love me." Then I thought "Wow, look how reduced my notion of Jesus is." I finally and freely and wonderfully concluded, "Wow, Jesus is loving me through these friends!"

This seems to be what is happening to Peter. He is likely downtrodden over his betrayals of Jesus. He wants to go fishing, and he doesn't invite anyone along; but his friends invite themselves. Peter's gaze upon himself is likely devoid of mercy and full of harsh measure. It only sees the sin. His friends, instead, are concerned for him. For his friends, Peter is much more than what he has done. In their tenderness for Peter, they will not leave him alone.

Peter is destined that morning to see the tender gaze of Jesus. But the gaze of Christ is already present to Peter in the gaze with which his friends look upon him, a gaze full of affection and full of truth. A gaze that seeks to break through the false gaze with which Peter is looking upon himself.

Jesus has fulfilled the promise of his presence by giving the Apostles the Holy Spirit, and already their love for a friend is revealing the very embrace of Christ.

Most merciful Father, continue to reveal the love of Christ to us through the companions you have given us, that our love for Christ might not be merely pious, but fully human.

A Term of Endearment

Father Richard Veras

When it was already dawn, Jesus was standing on the shore; but the disciples did not realize that it was Jesus. Jesus said to them, "Children, have you caught anything to eat?" They answered him, "No." So he said to them, "Cast the net over the right side of the boat and you will find something." So they cast it, and were not able to pull it in because of the number of fish. (Jn 21:4-6)

Before my grandfather died, when I was about twenty-three years old, he would sometimes call me "Ri." He used it mainly as an opening greeting, as in, "How ya doin', Ri?" After that he would call me "Richie" like the rest of my family. No one else has ever called me that, and when I recall that greeting it reminds me of being a beloved grandson, of being a child. Whenever I heard that greeting I would be filled with expectation, for I knew that the next few hours with my grandfather would be wonderful.

What must the Apostles have thought about this seeming stranger on the shore who greets them by calling them "children"? These were men, some of whom had fishing businesses. These Apostles had gone out to towns of Israel preaching Jesus, they healed the sick, and even demons had been subject to them. In what sense were they being called "children"? This stranger also has a fatherly concern for them, wanting to know if they have caught anything that would sustain them.

They do what the stranger asks, so they don't seem to mind the greeting. Although they do not yet recognize the stranger as Jesus, perhaps they recognize that his greeting rings true. For it was not their own cleverness or strength that healed the sick or expelled demons, it was their childlike dependence upon Christ. Even now, they are waiting like children: How will Peter find the peace that will penetrate his sadness? How will they once again enjoy the presence of Christ who changed their lives for ever?

When I recall being greeted as "Ri" it is with a nostalgia and a longing for the call of that strong and loving presence. The Apostles are longing for Christ, and so before they recognize this man to be Jesus, their hearts respond with great expectation to his unexpected way of calling them back into the embrace of his tender love.

Most loving Father, may our hearts leap with expectant joy before the faces and the encounters that your beloved Son offers us to recall us to an awareness of his preferential love.

The Beloved Friend

Father Richard Veras

So the disciple whom Jesus loved said to Peter, "It is the Lord."
When Simon Peter heard that it was the Lord, he tucked in his
garment, for he was lightly clad, and jumped into the sea.
(Jn 21:7)

How moving it is to see selfless love that is full of tenderness and affection. Like the altar server who was given an ice cream pop for doing some extra work and got into the car and gave it to his little brother. The ninety-one-year-old parishioner who cooks a full dinner for a friend whose husband is ill. Or a dear friend who drove me two hours to a speaking commitment I had made months previously, when I couldn't have known how under the weather I would feel that night. I could have gotten myself there, but it was beautiful to be so loved, so cared for.

John must have been so concerned for Peter. He may not have known the details of Peter's betrayals, but he knew that Peter was not with Jesus at the cross, as he had promised. Peter seemed beyond consolation; but John was ready to do anything for his friend.

John is the first to recognize that the man on the shore is Jesus. John was the Beloved Disciple, perhaps the closest to Jesus. He was attentive and ready to respond to any signs of Christ's presence. Peter was perhaps too distracted by his introspection to be aware that Christ is once again among them.

John could have swum ashore to enjoy some few precious moments alone with Jesus; but his thought, his love, goes to Peter, whose good John desires as much, or even more so, than his own. He sees this moment as a gift to Peter. And Peter's peace would be a gift to John, who so loved his friend, the chosen rock of the Church.

Peter is awakened to reality by John's love. He does not hesitate through misplaced humility but rather embraces the moment through which Christ promises to embrace him. He dives in and hurries to his only hope for peace—the tender and affectionate presence of that man on the shore.

Most merciful Father, may there never be any hesitation or timidity to embrace those opportunities you offer us for our peace, which comes through the repeated restorations of our relationship with you, through the grace of your Son, our Lord Jesus Christ.

The Look of Love

Father Richard Veras

The other disciples came in the boat, for they were not far from shore, only about a hundred yards, dragging the net with the fish. When they climbed out on shore, they saw a charcoal fire with fish on it and bread. Jesus said to them, "Bring some of the fish you just caught." So Simon Peter went over and dragged the net ashore full of one hundred fifty-three large fish. Even though there were so many, the net was not torn. (Jn 21:8-11)

Have you ever had something important you needed to say to someone: an affirmation of love, a sincere apology, an attempt at explanation for a grave shortcoming? Then in the moment you plan to broach the difficult subject, when you are on the cusp of having the courage to speak, a phone rings, or someone else comes into the room? There is a sinking feeling. Have I blown it? Will there be another chance? How much longer will I have to last with this weight on my heart?

This is what seems to have happened to Peter. He has swum ashore. He is searching for the words, but what words could possibly exist? What explanation could possibly be given. What affirmation of love would not ring hollow after what he has done? And yet, he somehow knows that it is not possible that his belonging to Jesus has been broken. It is not possible that this friendship can die.

Dismayed and speechless, Peter walks away from Jesus in order to drag the net full of fish ashore.

Jesus does not need Peter's words. He doesn't even need his own divine knowledge. His divine love sees everything. It sees Peter, dripping wet from head to toe. Why? Because he has jumped into the water to come to Jesus as quickly as possible. Whatever words he might have mustered would not have spoken as eloquently of the position of Peter's heart as this impromptu baptism of repentance into which he has plunged his whole self.

It is as if his entire body, indeed his very soul, are not large enough to house the greatness of the desire he has to be with Jesus, his desire to experience once again this friendship which has always seemed impossibly beyond his capacity, and yet which is really and truly becoming who he is. He is like the net, full of so many fish, and yet is not torn.

Eternal Father, by the tender love you reveal to us through your Son, increase in our souls the capacity to receive your mercy and your friendship. May you for ever expand our hearts toward the Infinite that is you.

Christ: Ever Risen, Ever New

Father Richard Veras

*Jesus said to [the disciples], "Come, have breakfast." And none
of the disciples dared to ask him, "Who are you?" because they
realized it was the Lord. Jesus came over and took the bread
and gave it to them, and in like manner the fish. This was now
the third time Jesus was revealed to his disciples after being
raised from the dead. (Jn 21:12-14)*

My father's mother died the day after he was born. Her sisters
helped raise him until my grandfather remarried and
moved the family to New York. I didn't know my grandmother's sisters very well, and was surprised when they traveled to
New York to attend my ordination. None of us expected them to
make the trip; and when they received my blessing I was completely
unprepared to hear them say through tears of joy, "Laura is so proud,
Laura…Laura!" I had never heard my grandmother called in such
a familiar way by her first name, referred to not as a memory, but
as a person, a living person with whom they were rejoicing. It was
clear and mysterious that, for my great-aunts, my newly ordained
hands which they were kissing was the flesh of their sister Laura,
alive and present.

At no point in this Resurrection appearance does Jesus look
physically as the disciples remembered him. He looked like an
ordinary man on the shore, but not like Jesus had looked when they
accompanied him through his public ministry. John tells us that no
one dared to ask who he was. There would be no temptation to ask
who he was if he looked exactly like they had known him to look.

Why did Jesus do that? He did it for us! The ordinary way that we
encounter Jesus in the flesh today is through the flesh of those who
believe in him now. The faces of men and women who don't look like
Jesus, but in whom we see Jesus alive. The Apostles knew that this
man with a stranger's face was Jesus, for he did what Jesus does, in
this case having them throw over their nets for a great catch of fish.

Through our baptism, we belong to the Body of Christ, and we
have the possibility to be recognized clearly yet mysteriously as
Christ, alive and present today.

*Ever loving Father, your Son was loving us even as he was appearing
to his Apostles. May we ever recognize and rejoice before the faces
through whom he loves us now, in the risen flesh which lives today
in his Mystical Body, the Church.*

Love That Is Measureless

Father Richard Veras

When they had finished breakfast, Jesus said to Simon Peter,
"Simon, son of John, do you love me more than these?" He said
to him, "Yes, Lord, you know that I love you." He said to him,
"Feed my lambs." (Jn 21:15)

In his general audiences on the Apostles, Pope Benedict reminded us that this exchange between Peter and Jesus contains more nuance than translations into modern languages can convey.

When Jesus asks Peter, "Do you *love* me," he uses the word *agape*, which means total and unconditional *love*. When Peter responds, "You know that I love you," he uses the word *fileo*, which means the love of friendship, which is not as all-encompassing.

But before Jesus addresses himself to Peter, he joins with all the Apostles in eating the breakfast that he has prepared for them. Thus Peter sees that he is welcomed as one of the Apostles, as he had always been before. Does Peter eat much? Is his mind on the food? Does he dare to look at Jesus or make eye contact with him during that meal, which must seem to Peter to last for ever? The last meal they had eaten together was in the Upper Room, when Peter proudly and a bit rashly promised Jesus that he would remain faithful to him even unto death.

How Peter's heart must leap when, after breakfast, Jesus speaks directly to him. Peter has no words, and so Jesus initiates the conversation, for Jesus' love for Peter has never waned. Jesus' tender pity for Peter, and for each one of us, is expressed in his words, "Do you love me?"

Peter replies that he does love Jesus, however after his betrayals he is not able to claim that he loves him unto death. Though his desire is to love Jesus unconditionally, his weakness falls short. Jesus replies, "Feed my lambs." Peter is not only welcomed among the Apostles as before, even his designation as the rock of the Church is not taken away! Jesus' love is total and unconditional, infinitely beyond our human measure of justice. Peter remains speechless, only beginning to grasp this new and unforeseen depth of love, whose name is Jesus.

Heavenly Father, may I never define myself or anyone else according to my measures of justice, but rather allow me the grace and the humility to see with the infinitely merciful eyes of Jesus.

Love That Clings

Father Richard Veras

*[Jesus] then said to [Simon Peter] a second time, "Simon,
son of John, do you love me?" He said to him, "Yes, Lord,
you know that I love you." He said to him, "Tend my sheep."*
(Jn 21:16)

Jesus asks Peter again, "Do you love me (unconditionally)?"
and Peter replies that he loves Jesus with the love of a friend.
And once gain, Jesus commands him to lead his followers.

Servant of God Luigi Giussani called this exchange the birth of
morality. For more important than Peter's coherence or incoherence
in regard to moral law is his attachment to Christ. Peter's betrayals
don't stop Jesus from faithfully imposing himself as a presence in
Peter's life. The attractiveness of Jesus overcomes any temptation
Peter might have to hide from him, as Adam and Eve hid from God
in the garden, for Peter's human affection is for Jesus. And Peter's
affection is a response to the overwhelming fact that the fullness
of Jesus' divine and human affection is for Peter! No amount of
betrayals can put a stop to this affection.

When I began to work with high school students, I brought a
large group on a trip to Manhattan. I was nervous about losing
someone. My pastor told me that the kids would be more fearful
of losing me than I was of losing them, and if they got lost for even
a minute, they would quickly find their way back to me.

Peter's human affection is for Jesus, his attachment is to Jesus,
and his experiential knowledge of Jesus' faithful love and mercy
makes him the rock of the Church.

Jesus knows Peter is weak, he knows that he is a sinner. But he
knows that Peter is for ever marked and generated by the presence
of his friend and Lord. Peter is the rock because he knows that
his hope is not in the law and not in his coherence. Peter's hope,
indeed the hope of the entire apostolic Church, is in the One who
faithfully waits for us and ever prepares for us the food that sustains
us, the food that worldly measures cannot know or understand—
his Loving Presence.

*Merciful Father, may the attractive presence of your Son be the
rock of my life. May Christ's longing for me and my longing for
him vanquish any hesitation to return to him that my sins and
betrayals may cause.*

Love That Saves

Father Richard Veras

[Jesus] said to [Simon Peter] the third time, "Simon, son of John, do you love me?" Peter was distressed that he had said to him a third time, "Do you love me?" and he said to him, "Lord, you know everything; you know that I love you." [Jesus] said to him, "Feed my sheep." (Jn 21:17)

The first two times Jesus asks Peter if he loves him unconditionally (*agape*), Peter responds that he loves Jesus as a friend (*fileo*). The third time, Jesus asks Peter, "Do you love me (*fileo*)?" Jesus doesn't wait for Peter to love him unconditionally; he accepts the love that Peter is able to give now. Christianity is a journey on which Jesus accompanies us. He doesn't stand way down at the finish line rooting for us; he promises to remain with us. Destiny has come to meet us!

In the Rite of Marriage, immediately after accepting the couple's vows, the priest says, "May the Lord in his goodness strengthen your consent." Thus the Church recognizes that the love the bride and groom have for one another falls short! It is not quite up to the love stated by their vows. And yet the marriage begins now! Why is this possible? Because the couple is bound together by the Lord! The most important condition of the wedding vows is the presence of Christ!

A woman once came to me with a long list of complaints about her husband. I finally asked her, "Do you want your marriage to end?" She stopped complaining and began to cry as she said, "No!" I knew that would be her answer since she came to see a priest and not a lawyer. But the marriage could only continue if Christ, with his mercy, would be recognized as the cornerstone of the marriage, the bearer of a love that is bigger than betrayal.

Peter is distressed that Jesus asks a third time. Yet Jesus is perhaps insisting that Peter's three betrayals are not being made light of, but are being redeemed. Jesus' mercy doesn't pretend that sin is not there, for no one knows better than Peter the weight of his betrayals. Christ rather reveals himself to be truer and more solid than even the longest list of betrayals.

Father of mercies, may true sorrow for my sins lead me to the joy of repentance, and the hope that comes from my awareness that you have sent your Son to remain with us always.

The Comfort of a Presence

Father Richard Veras

"Amen, amen, I say to you, when you were younger, you used to dress yourself and go where you wanted; but when you grow old, you will stretch out your hands, and someone else will dress you and lead you where you do not want to go." [Jesus] said this signifying by what kind of death [Peter] would glorify God. And when he had said this, he said to him, "Follow me."

(Jn 21:18-19)

Almost anyone who has followed a vocational path, whether to virginity such as priesthood or consecrated life, or to marriage, has experienced fear at the beginning of that path, most especially the fear of sacrifice.

Most priests and religious can name someone in particular who was living the vocation to virginity and whom they came to know as a friend or teacher or pastor. It was that person's exceptional joy or certainty or way of loving that attracted the young man or woman. That initial attraction developed into a desire to follow that person's path, to experience the newness of life that person is living.

Likewise with the vocation to marriage. A commitment that seems so daunting becomes less so in light of the unexpected love that a person brings into my life. In preparing couples for marriage, I have seen that one of the most helpful resources is a true friendship with another couple who are living marriage and family in a lively way.

We see Jesus recommending this same dynamic to Peter. Jesus offers a daunting prophecy regarding Peter's death. Scripture and tradition reveal that Peter was very frightened of the kind of martyrdom that he saw Jesus die. How will dying this kind of death be possible for Peter? Jesus explains by saying, "Follow me."

The risen Christ himself was led where he did not want to go, to drink of a cup from which he did not want to drink. Jesus' trust in his Father's love made it possible for him to drink of that cup. Jesus is inviting Peter to experience that same love, that same resurrection by uniting himself to the will of God revealed in Jesus' love.

"Follow me" is not a militaristic command of Jesus, but an invitation to enter into the sacrificial trust which brings me to the experience of what real love is, and what real love can make possible.

Merciful Lord, may my trust in your fatherly affection overcome any temptations to draw back from the daily and vocational sacrifices required of me by your providential and educative love.

Looking to Christ

Father Richard Veras

*Peter turned and saw the disciple following whom Jesus loved,
the one who had also reclined upon his chest during the supper
and had said, "Master, who is the one who will betray you?"
When Peter saw him, he said to Jesus, "Lord, what about him?"*
(Jn 21:20-21)

A friend of mine was worrying as the birth of her first child approached. She was concerned about being inadequate as a mother. Her own mother was so loving and seemed so nearly perfect in the way she raised her children. My friend saw virtues and qualities in her own mother that she was certain she lacked. Could she be as loving as her mother? Could she love this child in the proper way that this child needed to be loved?

When she confided these worries to her mother, her mother told her that she was thinking too much about herself. Her mother told her to be attentive to the child and through this the Lord would bring out the love that was needed and make her the mother that he was calling her to be.

Perhaps Peter is comparing himself to John. John did not make the promise that Peter made at the Last Supper, yet John did stay with Jesus right up to the cross. John was faithful to Peter even after Peter's betrayals; could Peter imagine himself being so full of love and respect for another Apostle who had betrayed? John seems to follow so easily, while Peter sees only his flaws in following.

Peter has been told to feed Jesus' sheep. He will continue as the reference point for the Apostles, the rock of the Church; and yet John must seem to Peter to be so much more qualified for that task.

As my friend's mother invited her worried daughter into motherhood, Jesus will lead Peter into the mystery of vocation, the mystery of God's choice, which is beyond our measures. At the core of Peter's vocation is not his virtues and good qualities, but the call of Jesus. In this call, which is reiterated and reaffirmed in this meeting on the shore, Peter will find all the peace and strength which is necessary to follow...and to lead.

All-powerful Father, you have called me from nothingness into existence. May your Son's presence in my life grab my attention, so that I may follow my vocation with confidence in your call, and not be stopped by the nothingness that remains in me.

Living Stones in the Temple

Father Richard Veras

*Jesus said to [Peter], "What if I want him to remain until
I come? What concern is it of yours? You follow me."*
(Jn 21:22)

I thought I had Jesus' plan for me all figured out. As a priest,
I had the great honor of being assigned to teach high school.
During that assignment, someone told me, "You know, once
they send you to high school, they forget about you…. You might
be there for the rest of your priesthood."

At first, I was horrified. All that discernment, all that study and
preparation so I could be in Room 111 for the rest of my life?! Then,
as time went by, I enjoyed the thought. After all, every year I had
one hundred and twenty-five new students before me. What an
opportunity for evangelization! I was thankful for what I assumed
would be my life's work.

I had begun to settle into what I thought was an accurate reading
of God's will, and I smugly approved of God's brilliant idea of how
my life should be used to build his kingdom. Then, about a week
before the new school year, I got an old-fashioned "we need you
there by next week" transfer. I went from teacher to first time pastor
before I knew what hit me. The suddenness of the change was God's
mercy to me. I had no time to worry about qualifications or personal
preferences or how well my gifts were being used, or who would
have been a better choice for the parish to which I was assigned.
I had no choice but to follow.

The building of God's kingdom is God's concern. If Christ is not
the builder, all of our strategies and programs and good ideas (which
we might mistakenly perceive as God's ideas) are vain. I may not
always be a teacher, or a pastor, but I will always be a student of
Jesus Christ, who continues to educate me to follow him through
reality. My concern is my relationship with Christ, Christ's concern
is the building of the Church, and I am learning that my greatest
contribution is my simple "yes."

*God our Father, through the simplicity of our "yes" may we offer
everything to you by following your Son, Jesus Christ, as he calls us
into the unfathomable design of your earthly and eternal kingdom.*

The Simplicity of a Witness

Father Richard Veras

So the word spread among the brothers that that disciple would not die. But Jesus had not told him that he would not die, just "What if I want him to remain until I come? [What concern is it of yours?]" It is this disciple who testifies to these things and has written them, and we know that his testimony is true. (Jn 21:23-24)

Many know of the apparitions of Our Lady of Lourdes and the miracles that have followed. Less known, but just as striking, is the simplicity of Bernadette, the young girl to whom Mary appeared. Bernadette was remarkably consistent in her reports of what happened during each apparition. She never assumed beyond what she saw and heard. Before church officials who wanted to verify her story, and journalists who wanted to parody it, Bernadette was unshakeable. She would not even give in to premature notions that the lady in the grotto was the Virgin Mary. She would simply and faithfully repeat what the lady said to her, and she allowed the Church to discover the truth behind what she saw and heard. Her humility and simplicity allowed God to work through Mary, and was perhaps the bedrock of all the miracles that would follow.

We see this same simplicity in John, as he refuses to interpret beyond what he saw and heard in following Jesus. The core of the Gospel is the event of Christ. The rumor of the Beloved Disciple not dying does not add anything to the event of Christ, and can likely distract from it.

John emphasizes that he is neither a philosopher nor a weaver of mythic tales; he is rather a witness who wants to testify to what he has seen with his eyes and touched with his hands and heard with his ears. John is the one who clings to Christ at the Last Supper, who stays by Jesus all the way to Calvary—not because he is a hero, but because, in his simplicity, he knows that his hope is in staying with Christ.

He is certain that our hope is the same, and so he simply witnesses to this man, this friend, this Messiah, this Word made flesh who is the meaning of everything. May John's simplicity help us to cling to the same Jesus who dwells with us.

Heavenly Father, you have brought heaven to earth through the Incarnation of your beloved Son; may we cling to Christ as he shows himself in our world so that we may experience now the love whose source and destiny is the infinity of your Fatherhood.

An Open Invitation

Father Richard Veras

There are also many other things that Jesus did, but if these were to be described individually, I do not think the whole world would contain the books that would be written.

(Jn 21:25)

In a meeting with high school students of Communion and Liberation, I once asked why John didn't tell us what happened on that first day he spent with Jesus after he met him at four in the afternoon. All we know is that he spent time with Jesus, and after spending those first hours with this man, he and Andrew were convinced that they had found the Messiah.

One of the girls at that meeting proposed that John purposefully did not give details of that day. She said that when she would try to explain to friends what we do at our high school meetings and retreats and vacations, the list of details never adequately conveyed the exceptionality of what we were experiencing, never fully communicated the presence of Christ which was beginning to become evident among us. To experience this presence, the only true method was to follow the advice of Jesus himself: "Come and see." She herself had thought that this group of high school students that was meeting at her parish was merely a curious group, until she accepted the invitation to come; and only then did she experience something so much greater and truer than she had in her "normal" friendships.

John didn't give details of that first day with Jesus because his Gospel is not an end in itself, but an invitation to come and see—to spend time with the community created and generated by Christ in order to experience the same exceptional presence that cannot be fully communicated in words.

John's simplicity and his trust in Jesus who dwells with him is revealed in these closing sentences. In concluding his Gospel, John is not fretting over what details might have been left out. He is not concerned that it is a completed book, because he is offering it to us as an open invitation.

Almighty Father, may the lives of all those who follow you with simplicity be open invitations to see, touch, and hear the same Christ to whom John testifies so faithfully. We ask this through the same Christ our Lord, who dwells among us in the Scriptures, the sacraments, and the members of his Body, the Church.

Brief Biographies of Contributors

■ **Father Timothy Bellamah, O.P.**, teaches historical and systematic theology at the Pontifical Faculty of the Immaculate Conception in Washington, DC. He is also the editor of the *The Thomist* and is a member of the Leonine Commission, editors of the works of Saint Thomas Aquinas.

■ **Father Herald Joseph Brock, C.F.R.**, a Franciscan Friar of the Renewal, was a missionary in Honduras and Africa; he now coordinates evangelization and missionary efforts through Franciscan Mission Outreach.

■ **Douglas Bushman** is director of the Institute for Pastoral Theology at Ave Maria University. He received his S.T.L. degree from the University of Fribourg, Switzerland.

■ **Father Peter John Cameron, O.P.**, is editor-in-chief of MAGNIFICAT and author of *Blessing Prayers: Devotions for Growing in Faith* (MAGNIFICAT).

■ **Father Gary C. Caster**, a priest of the Diocese of Peoria, IL, currently serves as the Catholic chaplain of Williams College in Massachusetts. He is the author of *Mary, in Her Own Words: The Mother of God in Scripture* and *The Little Way of Lent: Meditations in the Spirit of St. Thérèse of Lisieux* (St. Anthony Messenger Press).

■ **Father Romanus Cessario, O.P.**, serves as senior editor for MAGNIFICAT and teaches theology at Saint John's Seminary in Boston, MA.

■ **Father John Dominic Corbett, O.P.**, teaches moral theology at the Pontifical Faculty of the Immaculate Conception in Washington DC. He also assists in formation work and spiritual direction and preaches retreats.

■ **Father Lawrence Donohoo** is associate professor of systematic theology at Mount Saint Mary's Seminary in Emmitsburg, MD, and assigned priest for Saint Anthony Shrine/Our Lady of Mount Carmel Parishes.

■ **Anthony Esolen** is professor of English at Providence College, a senior editor of *Touchstone Magazine*, and a regular contributor to MAGNIFICAT. He is the translator and editor of Dante's *Divine Comedy* (Random House) and author of *The Beauty of the Word: A Running Commentary on the Roman Missal* (MAGNIFICAT).

■ **J. David Franks** is a professor of theology at Saint John's Seminary in Boston, MA, serving as vice president for mission of the seminary's Theological Institute for the New Evangelization. He also serves as chairman of the board of Massachusetts Citizens for Life.

■ **Father Michael Gaudoin-Parker**, a British priest, has been living a contemplative lifestyle near Assisi, Italy, for over twenty years. He is a frequent author of articles and books on Eucharistic spirituality.

■ **Father Anthony Giambrone, O.P.**, is a Dominican priest of the Province of Saint Joseph and a doctoral student in Scripture at the University of Notre Dame.

■ **Father Stephen Dominic Hayes, O.P.**, is a Dominican priest and has served as pastor, writer, and preacher. He is currently associate pastor at Saint Thomas Aquinas Church, Zanesville, OH.

■ **John Janaro** is a professor of theology currently engaged in research and writing. His most recent book is *Never Give Up: My Life and God's Mercy* (Servant Books).

■ **Father William M. Joensen**, a priest of the Archdiocese of Dubuque, IA, is dean of Campus Spiritual Life at Loras College, where he also teaches philosophy and is spiritual director for seminarians.

■ **Heather King** is a convert, a contemplative, and the author of three memoirs. She lives in Los Angeles and blogs at shirtofflame.blogspot.com.

■ **Father Joseph T. Lienhard, S.J.**, teaches patristic theology at Fordham University in the Bronx and Saint Joseph's Seminary in Yonkers, NY. He is currently translating Saint Augustine's commentaries on the Old Testament.

■ **Monsignor Gregory E. S. Malovetz** is a priest of the Diocese of Metuchen, NJ, and serves as pastor of Saint Charles Borromeo Church in Montgomery Township.

■ **Father Francis Martin** currently hosts a web site designed to aid priests in their sermon preparation and lay people in acquiring a deeper knowledge of Sacred Scripture (www.frfrancismartin.com).

■ **Regis Martin** is professor of theology at Franciscan University in Steubenville, OH, and the author of half a dozen books, including most recently *Still Point: Loss, Longing, & Man's Search for God* (Ave Maria Press).

■ **Andrew Matt** is a member of the MAGNIFICAT editorial team and holds a doctorate in comparative literature. He lives with his wife and two sons in Chester, CT.

■ **Father Vincent Nagle, F.S.C.B.**, is a missionary of the Fraternity of St. Charles Borromeo and is currently serving in Rome, Italy.

■ **Father Jacob Restrick, O.P.**, is a Dominican priest, presently serving as chaplain to the Hawthorne Dominican Sisters at Rosary Hill Home in Hawthorne, NY.

■ **Father George William Rutler** is pastor of the Church of Our Saviour in New York City. His latest book is *Cloud of Witnesses* (Scepter Publishers).

■ **Father Richard G. Smith**, a priest of the Archdiocese of New York, currently serves as pastor of Saint Joachim–Saint John the Evangelist Parish in Beacon, NY.

■ **Father James M. Sullivan, O.P.**, serves as novice master for the Dominican Province of Saint Joseph at Saint Gertrude Priory in Cincinnati, OH.

■ **Father Richard Veras** is pastor of the Church of Saint Rita in Staten Island, NY, and a regular contributor to MAGNIFICAT. He is the author of *Jesus of Israel: Finding Christ in the Old Testament* (St. Anthony Messenger Press) and *Wisdom for Everyday Life from the Book of Revelation* (Servant Books).

MAGNIFICAT®

Praying with…

A Day-by-Day Series
on the Four Gospels and Saint Paul

Scripture reflections for listening to God's voice speak in your daily life – presented in a handy page-a-day format

You will find an entry for each day of the calendar year that includes:

- ❖ A short quotation from Scripture
- ❖ An original, down-to-earth reflection composed by gifted spiritual authors
- ❖ A thought-provoking final prayer

Titles in this best selling series (over 150,000 copies sold):

- ► *Praying with Saint Paul*
- ► *Praying with Saint Matthew's Gospel*
- ► *Praying with Saint Mark's Gospel*
- ► *Praying with Saint Luke's Gospel*
- ► *Praying with Saint John's Gospel*

An ideal way to incorporate Scripture reading into your daily prayer life

A great guide for Bible study or faith-sharing groups

Answers Pope Francis's call for a renewed encounter with Sacred Scripture

Generous bulk rates available!

For more information and to order
visit www.magnificat.com
or call 1-970-416-6670